D1032062

www.coralrealm.com
CLiBANARiuS

Basslets, Dottybacks & Hawkfishes

TO PATRICIA,

BEST OF LUCK IN YOUR DOTTYBACK
KEEPING ENDEAVORS!

BEST FISHES,

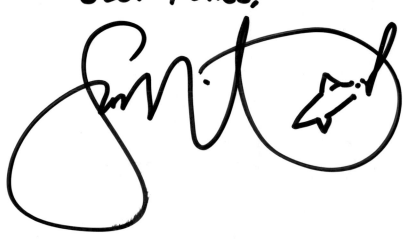

You'll want to own all six books in Scott Michael's authoritative *Reef Fishes Series* as soon as they become available:

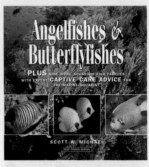

Moray Eels, Lionfishes & Anthias, plus Frogfishes, Squirrelfishes, Seahorses, Dwarf Seabasses, and more.
REEF FISHES, 1

Basslets, Dottybacks & Hawkfishes, plus Jawfishes, Grammas, Cardinalfishes, Tilefishes, and more.
REEF FISHES, 2

Angelfishes & Butterflyfishes, plus Sweepers, Goatfishes, Drums, Remoras, Snappers, and more.
REEF FISHES, 3

Wrasses, Damselfishes, & Blennies, plus Dragonets, Parrotfishes, Clingfishes, Triplefins, and more.
REEF FISHES, 4

Triggerfishes & Surgeonfishes, plus Gobies, Rabbitfishes, Pufferfishes, Moorish Idols, and more.
REEF FISHES, 5

A comprehensive photographic index to all fishes covered in this series, plus aquarium sharks and rays.
REEF FISHES ATLAS

Front Cover (background photograph by Fred Bavendam; inset photographs by Scott W. Michael)
Background: Gorgonian sea fans (*Subergorgia mollis*) thriving in a current-swept channel
between two islands in the Vavau Island Group, Tonga.
Left: Candy Basslet (*Liopropoma carmabi*)
Center: Royal Dottyback (*Pitichromis paccagnellae*)
Right: Flame Hawkfish (*Neocirrhites armatus*)

Back Cover
Top: Photograph by Roger Steene
Center and Bottom: Photographs by Scott W. Michael

Basslets, Dottybacks & Hawkfishes

PLUS SEVEN MORE AQUARIUM FISH FAMILIES
WITH EXPERT **CAPTIVE CARE ADVICE** FOR
THE MARINE AQUARIST

TEXT AND PRINCIPAL PHOTOGRAPHY BY

SCOTT W. MICHAEL

REEF FISHES SERIES • BOOK 2

Major Photographic Contributors
Fred Bavendam, Paul Humann, Rudie Kuiter, Dr. John Randall,
Roger Steene, and Takamosa Tonozuka

MICROCOSM

t.f.h.
PROFESSIONAL
SERIES™

T.F.H. Publications
One T.F.H. Plaza
Third and Union Avenues
Neptune City, NJ 07753
www.tfh.com

Copyright © 2004 by T.F.H. Publications, Inc.
Illustrations copyright © Joshua Highter

All rights reserved. No part of this publication may be reproduced, stored, or transmitted
in any form, or by any means electronic, mechanical, or otherwise, without written permission
from the publisher, except where permitted by law. Requests for permission or
further information should be directed to the above address.

This book has been published with the intent to provide accurate and authoritative information
in regard to the subject matter within. While every precaution has been taken
in preparation of this book, the publisher and author assume no responsibility for
errors or omissions. Neither is any liability assumed for damages resulting
from the use of the information herein.

ISBN 1-890087-33-5

If you purchased this book without a cover, you should be aware that this book is stolen.
It was reported as unsold and destroyed to the publisher, and neither the author nor
the publisher has received any payment for this "stripped book."

Printed and bound in China

Library of Congress Cataloging-in-Publication Data available upon request.

Designed by Eugenie Seidenberg Delaney, Alice Z. Lawrence, and Alesia Depot
Color separations by Digital Engine, Burlington, Vermont

Co-published by
Microcosm Ltd.
P.O. Box 550
Charlotte, VT 05445
www.microcosm-books.com

This series of books is dedicated to my lifelong dive buddy,
my soulmate, and my reason for living,
Janine Cairns-Michael.
Without her constant guidance, patience,
encouragement, and companionship, these books
would still be a dream, not a reality.

Contents

Preface

T HE INFORMATION IN THIS BOOK is designed to assist anyone interested in these fishes to maintain them in peak condition in the aquarium. This book is also part of a larger effort—a reference tool for marine aquarists as well as divers, snorkelers, and underwater naturalists with an interest in fish species associated with the coral reefs of the world. Because of the scope and volume of this work, the family groupings have been divided into several books, as follows. Each book is designed to be used and enjoyed individually as well as in the series. A special comprehensive *Reeef Fishes Atlas* will provide a full photographic index to all species covered in the set.

BOOK 1

Muraenidae	Moray Eels
Heterocongridae	Conger & Garden Eels
Ophichthidae	Snake Eels
Plotosidae	Eel Catfishes
Synodontidae	Lizardfishes
Bythitidae	Livebearing Brotulas
Batrachoididae	Toadfishes
Antennariidae	Frogfishes
Ogcocephalidae	Walking Batfishes
Anomalopidae	Flashlight Fishes
Monocentridae	Pineapple Fishes
Holocentridae	Squirrelfishes & Soldierfishes
Aulostomidae	Trumpetfishes
Pegasidae	Sea Moths
Solenostomidae	Ghost Pipefishes
Syngnathidae	Seahorses & Pipefishes
Centriscidae	Shrimpfishes
Caracanthidae	Coral Crouchers
Tetrarogidae	Waspfishes
Scorpaenidae	Scorpionfishes, Lionfishes
Platycephalidae	Flatheads
Dactylopteridae	Helmet Gurnards
Serranidae	Dwarf Seabasses, Hamlets, Anthias

BOOK 2

Serranidae	Groupers, Soapfishes, Reef Basslets
Pseudochromidae	Dottybacks
Grammatidae	Grammas
Plesiopidae	Longfins
Opistognathidae	Jawfishes
Priacanthidae	Bigeyes
Cirrhitidae	Hawkfishes
Cheilodactylidae	Morwongs
Apogonidae	Cardinalfishes
Malacanthidae	Tilefishes

BOOK 3

Echeneidae	Remoras
Carangidae	Jacks
Lutjanidae	Snappers & Fusiliers
Haemulidae	Grunts
Nemipteridae	Spinecheeks
Sciaenidae	Drums & Croakers
Mullidae	Goatfishes
Pempheridae	Sweepers
Monodactylidae	Monos
Chaetodontidae	Butterflyfishes
Pomacanthidae	Angelfishes

BOOK 4

Pomacentridae	Damselfishes
Labridae	Wrasses
Scaridae	Parrotfishes
Pholidichthyidae	Convict Blenny
Trichonotidae	Sand Divers
Pinguipedidae	Sand Perches
Tripterygiidae	Triplefins
Labrisomidae	Weed Blennies
Chaenopsidae	Tube & Pike Blennies
Blenniidae	Blennies
Gobiesocidae	Clingfishes
Callionymidae	Dragonets

BOOK 5

Gobiidae	Gobies
Microdesmidae	Dartfishes & Wormfishes
Ephippidae	Spadefishes & Batfishes
Siganidae	Rabbitfishes
Zanclidae	Moorish Idol
Acanthuridae	Surgeonfishes
Bothidae	Lefteye Flounders
Soleidae	Soles
Balistidae	Triggerfishes
Monacanthidae	Filefishes
Ostraciidae	Trunkfishes
Tetraodontidae	Pufferfishes & Tobies
Diodontidae	Porcupinefishes

Acknowledgments

I T IS IMPOSSIBLE TO IMAGINE CREATING THIS SERIES of books without the help, expertise, contributions, advice and unfailing encouragement of a great many generous people in many disciplines and many countries. For more than the decade that I have been gathering material for this book and its companion volumes, I have been aided by countless folks from the worlds of marine biology, ichthyology, diving, aquarium keeping, and underwater photography. The following acknowledgments are painfully incomplete, and I apologize to any of you who have contributed and whose assistance is not noted here.

I must begin by expressing my gratitude to an international group of scientists and reef fish experts who have unselfishly aided my efforts to identify fishes, gather photographs and ecological information, and provide behavioral observations on many species. These include Dr. Gerald R. Allen, Dr. Bruce Carlson, Neville Coleman, Dr. Anthony Gill, Keisuke Imai, Rudie H. Kuiter, Dr. John E. McCosker, Robert Myers, Richard Pyle, Dr. John E. Randall, Roger Steene, Dr. Hiroyuki Tanaka, and Fenton Walsh.

My colleagues in marine fishkeeping circles have also provided a constant source of new information and insights on the species of interest to aquarists. My sincere thanks to Chip Boyle, Mitch Carl, J. Charles Delbeek, Tom Frakes, Kevin Gaines, Richard Harker, Jay Hemdal, Larry Jackson, Kelly Jedlicki, Martin A. Moe, Jr., Bronson Nagareda, Tony Nahacky, Alf Jacob Nilsen, Michael S. Paletta, Vince Rado, Gregory Schiemer, Frank Schneidewind, Mike Schied, Matt Schuler, Terry Siegel, Julian Sprung,

Forrest Young and Angus Barnhart (Dynasty Marine Associates), and Bill Zarnick.

I am especially appreciative of years of support from many fine friends and acquaintances in the aquarium trade, including Bill Addison (C-Quest), Wayne Sugiyama (Wayne's Ocean World), Millie, Ted, and Edwin Chua (All Seas Marine), Kyle and Mark Haeffner (Fish Store Inc.), Roy and Teresa Herndon (Sea Critters), Eric Kohen, Kevin Kohen, Betsey Moore (CaribSea), George Teodora and Robert Stern (Sea Dwelling Creatures), Jeffrey Turner (Oceans, Reefs & Aquariums), Jeff Voet (Tropical Fish World), Randy Walker (Marine Center), Jim Walters (Old Town Aquarium), and Forrest Young and Angus Barnhart (Dynasty Marine). My friend and expert fishfinder Dennis Reynolds and his son Erik (Aqua Marines, Hermosa Beach, CA) deserve special recognition for all the unusual fishes and reliable information they have provided over the years. Thanks Dennis for your enthusiastic support and for providing me with more amazing fishes than all the other wholesalers and fish collectors combined! Fenton Walsh has also sent me some rare and unusual Australian fishes, as well as some beautiful photos for future volumes.

Many individuals, companies, and resorts have also assisted me in traveling to exotic locations to photograph the fishes contained within these volumes. They include Debbie Baratta, Garuda Indonesia, Karen Gowlett-Holmes, Avi Klapfer (Undersea Hunter, Coco Island), Carol Palmer (Ambon Dive Centre), Larry Smith, and Martin and Lori Sutton (Fisheye, Grand Cayman). Several dive operators deserve special recognition: Rob Vanderloss (Chertan, Papua New Guinea), one of the nicest people in the dive travel industry, has provided great diving opportunities for the author in Milne Bay, and Mark Ecenbarger (Kungkungan Bay Resort, Sulawesi) has been incredibly helpful in enabling Janine, Roger Steene and I to study and photograph the amazing marine life of Lembeh Strait. Toshikazu and Junco Kozawa (Anthis Corp.) were incredibly gracious hosts to the author and Roger during dive travel to Japan, and Takamosa and Miki Tonozuka (Dive and Dives) provided wonderful photo opportunities in Bali.

I would never have been able to assemble a comprehensive collection of species photographs without the help of some of the best fish photographers in the world. I thank Mary Jane Adams, Dr. Gerald R. Allen, Laddie Atkins, Glen Barnell, Fred Bavendam, Clay Brice, Janine Cairns-Michael, Helmut Debelius (IKAN), Dieter Eichler, Klaus Fiedler, Fred Good, John P. Hoover, Paul Humann, Keisuke Imai, Rudie H. Kuiter, Ewald Lieske, Boo Nillson, Aaron Norman, Robert F. Myers, Dr. John E. Randall, Roger Steene, Denise Nielsen Tackett, Takamosa Tonozuka, and Toshio Tsubota who helped to fill the gaps with their own magnificent photographs.

I can't fail to recognize my diving companions over the years. This list includes, Mary Findlay, John Greenamyer, Joe and Melisa Hancock, Richard Harker, Larry Jackson, Phyllis Randall, David Salmanowitz, Ron and Midge Silver, Cameron Snow, and George Willoughby. I need to give special recognition to one of my favorite travel companions, Roger Steene. It has been a great pleasure to share some memorable trips with Roger. Not only has his company been good for lots of laughter and informative fish talk, my photographic skills have been honed as a result of his tutelage. I also want to extend a big thanks to my dive buddies and Coral Realm business partners, Terry Majewski and Terri Parson, for their support.

I am extremely appreciative of the work of my publishing team at Microcosm, especially my editor James Lawrence, as well as Alesia Depot, Alice Lawrence, and Kate Robinson for the many months they have invested in editing, designing, and organizing these volumes and their dedication to book-publishing excellence. Thanks also to the folks at TFH Publications, Inc., especially Glen Axelrod, for helping this effort come to fruition.

On a more personal level, I want to express sincere thanks to my family, especially the late Duane and Donna Michael, my parents, for encouraging my interest in the ocean's inhabitants and saltwater aquarium keeping. Thanks also to my New Zealand mum, Margaret, and to the late, great William Cairns for providing a friendly waystation during our South Pacific expeditions, and for letting me use their compost pile as a post dissection repository for Carpet Shark remains. My sister Sandy Michael took me to my scuba classes before I was able to drive and my sister Suzie McDaniel and her husband Tommy provided a lab in their garage during my summer trips to the Gulf of Mexico. I would also wish to express thanks to our Creator for the marvelous planet on which we dwell, and for the extraordinary creatures and natural wonders we marvel at and which demand our responsible stewardship.

Finally, along with ichthyophiles everywhere, I am forever indebted to Jack Randall for dedicating his life to the study of coral reef fishes. Through his astonishing volume of scientific papers and books, and our regular communications, he was a constant influence for me over the many years that I was writing this text. Without his enormous contribution to the science of ichthyology, our knowledge about the taxonomy and ecology of this wonderful guild of fishes would be sorely lacking.

—*Scott W. Michael*
Lincoln, Nebraska

The Fishes

THE GROUPERS (SERRANIDAE)
TO THE TILEFISHES (MALACANTHIDAE):
A GUIDE TO THE FAMILIES, GENERA, AND SPECIES

"In all things of nature, there is something of the marvelous."
—ARISTOTLE, *Parts of Animals*

A CORAL REEF OR A MARINE AQUARIUM WITHOUT FISHES HAS BEEN likened to a garden without birds or butterflies—beautiful but lacking the flashing colors, the dynamics of movement, and the captivating behaviors that truly complete the scene.

While the gardener must rely on nature to provide the desirable avian and insect life, an aquarist has almost divine control over the fish species that populate his or her created piece of ocean. Given the astonishing diversity of choices available, with fishes from the far reaches of the tropical world, the aquarium keeper today can assemble groupings of marine species that provide endless hours of pleasure—or unhappy scenes of strife, territoriality, and unwanted predation.

Matching species in a marine aquarium is both science and art. Doing it well may take years of experimentation and reading, and it is far from uncommon for inexperienced or bewildered aquarists to select fishes that are inappropriate for one reason or another. The accounts that follow are intended to provide the aquarium keeper with a tool to better understand the families and species available, to choose intelligently among them and, once the

Priacanthus hamrur, Crescent-tail Bigeye (Great Barrier Reef, Queensland, Australia): knowing the native habitats and behaviors of reef fishes is an aquarist's best start in successful husbandry.

11

Paracheilinus filamentosus, Filamented Flasher Wrasse: male displays his flamboyant pigments and finnage. Such fish often trigger the "must-have syndrome" in a marine aquarist, but it is imprudent to bring home such a fish without an appreciation for its care and feeding needs, along with its ability to fit into a particular captive community.

choices have been made, to keep the fishes alive and well.

In these pages and the companion volumes to this work, the aquarist will find information about, and photographs of, the majority of coral reef fishes that can be encountered in the trade by aquarists and by divers exploring reefs around the world. This is not to say that all of these fishes are readily or constantly available. Some of the species covered rarely enter the ornamental marine fish trade, but are included because they would make desirable aquarium specimens—or are of general interest to fishkeepers.

Others, as will be clear from the descriptions, are not suitable for home aquariums, even though they may frequently be offered for sale to marine hobbyists. While even experienced fishkeepers sometimes fall prey to the "must have" or "love at first sight" syndrome when encountering a new species that turns up in the local aquarium shop, uninformed purchases very often have unhappy endings.

The simple rule of thumb is to examine the care requirements of each species very carefully before seeking out or purchasing a particular fish. I have made every attempt to discourage aquarists from purchasing those species that do not fare well in captivity. Although things are improving, it is still possible to see innocent hobbyists heading home with fishes that have, for decades, defied the best efforts of experts—even professional public aquarists—to keep them alive. If you observe such species in your local aquarium store, please point them out to the management. If the store doesn't discontinue the selling of unkeepable species, please shop elsewhere. It is critical that we police our own hobby.

An overview of the systematics, biology, behavioral ecology, and captive care of the group—whether it is a family, subfamily, or genus—is provided in each section. The reader is urged to examine these overviews before moving into the species accounts, as there is often important general information covering a family group that is not repeated for each and every species.

In order to make information more readily available to the hobbyist or diver, the species accounts are broken down into the following divisions.

Scientific Name

This is the most current Latin name applied to the fish by the scientific community. The name is in the form of a binomial. The first name indicates the genus to which the fish belongs, while the second name is the species name. At first mention of a scientific name, the "author" is listed after it. This is the ichthyologist or naturalist who formally described the fish. If the name is in parentheses, it indicates that the species was originally placed in a different genus. For example, the Hispid Frogfish (*Antennarius hispidus*) (Bloch & Schneider, 1801) was originally placed in the genus *Lophius* by its describers, but has since been moved to the genus *Antennarius*.

Common Name

One or more common names are listed for each species. The first name provided is the name most frequently used in the authoritative checklists and field guides written by ichthyologists. It is the name we will use in this series. In many cases, the names used in the aquarium trade are not given as the preferred name. This is often because the trade name(s) are confusing and lend little insight into the systematics or relatedness of various species. For example, in the aquarium trade, the name "scooter blenny" is applied to members of the Family Pinguipedidae and the Family Callionymidae. Members of these two families are referred to as sand perches and dragonets by ichthyologists, while blennies belong to the Family Blenniidae. In assigning the preferred common name to each species, I have attempted to steer away from such misnomers and toward names that will minimize confusion and bring science and hobby closer together. For example, the names used in ichthyological circles often incorporate the scientific name into the common name. For instance, *Dendrochirus biocellatus* is called the Twinspot Lionfish—*biocellatus* means "two ocelli" or "two spots"—hence the name Twinspot.

I believe that by using a common name that is derived from the scientific name, amateur aquarists, divers, and marine scientists can better communicate with one another. However, to make the book more user-friendly, I have tried to include most of the common names used in the aquarium hobby in

> *"In assigning the preferred common name to each species, I have attempted to steer away from misnomers and toward names that will minimize confusion and bring science and hobby closer together."*

Chaetodontoplus septentrionalis, Bluestriped Angelfish: when thinking about the long-term suitability of a particular species for your aquarium, Maximum Length (the size a particular species can reach, measured from the end of the snout to the tip of the tail) is an essential bit of information.

the list of common names and in the index.

Maximum Length

This refers to the greatest length that an individual of that particular species can attain—or the longest ever reported—measuring from the end of the snout to the tip of the tail. In most cases, the length of a specimen will fall short of this measure, but the aquarist should always infer that his or her fish will reach a maximum length near to that presented. In some cases, the standard length (SL)—which is measured from the tip of the snout to the base of the caudal (tail) fin—may be given.

Range

The distribution of a fish is presented from its eastern, western, northern, and southern geographical limits. This information is of great value to those aquarists who want to set up a tank that represents a fish community from a specific geographical location. It may also provide clues to the environmental conditions to which a species is subjected (e.g., fishes from Easter Island will tolerate cooler water temperatures than species limited to coral reefs around the Philippines).

Biology

In this section, information is provided on the natural history of the fish. This includes details on the habitats and reef zones occupied by the fish, its depth range, food habits, feeding behavior, reproductive behavior, social organization, and any interspecific relationships. The information was compiled from scientific papers, fish guides, and personal observations.

Captive Care

This section includes specific husbandry requirements, food preferences, color fastness, how aggressive a species is toward conspecifics and heterospecifics, unusual habits, suitability of the species for the invertebrate aquarium, and captive breeding information, if available.

Aquarium Size

This is the minimum suitable aquarium size for an adult individual of the species. Of course, juveniles and adolescents can be housed in smaller tanks. Activity levels and behavior patterns of a particular species have been accounted for whenever possible. As this is the minimum suitable size, please note that providing as much room as possible will allow any fish to acclimate better and display less aggression toward its tankmates.

Temperature

This is the temperature range most suitable for the species. The data is based on captive observation and/or examination of the geographical distribution of the species. For example, a species that is found around Pitcairn Island can withstand lower water temperatures than a fish that is limited in its distribution to Micronesia. In many cases, the fish would survive at higher and lower water temperatures than recommended.

Aquarium Suitability Index

I have provided a number from 1 to 5 to give the reader some indication of the durability, hardiness, and/or adaptability of each species. Factors such as readiness to feed, dietary breadth, competitiveness, tolerance of sudden changes, and deteriorating conditions were taken into account when applying a captive suitability rating. A species typically loses one rating point on my scale if live food is usually required. The origin of an individual also influences its likelihood of survival in captivity. In some regions, the fishes being collected are handled with less care or are captured using chemicals. This makes them stressed and less likely to acclimate.

Pseudanthias hypselosoma, Stocky Anthias: All species in this volume are assigned an Aquarium Suitability Index number, from 1 to 5, to give the reader some indication of the durability, hardiness, and/or adaptability of each species.

Enchelycore pardalis, Dragon Moray: an example of a species highly coveted by marine aquarists, but one demanding special conditions and precautions.

Although fishes from the Philippines and Indonesia are most often considered "handicapped" because of the stress they are exposed to before being shipped, I have seen collectors and wholesalers in Florida who housed and handled fish with little regard for their long-term health. The following is a breakdown of the rating system:

1 These species are almost impossible to keep and should be left on the reef. These fishes may rarely feed, may be prone to disease, may be incurably shy, and, for one or more of these reasons, will almost always waste away and die in the home aquarium.

2 Most individuals of these species do not acclimate to the home aquarium, often refusing to feed and wasting away in captivity. However, the occasional individual may adapt if kept in optimal water conditions and housed on its own or with noncompetitive tankmates. These species are best left in the wild or ordered only by the experienced aquarist with the aptitude and willingness to devote the time and energy to maintaining them.

3 These species can be successfully kept, but special care may need to be provided if they are to thrive. This may include offering live food to induce a feeding response, keeping them with less competitive (and less aggressive) tankmates, and providing aquarium conditions that resemble those of their natural habitats. For some of these species, a lush growth of filamentous algae may also provide a natural source of food and increase the chances of their successful maintenance.

4 These species are durable, with most individuals acclimating to the home aquarium. Even so, they should not be exposed to dramatic changes in environment or to poor water conditions. They will accept a wide range of commercially available foods. In the case of some fish or crustacean feeders, live food may either be required to induce feeding or may be the only type of food accepted. These fishes could be kept by aquarists with limited experience (e.g., 6 months).

5 These species are very hardy with almost all individuals readily acclimating to aquarium confines. They are undemanding and are more likely to withstand some neglect and deteriorating conditions. They will accept a wide range of commercially available fish foods and will not require live food to survive. These fish are great for the beginning hobbyist.

While these rankings are arbitrary, they are based on the collected experiences of hundreds of amateur and professional aquarists, marine biologists, aquarium trade importers, distributors, retailers, and others. (Readers with additional information—or contrary opinions—are invited to contact the author or publisher.)

Remarks

If sexual dimorphism and sexual dichromatism exist for the species, details are provided in this section. In addition, information on salient identifying characteristics and color variation is included. In some cases, morphological and chromatic differences between similar species and incorrect or obsolete scientific names often used in the aquarium literature are given—as well as interesting anecdotes about the species.

Wherever possible, at least one photograph is provided for each of the species accounts. In some cases, two or more photographs of the same fish are provided to show color differences between males and females or between adults and juveniles. Multiple photos may also be used to demonstrate the chromatic variability within a species. A complete listing of salient distinguishing characteristics and detailed descriptions of the color pattern is not included, but can be found in more technical reference works listed in the bibliography. Instead, photographs are provided to enable the hobbyist to make a correct identification.

One additional note: while the organization of these books follows standard taxonomic order, the reef-

Pseudanthias tuka, Yellowstripe Anthias (male): Care and husbandry advice for the fishes in this series are based on the collected experiences of hundreds of amateur and professional aquarists, marine biologists, aquarium trade importers, distributors, retailers, and others.

GENERALIZED BONY FISH ANATOMY

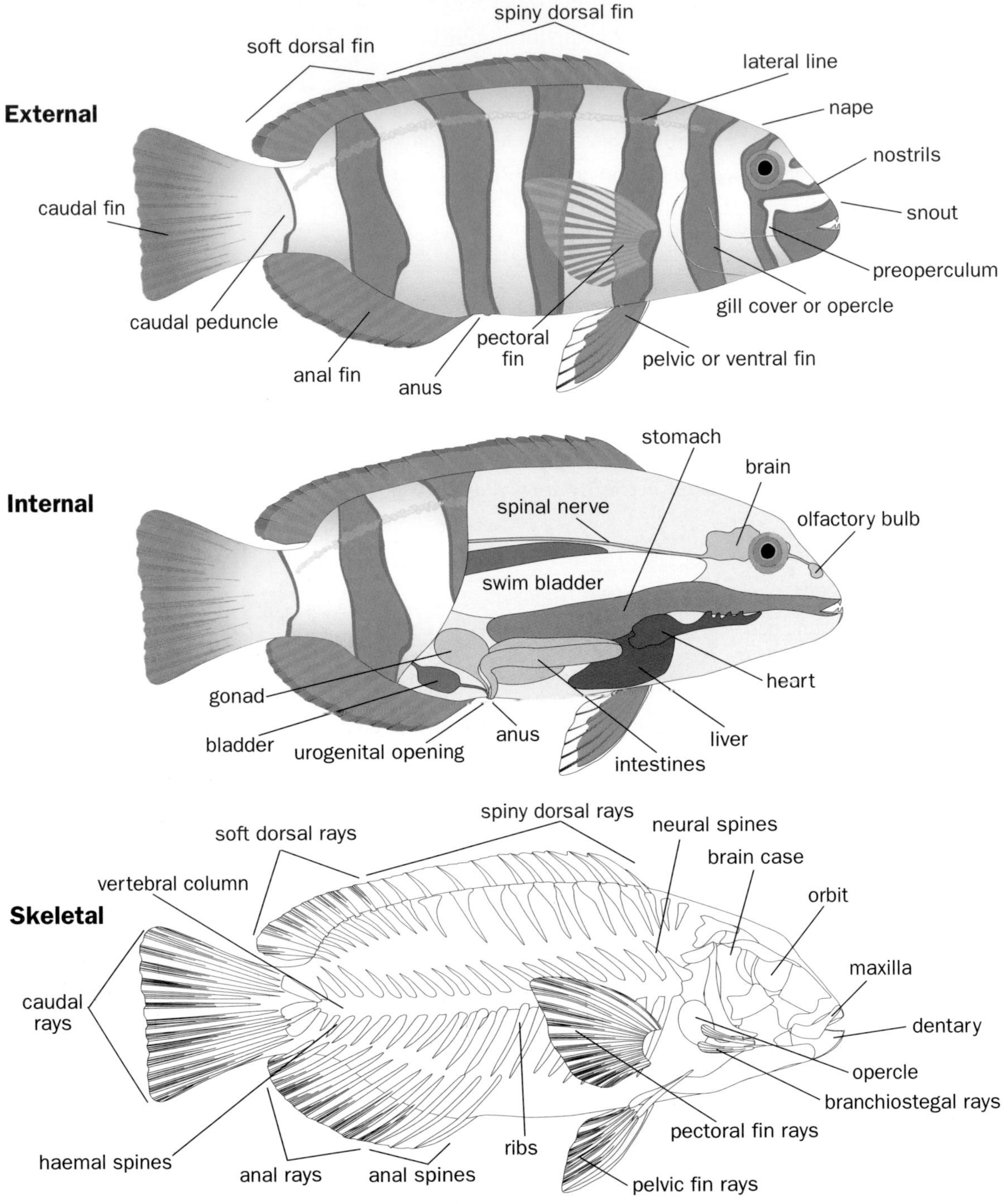

External

soft dorsal fin
spiny dorsal fin
lateral line
nape
nostrils
snout
preoperculum
gill cover or opercle
caudal fin
caudal peduncle
anal fin
anus
pectoral fin
pelvic or ventral fin

Internal

stomach
brain
spinal nerve
olfactory bulb
swim bladder
gonad
bladder
urogenital opening
anus
intestines
liver
heart

Skeletal

spiny dorsal rays
soft dorsal rays
neural spines
brain case
vertebral column
orbit
caudal rays
maxilla
dentary
opercle
branchiostegal rays
haemal spines
anal rays
anal spines
ribs
pectoral fin rays
pelvic fin rays

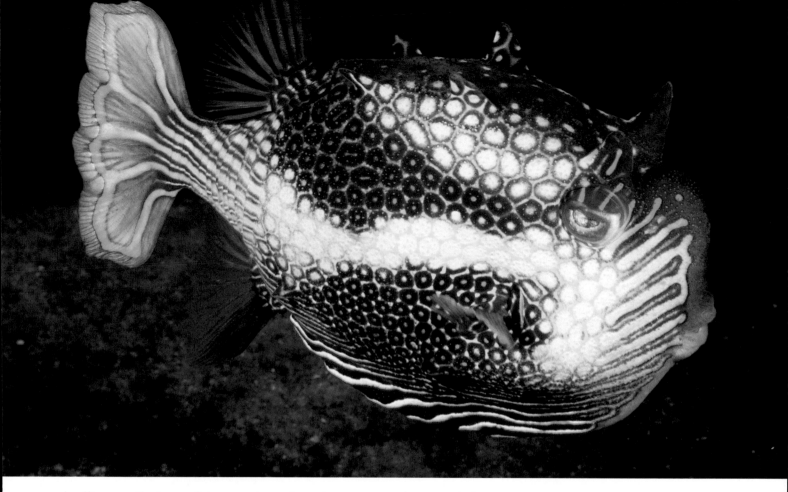

dwelling cartilaginous fishes, or elasmobranchs, are covered separately in *Aquarium Sharks & Rays* and *The Reef Fishes Atlas* (Microcosm/TFH).

Finally, I hope that this series will help the aquarist target the species that he or she finds most appealing and that are appropriate for his or her intended aquarium and tankmates. Just using one's buying power to bring home a fish without foresight and planning is something the thoughtful aquarist will want to avoid.

In the words of John Berry, "The bird of paradise alights only upon the hand that does not grasp." Simply acquiring fishes without studying their natural histories and biological requirements too often leads to problems for the animals and expensive and unhappy experiences for their owners—there are better ways of approaching and enjoying these wonderful works of nature.

Aracana ornata, Ornate Cowfish: a gorgeous fish that embodies the exotic allure of coral and rocky reefs and their ability to captivate the imagination of the involved aquarist.

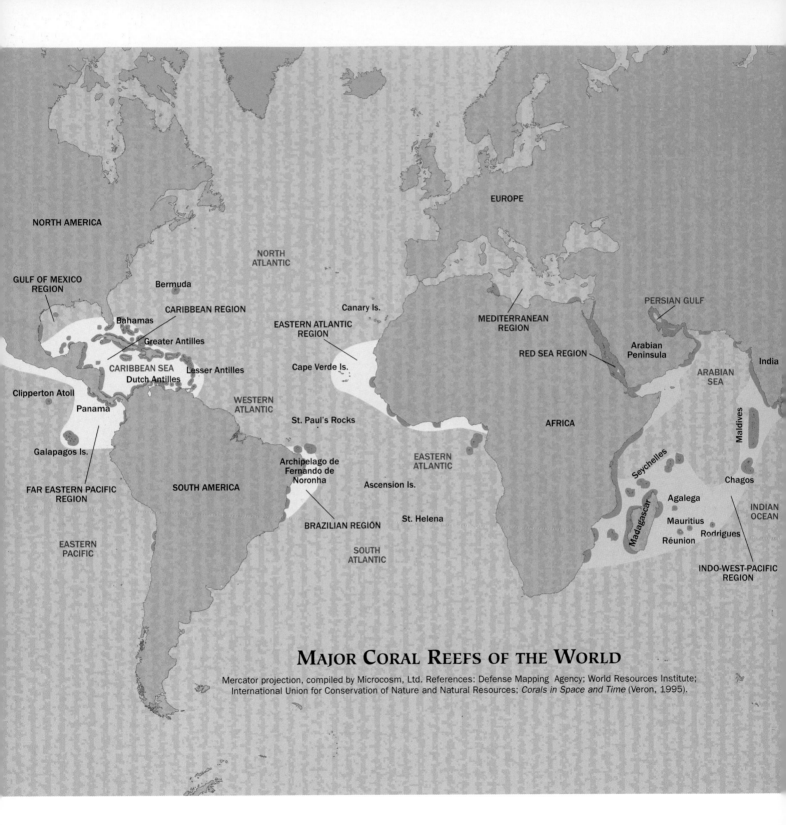

NORTH AMERICA

GULF OF MEXICO
REGION

Bermuda

NORTH
ATLANTIC

CARIBBEAN REGION

Canary Is.

EUROPE

Bahamas

Greater Antilles

CARIBBEAN SEA

Dutch Antilles

Clipperton Atoll

Panama

Lesser Antilles

EASTERN ATLANTIC
REGION

Cape Verde Is.

WESTERN
ATLANTIC

St. Paul's Rocks

MEDITERRANEAN
REGION

PERSIAN GULF

RED SEA REGION

Arabian
Peninsula

India

ARABIAN
SEA

Maldives

Galapagos Is.

FAR EASTERN PACIFIC
REGION

SOUTH AMERICA

Archipelago de
Fernando de
Noronha

EASTERN
ATLANTIC

Ascension Is.

AFRICA

Seychelles

Chagos

Agalega

Madagascar

Mauritius

INDIAN
OCEAN

EASTERN
PACIFIC

BRAZILIAN REGION

St. Helena

Rodrigues

Réunion

SOUTH
ATLANTIC

INDO-WEST-PACIFIC
REGION

MAJOR CORAL REEFS OF THE WORLD

Mercator projection, compiled by Microcosm, Ltd. References: Defense Mapping Agency; World Resources Institute;
International Union for Conservation of Nature and Natural Resources; *Corals in Space and Time* (Veron, 1995).

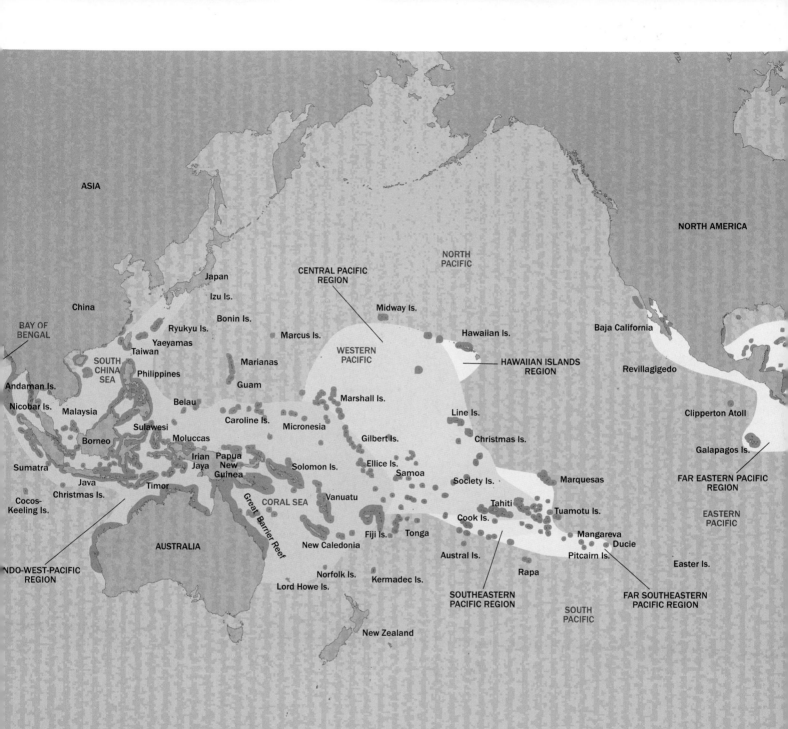

ASIA

NORTH AMERICA

NORTH
PACIFIC

Japan

CENTRAL PACIFIC
REGION

Izu Is.

Midway Is.

China

Bonin Is.

Hawaiian Is.

Baja California

BAY OF
BENGAL

Ryukyu Is.

Marcus Is.

WESTERN
PACIFIC

Yaeyamas

Taiwan

SOUTH
CHINA
SEA

Philippines

Marianas

HAWAIIAN ISLANDS
REGION

Revillagigedo

Andaman Is.

Guam

Belau

Marshall Is.

Line Is.

Clipperton Atoll

Nicobar Is.

Malaysia

Caroline Is.

Micronesia

Christmas Is.

Sulawesi

Galapagos Is.

Borneo

Moluccas

Gilbert Is.

Sumatra

Irian
Jaya

Papua
New
Guinea

Solomon Is.

Ellice Is.

Samoa

Society Is.

Marquesas

FAR EASTERN PACIFIC
REGION

Java

Christmas Is.

Timor

Vanuatu

EASTERN
PACIFIC

Cocos-
Keeling Is.

Great Barrier Reef

CORAL SEA

Tahiti

Cook Is.

Tuamotu Is.

Mangareva

Ducie

Fiji Is.

Tonga

NDO-WEST-PACIFIC
REGION

AUSTRALIA

New Caledonia

Pitcairn Is.

Easter Is.

Austral Is.

Norfolk Is.

Kermadec Is.

Rapa

Lord Howe Is.

SOUTHEASTERN
PACIFIC REGION

FAR SOUTHEASTERN
PACIFIC REGION

SOUTH
PACIFIC

New Zealand

THE FISHES 21

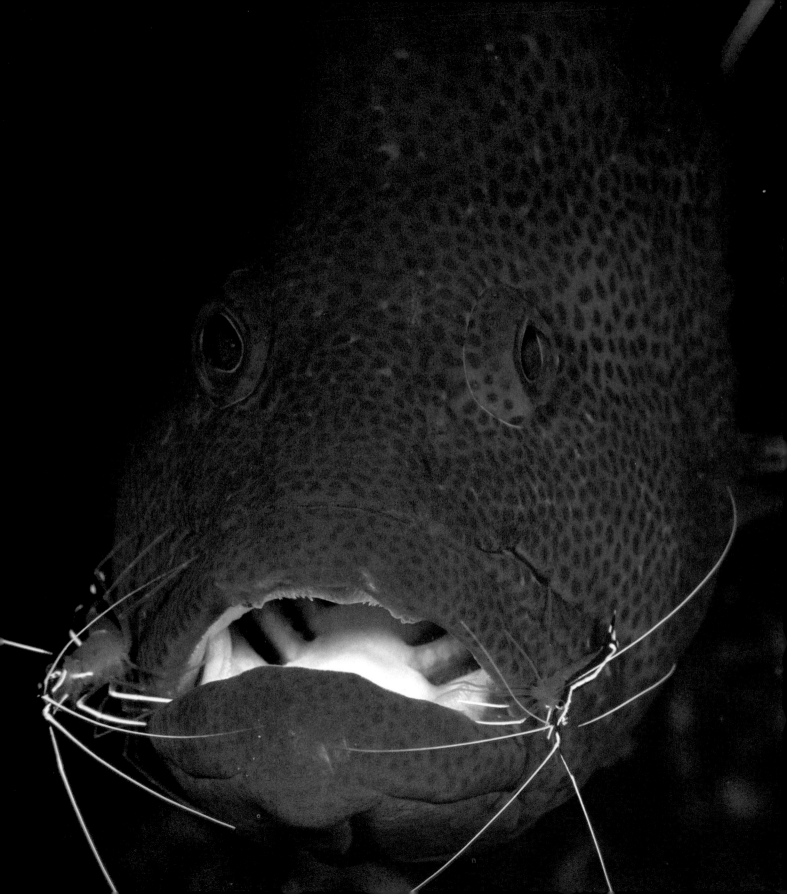

HIGHLY REGARDED BY THE WORLD'S FISHERFOLK FOR their eating qualities, beloved by aquanauts who frequently encounter "personable" specimens at favorite dive sites, and ever-popular among aquarists for their beauty and hardiness, the groupers form one of the most familiar groups of coral reef fishes.

The Subfamily Epinephelinae—the fishes most of us think of when we hear the name grouper—is one of three subfamilies in the Family Serranidae, the others being the Serraninae (dwarf seabasses and hamlets) and the Anthiinae (anthias), both of which were covered in Volume 1 of this series.

Five tribes make up the Subfamily Epinephelinae: the Niphonini (a lone species of primitive serranid), the Epinephelini (groupers), the Diploprionini (deep-bodied soapfishes), the Liopropomini (reef basslets), and the Grammistini (soapfishes). The largest of these is the Epinephelini, with about 164 described species and most of these (over 100 species) belonging to the genus *Epinephelus*.

Some Epinephelini are exquisitely colored—few fish can rival the combination of brilliant red and overall peppering of fluorescent blue spots of the Coral Hind (*Cephalopholis miniata*). Also variously known as coral groupers and hinds, the groupers include in their ranks the largest reef-dwelling bony fishes in the world, such as the Giant Grouper (*Epinephelus lanceolatus*) and the mighty Jewfish (*Epinephelus itajara*), which has been reported as long as 2.4 m (7.9 ft.) and weighing over 455 kg (1,003 lbs.). (Both of these behemoths have been implicated in attacks on humans.) There are also some smaller, related forms, but most are not as diminutive as members of the anthias and dwarf seabass subfamilies. In fact, the average size of the members of the Epinephelini is about 70 cm (27.6 in.).

Because of their commercial importance as food fishes throughout the world's tropics and subtropics, the groupers and their biology have been the subject of a significant amount of research. Many reef fishes of interest to aquarists are seldom studied, for the simple economic fact that the total worldwide catch of all "ornamental" species for export to the aquarium trade is approximately 110 tons (OATA, 1999). In contrast, in 1990 it was reported that 97,000 tons of grouper alone were

Cephalopholis sonnerati, Tomato Hind, being groomed by a pair of cleaner shrimp. Groupers are favorites of aquarists, divers, and fishermen alike.

landed worldwide for human consumption. (This figure is an underestimate that does not include those groupers caught in artisanal fisheries, which land significant quantities of grouper for table use.)

Biology

The majority of groupers are most abundant in tropical seas, especially in relatively shallow water. However, some species prefer offshore banks and walls. For example, the Goldbar Grouper (*Cephalopholis igarashiensis*) and the Reticulate Grouper (*Epinephelus tuamotuensis*) have been reported to depths of 250 m (820 ft.); the Seamount Grouper (*E. suborbitalis*) occurs to depths greater than 300 m (984 ft.); and the Eightbar Grouper (*E. octofasciatus*) ranges to a depth of 350 m (1,148 ft.). But the serranids reach their peak of diversity on shallow coral reefs.

Coral reef-dwelling groupers can be separated into groups based on the habitat they favor. There are those that prefer quiet, inshore reefs, often in protected bays or lagoons. The reefs may be silt-covered, with poor coral growth or even dead and dying coral. This group includes the Bluelined Hind (*Cephalopholis formosa*), the Panther Grouper (*Cromileptes altivelis*), and the Longfin Grouper (*Epinephelus quoyanus*). Other groupers are usually found on coral-rich exposed reefs with clear water. The ever-popular Coral Hind (*Cephalopholis miniata*), the Whitemargin Grouper (*Gracila albomarginata*), and the Lyretail Grouper (*Variola louti*) are members of this guild. Some groupers are most abundant on coastal or lagoon coral heads and patch reefs. Members of this group include the Bluespotted Hind (*Cephalopholis cyanostigma*) and the Summan Grouper (*Epinephelus summana*). Finally, there is a small group of reef-dwelling groupers that prefer caves and/or fore-reef dropoffs. This group is comprised of the Harlequin Hind (*Cephalopholis polleni*) and the Sixspot Hind (*C. sexmaculata*).

Foods and Feeding

The food habits of many groupers have been studied quite extensively, and it is well known that groupers feed primarily on fishes and crustaceans—the proportion of either in a grouper's diet being dependent on the species in question. For example, the diet of the Peacock Hind (*Cephalopholis argus*) consists mainly of fishes, while crustaceans make up the bulk of the diet of the

Plectropomus leopardus, Leopard Coral Grouper: apex predator.

Food Habits of the Leopard Coral Grouper: A Case Study

The Leopard Coral Grouper (*Plectropomus leopardus*) (or Coral Trout as it is popularly referred to in Australia) is a common apex predator in certain parts of the Western Pacific. It is a large grouper, attaining a maximum length of 70.5 cm (27.8 in.), and has been known to reach an age of 14 years. Because it is an important target of sport fisherman, it has been the subject of intense ecological study. In one such survey, the researcher examined the stomachs of 2,500 Leopard Coral Groupers taken off the Great Barrier Reef (St. John, 1999) to better understand the feeding habits of this top carnivore.

Four-hundred and twenty-two prey species, representing 28 different families, were taken from the stomachs of groupers ranging in size from 4.7 to 70.5 cm standard length (1.9 to 27.8 in. SL). (Standard length is the length from the tip of the snout to the origin of the caudal fin.) Three families, the Clupeidae (menhaden), Pomacentridae (damselfishes), and Labridae (wrasses), comprised more than 60% of the diet of this species. The Leopard Coral Groupers consumed an average of 2.8% of their relative body weight per day. All size classes ingested fish prey that measured from 2 to 5 cm (0.8 to 2 in.) in standard length (SL). At about 20 cm (7.9 in.) SL there was a distinct dietary shift. Smaller individuals fed more on benthic crustaceans (mostly penaeid shrimps), while adults fed almost entirely on fishes. Larger individuals also fed more on deep-bodied fishes, while juvenile coral groupers consumed more slender fishes. The size of the prey was related to the size of the predator in juvenile and small adult specimens—as expected, larger fish ate larger prey. Triplefins and dragonets were only eaten by juveniles, while fusiliers and lizardfishes were only consumed by adults. Adults also fed frequently on small, schooling fishes.

Chocolate Hind (*Cephalopholis boenak*), the Tomato Hind (*C. sonnerati*), and the Blacktip Grouper (*Epinephelus fasciatus*). The types of crustaceans consumed include crabs, shrimps, and mantis shrimps. The proportion of fishes and crustaceans in a grouper's diet may also change as the individual grows. For example, in some grouper species, smaller individuals feed infrequently on fishes, consuming more crustaceans than adults of the same species. Other grouper food items include squids, octopuses, gastropods, polychaete worms, and small sea turtles.

Research has shown that groupers increase their hunting activity after dark, while others are crepuscular, feeding most heavily at dusk and dawn. Most groupers are opportunistic, feeding any time the opportunity presents itself, no matter the time of day.

Groupers use two primary hunting strategies: ambush and interspecific association. Ambush is the most important tactic and can take one of three forms. One classic mode of grouper ambush starts with the predator resting on the seafloor, hiding among corals or in a crevice. It is poised to dash out with great speed to snatch any appropriate-sized fish that moves past in the water column. The Coral Hind (*C. miniata*) uses this technique to capture its favorite food, Lyretail Anthias (*Pseudanthias squamipinnis*). In the Gulf of California, groups of Leopard Groupers (*Mycteroperca rosacea*) have been observed to move under large schools of herring as dusk approaches. They sit among rocks under the herring and occasionally dash up off the bottom to attack the school above. These explosive attacks sometimes result in the grouper leaping clear of the water's surface. When ambushing prey while lying on the substrate, groupers often change color pattern, assuming a more disruptive coloration to avoid being detected by their quarry.

In a second form of ambush, a grouper launches an attack on a bottom-dwelling prey item from its ambush site. The Halfspotted Hind (*Cephalopholis hemistiktos*) uses this tactic to capture the crustaceans that make up the bulk of its diet. A third variation of ambushing is seen when a grouper hunts in midwater. If a swimming grouper sees a potential prey item moving over the reef, it may cease cruising and, except for the sculling action of its pectoral fins, hold itself motionless in the water column. From this position, the grouper may initiate a sudden attack on its quarry. This hunting strategy is employed by the Coral Hind (*C. miniata*) when feeding on Red Sea Slender Sweepers (*Parapriacanthus guentheri*) and by the Halfspotted Hind (*C. hemistiktos*) when feeding on Dascyllus damselfishes.

The other primary hunting tactic employed by groupers is to associate with other fish species or even invertebrates to gain access to food. Groupers will follow octopuses and fishes that

Cephalopholis formosa, Bluelined Hind (Andaman Sea, Thailand): note tiny cleaner shrimps searching for parasites or bits of debris on the fish's lower jaw.

crawl over the substrate or that enter reef crevices and the interstices between coral branches in search of food. By associating with these species, the grouper can capture prey items flushed out from hiding. For example, the Coral Hind has been observed following the Common Octopus (*Octopus cyaneus*) and the Gray Moray (*Siderea grisea*), while the Coney (*Cephalopholis fulva*) will follow Spotted Morays (*Gymnothorax moringa*) and snake eels. In the Gulf of California, juvenile Leopard Groupers (*Mycteroperca rosacea*) follow a number of fish species (including rays, jacks, morays, angelfishes, hogfishes, parrotfishes, and triggerfishes) as well as an octopus, while adult *M. rosacea* associate with mobile or foraging morays. Groupers will also use schools of roving herbivores as a natural blind to sneak up on their prey. For example, I have seen small groups of Leather Bass (*Dermatolepis dermatolepis*) swimming among groups of roving herbivores (mainly surgeonfishes). When the school of herbivores descended to feed, the Leather Bass would race out from among the group and attempt to capture unwary fishes and crustaceans.

Social Behavior and Reproduction

Many of the groupers studied thus far defend a permanent territory, which usually contains one or several preferred shelter sites.

The territory of a male grouper may include the smaller territories of up to 12 females. Groupers not only exclude members of their own species, but they will also behave aggressively toward other fishes that compete with them for shelter sites or food. When interacting with a rival, these fishes will engage in lateral displays and yawning behavior, in which the grouper's impressive maw is exhibited. If aggression escalates, a grouper's color will change dramatically, and it may chase or nip at its opponent. Two groupers may face each other and then lock jaws. They will then shake each other violently, with intermittent bouts of resting on the sea floor. A jaw-locking match lasts until the combatants release and one swims off—these bouts may last as long as 5 minutes. Occasionally, smaller groupers are evicted from hiding places by large damselfishes, like the Jewel Damselfish (*Plectroglyphidodon lacrymatus*).

Groupers often spend the majority of the day resting on their pectoral fins on the substrate. They frequently visit cleaning stations of cleaner wrasses (e.g., *Labroides* spp.), cleaner gobies (*Gobiosoma* spp.), and cleaner shrimps (e.g., *Periclimenes* and *Lysmata*). They will also chafe against the substrate, possibly in an attempt to relieve themselves of annoying parasites. At night, many groupers retreat to shelter sites where they refuge until morning.

Plectropomus oligocanthus, Vermiculate Coral Grouper: a typical aggressive display in this family includes "yawning" to exhibit a fearsomely large maw.

Many groupers are sexually dimorphic, with males attaining a larger size than females. This is consistent with the fact that most groupers studied to date are protogynous hermaphrodites, that is, males result from female sex change. There is considerable overlap in the size of male and female groupers of some species, and some females apparently never change sex. Age, rather than size, is apparently the factor that determines when sex change occurs, at least in some species. For example, in the Red Grouper (*Epinephelus morio*) the majority of individuals of less than 17 years of age were females, most over 17 years of age were male, while the sex of the individuals between 15 and 17 years of age was about 50% female and 50% male. It does not appear that the social context is the major factor determining whether a grouper changes sex, as is the case in the related anthiines.

There are some recognizable trends in grouper reproduction. All tend to spawn around dusk. The lunar cycle influences their spawning, with peaks in activity occurring at the new or full moon. Many groupers migrate to traditional spawning grounds that have been used by their kin for decades (and perhaps centuries). In some cases, larger groups will cover great distances (up to 560 km [348 mi.]) during their migration to specific spawning areas. These massive spawning aggregations usually coincide with the full moon. As many as 100,000 Nassau Groupers (*Epinephelus striatus*) have been observed aggregating at spawning sites in the Caribbean. Some of the larger groupers

exhibit leklike mating behavior—that is, males form contiguous, temporary territories that females visit.

All groupers studied thus far produce pelagic eggs that are spherical and nonadhesive. The eggs are broadcast into the water column, becoming part of the planktonic mass. The fecundity of the female is a function of her body size. Larger species release from several thousand to over a million eggs at a time, probably spawning only once or twice a year, and are more likely to form reproductive assemblages. Smaller individuals release fewer eggs per clutch, but spawn more often during the year.

Captive Care

The groupers are incredibly hardy, disease-resistant fishes that can live for many years in the home aquarium. (Longevity records from the wild range anywhere from 9 to 37 years for some of the larger species.) Many species are brightly colored and eye-catching, but others are better at camouflage than dazzlement. For example, the predominant color in several members of the genus *Cephalopholis* is a brilliant red, while many of the members of *Epinephelus* are more drably attired, exhibiting a variety of earth-tone colors and mottled patterns.

A grouper can make a great pet, learning to recognize the aquarist and putting on a fascinating display of predatory speed and appetite at every feeding. Some groupers even become so tame that they will take food from the fingers of their caretaker. However, there are some drawbacks associated with keeping these fishes in the home aquarium. The first, and most obvious, is that many outgrow their captive homes. For example, the Giant Grouper (*Epinephelus lanceolatus*) attains a maximum length of 2.7 m (8.9 ft.). Also, groupers are crustacean and fish eaters and will make short work of any tankmate that can be swallowed whole. Some groupers, like the hinds (genus *Cephalopholis*), are often very secretive, spending much of the day peering out from under ledges and caves. However, as they become accustomed to their surroundings and a new source of food, they will begin to spend more of the daylight hours hovering near or sitting on the bottom, close to their favorite shelter site.

Although some juvenile groupers can be kept in aquariums as small as 20 or 30 gallons, the aquarist should be prepared to move them to larger accommodations as they grow. The appropriate aquarium size for an adult grouper is obviously dependent on the species you intend to keep. Some of the smaller species can be housed in tanks as small as 55 gallons for their entire lives, while some of the larger forms will do best if kept in a tank of 180 gallons or larger. Some species will even outgrow tanks as large as 240 gallons, and a large grouper that is heavily fed can place severe demands on a typical home filtration system.

Variola louti, Lyretail Grouper (adult): named for its classic lunate tail, this is one of the most active and elegant groupers, but one demanding a large aquarium.

Feeding

The groupers are carnivores and should be fed a varied diet consisting, in part, of fresh marine fish and crustacean flesh. They will also eat freeze-dried and frozen krill, mysid shrimp, brine shrimp, and pelletized foods. Smaller specimens will even take flake food. An occasional grouper may require live feeder fish, grass shrimp, or small freshwater crayfish to initiate the feeding response, but it should be switched to nonliving foods over time. Although feeding live food, such as feeder goldfish, to your grouper can be interesting to watch, a diet consisting only of freshwater fish can result in long-term health problems.

It is important to avoid overfeeding captive groupers. This can result in fatty tissue being deposited around the liver, which can impair its functioning. Feeding to satiation two or three times a week should provide enough nutrients to meet a grouper's metabolic and growth needs. However, feeding frequency is somewhat dependent on the water temperature and age of the fish (i.e., feed more at higher water temperatures and feed juvenile fishes more frequently). Newly settled groupers are especially voracious. For example, larval groupers (between 4 and 10 mm) will consume about 30% of their body weight in food per day—that is equivalent to 193 rotifers for a 4 mm fish and 293 brine shrimp nauplii for a 10 mm individual in one day's time. They increase food intake at dusk and dawn and do not feed at all at night. Daily consumption rates for young, captive red groupers ranged from 0.9 to 4.7% of the total body weight (Brule et al., 1996).

Do not be fooled into thinking you can keep a juvenile of one of the larger grouper species in a small tank for an extended period of time. Most groupers grow very quickly. Also, because of their high rate of food intake and the immense amounts of waste they are likely to produce, an aquarium that contains a grouper is best outfitted with a good protein skimmer and/or some effective chemical filtration.

The groupers are relatively indiscriminate predators that will eat any fish or crustacean they can swallow. In some cases, depending on the prey item's shape, they can ingest fishes almost as long as they are. Long, slender fishes, like eels, certain wrasses, blennies, gobies, and dartfishes, are easily engulfed and will curl up in the grouper's stomach until digested. For example, a 92 cm (36.2 in.) Black Grouper (*Mycteroperca bonaci*) was found to contain a Bluespotted Cornetfish (*Fistularia tabacaria*) that was

Bullisichthys caribreus: a deep-water serranid that is seen in the aquarium trade on rare occasions. Little is known about its biology.

81 cm (31.6 in.) in standard length. Deep-bodied spiny fishes, like butterflyfishes, angelfishes, and Dascyllus damselfishes, are more difficult for groupers to ingest and will usually be ignored by all but the most determined or food-deprived individual. It is possible for an overzealous grouper to get one of these fishes lodged in its mouth or pharynx. The aquarist may have to intervene to extract the oversized prey item.

Compatibility

Interspecific aggression is not a particular problem with groupers, which will usually ignore unrelated species, especially in a larger aquarium, unless their favorite hiding places are invaded. However, they may bully newly introduced tankmates, especially if space is in short supply and the newcomers are related or similar in shape to the established grouper. Therefore, in most community tanks, the grouper should be the last fish introduced.

Epinephelids will behave aggressively toward conspecifics and will often fight with their relatives. To minimize this possibility, keep only one grouper per aquarium, although if you have a large tank (e.g., 135 gallons or more) with ample shelter sites, individuals with disparate color patterns can be housed together successfully. Some species are more aggressive and will dominate other forms, but in most cases the grouper's size and order of introduction to the aquarium will determine who is at the top of the social ladder.

The groupers can be kept in a predatory reef aquarium, but, as mentioned earlier, they will eat crustaceans, including anemone shrimps, cleaner shrimps, and decorative crabs. If you want to attempt to keep cleaner (*Lysmata* spp.) or boxer shrimps (*Stenopus* spp.) with a grouper, adding the crustaceans to the tank before the fish will increase your chances of success. A food-deprived grouper is also more likely to ingest its cleaner tankmates than a well-fed specimen.

Health

A study conducted on wild and cultured Malabar Groupers (*Epinephelus malabaricus*) demonstrated that all those examined were infected by one or more parasites. Sixteen species of parasite were found on the cultured groupers, while 11 species were present on the wild-caught individuals. These included, in order of abundance, monogenetic flukes, trematodes, nematodes, cestodes, copepods, isopods, acanthocephalans, and protozoans (*Cryptocaryon irritans* and *Trichodina*). Certain parasites were found only on either cultured or wild-caught groupers. For example, protozoa, cestodes, acanthocephalans, and leeches were found only on cultured specimens, while isopods were found only on wild-caught individuals. Studies have shown that the larger/older the grouper, the more parasites it is likely to host. The aquarist should be aware that groupers they purchase at the local aquarium store are likely to be hosting one or more species of parasite. Thus, as with any new fish, groupers should be quarantined and, if necessary, treated before they are introduced to the display aquarium. Fortunately, most groupers are durable aquarium fishes that rarely succumb to parasitic infections. They are also not sensitive to the common treatment protocols instigated to deal with parasites.

Captive Reproduction

Twenty-three species of groupers have "voluntarily" spawned in captivity. Numerous others have been induced to spawn by the administration of hormone injections. The ingredients to spawning these animals successfully in captivity include: placing them in an extra-large living space (most captive spawning has occurred in saltwater ponds), feeding them frequently, and not crowding them. Temperature is also critical to induce spawning. Simply raising the tank temperature several degrees (Fahrenheit) will catalyze some species to spawn. Daylength, although less important than water temperature, may also stimulate spawning, with most species spawning when daylength is longest. (Gradually increasing water temperature and simulating an increase in daylength by keeping the lights on longer are two time-tested methods of triggering captive-spawning events.)

Genus *Aethaloperca* (Redmouth Grouper)

This genus contains one very distinct species, the Redmouth Grouper. It is deep-bodied with a truncate tail; the interior of the mouth is light pink or crimson. A resident of the Indo-Pacific, it is most frequently found on coral reefs and shipwrecks. Juveniles occasionally make their way into the aquarium trade.

Aethaloperca rogaa (Forsskål, 1775)

Common Name: Redmouth Grouper.
Maximum Length: 60 cm (23.6 in.).
Distribution: Red Sea to Kiribati and Vanuatu, north to Japan, and south to the Great Barrier Reef.
Biology: The Redmouth Grouper lives on coastal reefs and fore-reef slopes at depths of 3 to 54 m (9.8 to 177 ft.). It rarely sits on the substrate, but often hangs or swims 1 to 2 m (3.3 to 6.6 ft.) above it. The Redmouth Grouper does not roam over large areas of the reef, but usually remains near a cave, crevice, or shipwreck in which it will hide if threatened. This grouper feeds almost exclusively on fishes, especially schooling species that inhabit caves, like sweepers (Pempheridae). It will eat crustaceans (including mantis shrimps) on occasion. There is a striking resemblance between the juvenile Redmouth Grouper and some of the small, dark-colored pygmy angelfishes (genus *Centropyge*), including the Midnight Angelfish (*Centropyge nox*) in the Western Pacific and the Many-spined Angelfish (*C. multispina*) in the Red Sea and Indian Ocean. Not only do young Redmouth Groupers share a likeness in color and general body shape to these pygmy angelfishes, they also swim in a similar fashion. If, indeed, this is a case of mimicry, it would most probably be aggressive mimicry. That is, the carnivorous grouper mimics these angelfishes, which feed mainly on algae and detritus, in order to approach the fishes and crustaceans on which the grouper preys without causing them to flee. It is also possible that juvenile *A. rogaa* may be aggressive mimics of some of the larger, dark-colored damselfishes of the genus *Stegastes*.

Captive Care: Juvenile Redmouth Groupers occasionally show up in the aquarium trade. Aquarists should be aware that this active species attains larger sizes. It will need a large tank (i.e., 200 gallons or more) if it is to be kept for its entire life. It should be provided with plenty of swimming room as well as a large cave or ledge in or under which it can retreat. It will be quite shy when initially placed in the aquarium, but will become more bold as it grows accustomed to its surroundings. The Redmouth Grouper will eat any fish or crustacean that can be ingested whole, including fish tankmates that measure up to two-thirds of its own body length. Although only one of these groupers should be housed per tank, it will rarely behave aggressively toward fishes larger than itself and can be kept with other species of groupers if the tank is large enough and replete with hiding places. The Redmouth Grouper can be kept in a shallow- or deep-water reef aquarium, but the tank should have plenty of swimming room (ordinarily lacking in most reef aquariums). The Redmouth Grouper will thin out ornamental shrimp and crab populations. On a more positive note, it may consume mantis shrimps.

Aquarium Size: 200 gal. **Temperature:** 24 to 28°C (75 to 82°F).
Aquarium Suitability Index: 4.
Remarks: The body and fins of the Redmouth Grouper are black, although some adults sport a pale band on the belly, just behind

Aethaloperca rogaa, Redmouth Grouper: juvenile resembles pygmy angelfish.

Aethaloperca rogaa, Redmouth Grouper: adult being cleaned by shrimp.

Alphestes afer, Mutton Hamlet: colors are highly variable.

the pectoral fin. It may be that these color differences are related to the sex of the fish, although this needs to confirmed by internal examination. Juveniles are black or dark gray with a white distal margin on the caudal fin.

Genus *Alphestes* (Mutton Hamlets)

This small family of serranids should not be confused with the hamlets of the genus *Hypoplectrus*. There are three species in the family: one in the Western Atlantic and two in the Eastern Pacific. These fishes have strongly compressed bodies with a small head much like the Leather Bass (*Dermatolepis dermatolepis*). They also have a spine on the preopercle that is directed forward and down. Their variegated color pattern consists of bars, spots, and blotches. They are smaller fishes, the largest attains a maximum length of about 30 cm (11.7 in.). At least one species is occasionally seen in the aquarium trade.

Alphestes afer (Bloch, 1793)
Common Name: Mutton Hamlet.
Maximum Length: 30 cm (11.7 in.).
Distribution: Bermuda, Florida, and the Bahamas south to Argentina and the Falkland Islands.
Biology: While it can be found on rocky and coral reefs, *A. afer* is most common in seagrass meadows. On the reef, it is often found under ledges and in crevices. It is a nocturnal predator that feeds mainly on crustaceans (primarily crabs). It will also consume fishes (including morays and surgeonfishes) and octopuses. The Mutton Hamlet incidentally ingests seagrasses.
Captive Care: This is a very durable aquarium fish. It tends to hide in holes, under ledges, or among macroalgae until food is added to the tank. It will dash into the water column to snatch food,

then dart back to the bottom. Once it is fully acclimated, it will spend more time in the open and learn to associate the aquarist with food. Keep only one individual per tank. It will eat small fishes and crustaceans, but is not overly aggressive toward other fish species.
Aquarium Size: 55 gal. **Temperature:** 20 to 28°C (68 to 82°F).
Aquarium Suitability Index: 5.
Remarks: Those Mutton Hamlets found in seagrass beds are usually olive overall with darker blotches and bands. Individuals from reefs, especially those in deeper water, are often reddish brown. The **Pacific Hamlet** (*Alphestes immaculatus*) **Breder, 1936** was once considered to be synonymous with *A. afer.* It is now thought, at least by some, to be a distinct species. It ranges from the Gulf of California to Peru (including the Galapagos Islands). It tends to reside in macroalgae patches, especially among the algae *Blossivilla, Padina,* and *Sargassum.*

Genus *Anyperodon* (Lined Groupers)

This genus contains one described and one undescribed species. These serranids are built for speed with bodies that are more slender and torpedolike than any of the other groupers. They also lack palatine teeth. In the Whitelined Grouper (*Anyperodon leucogrammicus*), the juvenile and adult differ in color. Neither species is common in the aquarium trade.

Anyperodon leucogrammicus (Valenciennes, 1828)
Common Names: Whitelined Grouper, Slender Grouper.
Maximum Length: 65 cm (25.6 in.).
Distribution: Red Sea to the Line Islands, north to the Ryukyus, and south to New Caledonia.
Biology: The Whitelined Grouper occurs on lagoon patch reefs and protected fore-reef slopes, preferring clear water and areas with rich hard-coral growth. It occurs at depths of 5 to 80 m (16 to 262 ft.). A rather secretive species, it is strongly attached to the substrate and will reside in caves and crevices, under ledges, or among branching corals. The Whitelined Grouper feeds mainly on small reef fishes, but it will also consume crustaceans and cephalopods. *Anyperodon leucogrammicus* is an ambush predator that sits, or hangs, motionless among sponges or hard corals until potential prey comes within striking range. At that point it dashes out at great speed to capture its quarry. The juveniles (2 to 7 cm [0.8 to 2.8 in.] in length) are apparently aggressive mimics of the initial phases of several species of wrasses in the genus *Halichoeres*, including the Tailspot Wrasse (*H. melanurus*), Purplestriped Wrasse (*H. purpurescens*), Chainlink Wrasse (*H. richmondi*), and the Indian Ocean Pinstriped Wrasse (*H. vrolikii*). (It resembles *H. purpurescens* most closely.) By looking

like one of these microcarnivore wrasses, which feed selectively on tiny invertebrates, the juvenile Whitelined Grouper is able to move into striking distance of the small fishes on which it feeds. Juvenile *A. leucogrammicus* have been observed associating with some of these wrasses, and in one instance a Whitelined Grouper swimming with two *H. melanurus* was observed to eat a small damselfish. This grouper occurs singly or in pairs, although adults are occasionally found in loose groups.

Captive Care: This is a large grouper that should be kept in an aquarium with plenty of swimming room. Although juveniles and subadults can be kept in smaller aquariums, adult specimens need to be housed in a tank of 180 gallons or larger. It is also extremely important to provide suitable hiding places for this secretive fish, which will otherwise lie in the corner of the tank, refuse to eat, and pine away. A large overhang or cave would provide this fish with a microhabitat similar to one it occupies in nature. If startled, this fish will dash about the aquarium and may jump out of an open tank. It is definitely not a good choice for aquariums in high-traffic areas. Captive Whitelined Groupers will snap up smaller fishes and crustaceans, including those species that often remove parasites from them in the wild (e.g., cleaner wrasses). This species should not be kept with its own kind, but it rarely displays aggression toward heterospecifics. It is possible that young Whitelined Groupers are occasionally sold in the aquarium trade as the wrasses that they mimic.

Aquarium Size: 180 gal. **Temperature:** 24 to 28°C (75 to 82°F).

Aquarium Suitability Index: 4.

Remarks: Subadult and smaller adult *A. leucogrammicus* are greenish to brownish gray overall with three to five longitudinal "racing" stripes and orangish red spots on the head and body. Larger adults lack the white lines. Juveniles of less than about 9.5 cm (3.7 in.) have alternating longitudinal stripes of orangish yellow and blue, with one or two blue-edged black spots at the base of the tail and on the dorsal fin. There is a second species, the **Metallic Blue Grouper** (*Anyperodon* **sp.**), in this genus that is one of the most spectacular of all the groupers. This species is reported in deep-water (62 m [203 ft.]) off Saudi Arabia. It is brilliant blue with black lines down the body, white blotches between the lines, and a black band at the base of the tail. I received this fish from Jim Walters (Old Town Aquarium) and kept it in my aquarium for several months before sacrificing it for scientific purposes. It is a great aquarium fish, quickly acclimating to captivity and accepting live and frozen foods. It spends much of its time in hiding (in holes and crevices). When live food is introduced to the tank, it will dart around the tank like a torpedo, snatching its prey. Although my specimen did not behave aggressively toward

Anyperodon leucogrammicus, Whitelined Grouper (Indonesia): small adult.

Anyperodon leucogrammicus, Whitelined Grouper (adult): may lack lines.

Anyperodon sp., Metallic Blue Grouper: stunning but extremely rare.

Cephalopholis argus, Peacock Hind: very common Indo-Pacific grouper.

Cephalopholis cyanostigma, Bluespotted Hind: Padang, Sumatra.

the butterflyfishes and anthias it was housed with, this fish should not be housed with members of its own species (unless the aquarium is quite large). It would aggressively display toward its reflection in a mirror, flaring its operculum and opening its mouth wide. It suffered from an infestation of *Amyloodinium*, which I treated with formalin.

Genus *Cephalopholis* (Hinds)

The genus *Cephalopholis,* whose members are commonly referred to as hinds, contains 22 reef-dwelling species. (The common names for this genus in Australian references are "cod" and "rock-cod," but there is no relation to the temperate-water cods of the Family Gadidae, so important to the North Atlantic fishery.) Seventeen of these species are found in the Indo-Pacific, two in the Western Atlantic and one in the Eastern Pacific. Most hinds

attain relatively small sizes, compared to other groupers, making them more suitable candidates for home aquariums.

Cephalopholis argus (Schneider, 1801)

Common Names: Peacock Hind, Bluespotted Grouper.
Maximum Length: 44 cm (17 in.).
Distribution: Red Sea to the Pitcairn Group, north to southern Japan, south to Lord Howe Island. This species was introduced to the Hawaiian Islands.
Biology: *Cephalopholis argus* is most abundant in the clear, shallow water of the exposed reef crest and reef face, in areas with profuse coral growth. Smaller individuals often frequent more protected areas. It is also found in lagoons and on fore-reef slopes. While it occurs at a depth range of 1 to 40 m (3.3 to 131 ft.), it is most abundant at depths of less than 10 m (33 ft.). Food studies have shown that its diet consists primarily of bony fishes. Crustaceans, including crabs, decapod shrimps, mantis shrimps, and spiny lobsters (*Panulirus* spp.), are of secondary importance. In a study conducted on this species in the Red Sea, of 56 individuals with food in their stomachs, 95% contained fishes, while 5% contained crustaceans. Crustaceans, especially shrimps, make up a more substantial part of the diet in other localities. In the Red Sea study, the most important species of fish in the diet was the Dusky Surgeonfish (*Acanthurus nigrofuscus*), but Purple Tangs (*Zebrasoma xanthurum*), Indian Ocean Sailfin Tangs (*Z. desjardinii*), lizardfishes, Gray Morays (*Siderea grisea*), Lyretail Anthias (*Pseudanthias squamipinnis*), Klunzinger's Wrasse (*Thalassoma klunzingeri*), sweepers, and Blue Green Chromis (*Chromis viridis*) were also eaten. The Peacock Hind was observed to increase its hunting activity at dawn (0600 to 0800 hours) and at dusk (1700 to 1800 hours), although it is also known to feed after dark. It has been observed associating with foraging octopuses and the Gray Moray and stalking prey by joining schools of feeding herbivores, such as parrotfishes. The Yellowface Soapfish (*Diploprion drachi*) will hunt by "riding" (swimming alongside) *C. argus.*

The Peacock Hind ranges over a much larger home area than many of its congeners. It is a polygamous species, with a social unit of one male and up to six females. The male defends a territory of 1,500 m² (16,146 ft.²) on average, which contains the territories of each of the females. Adult specimens usually occur singly, but are occasionally observed in pairs, or in small groups. During the spawning period, Peacock Hinds form mating aggregations that consist of one male and four or five females. Individuals that make up these mating groups assume a darker color than normal and a white keyhole-shaped mark appears on each side of the body. The male courts with each female sequentially and the group disperses at dusk. This is one of the most abundant piscivores in the Indo-Pacific.

Captive Care: The Peacock Hind is a secretive species that will spend much of its time hiding, especially when first introduced to the aquarium. Over time, many specimens will become bolder, to the point where they will take food from the aquarist's hand. Although it can be kept with other groupers, only one Peacock Hind should be kept per tank; this large species needs plenty of swimming space and one or two good shelter sites. Although it can be housed in a shallow- or deep-water reef aquarium, it will eat small fishes and crustaceans.

Aquarium Size: 180 gal. **Temperature:** 22 to 27°C (72 to 81°F).

Aquarium Suitability Index: 5.

Remarks: Male Peacock Hinds are 30 to 40% larger than females. The Peacock Hind should not be confused with the Bluespotted Hind (*Cephalopholis cyanostigma*). The **Starry Hind** (*Cephalopholis polyspila*) **Randall & Satapoomin, 2000** is similar to the Peacock Hind, but it has smaller, more numerous spots that are white or light blue, while lacking spots on the distal portions of the dorsal, caudal, and anal fins. The Starry Hind is found from the Similan Islands to Sumatra. It has been reported from patch reefs at depths of 3 to at least 20 m (9.8 to 66 ft.).

Cephalopholis aurantia (Valenciennes, 1828)

Common Name: Golden Hind.

Maximum Length: 29 cm (11.4 in.).

Distribution: East Africa to the Society Islands, north to the Ryukyus, and south to New Caledonia.

Biology: The Golden Hind is a resident of steep fore-reef slopes, where it occurs at a depth range of 40 to 300 m (131 to 984 ft.). However, it is generally found at depths greater than 100 m (328 ft.). This species is reported to feed on crabs.

Captive Care: Because of its predilection for deep-reef habitats, it is highly unusual for this species to appear in the aquarium trade. If the aquarist does encounter a *C. aurantia*, it will surely be priced near its weight in gold. This species should be housed in a dimly lit tank with numerous hiding places. As with any hind that frequents great depths, be sure it is swimming normally and does not have problems resting on the substrate or maintaining its position in the water column, which is a sure sign of injuries related to improper decompression by collectors.

Aquarium Size: 75 gal. **Temperature:** 22 to 27°C (72 to 81°F).

Aquarium Suitability Index: 5.

Remarks: Those individuals from the Pacific lack the black band near the tail margin and were once considered to be a distinct species known as *Cephalopholis analis*.

Cephalopholis aurantia, Golden Hind: cleaners work over a coveted rarity.

Cephalopholis boenak, Chocolate Hind: threat display shows large mouth.

Cephalopholis boenak (Bloch, 1790)

Common Names: Chocolate Hind, Brown Grouper.

Maximum Length: 26 cm (10.2 in.).

Distribution: East Africa to Vanuatu, north to southern Japan, and south to Queensland. This species is absent from oceanic islands.

Biology: The Chocolate Hind is most common on lagoon patch reefs and back-reef areas, at depths from 1 to at least 30 m (3.3 to 98 ft.). It often occurs in more turbid water. I have seen numerous Chocolate Hinds in murky water on a shipwreck that was covered with soft corals and large-polyped stony corals. It is also found on coral-rich reef-face habitats. This hind feeds mainly on shrimps and crabs, but also eats some small fishes (including damselfishes) and squids. One study demonstrated that this species captures most of its fish prey in less structurally complex

Cephalopholis cruentatus, Graysby (juvenile): note yellow cap.

Cephalopholis cruentatus, Graysby (adult coloration): effective camouflage.

reef habitats. The Chocolate Hind spawns in pairs. Courtship begins about 20 minutes before sunset. The male swims parallel to the female, remaining stationary with his body tilted at 90°. The pair will then settle to the bottom and repeat the parallel swimming behavior. Courtship culminates in the pair making a spawning ascent (male following female with his snout pressed against her side) up to 6 m (20 ft.) above the bottom. The duration of the courtship act is about 5 minutes.

Captive Care: Although regularly encountered at fish wholesalers, the Chocolate Hind is not highly sought after because of its muted coloration. It is even more secretive than many of its close relatives and will spend most of its time hiding, at least when initially placed in the aquarium. It can be aggressive toward fishes that try to intrude into its hiding places. For example, I once had a smaller specimen that thrashed a similar-sized Steene's Dottyback (*Pseudochromis steenei*)—one of the most aggressive fishes in the dottyback family. It can be kept in a shallow- or deep-water reef aquarium, but it will eat crustaceans and smaller fish tankmates.

Aquarium Size: 55 gal. **Temperature:** 22 to 28°C (72 to 82°F).

Aquarium Suitability Index: 5.

Remarks: In older aquarium literature, the name *Cephalopholis boenak* is often used incorrectly for *C. formosa*, the Bluelined Hind. The Chocolate Hind has dusky bars on the body, a spot on the edge of the operculum and lacks blue stripes on the body.

Cephalopholis cruentatus (Lacépède, 1803)

Common Name: Graysby.

Maximum Length: 35 cm (13.8 in.).

Distribution: Northern Gulf of Mexico, North Carolina, and Bermuda to southeast Brazil.

Biology: The Graysby is one of the most abundant of the tropical Atlantic groupers on offshore reefs. It occurs on coral-rich reef faces and fore-reef slopes at depths ranging from 2 to 170 m (6.6 to 558 ft.). It is particularly common in areas with extensive growths of *Montastraea annularis* and *Agaricia* spp. corals whose growth forms provide numerous hiding places for these fish. Its mottled, spotted color pattern helps it to disappear among the corallites of these stony corals. Juvenile Graysby occur in seagrass meadows and reef habitats. Studies have shown that juveniles use habitats of lower relief in deeper water, while adults are more often found in high-relief habitats at shallower depths. Juveniles often refuge in the lumens of tube sponges or among the ridges of barrel sponges.

Adult *C. cruentatus* are bold, spending most of the daylight hours in repose on the substrate, often sitting at the entrance of a small cave or near a crevice. During the day, adults feed primarily on fishes (especially the Yellow-edge Chromis, *Chromis multilineata*), but also on cardinalfishes, gobies, grunts, and squirrelfishes. At night, they feed more on crustaceans, including pistol shrimps, mantis shrimps, and crabs. The stomach of one specimen was reported to contain a Queen Conch. Juveniles feed more on crustaceans, at all times of the day, than do the adults. There is a peak in feeding activity at dusk and dawn. The Graysby sometimes follows hunting morays and may chafe against a stationary eel to encourage it to move. Up to four individuals may associate with a single eel. When there is more than one Graysby present, individuals may fight among themselves for the best vantage point to capture flushed prey. Males maintain a territory that contains one to three females. Territorial boundaries are aggressively defended. When fighting, males will perform lateral displays, mouth gaping, and jaw locking. This species is a protogynous hermaphrodite, with females maturing at about 16 cm (6.3 in.) and transforming to males between 20 and 23 cm (7.9 to 9.1 in.). Sex change usually occurs during the fourth or fifth years of life. Spawning occurs within male territories between May and September in the southern Caribbean. During the first years of life, the Graysby will grow about 5 cm (2 in.) per year. This growth rate drops to less than 2.5 cm (1 in.) as the fish ages. It is reported to live for up to 9 years in the wild.

Captive Care: The Graysby will spend more time resting on the bottom in full view than many of the other hinds. Most individuals are quick to adjust to aquarium life and will readily accept food from their keeper's fingers. Like any of the groupers, this species should not be housed with smaller fishes and has even been known to attempt to eat tankmates equal to its own length. The Graysby will usually fight with members of its own species, and although it may display aggression toward related forms, it is more likely to be dominated by other groupers if they are of similar size or larger. It can be kept in a shallow- or deep-water reef aquarium, although it will eat ornamental crustaceans.

Aquarium Size: 75 gal. **Temperature:** 22 to 28°C (72 to 82°F).

Aquarium Suitability Index: 5.

Remarks: This species is easily recognized by the row of three or four black spots running along the base of the dorsal fin. These spots can change rapidly from black to white. The Graysby can also change its overall coloration, from darker shades of brown to gray or almost white. Some juveniles may have yellow on the head and back. The **Panamic Graysby** (*Cephalopholis panamensis*) (**Steindachner, 1876**) is the sister species of *C. cruentatus.* The two species are almost identical, although *C. panamensis* is a resident of the tropical Eastern Pacific. It should be noted that some ichthyologists (and field guides) place the Graysby in the genus *Epinephelus.*

Cephalopholis cyanostigma (Valenciennes,1828)

Common Names: Bluespotted Hind, Bluespotted Grouper.

Maximum Length: 35 cm (13.8 in.).

Distribution: Thailand, Western Australia and the Solomon Islands, north to the Philippines and south to Queensland.

Biology: The Bluespotted Hind is a resident of protected coastal reefs. Found in seagrass and algae beds and on coral-rich reef slopes, it tends to be very site-specific and is probably territorial. (I have observed what appeared to be the same individuals in the same spots, day after day for weeks.) It occurs at depths from 1.5 to 50 m (4.9 to 164 ft.). This hind feeds on fishes and crustaceans and tends to spend most of its time in repose on hard substrates, often sitting in the open among stony corals or sponges. It will also rest in crevices and under overhangs.

Cephalopholis cyanostigma, Bluespotted Hind (adult): resting on bed of coral.

Captive Care: *Cephalopholis cyanostigma* is a medium-sized species not regularly seen in the aquarium trade. Like many of its relatives, this species is shy when initially placed in the aquarium, but after it has fully adjusted to its new home and the presence of the aquarist, it will begin to spend more time in the open. It can be kept in a shallow- or deep-water reef aquarium, although it will eat crustaceans and small fish tankmates.

Aquarium Size: 75 gal. **Temperature:** 23 to 28°C (73 to 82°F).

Aquarium Suitability Index: 5.

Remarks: Subadults of this species have a dark brown head and body and dark brown pectoral fins, but all the other fins are bright yellow. At approximately 12 cm (4.7 in.) bright blue spots begin to develop on the head and body and the fins begin to darken. Adults are brown to reddish brown with dark-edged blue spots on the head, body, and fins. Pale spots may join on the body to form irregular bars.

Cephalopholis formosa (Shaw & Nodder, 1812)

Common Names: Bluelined Hind, Bluelined Grouper.

Maximum Length: 34 cm (13.4 in.).

Distribution: Sri Lanka and western India to Papua New Guinea, north to southern Japan, and south to the Great Barrier Reef.

Biology: The Bluelined Hind occurs on sheltered coastal reefs, often where the coral is dead and silt-covered. It is sometimes found in crevices where it is cleaned by *Lysmata* shrimps. Little else is known about its biology.

Captive Care: This shy species will hide most of the time. When it detects any movement outside the tank, it will quickly dart for cover. With time, however, an individual will become bolder and will start spending time in full view. This fish will eat a wide variety of fresh, frozen, and prepared foods, as well as live feeder

Cephalopholis formosa, Bluelined Hind: beautiful but aggressive for a hind.

Cephalopholis formosa, Bluelined Hind (Andaman Sea): pale coloration phase.

fish and grass shrimp. When food its presented, it will dash out to ingest it and then quickly return to its favorite shelter site. It is one of the more aggressive hind species, and should not be kept with members of its own species, closely related groupers, or docile fish species, although it can coexist with fishes too large for it to eat. In a shallow- or deep-water reef tank, it may be seen only infrequently and will eat crustaceans.

Aquarium Size: 75 gal. **Temperature:** 22 to 28°C (72 to 82°F).

Aquarium Suitability Index: 5.

Remarks: The Bluelined Hind is easily recognized by its distinct color pattern. Although it always has blue lines running down the head and body, the overall color can vary from olive green to dark brown. In the older aquarium literature, this species is often referred to as *Cephalopholis boenak*.

Cephalopholis fulva (Linnaeus, 1758)

Common Name: Coney.

Maximum Length: 33 cm (12.9 in.); in Bermuda to 37 cm (14.6 in.).

Distribution: Bermuda to south Florida and the Bahamas to southern Brazil.

Biology: The Coney is one of the most common reef-dwelling groupers in the Caribbean. It prefers clear water and is most abundant on sand substrates with scattered coral heads and small patch reefs. Although often found in lagoons and back-reef areas at a depth range of 3 to 45 m (9.8 to 148 ft.), Coneys are most abundant at depths of 5 to 12 m (16 to 39 ft.). This species is often seen sitting prone on the bottom, or moving just above it, during the day. It is an ambush predator that feeds mainly on fishes, including trumpetfishes, juvenile surgeonfishes, parrotfishes, clinid blennies, filefishes, and pufferfishes, but also eats de-

capod shrimps, including the Banded Coral Shrimp (*Stenopus hispidus*), crabs, and mantis shrimps. In Brazil, the Coney regularly preys upon the Noronha Wrasse (*Thalassoma noronhanum*), which is a facultative cleaner as a juvenile and subadult. It usually preys upon wrasses that are foraging near the substrate, not those soliciting at cleaning stations. *Cephalopholis fulva* commonly follows snake eels, often with an entourage of other predatory fishes, as the eels forage among coral rubble and probe the crevices of small patch reefs. The Coney often occurs in small aggregations. For example, I have seen as many as four of these fish following the same Sharptail Snake Eel (*Myrichthys breviceps*). This species is a protogynous hermaphrodite: females become mature at approximately 16 cm (6.3 in.) and change into males at about 20 cm (7.9 in.) in total length. Males defend a territory that contains one to several females. The male spawns with each female daily, just before sunset. During courtship, the male develops a dark band from the pectoral fin base to the end of the tail, the edge of the soft portion of the dorsal fin turns black, a dark stripe appears through the eye, and a white spot appears on the body near the middle of the dorsal fin base. During the spawning ascent, this species will swim up to 3 m (9.8 ft.) into the water column. The Coney has been reported to cross-breed with the Creolefish (*Paranthias furcifer*)—the two species have concurrent spawning seasons in at least some locations. The product of this hybridization was originally described as a new genus and species, *Menophorus dubius*.

Captive Care: This durable species is occasionally encountered in the aquarium trade. One desirable attribute is that it is not as secretive as many of the other hinds and will spend much of its time either sitting on the bottom or hovering in the water column. It is easily tamed and will readily take food from the aquar-

Cephalopholis fulva, Coney: juvenile shows the rare yellow, or xanthic, color morph.

Cephalopholis fulva, Coney: bicolor adult, which can be the excited state of a brown specimen.

Cephalopholis fulva, Coney: brown adult, showing a common color phase seen in shallow water.

Cephalopholis fulva, Coney: yellow adult occasionally seen in both shallow and deep water.

Cephalopholis fulva, Coney: red adult, common color phase often observed in deeper water.

Cephalopholis fulva, Coney: rare hybrid specimen resulting from Coney-Creolefish crossbreeding.

ist's fingers. Unfortunately, red juveniles often change to the dark brown or bicolored phase within several weeks of being placed in an aquarium and will usually retain these less dramatic colors indefinitely. This species has been reported to live for at least 9 years in the wild, and may exceed this in the aquarium.
Aquarium Size: 100 gal. **Temperature:** 22 to 28°C (72 to 82°F).
Aquarium Suitability Index: 5.
Remarks: This hind displays at least four distinct color phases. One, which is most often found in deep water, is red overall (this phase appears brown underwater because of the lack of red light at depth). Another color phase, which is most common in shallow water, is chocolate brown overall. Some individuals exhibit a bicolor phase, where they are dark brown above and creamy white below. The third phase, the rarest form, is xanthic (bright yellow) and is found in both shallow and deep water. Coneys are able to change color—for example, dark brown individuals can transform to the bicolored phase when excited, while bicolored fish can become brown overall. Individuals display the bicolored phase most during the morning and late afternoon, while at midday these same individuals often turn all brown. This change in color may reflect differences in feeding ac-

tivity that occur during the day. The Coneys are crepuscular hunters. At dawn and dusk (when light levels are reduced) many will exhibit the bicolored pattern, which would provide more obliterative countershading as they sit on or hang over sandy substrates. All these color forms have bright blue spots (xanthic individuals have fewer), two dark spots on top of the caudal peduncle, and two black spots on the lower lip. Some of the older literature places this species in the genus *Epinephelus*.

Cephalopholis hemistiktos (Rüppell, 1830)
Common Names: Halfspotted Hind, Yellowfin Hind.
Maximum Length: 35 cm (13.8 in.).
Distribution: Northern Red Sea to Pakistan.
Biology: The Halfspotted Hind is most common on patch reefs or rocky outcroppings on open sandy bottoms, at depths from 4 to 55 m (13 to 180 ft.). In a study conducted on the food habits of this fish in the Red Sea, 64% of 98 individuals with food in their stomachs had fed on fishes, including gobies, damselfishes, cardinalfishes, and the Lyretail Anthias (*Pseudanthias squamipinnis*), while 36% had eaten crustaceans, including *Carpilius* crabs, pistol shrimps, and spiny lobsters. When hunting fishes,

Cephalopholis hemistiktos, Halfspotted Hind (Egypt): Red Sea specimen.

Cephalopholis leopardus, Leopard Hind (Madives): note identifying saddle.

Cephalopholis microprion, Freckled Hind: smaller species with blue spots.

this hind most often attacks those species that live near the bottom. Unlike some sympatric *Cephalopholis* species, the Halfspotted Hind does not engage in increased hunting efforts at specific times of the day. These hinds are usually found in monogamous pairs that exclude conspecifics from an area that can measure as large as 62 m² (667 ft.²). *Cephalopholis hemistiktos* is subordinate to the Peacock Hind (*C. argus*) and Coral Hind (*C. miniata*) where they co-occur.

Captive Care: This medium-sized species is uncommon in the aquarium trade. It should be kept in a larger tank with a sandy substrate and several small patch reefs with suitable shelter sites. It will eat any fish that it can swallow whole. Although it can be kept in a shallow- or deep-water reef aquarium, it will eat crustaceans and small fish tankmates.

Aquarium Size: 75 gal. **Temperature:** 22 to 27°C (72 to 81°F).

Aquarium Suitability Index: 5.

Remarks: Males of this species are larger than females. Color depends on the depth at which the individual lives: in shallow water (less than 15 m [49 ft.]) the fish are brown; between 15 and 30 m (49 and 98 ft.), individuals are more brown than red; and at depths greater than 30 m (98 ft.), they are red.

Cephalopholis leopardus (Lacépède, 1801)

Common Names: Leopard Hind, Leopard Grouper.

Maximum Length: 24 cm (9.4 in.).

Distribution: East Africa to the Line and Tuamotu Islands, north to Yaeyama Island, and south to the Great Barrier Reef.

Biology: The Leopard Hind is a resident of lagoon patch reefs, channels, reef faces, and fore-reef slopes at depths of 3 to 38 m (9.8 to 125 ft.). It is most common on well-developed reefs, in clear water, with rich hard-coral cover. Rarely straying far from its preferred hiding places, it is a solitary, secretive, site-attached species that feeds on fishes and crustaceans.

Captive Care: Usually sold in the hobby as an "assorted" grouper, it is a very durable species that should be housed in a tank replete with hiding places. This is one of the more secretive hinds and will spend more time hiding than some of the bolder members of the genus. Its smaller maximum length means it can be kept with a wider range of fish tankmates. In a smaller tank, it may bully fishes of similar size or those introduced after it has become a well-established resident. It can be kept in a shallow- or deep-water reef tank, although it will eat smaller fishes and crustaceans.

Aquarium Size: 55 gal. **Temperature:** 22 to 27°C (72 to 81°F).

Aquarium Suitability Index: 5.

Remarks: Some color forms of this species can easily be mistaken for the Darkfin or V-tail Hind (*Cephalopholis urodeta*), but the

Cephalopholis miniata, Coral Hind (Papua New Guinea): typical hind aggression, show here, includes jaw gaping, pushing with the snout, and color changes.

Leopard Hind can always be distinguished by the presence of a dark saddle mark on the caudal peduncle.

Cephalopholis microprion (Bleeker, 1852)
Common Names: Freckled Hind, Freckled Grouper.
Maximum Length: 23 cm (9 in.).
Distribution: Andaman Sea to the Great Barrier Reef and New Caledonia, north to the Philippines.
Biology: The Freckled Hind is found on coastal fringing reefs, on lagoon patch reefs, and in back-reef areas. It can also be found on silt-covered reefs. I have encountered *C. microprion* on inshore reefs composed principally of large-polyped stony corals, such as Anchor Coral (*Euphyllia ancora*). It occurs at a depth range of 4.5 to 30 m (15 to 98 ft.). *C. microprion* is a site-attached species that rarely strays far from its shelter position.
Captive Care: Because of its smaller maximum size, the Freckled Hind can be kept in a medium-sized tank with a variety of fish tankmates. It can be housed in a shallow- or deep-water reef aquarium, although it will eat crustaceans. See the Captive Care section in the tribe account, page 26, for more general care information.
Aquarium Size: 55 gal. **Temperature:** 22 to 27°C (72 to 81°F).
Aquarium Suitability Index: 5.

Remarks: The overall coloration of the Freckled Hind is dark brown, while the head and anterior part of the body has numerous small blue spots. The dorsal, caudal, and anal fins have gray-blue distal margins, and some individuals are greenish yellow on the dorsum.

Cephalopholis miniata (Forsskål, 1775)
Common Names: Coral Hind, Miniata Grouper, Coral Grouper.
Maximum Length: 41 cm (16 in.).
Distribution: Red Sea to the Line Islands, north to southern Japan, and south to Lord Howe Island.
Biology: The Coral Hind is one of the most photographed reef fishes and is typically found on isolated lagoon pinnacles and reef faces with rich coral growth, where it occurs at a depth range of 2 to 150 m (6.6 to 492 ft.). It is most commonly seen at depths of 17 to 33 m (56 to 108 ft.). This species feeds predominantly on bony fishes, but does eat some crustaceans. For example, in a study conducted in the Red Sea, of 124 Coral Hinds that had food in their stomachs, 86% had ingested fishes. The Lyretail Anthias (*Pseudanthias squamipinnis*) was by far the most important prey item, but Blue Green Chromis (*Chromis viridis*), sweepers, surgeonfishes, and squirrelfishes were also eaten. The stomachs of 14% of these individuals contained crustaceans, including crabs

Cephalopholis miniata, Coral Hind: juvenile showing orange color phase.

Cephalopholis miniata, Coral Hind: brilliant scarlet Red Sea specimen.

Cephalopholis miniata, Coral Hind: accepting grooming services of a wrasse.

Cephalopholis oligosticta, Vermilion Hind: fewer spots than *C. miniata*.

and decapod shrimps. In other areas, the Coral Hind is also reported to eat mantis shrimps and cephalopods. This grouper is crepuscular, doing most of its hunting between 0700 and 0900 hours and 1400 and 1600 hours. In the Red Sea, the Coral Hind has been observed associating with foraging octopuses and the Gray Moray (*Siderea grisea*).

Captive Care: The Coral Hind is a durable species that will thrive in captivity. Although it can be quite shy when initially introduced to the aquarium, when acclimated it will spend more time in the open. This fish, like all other members of the genus, will eat chopped fresh or frozen seafoods, other frozen preparations, and freeze-dried krill. Only one Coral Hind should be kept per aquarium, as they are prone to intraspecific fighting. It will eat any fish it can swallow whole and will behave aggressively toward tankmates that invade its preferred hiding places. This grouper will sometimes eat cleaner wrasses, such as the Bluestreak Cleaner Wrasse (*Labroides dimidiatus*) and the Fourline Cleaner (*Larabicus quadrilineatus*), in captivity. The Coral Hind can be kept in a shallow- or deep-water reef aquarium, but it will eat crustaceans.

Aquarium Size: 100 gal. **Temperature:** 22 to 28°C (72 to 82°F).

Aquarium Suitability Index: 5.

Remarks: The juvenile Coral Hind is orange, rather than red, with more broadly scattered blue spots. Adults will often assume a mottled appearance when interacting with other hinds or when hunting.

Cephalopholis oligosticta Randall & Ben-Tuvia, 1983

Common Name: Vermilion Hind.

Maximum Length: 30 cm (11.8 in.).

Distribution: Red Sea.

Cephalopholis polleni, Harlequin Hind (Christmas Island): a glorious fish and a true "Holy Grail" species among collectors of rare groupers.

Biology: The Vermilion Hind is a resident of open sand and rubble flats and dead, silt-covered reefs at a depth range of 15 to 48 m (49 to 157 ft.). However, it is most common in water deeper than 30 m (98 ft.). This species is known to feed on fishes.

Captive Care: *Cephalopholis oligosticta* will acclimate more quickly in a dimly lit tank. See the Captive Care section in the tribe account, page 26, for more general care information.

Aquarium Size: 75 gal. **Temperature:** 22 to 27°C (72 to 81°F).

Aquarium Suitability Index: 5.

Remarks: This beautiful species is similar to the Coral Hind but has fewer blue spots (more widely scattered over the head and body), fewer lateral-line scales, a smooth preopercular margin, and shorter pelvic fins.

Cephalopholis polleni (Bleeker, 1868)

Common Name: Harlequin Hind.

Maximum Length: 35 cm (13.8 in.).

Distribution: Comoros to the Line Islands, north to the Ryukyus, and south to Mauritius.

Biology: This species is a resident of steep reef dropoffs, where it can be found in caves or under ledges or archways. It occurs at a depth range of 10 to 120 m (33 to 394 ft.), but is uncommon in less than 45 m (148 ft.). Juveniles are solitary, while adults often occur in pairs or small groups. They often swim upside down, with their ventral surfaces facing the ceiling of a cave or overhang.

Captive Care: The Harlequin Hind is a glorious fish that is infrequently seen in the aquarium trade. It should be provided with a large cave or overhang-like structure to serve as a natural hiding place, and the tank should be dimly lit, to replicate a deep-reef environment. It is flighty when first introduced to the aquarium, spending most its time hiding or near the entrance of a hole or crevice. It will dash out from a hiding place to capture passing morsels and will defend a preferred hiding place from intrusion, especially if the intruder is a conspecific or a related species. This species will eat any fish that can fit into its mouth. It can be kept in a deep-water reef aquarium, but ornamental crustaceans are potential fodder (I have kept it with cleaner shrimps, which were introduced before the hind). Because of its proclivity for deep water and relative rarity over most of its range, it commands a high price when occasionally imported.

Aquarium Size: 75 gal. **Temperature:** 22 to 27°C (72 to 81°F).

Aquarium Suitability Index: 5.

Remarks: Juvenile Harlequin Hinds are orange overall without the magenta markings. Subadults have magenta dots, arranged in rows, along the dorsal half of the body. In adults, the lines on the body are often blue or purple.

Cephalopholis sexmaculata, Sixspot Hind (juvenile): note blue lines on head.

Cephalopholis sexmaculata, Sixspot Hind: displaying six dusky bars.

Cephalopholis sexmaculata (Rüppell, 1830)
Common Names: Sixspot Hind, Sixspot Grouper.
Maximum Length: 47 cm (18.5 in.).
Distribution: Red Sea to the Marquesas, north to southern Japan, and south to Lord Howe Island.
Biology: The Sixspot Hind is most abundant on fore-reef dropoffs. It occurs at depths of 6 to 150 m (20 to 492 ft.). At depths of less than 30 m (98 ft.) it competes with other hinds for space and food, this species spends the day in caves, under large overhangs, or in expansive crevices and comes out at night to hunt. In deeper water, it often exhibits a diurnal activity pattern, swimming out in the open during the day, above the reef. It often swims upside down along cave roofs and occurs singly, in pairs, or in small groups. This hind feeds mainly on bony fishes, including cardinalfishes, anthias, surgeonfishes, and even tobies (e.g., the Pearl Toby, *Canthigaster margaritata*), which are toxic, but it also eats the occasional shrimp. It is frequently groomed by cleaner species, like the Elegant Cleaner Shrimp (*Periclimenes elegans*).
Captive Care: The Sixspot Hind should be housed in a larger aquarium. In order to imitate its natural habitat, the tank should have one or more large caves and/or overhangs. It is a secretive species that will spend much of its time in hiding. Keep one Sixspot Hind per aquarium and be careful when housing it with closely related forms. It will rarely bother tankmates of equal size or larger, except when they invade its hiding place. Although this grouper can be housed in a shallow-water reef aquarium if suitable shelter sites are constructed, it will spend more time in the open in a dimly lit tank. Like its relatives, it will consume crustaceans, even cleaner shrimps, in captivity. (If cleaner shrimps are added to the tank first, they may survive for a while with

the Sixspot Hind.) It is a threat to small fishes.
Aquarium Size: 135 gal. **Temperature:** 22 to 27°C (72 to 81°F).
Aquarium Suitability Index: 5.
Remarks: *Cephalopholis sexmaculata* is similar to the Coral Hind (*C. miniata*), but it is peppered with smaller blue dots, has blue lines on the head, and six dusky bars on the body.

Cephalopholis sonnerati (Valenciennes, 1828)
Common Name: Tomato Hind.
Maximum Length: 57 cm (22.4 in.).
Distribution: East Africa to Samoa, north to southern Japan, and south to Great Barrier Reef and Tonga.
Biology: The Tomato Hind is a resident of deep lagoon reefs, reef faces, and steep fore-reef slopes at depths from 10 to 150 m (33 to 492 ft.). It is rare at depths of less than 30 m (98 ft.). In some areas, it is most common around large patch reefs on sand slopes. It is often found at shrimp cleaning stations, allowing the shrimp to clean its body, fins, gills, and mouth. It changes color to facilitate the shrimp's cleaning efforts. The Tomato Hind feeds primarily on crustaceans, including galatheid crabs, brachyuran crabs, decapod shrimps, mantis shrimps, and small spiny lobsters, but it also eats bony fishes, including cardinalfishes. This species will follow foraging octopuses, pouncing on morays, small fishes, and crustaceans flushed by the cephalopods. Juveniles usually occur singly, while adults are also found in pairs or in small groups (e.g., at cleaning stations).
Captive Care: Although juvenile Tomato Hinds most commonly enter the aquarium trade, this is one of the larger hind species and adults need to be housed in a large aquarium. Because of its potential to reach greater sizes, it is also a threat to a wider range of

Cephalopholis sonnerati, Tomato Hind: juvenile is cute, but ready to grow.

Cephalopholis sonnerati, Tomato Hind: dark variant juvenile form.

Cephalopholis sonnerati, Tomato Hind (Bali): handsome adult specimen.

Cephalopholis spiloparaea, Strawberry Hind: prefers deeper-water habitats.

fish tankmates. See the Captive Care section in the tribe account, page 26, for more general care information.

Aquarium Size: 180 gal. **Temperature:** 22 to 27°C (72 to 81°F).

Aquarium Suitability Index: 5.

Remarks: Adults from the Indian Ocean and Pacific Ocean differ in color. Indian Ocean specimens have an orangish red to reddish brown body, often with scattered light blotches and a purplish or reddish brown head with orange spots. Individuals from the Pacific are light red to yellowish brown with numerous reddish brown spots on the head, body, and fins. Juveniles are reddish brown to black overall with a white border on the caudal fin margin. Some specimens may have yellow spots on the head, black spots on the body (which can be quickly changed to a pale green), and white diagonal lines on the tail reminiscent of the Darkfin Hind (*Cephalopholis urodeta*).

Cephalopholis spiloparaea (Valenciennes, 1828)
Common Name: Strawberry Hind.

Maximum Length: 27.5 cm (10.8 in.).

Distribution: East Africa to the Pitcairn Group, north to the Ryukyus and Ogasawara Islands, and south to New Caledonia.

Biology: The Strawberry Hind is a resident of fore-reef slopes and walls with heavy coral growth, holes, ledges, and caves in which it can seek shelter. It is more common on seaward or offshore reefs than on continental reefs. In some areas, it is most abundant on slightly silty inner-reef slopes. This fish occurs at depths ranging from 15 to 108 m (49 to 354 ft.), but are most abundant at depths in excess of 30 m (98 ft.). Crustaceans, especially crabs, are important prey items. Male Strawberry Hinds defend a territory that covers an area of 6.6 to 73 m^2 (71 to 786 ft.^{2}) and contains shelter sites attractive to females. From two to

Cephaolopholis urodeta, Darkfin Hind: also sold as the V-tail Grouper.

Cephalopholis urodeta, Darkfin Hind: mottled color phase.

Cephalopholis urodeta nigripinnis (Andaman Sea, Thailand): regional variant.

six females will live within the male's territory. During the mating period, females at adjacent courtship sites regularly behave aggressively toward each other, which often interrupts courtship behavior. Spawning occurs just after sunset.

Captive Care: This small hind is not common in the marine fish trade because of its deep-water habits. It should be housed in a dimly lit tank containing numerous hiding places. It will fight with members of its own species and possibly with its close relatives. It can be kept in a deep-water reef aquarium, but will eat any fish or crustacean that will fit into its capacious jaws.

Aquarium Size: 55 gal. **Temperature:** 22 to 27°C (72 to 81°F).

Aquarium Suitability Index: 5.

Remarks: This species is similar to the Golden Hind (*C. aurantia*), but has markings on the tail margin. Some individuals from the Western Indian Ocean have seven to eight saddlelike blotches on the body and one at the anterior end of the caudal peduncle. The Strawberry Hind has small orange spots on the head, pale pectoral fins, and a white margin on the edge of the caudal fin. The **Rusty Hind** (*Cephalopholis aitha*) **Randall & Heemstra, 1991** is somewhat similar to *C. spiloparaea*, but less colorful. The Rusty Hind is reddish brown, with a distinct blotch on the base of the pectoral fin. The rear margin of the caudal fin is bluish, especially toward the center of the fin. This species attains a maximum length of 17 cm (6.7 in.) and ranges from Papua New Guinea to Indonesia and the Philippines. It is most commonly seen on silt-covered reefs at depths of 5 to 33 m (16 to 108 ft.). The small size attained by *C. aitha* makes it well suited to the home aquarium.

Cephalopholis urodeta (Forster, 1801)

Common Names: Darkfin Hind, V-tail Grouper, Flagtail Grouper.

Maximum Length: 27 cm (10.6 in.).

Distribution: East Africa to Similan and Christmas Islands (*C. urodeta nigripinnis*); Christmas Island to the Marquesas and Gambier Island, north to southern Japan, and south to New Caledonia and Rapa Island (*C. urodeta urodeta*).

Biology: The Darkfin Hind is a resident of lagoon patch reefs, the reef face, and fore-reef slopes, at depths from 1 to 40 m (3.3 to 131 ft.). It is most common in clear water, in areas of rich coral growth, or on fore-reef rubble tracts. It usually hovers just above or hides in holes among hard corals and coral boulders, or sits on coral pavement. In a study conducted on the food habits of this species on the reefs of Tahiti, of 25 specimens examined that had food in their stomachs, 68% had ingested fishes, including squirrelfishes, surgeonfishes, and a blenny, while 32% had eaten crustaceans, including decapod and mantis shrimps. It has also been reported to feed on goatfishes, damselfishes, xanthid and porcelain crabs, and squids. Males defend an area that contains the smaller territories of six to eight females. It is not unusual to see specimens in the wild with torn fins and abrasions on their sides. This may be the result of aggressive encounters with members of their own species or other hinds.

Captive Care: This average-sized hind is one of the most popular members of the genus in the aquarium trade. It tends to be slightly less secretive, spending more of the day sitting out in the open than some of its relatives. Only one should be kept per aquarium and it should not be housed with fishes small enough for it to swallow whole. It can be introduced to a shallow- or deep-water reef aquarium, but it will eat ornamental crustaceans.

Aquarium Size: 55 gal. **Temperature:** 22 to 27°C (72 to 81°F).

Aquarium Suitability Index: 5.

Remarks: This species is known to be sexually dimorphic, with male Darkfin Hinds being larger than females. There are two subspecies of *C. urodeta* (Kuiter [1998] elevates these to valid species level), which can be easily separated by the coloration of the caudal fin. The Indian Ocean form, *C. urodeta nigripinnis*, has a dark reddish brown to almost black tail, with numerous pale blotches. The Pacific form, *C. urodeta urodeta*, has white to whitish blue diagonal bands that converge as they near the posterior edge of the tail. In the Maldives, adult *C. urodeta nigripinnis* may have black on the posterior one-third to one-half of the body, while small juveniles have been reported with a red head and a black body. In dimly lit habitats in the Comoros, the Darkfin Hind is reported to be uniformly brown.

Genus *Cromileptes* (Panther Grouper)

This monotypic genus contains one of the most popular groupers in the marine aquarium trade. It is distinctive in appearance, with a small head, humplike nape, large pectoral fins, and conspicuous color pattern. The coloration of the juveniles is particularly interesting. The body is white with large black spots, but there is also an iridescent hue that reflects green, pink and other colors when viewed at certain angles.

Cromileptes altivelis (Valenciennes, 1828)

Common Names: Panther Grouper, Panther Fish, Polkadot Grouper, Barramundi Cod, Humpback Grouper.

Maximum Length: 70 cm (27.6 in.).

Distribution: East Africa to Vanuatu, north to southern Japan, and south to New Caledonia. Several individuals, apparently fish released by thoughtless aquarists, also reside on reefs off the Hawaiian Islands.

Biology: Although the Panther Grouper is most abundant on dead, silty coastal reefs, it also occurs on well-developed reefs with

Cromileptes altivelis, Panther Grouper (Sulawesi, Indonesia): radiant juvenile.

healthy coral growth, in lagoons, on reef flats, reef faces, and fore-reef slopes. On the Great Barrier Reef, this species is most common in lagoons and on back-reef zones. Juveniles have also been observed in shallow tide pools. The Panther Grouper occurs at a depth range of 0.4 to at least 40 m (16 in. to 131 ft.). Juveniles are solitary animals, occurring around coral heads, among macroalgae, sponges, and ramose corals on coastal fringing reefs. Adults, on the other hand, occur singly or in small aggregations. The largest concentration of Panther Groupers I have ever seen was on a shipwreck off the coast of northern Sulawesi, Indonesia. On this wreck, adult Panther Groupers live in small aggregations and refuge under large table-forming *Turbinaria* corals that are growing on the hull of the sunken vessel. The diet of this grouper consists of fishes, crustaceans (including shrimps), and squids.

Captive Care: The Panther Grouper is a mainstay in the aquarium hobby because of its striking color pattern, unusual appearance, amusing swimming behavior (its pectoral fins are constantly undulating), and charming personality. It is a durable, long-lived fish that is suitable for aquarists at all levels. Although juveniles are a tempting acquisition for the smaller home aquarium, be warned: this species grows at a rapid rate if fed frequently. The only prerequisite is that the aquarist be willing to invest in a tank big enough to house it for its entire life and great quantities of food to meet its nutritional needs. This species could be housed indefinitely in an aquarium of 180 gallons. The tank should have several suitable hiding places, especially when the

Cromileptes altivelis, Panther Grouper: subadult displaying yellow hue.

Cromileptes altivelis, Panther Grouper (Solomon Islands): large adult.

fish is first introduced, but it is also important to provide plenty of swimming room. The Panther Grouper will readily accept all types of frozen, pelletized, and fresh foods commonly available to the aquarist. One favorite food is fresh table shrimp, either whole or in pieces. From the outset, the Panther Grouper tends to be bolder than many members of this family. As it becomes more accustomed to its new home, and begins to recognize where its food comes from (i.e., the aquarist), it will often put on an impressive performance. When its sees its owner enter the room, it is not unusual for the Panther Grouper to swim back and forth along the front of the tank in anticipation of a meal. This grouper is rarely aggressive and will ignore its fish tankmates unless they are small enough to swallow whole. Adult individuals can even be housed together in an extra-large system. The mouth of this species is small relative to its body size, making it unable to eat

prey items as large as those consumed by other comparably sized groupers. However, it is best to keep it with fishes of similar size.
Aquarium Size: 180 gal. **Temperature:** 22 to 27°C (72 to 81°F).
Aquarium Suitability Index: 5.
Remarks: The juvenile has a white body with large black polka-dots. As the fish grows, the spots become smaller and more numerous and the overall coloration becomes gray to reddish brown, with dusky blotches often appearing on the body and fins. An occasional individual may have yellow dorsal, caudal, and anal fin margins. The size of the spots and the amount of blotching on the body can change quite rapidly. Although this fish normally exhibits some of these chromatic changes in captivity, an individual may adopt a more mottled appearance for long periods of time when the physical parameters (especially the pH) of the aquarium are suboptimal. When swimming slowly or maintaining its position in the water column, this fish will assume a head-down position, undulate the posterior part of the body, and scull with the enlarged pectoral fins. This species is highly prized in Asian food markets, and adults are under intense fishing pressure in many areas.

Genus *Dermatolepis* (Leather Bass)

This genus consists of three species: the Smooth Grouper (*Dermatolepis striolata*) from the Indian Ocean, the Marbled Grouper (*D. inermis*) from the Western Atlantic, and the Leather Bass (*D. dermatolepis*) from the tropical Eastern Pacific, with only the latter two likely to be encountered in the aquarium trade. These species have relatively deep bodies, a steep head profile, and are humpbacked. Although they are not chromatically noteworthy, they do exhibit pleasing color patterns.

Dermatolepis dermatolepis Boulenger, 1895
Common Names: Leather Bass, Leatherback Bass.
Maximum Length: 1 m (3.3 ft.).
Distribution: Bahia Magdalena and Central Gulf of California to Ecuador, including all offshore islands (e.g., Galapagos, Cocos).
Biology: This grouper is found on rocky reefs at depths of 2 to 38 m (6.6 to 125 ft.). Juvenile Leather Bass seek refuge in the spines of the sea urchins *Diadema mexicanum* and *Centrostephanus coronatus*. The color of the juveniles—bold black and white bands—helps them to blend in among the spines of these echinoderms while they apparently forage on small fishes and invertebrates that live around them. Adults are cunning predators, often using other fishes to gain an advantage over their prey. For example, they often swim with schools of roving herbivores, like Whitecheek Surgeonfish (*Acanthurus nigricans*), Spotted Surgeonfish (*Prionurus punctatus*), Yellowtail Surgeonfish

(*P. laticlavius*), and Striped Chubs (*Kyphosus analogus*). At Cocos I have observed solitary or pairs of adolescent Leather Bass swimming amid large schools of Whitecheek Surgeonfish. When in the company of these herbivores, the Leather Bass is often blanched in color so it is less conspicuous. It may be that the bass is exhibiting aggressive mimicry: resembling a harmless or nonpredatory species in order to gain access to its prey.

These schools of herbivores raid territories of aggressive damselfishes and feed on the algal turf that they so pugnaciously defend. By hiding in these groups, smaller Leather Bass (most attendant bass are under 30 cm [11.8 in.]) gain access to the rich invertebrate communities that inhabit a damsel's algae patch. These territories support a higher density of crustaceans, worms, and serpent stars than the surrounding areas because the algae growth is more luxuriant, providing suitable hiding places, and many of their predators are chased off by the damselfishes. The feeding activities of the grazing herbivores flush crustaceans and even small fishes—such as blennies, clinids, and gobies—out from hiding and make them vulnerable to Leather Bass attack. Many of these little fishes are very cryptic and when stationary are hard to see, but the feeding herbivores often cause them to change position and make them conspicuous to the hunting bass. The damselfish itself is vulnerable to attack by larger bass when it comes out to fend off the school. In fact, the herbivores may actually be luring the damselfish into striking distance of an attendant leather bass. If this is the case, this could be classified as a mutualistic relationship (all members benefit). The school of herbivores would benefit if the damselfish were eaten, because they would then have free access to the damsel's productive territory.

Small to medium-sized Leather Bass also associate with solitary herbivores, omnivores, and carnivores. This association usually consists of the bass approaching the nuclear (target) species from the side or rear, then pitching its body forward and taking a position so its "nape" is near the pectoral fin of the other fish. The bass maintains body contact with the nuclear species until it breaks away to strike at a prey item or look for another fish to "ride." This behavior is called "hunting by riding" or "shadow stalking." In the Gulf of California, the Leather Bass is particularly fond of the Guinea Fowl Puffer (*Arothron meleagris*), possibly because this slower fish has a difficult time shaking off an attendant bass. As the puffer sculls along above the reef, the bass uses it as a moving blind. The Cortez Hogfish (*Bodianus diplotaenia*), parrotfishes, and Orange-sided Triggerfish (*Balistes verres*) are also followed by the Leather Bass, because these fish nip at the substrate and scare out small organisms, which are then pounced on by the bass. The Leather Bass also associates with the Giant Damselfish (*Microspathodon dorsalis*) and Cortez Damselfish

Dermatolepis dermatolepis, Leather Bass: juvenile hides with spiny urchins.

Dermatolepis dermatolepis, Leather Bass (Cocos Island): large adult.

(*Stegastes rectifraenum*), possibly to feed on small fishes that the damsels chase from their territories. When associating with solitary fishes, the Leather Bass is often dark gray or black with almost indistinguishable markings; of the associate fishes, only two (parrotfishes and the Cortez Hogfish) are not dark in color.

The Leather Bass is not only an attendant species, it also serves as a nuclear species for the Pacific Trumpetfish (*Aulostomus chinensis*). On numerous occasions, I have observed this trumpetfish, which is very common at Cocos, riding along the back of the Leather Bass. This serves the same function as the Leather Bass riding the pufferfish (i.e., a moving blind is used to approach unwary prey).

When hunting on their own, Leather Bass slowly cruise over the reef and inspect the algal mat. They feed on small fishes, crustaceans, and octopuses, primarily during the day. When they

Dermatolepis striolata, Smooth Grouper (South Oman): seldom-seen species.

Dermatolepis inermis, Marbled Grouper: juveniles display attractive patterns.

see a prey item, they dart forward and attempt to ingest it. When feeding on their own, Leather Bass assume a medium gray color overall with several darker broad bars and small dark and light spots.

Captive Care: The Leather Bass is a durable aquarium inhabitant. Juveniles are more readily available in the marine trade and can be housed in smaller aquariums (e.g., 30-gallon). One or more juveniles in a tank with several pieces of live rock and some larger long-spined urchins (*Diadema* spp.) make an interesting display. Smaller specimens acclimate to aquarium confines more readily than larger individuals. As this fish grows, it will need to be placed in a tank of 180 gallons or larger. Feed this fish chopped fresh shrimp, squid, and pieces of marine fish flesh. Juveniles will also readily accept brine shrimp, pelletized food, and even flake food. The Leather Bass can be kept in a community tank, although it will eat any fish that can be swallowed whole. It can also be kept in a shallow- or deep-water reef aquarium, although it will eat ornamental crustaceans.

Aquarium Size: 180 gal. **Temperature:** 18 to 24°C (64 to 75°F).

Aquarium Suitability Index: 5.

Remarks: The **Smooth Grouper** (*Dermatolepis striolata*) (Playfair & Günther, 1867) is known from the Gulf of Oman to southern Africa. It is yellow to red-brown with small dark spots (the spots sometimes form lines on the body) and pale blotches.

Dermatolepis inermis (Cuvier & Valenciennes, 1833)

Common Name: Marbled Grouper.

Maximum Length: 81 cm (31.9 in.).

Distribution: Southern Florida, Bermuda, and the northern Gulf of Mexico, south to Brazil.

Biology: The Marbled Grouper occurs on coral and rocky reefs at depths of 3 to 215 m (9.8 to 705 ft.). It frequently associates with caves, overhangs, and crevices. It has not been reported to hunt by riding like *D. dermatolepis*.

Captive Care: The care requirements of this species are similar to those of the Leather Bass (*D. dermatolepis*). Be sure to provide this species with a suitable cave or overhang to refuge in or under.

Aquarium Size: 180 gal. **Temperature:** 21 to 27°C (70 to 81°F).

Aquarium Suitability Index: 5.

Remarks: The tail of *D. inermis* is rounded in juveniles and emarginate or notched in adults. Juveniles are dark brown and have scattered white spots on the body and fins. Adults have rings of small black spots and are mottled with brown.

Genus *Epinephelus* (Spotted Groupers)

This is the largest genus in the family, with more than 100 species described. Of these, 76 species occur in the Indo-Pacific, 8 in the Eastern Pacific, 10 in the Western Atlantic, and 7 species in the Eastern Atlantic. Although members of this genus do show up in aquarium stores from time to time, most are not as highly sought after as members of the genus *Cephalopholis* or *Variola*. This is explained by the more subdued colors often displayed by the *Epinephelus* species (dark or light spots on a light or dark body is a common chromatic theme). There are, however, some very attractive species in this genus, such as the stunning Powder Blue Grouper (*Epinephelus flavocaeruleus*), which is blue overall with yellow fins. Another drawback to members of this genus is the larger sizes they attain, requiring a huge aquarium to maintain them into adulthood. In fact, this genus contains the two largest bony fishes known, the Goliath (*Epinephelus itajara*) and the Giant Grouper (*E. lanceolatus*). These fishes exceed 2.5 m (8.2 ft.) in length and can weigh over 300 kg (660 lbs.).

Most of the *Epinephelus* species are found at relatively shallow or moderate depths, on coral and rocky reefs. There are, however, a few species that live over open sand or mud plains and lurk at depths of up to 525 m (1,722 ft.). Many of the coral-reef-associated species spend their time during the day in repose on exposed hard substrates or in crevices and caves. Others will rest on sandy bottoms, but usually do not stray far from a shelter site.

Although opportunistic feeders, many of the *Epinephelus* species are nocturnal or crepuscular. They feed primarily on bony fishes (from morays to porcupinefishes) and crustaceans (including spiny lobsters, crabs, shrimps, and mantis shrimps). However, polychaete worms, peanut worms, cephalopods (including octopuses, cuttlefishes, and squids), gastropods, bivalves, sharks, and juvenile sea turtles form a minor portion of some grouper diets. At least one species sometimes ingests zooplankton, particularly pelagic tunicates. This species, the Wavy-lined Grouper (*Epinephelus undulosus*), has modified gill-rakers that enable it to feed on these smaller planktonic prey items. Most of these groupers employ a sit-and-wait feeding strategy, ambushing prey species that move past their resting sites. Their reef-tone color patterns help them to disappear when lying on the substrate, and the spots on the head, which many of these groupers possess, may make it difficult for prey species to see their eyes and recognize them as potential predators. (In piscivores, the distance between the eyes is usually greater than in herbivores, and they have an upturned mouth—prey species apparently cue in on the distance between a larger fish's eyes to determine if they should flee.) Other groupers will take advantage of the foraging activities of eels, following close beside them and pouncing on any fish or crustacean that is flushed from cover.

All the *Epinephelus* species studied to date are protogynous hermaphrodites, although this may not be true for all species. Some species form massive spawning aggregations, at specific locations, during certain times of the year (usually a few days to a few weeks in duration). In most cases, spawning aggregations form during the full moon. These aggregations routinely number in the hundreds (e.g., 200 to 300 individuals), but can consist of more than 100,000. In some *Epinephelus* species, individuals form clusters (usually composed primarily of females) within these larger aggregations, and the members in this smaller subunit spawn together.

Some of the *Epinephelus* species are quite aggressive on the reef and in captivity. They will often defend a preferred hiding place and will evict any intruders. In smaller aquariums, they may spend a good deal of time chasing and biting their tankmates.

Epinephelus adscensionis, Rock Hind: known to eat young sea turtles.

In captivity, they will, of course, ingest any fish or crustacean they can swallow whole.

Epinephelus adscensionis (Osbeck, 1765)
Common Name: Rock Hind.
Maximum Length: 61 cm (24 in.).
Distribution: Massachusetts and Bermuda, south to southeast Brazil, east to Ascension and St. Helena.
Biology: The Rock Hind occurs on rocky and coral reefs at depths of 1 to 50 m (3.3 to 164 ft.). In the Bahamas, it is often found at depths of less than 4 m (13 ft.). It feeds most heavily on crabs (including decorator and arrow carbs), but also eats fishes and shrimps. It is also known to eat young sea turtles. This fish is often found mixing with spawning aggregations of Red Hinds (*Epinephelus guttatus*).
Captive Care: See the Captive Care section in the tribe account, page 26, for more details on its husbandry.
Aquarium Size: 200 gal. **Temperature:** 22 to 27°C (72 to 81°F).
Aquarium Suitability Index: 5.

Epinephelus areolatus (Forsskål, 1775)
Common Name: Areolate Grouper.
Maximum Length: 40 cm (15.7 in.).
Distribution: East Africa and the Red Sea, east to the Fiji Islands, north to southern Japan, south to northern Queensland.
Biology: *Epinephelus areolatus* is a resident of relatively turbid coastal areas, including seagrass beds and isolated patch reefs (consisting of rock, sponge, soft, or dead stony corals). It is also found resting on open sand bottoms. This serranid occurs at depths of 6 to 200 m (20 to 656 ft.). It is usually a solitary species.
Captive Care: The Areolate Grouper is occasionally sold as a "spot-

Epinephelus areolatus, Areolate Grouper: often frequents seagrass beds.

Epinephelus bleekeri, Bleeker's Grouper (Bali): note orange spots on head.

Epinephelus bontoides, Palemargin Grouper (Indonesia): eating a damselfish.

ted grouper" in the aquarium trade. This a durable species can be kept in moderate-sized aquariums. Provide it with plenty of shelter sites and be aware that it will eat any fish or crustacean that it can swallow whole. See the Captive Care section in the tribe account, page 26, for more details on its husbandry.
Aquarium Size: 100 gal. **Temperature:** 22 to 27°C (72 to 81°F).
Aquarium Suitability Index: 5.
Remarks: The adult Areolate Grouper has brown to yellowish brown spots on the head, body, and fins that are about the size of the pupil. **Bleeker's Grouper (*Epinephelus bleekeri*) (Vaillant, 1877)** is another spotted species that is found from Taiwan, the Philippines, and the coast of China to the Persian Gulf. It inhabits coastal habitats (often in silty or turbid conditions) where it usually shelters near trash (e.g., cans, bottles), waterlogged tree branches, and rocky outcrops. It is usually not found on well-developed coral reefs. It has been reported from depths of less than 1 to 45 m (3.3 to 148 ft.). This attractive species is purplish gray overall with many small, orangish yellow spots on the head, body, and fins. It attains a maximum length of at least 76 cm (30 in.), which means it will require an extra-large aquarium.

Epinephelus bontoides (Bleeker, 1855)
Common Name: Palemargin Grouper.
Maximum Length: 30 cm (11.8 in.).
Distribution: Taiwan, the Philippines, Indonesia, and Papua New Guinea.
Biology: This grouper is found among stones, man-made debris, or large sponges on sand or mud bottoms. It occurs in protected bays and current-washed sand or reef slopes. It has been taken at depths of 2 to at least 30 m (6.6 to 98 ft.). Numerous individuals will reside along stretches of stony shoreline, sometimes with the Blacktip Grouper (*Epinephelus fasciatus*). In one case, I observed an individual with a damselfish sticking out of its mouth.
Captive Care: See the Captive Care section in the tribe account, page 26, for more details on its husbandry.
Aquarium Size: 75 gal. **Temperature:** 22 to 27°C (72 to 81°F).
Aquarium Suitability Index: 5.
Remarks: In the Palemargin Grouper, the caudal fin, the pectoral fins, and the soft portion of the dorsal fin are dark brown to blackish. The posterior margins of these fins are pale yellow to white.

Epinephelus caeruleopunctatus (Bloch, 1790)
Common Name: Whitespotted Grouper.
Maximum Length: 76 cm (29.6 in.).
Distribution: East Africa to Kiribati, north to the Persian Gulf

Epinephelus caeruleopunctatus, Whitespotted Grouper: colorful juvenile.

Epinephelus caeruleopunctatus, Whitespotted Grouper: large, muted adult.

Epinephelus macrospilos, Snubnose Grouper: note rounded, spotted tail fin.

Epinephelus corallicola, Coral Grouper: handsome Pacific species.

and south Japan, south to the Great Barrier Reef and New Caledonia.

Biology: The Whitespotted Grouper is found in lagoons, on the reef face, and on fore-reef slopes, at depths of 4 to 65 m (13 to 213 ft.). It usually occurs in areas with lush coral growth and often sits on the substrate near its home cave or overhang. Juveniles are sometimes found in tidepools. This species feeds on fishes and shrimps.

Captive Care: This is a larger fish that will need to be housed in a sizeable tank. Its size makes it a greater threat to a wider range of prey items. Provide this species with suitable hiding places as it tends to be rather shy when initially placed in the aquarium. See the Captive Care section in the tribe account, page 26, for more details on its husbandry.

Aquarium Size: 240 gal. **Temperature:** 22 to 27°C (72 to 81°F).

Aquarium Suitability Index: 5.

Remarks: Juvenile *E. caeruleopunctatus* have a darker brown body with larger white spots and a white margin on the median fins. The **Snubnose Grouper** (*Epinephelus macrospilos*) (**Bleeker, 1855**) is a similar species with large spots on a rounded caudal fin. It occurs from East Africa to French Polynesia and reaches 43 cm (17 in.) in length.

Epinephelus corallicola (Valenciennes, 1828)

Common Name: Coral Grouper.

Maximum Length: 49 cm (19.3 in.).

Distribution: Gulf of Thailand to the Solomon Islands, north to Taiwan, south to northwestern Australia and New South Wales.

Biology: The Coral Grouper is most abundant on silty coastal reefs, although it also occurs on clear fore-reef slopes at depths

Epinephelus cyanopodus, Speckled Grouper (juvenile): hardy but gets huge.

Epinephelus cyanopodus, Speckled Grouper (Great Barrier Reef): adult.

of 5 to 23 m (16 to 75 ft.). This species will enter estuaries. It has been reported to feed at least in part on lobsters.

Captive Care: This grouper can be kept in a large home aquarium. Provide it with plenty of shelter sites and be aware that it will eat any fish or crustacean that it can swallow whole. See the Captive Care section in the tribe account, page 26, for more details on its husbandry.

Aquarium Size: 135 gal. **Temperature:** 22 to 27°C (72 to 81°F).

Aquarium Suitability Index: 5.

Remarks: This species is somewhat similar meristically to the Whitespotted Grouper (*E. caeruleopunctatus*). The Coral Grouper differs in color; juveniles have white spots with black trim on the body, while adults have gray-black spots smaller than the pupil scattered on the head, body, and fins.

Epinephelus cyanopodus (Richardson, 1790)

Common Name: Speckled Grouper.

Maximum Length: 1 m (39.4 in.).

Distribution: East Africa to the Marshall Islands, north to the Ryukyus, south to the Great Barrier Reef and New Caledonia.

Biology: This distinctive grouper usually occurs on isolated coral heads in lagoons and bays, and occasionally on fore-reef slopes, at depths of 2 to 150 m (6.6 to 492 ft.). It often sits on the seafloor near a home patch reef. Fishes (including snake eels) and crabs (including calappid crabs) make up the bulk of this grouper's diet, but it will consume all cephalopods and shrimps.

Captive Care: The Speckled Grouper is a very hardy species that can be housed in larger home aquariums. Be aware that this is a fast-maturing species that will quickly outgrow smaller tanks (a juvenile may grow 30 cm [11.8 in.] in as little as a year). It tends to spend more time in the open then many of its tribe mates,

and it often hovers in the water column. Because of this tendency, and the fact that it is more active than many other groupers, it is a good idea to provide plenty of uncluttered swimming space. It is a formidable predator and will make short work of smaller fishes and crustaceans. Although it is possible to keep more than one of these groupers in an extra-large aquarium, individuals may fight if space is limited. See the Captive Care section in the tribe account, page 26, for more details on its husbandry.

Aquarium Size: 240 gal. **Temperature:** 22 to 27°C (72 to 81°F).

Aquarium Suitability Index: 5.

Remarks: The juveniles of this species are blue with yellow or orange fins. As the Speckled Grouper grows, the yellow on the fins disappears, and more speckles and large spots develop on the body and fins. Subadults sometimes have black margins on the median fins and black-tipped pelvic fins.

Epinephelus fasciatus (Forsskål, 1775)

Common Name: Blacktip Grouper.

Maximum Length: 40 cm (15.7 in.).

Distribution: Red Sea to the Marquesas and the Pitcairn Group, north to southern Japan, and south to Lord Howe Island.

Biology: The Blacktip Grouper is most often found in lagoons, on reef flats, and on back reefs at depths of 1 to 160 m (3.3 to 525 ft.). It is, however, most common at depths of less than 6 m (20 ft.). This species is usually closely associated with its shelter. It typically is seen in repose on live hard corals, rubble, algal mats, beds of macroalgae, or on the sand at the base of coral heads. The Blacktip Grouper feeds on octopuses, brachyuran crabs, galatheid crabs, pistol shrimps, mantis shrimps, serpent stars, and bony fishes (including cardinalfishes and fusiliers). It regularly associates with feeding octopuses, morays, and snake eels, patiently

Epinephelus fasciatus, Blacktip Grouper (Red Sea): highly variable colors.

E. fasciatus, Blacktip Grouper: color-change display by fish shown above.

E. fasciatus, Blacktip Grouper: red bands switch on and off almost instantly.

waiting for small fishes and crustaceans to be flushed out by the foraging activity of these predators. The Blacktip Grouper will rub against stationary morays, possibly to encourage them to continue their hunting activities.

Captive Care: This is a durable aquarium fish that can be housed in a large home aquarium. Its relatively modest maximum length also means it can be kept with a greater range of fish tankmates. It will spend most of its time sitting on the bottom near a potential hiding place and will accept a wide range of food items. This fish can be kept in a shallow- or deep-water reef aquarium, although it will ingest any crustacean or fish that it can swallow whole, and may also eat other motile invertebrates, including worms and serpent stars.

Aquarium Size: 100 gal. **Temperature:** 22 to 27°C (72 to 81°F).
Aquarium Suitability Index: 5.

Remarks: The color of this species can be quite variable. It ranges from light greenish gray to pale yellowish red. The body may or may not have five orangish brown to dark red bars, and there can be irregular whitish spots on the body. The red bands on the side can be turned off and on almost instantaneously. Individuals often exhibit the banded pattern when they are in a hunting mode. There are black triangles between the spines of the spinous dorsal fin. Six populations of this fish species have been recognized, which vary somewhat in meristic measurements and coloration. The **Redtipped Grouper** (*Epinephelus retouti*) **Bleeker, 1868** is a similar species that ranges from East Africa east to the Society Islands. It can be separated from *E. fasciatus* by the shape of the tail (it is truncate rather than rounded or nearly truncate) and the profile of the head (*E. retouti* has a straight head profile, while *E. fasciatus* has a convex profile). The Redtipped

Epinephelus flavocaeruleus, Blue-and-Yellow Grouper: highly prized beauty.

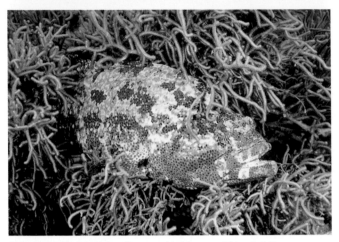

Epinephelus fuscoguttatus, Brownmarbled Grouper: big and gluttonous.

Grouper is also found on deep reefs (at depths of 70 to 220 m [230 to 722 ft.]).

Epinephelus flavocaeruleus (Lacépède, 1801)

Common Name: Blue-and-Yellow Grouper, Powder Blue Grouper.
Maximum Length: 90 cm (35.4 in.).
Distribution: East Africa to west Thailand and Sumatra, north to the Persian Gulf, and south to Mauritius.
Biology: The juveniles of the Blue-and-yellow Grouper occur on shallow rocky and coral reefs, while adults usually occur in deeper water. This species has been reported at depths of 10 to 150 m (33 to 492 ft.). Adults are often seen swimming high above the substrate. Fish make up a large portion of this grouper's diet (including species that would seemingly be inedible, such as the Longhorn Cowfish [*Lactoria cornuta*]), but it also eats shrimps,

spiny lobsters, crabs (especially calappids), squids, and small octopuses. One individual was even found with a sponge in its stomach (probably eaten incidentally). This species is reported to attain sexual maturity at about 35 cm (13.8 in.). Off East Africa, it is reported to spawn during the summer.
Captive Care: This attractive species can be kept in the extra-large home aquarium. It will, however, quickly outgrow smaller tanks. It spends much of its time swimming or hanging in the water column and should be provided with plenty of room to move. This species will eat any crustaceans and fishes that it can swallow whole (including moray eels), so choose its tankmates carefully. Most crowded reef tanks would be too confining for this large, active fish, and like its relatives, it will eat ornamental crustaceans and other motile invertebrates.
Aquarium Size: 300 gal. **Temperature:** 22 to 27°C (72 to 81°F).
Aquarium Suitability Index: 5.
Remarks: Small adults are deep blue, sometimes with blue flecks on the body, with yellow on the caudal peduncle and the fins. Some individuals may also have yellow on the front of the head. As adults grow larger, they may lose the yellow coloration and become deep blue, purplish, or nearly black overall. This species is very closely related to the Speckled Grouper (*E. cyanopodus*)—in fact, some ichthyologists consider them to be the same species.

Epinephelus fuscoguttatus (Forsskål, 1775)

Common Name: Brownmarbled Grouper.
Maximum Length: 90 cm (35.4 in.).
Distribution: Red Sea to Phoenix and Samoan Islands, north to the Ryukyus, south to the Great Barrier Reef.
Biology: *Epinephelus fuscoguttatus* inhabits lagoons, reef faces, and fore-reef slopes, at depths of 1 to 60 m (3.3 to 197 ft.). While a juvenile was collected from a mangrove swamp, this species usually occurs in clear water, in habitats with rich stony-coral growth. It commonly lies on the substrate, sometimes far from shelter, and also refuges under staghorn coral heads and rock ledges. The Brownmarbled Grouper feeds mainly on fishes (including squirrelfishes and goatfishes), but also dines on brachyuran crabs, shrimps, and cephalopods.
Captive Care: This grouper attains a size too large to be adequately housed in the majority of home aquariums. It will also require a hefty food budget to maintain for the long-term. The size and appetite of this fish makes it a threat to a large number of potential tankmates. If kept, this species must have one or two large caves to hide in and plenty of open bottom space to rest upon. For more information on keeping this species, see the Captive Care section in the tribe account, page 26.
Aquarium Size: 300 gal. **Temperature:** 22 to 27°C (72 to 81°F).

Aquarium Suitability Index: 5.

Remarks: The Brownmarbled Grouper is yellowish tan overall, with brown blotches of varying size on the body and fins, a black spot on the top of the caudal peduncle, and small dark spots on the head, body, and fins. When the fish is viewed in profile, there is a slight indentation adjacent to the eyes.

Epinephelus gabriellae Randall & Heemstra, 1991

Common Name: Gabriella's Grouper.

Maximum Length: 52 cm (20.5 in.).

Distribution: Oman and Somalia.

Biology: This species is found on coral reefs and rocky bottoms. It has been reported from "inshore" to depths of 40 m (131 ft.).

Captive Care: Nothing is known of its husbandry requirements, but they are probably similar to those of other medium-sized groupers. See the general captive care information in the genus account above (page 26).

Aquarium Size: 135 gal. **Temperature:** 22 to 27°C (72 to 81°F).

Aquarium Suitability Index: 5.

Remarks: *Epinephelus gabriellae* is pale brown to grayish overall with small orange to brownish orange spots on the head, body, and fins. There is a narrow white margin on the soft portion of the dorsal, anal, and caudal fins. There are five dark bars on the body that can be "turned on and off." It is similar to the **Brownspotted Grouper** (*Epinephelus chlorostigma*) (**Valenciennes, 1828**). *Epinephelus gabriellae* differs in having fewer soft dorsal rays (14 to 15 compared to 16 to 18), a more elongated body, and the spots on the body are orangish brown (they are a darker brown in *E. chlorostigma*) and the outer portion of the pectoral fins are not spotted (they are spotted in *E. chlorostigma*). The Brownspotted Grouper is found from South Africa east to Samoa, north to southern Japan, and south to New Caledonia. It attains a maximum length of 75 cm (29.5 in.). It is found in seagrass beds, on mud bottoms, rocky reefs, and coral reefs and is reported from depths of 4 to 280 m (13 to 919 ft.). Juveniles typically occur in shallower water than adults. It is reported to feed on fishes (including eels and anthias) and crustaceans (mantis shrimps and crabs).

Epinephelus guttatus (Linnaeus 1758)

Common Name: Red Hind.

Maximum Length: 67 cm (26.4 in.).

Distribution: North Carolina and Bermuda to Brazil.

Biology: This is a common grouper on coral and rocky reefs, occurring at a depth range of 3 to 80 m (9.8 to 262 ft.). It is most abundant in low-relief reef habitats. *Epinephelus guttatus* spends much of its time resting in reef crevices, behind small patch reefs,

Epinephelus chlorostigma, Brownspotted Grouper: similar to *E. gabriellae*.

Epinephelus guttatus, Red Hind: following a foraging snake eel.

and at cleaning stations during the daytime, while at night it seeks shelter in reef crevices. It feeds on crabs (including *Mithrax* spp.), fishes (including morays, trumpetfishes, goatfishes, wrasses, parrotfishes, and filefishes), mantis shrimps, shrimps (including the Banded Coral Shrimp [*Stenopus hispidus*] and pistol shrimps), lobsters (including slipper lobsters), octopuses, and sea urchins. This species will follow hunting Sharptail Snake Eels (*Myrichthys breviceps*), capturing prey items that the eels startle from cover. In a population of Red Hinds studied off Puerto Rico, it was shown that individuals occupy a home range of 112 to 5,636 m^2 (1,206 to 60,666 ft.^{2}). The home range of an individual may overlap with those of 1 to 18 conspecifics. However, individuals are not highly social, spending much of their time sitting on the substrate. Almost all individuals sexed on inshore patch reefs were females, suggesting that the sexes may remain segregated during much of the year. The majority of males are thought to spend their time over the insular shelf, in deeper water. This species is a protogynous hermaphrodite, with females changing to males as early as 2 years of age. Presence or absence of males apparently does not influence when or if a female changes sex, as it does in many other protogynous hermaphrodites.

This species forms female-dominated spawning aggregations, typically around the full moon. Red Hinds come from near and far to join these reproductive gatherings. The spawning occurs from January to April in the Caribbean; in Bermuda, aggregations form from April to July. A single male will associate with a group of two to six females (a male may join with more than one female group). It is possible that the males may form spawning territories or at least defend their group(s) of females. Males have been observed charging at each other with their mouths open and performing lateral displays along what appear to be territorial borders. This Red Hind will spawn in pairs. A female will swim off the bottom, where it is joined by a male. The gametes are released about 50 cm (19.7 in.) above the bottom, but there is no upward dash as seen in many of the other serranids. Both sexes spawn more than once during the reproductive period. It has been estimated that the Red Hind can live up to 18 years in the wild.

Captive Care: The Red Hind becomes very tame in captivity, although it attains a size too large to be adequately maintained in most home aquariums. Its size also makes it a greater threat to a wider range of tankmates, and large adults will produce a significant amount of waste. Provide this fish with several suitable shelter sites, as well as open bottom space where it can rest. See the Captive Care section in the tribe account, page 26, for more details on its husbandry.

Aquarium Size: 300 gal. **Temperature:** 22 to 27°C (72 to 81°F).
Aquarium Suitability Index: 5.
Remarks: This species has red spots over the entire body (although they are not larger on the belly as they are in the Rock Hind, *Epinephelus adscensionis*), and black margins on the soft portion of the dorsal, anal, caudal, and pelvic fins. During the spawning period, female Red Hinds are readily distinguishable from males. The females have a swollen abdomen and are lighter in color with dark spots. Males are darker with large vertical bars and squares posterior to the anus.

Epinephelus hexagonatus (Schneider, 1801)
Common Names: Starspotted Grouper, Hexagon Grouper.
Maximum Length: 26 cm (10.2 in.).
Distribution: South Africa to the Marquesas and the Pitcairn

Epinephelus hexagonatus, Starspotted Grouper: note five dark saddles.

Group, north to the Ryukyus and Izu Islands, south to New Caledonia and Rapa.
Biology: The Starspotted Grouper can be found on shallow outer-reef flats (often in areas exposed to surge), and in clear lagoons, at depths of less than 1 to at least 6 m (3.3 to 20 ft.). This species feeds mainly on small fishes, but also eats brachyuran crabs, mantis shrimps, and polychaete worms. It feeds both day and night.
Captive Care: Because of its smaller maximum length, *E. hexagonatus* is well suited to the home aquarium. Like any grouper, it is a threat to fishes and crustaceans that it can swallow whole, but its smaller size means that it is less of a threat than many other members of this tribe. It spends most of its time in repose on the aquarium bottom and will need suitable shelter sites, which can consist of a cave or crevice.
Aquarium Size: 75 gal. **Temperature:** 22 to 27°C (72 to 81°F).
Aquarium Suitability Index: 5.
Remarks: This species has dark, polygon-shaped spots on the body (separated at each corner by a white spot) and a large yellow blotch behind the eye.

Epinephelus itajara (Lichtenstein, 1822)
Common Names: Goliath Grouper, Jewfish, Itajara.
Maximum Length: 2.5 m (8.2 ft.).
Distribution: North Carolina and Bermuda south to southern Brazil, including Gulf of Mexico; in eastern Atlantic known from Senegal to the Congo (rare around the Canary Islands). Eastern Pacific from Gulf of California to Peru. Caribbean and Bahamas, as far north as the Carolinas and as far south as southern Brazil.
Biology: The Goliath Grouper exhibits some ontogenetic preferences when it comes to habitat utilization. It occurs at depths of less than 1 to 100 m (3.3 to 328 ft.); however, it is usually found at depths of less than 50 m (165 ft.). Post-larvae and juveniles

are often found in mangrove habitats (e.g., the Florida ever-glades are an important "nursery"), where they live among the mangrove prop roots. The juvenile fish are also found in estuarine habitats. They are reported to enter tidal creeks during hunting forays. The young fish move from mangroves and estuaries at a size of approximately 14 kg (31 lbs.). Adults occur on inshore and offshore reefs and ship wreckage (up to 22 km [14 mi.] offshore). They have also been reported near pier pilings and jetties in harbors and bays. It can be found over sand, mud, rock, or coral substrates. They have been taken in poorly oxygenated waters. Adults tend to occur near ledges, caves, and wrecks.

Epinephelus itajara has an eclectic diet. Juveniles feed mostly on shrimps, crabs, and bony fishes (including the Sea Catfish, *Arius felis*), while adult diets are more varied. Spiny and slipper lobsters are a favorite food of larger *E. itajara*, but they also eat octopuses, crabs, stingrays, small sharks, a variety of bony fishes (including relatively slow-moving forms, like trunkfishes, spiny boxfishes and spiny puffers) and young Hawksbill Sea Turtles.

It is apparently an ambush, as well as a stalking, predator. It is capable of sudden, explosive speed from a stationary position. This fish is quite "vocal." It is known to produce a highly audible "boom," which is apparently important for intraspecific communication. It may use this sound in territorial disputes and during courtship (male are reported to engage in this behavior more than females). Adults are solitary, territorial animals that tend to stay in the same area for long periods of time. When defending their territory, they will open their jaws wide and their body will quiver. The Goliath Grouper will also hover or rest on the substrate near cleaning stations. In the Gulf of California they will take advantage of the services of cleaner gobies (*Elacatinus* spp.). They can be very placid and easily approached when being "groomed." This grouper has also been reported to be cleaned by the Black Widow (*Stygnobrotula latebricola*) (although some doubt exists that this bythitid actually engages in cleaning). The Goliath Grouper is host to trematode, nematode, copepod, and isopod parasites.

It is thought to be a protogynous hermaphrodite, although more research is needed to verify this. The spawning season occurs between June and October, although it varies over the fish's range. For example, off the Florida coast, the spawning season occurs in August and September. In Belize, the reproductive period occurs in July and August, while in Colombia, spawning season lasts from September through October. During the reproductive season, *E. itajara* will aggregate in preferred habitats (e.g., around wrecks, around rocky ledges and on isolated patch reefs). They have been reported to move up to 100 km (62 mi.) to these spawning sites. Spawning aggregations can consist of 3 to

Epinephelus itajara, Goliath Grouper: a true behemoth, threatened in the wild.

over 100 individuals. The size of these aggregations was much larger many years ago, before spearfishing pressure depleted *E. itajara* stocks. In southern Florida thirty or forty years ago, it was not uncommon to see 50 to 100 adults in one of these spawning aggregations. But in the 1980s, a typical spawning group consisted of 10 individuals or fewer. Due to government protection, these reproductive groups are increasing in size. Spawning groups have been reported at depths of 30 to 46 m (98 to 151 ft.). In these aggregations, individuals sometimes occur in "stalked" layers over the seafloor.

During courtship, the head of the male becomes paler in color. Females do not change color. During courtship, a male will approach a female from behind and nuzzle her vent with his snout. A male will also approach a female, swim parallel to her, and the pair will then begin turning together in the water column. Males have been observed swimming away from the main aggregation with one to three females. Males are known to produce up to one "boom" every 15 to 20 seconds during courtship. It has been suggested that spawning occurs late in the day, although it has yet to be observed. Eggs are hatched in 23 to 40 hours (this is temperature-dependent). Both sexes reach maturity at a length of about 1.2 m (4 ft.) and 4 to 7 years of age. All males greater than 116 cm (45.7 in.) in total length and over 7 years are sexually mature (some are sexually mature at 5 years). All females over a total length of 123 cm (48.4 in.) and older than 6 years of age are sexually mature. The growth rate of this species decreases markedly after age 7. This giant grouper can live for

Centrogenys vaigiensis (False Scorpionfish):
perfect mimic of a venomous species.

Centrogenys vaigiensis (False Scorpionfish):
family classification is in question.

Centrogenys vaigiensis (False Scorpionfish):
colors vary wdely, but pectorals are striped.

Grouper, Scorpionfish, or Hawkfish?

Roger Steene came to my room bubbling over with excitement. He had just found a fish on a night dive that he had never seen before. Roger knows his fishes better than most of us, so when he said he had never seen it, my curiosity was on full alert. He set his bag in the sink and opened it wide. Hmm.... It looked like some type of scorpionfish. But I was certainly not familiar with it. The next day we took the strange fish back to the area where Roger had captured it and let it go, but not without subjecting it to a rigorous photo session. We sent one of the photos to Rudie Kuiter who identified it as a **False Scorpionfish (*Centrogenys vaigiensis*) Quoy & Gaimard, 1824**. What, not a scorpionfish? This scorpaenid mimic had done a great job at duping two fish enthusiasts, and there is no doubt that its resemblance to a venomous scorpionfish provides it with some degree of protection from roaming piscivores. It is a wonderful example of Batesian mimicry.

This fish is now thought to be a member of the Family Centrogeniidae, although many guide books classify it in the Serranidae (grouper) family. Its place in the ichthyological classification scheme is a bit of a mystery, and some taxonomists suggest it shares more likenesses with the hawkfishes (Family Cirrhitidae) than with the groupers. More study is needed to figure out who its relatives are. As the photographs attest, this fish's color is somewhat variable, but it always has bold stripes on the inside of the pectoral fins. It can reach a maximum length of around 22 cm (8.7 in.).

The False Scorpionfish has been reported from Nicobar Island in the eastern Indian Ocean, east to New Guinea and northern Australia, north to the Izu Peninsula. I have found that it is not uncommon in certain habitats in Lembeh Strait, northern Sulawesi. It has been reported from brackish estuaries and on coastal reefs. I have seen it most often on silty substrates, refuging among benthic debris (e.g., sunken logs, trash) and patches of macroalgae. It is also reported from rubble substrates. This fish is found at depths of 5 to 10 m (16.4 to 33 ft.). Preying on small fishes and crustaceans (including shrimps and crabs), it refuges during the day and probably does most of its hunting at night. Although it is not common in the aquarium trade, it is occasionally collected.

up to at least 37 years (some researchers have suggested it can live much longer).

Captive Care: This species has been successfully kept in large public aquariums. They are obviously a threat to a variety of tankmates because of their large mouths and predatory behavior.

Aquarium Size: 500 gal. **Temperature:** 20 to 27°C (68 to 80°F).

Aquarium Suitability Index: 0 (Gets much too large and is illegal to collect).

Remarks: The Goliath Grouper is usually brownish yellow or greenish gray with small black spots on the fins. Since 1991, these groupers have been protected in federal waters of the United States. They are also protected in the Caribbean. Their numbers have increased significantly since protection was granted. There are reports of it stalking and even attacking divers. In the latter case, *E. itajara* has grabbed an arm or a leg, then spat it out, sometimes leaving the diver with serious skin abrasions.

Epinephelus lanceolatus (Bloch, 1790)

Common Names: Giant Grouper, Queensland Grouper, Brindle Bass.

Maximum Length: 2.7 m (8.9 ft.).

Distribution: Red Sea to the Hawaiian, Line, and Society Islands, north to southern Japan, and south to New South Wales and New Caledonia.

Biology: The Giant Grouper occurs on reef faces and fore-reef slopes at depths of 5 to 100 m (16 to 328 ft.). Juveniles have been taken in brackish water estuaries and from the intertidal zone. Adults are often found in caves or among ship wreckage, although it is sometimes observed hanging in the water column above the reef. The Giant Grouper feeds on large crustaceans, like crabs and lobsters, and fishes, including sharks, skates, and a variety of bony fishes. It is usually a solitary species, although it has been observed in small aggregations. In some regions (e.g., South Africa) this species is known to spawn during the summer months. They are often escorted by groups of juvenile Golden Jack (*Gnathanodon speciosus*), which swim in front of the head and along the body of these immense fish, and/or the groupers may be accompanied by disc fishes.

Captive Care: *Epinephelus lanceolatus* should not be collected for the marine aquarium trade because of its scarcity in the wild and because of the enormous size that it can attain. In large public aquariums, Giant Groupers are usually at the top of the pecking order, even in those tanks that contain sharks. They will eat smaller shark and ray tankmates. (Giant Groupers are reported to be potentially aggressive toward scuba divers, and there are anecdotal reports of fatal attacks on humans.)

Aquarium Size: 1,000 gal. **Temperature:** 22 to 27°C (72 to 81°F).

Aquarium Suitability Index: 1.

Remarks: Juveniles are yellow with three black bars on the body. As they grow, the yellow becomes dingy and black blotches develop. Full-grown adults display dark brown mottling on the body and small black spots on the fins. Adults have very small eyes. Some authors have placed this fish in the genus *Promicrops*.

Epinephelus maculatus (Bloch, 1790)

Common Name: Highfin Grouper.

Maximum Length: 62 cm (24.4 in.).

Distribution: Cocos-Keeling Island to Samoa, north to southern Japan, and south to Lord Howe Island.

Biology: The Highfin Grouper is usually found on protected areas, often in atoll lagoons around patch reefs, at depths from 2 to 100 m (6.6 to 328 ft.). It eats small fishes, including the Onespot Wormfish (*Gunnelichthys monostigma*), crabs, including swimming and calappid crabs, and octopuses.

Captive Care: *Epinephelus maculatus* is regularly sold as an "assorted" or "spotted" grouper in the aquarium trade. This hardy aquarium fish should be provided with open sand substrate to rest upon and several suitable hiding places. It is quite shy when first added to the tank, but becomes bolder as it begins to recognize its caretaker as a source of food. Like others in the genus, it will make short work of smaller fishes and crustaceans.

Aquarium Size: 180 gal. **Temperature:** 22 to 27°C (72 to 81°F).

Aquarium Suitability Index: 5.

Epinephelus lanceolatus, Giant Grouper: grows to 8.9 feet (2.7 m) in length.

Epinephelus maculatus, Highfin Grouper (juvenile): hardy, but shy at first.

Remarks: Juvenile Highfin Groupers are yellowish brown with small black spots and large white blotches. Adults are light brown to whitish overall, with numerous hexagon-shaped dark brown spots on the head, body, and fins, two dusky saddles on the back, and no black streak on the lower cheek. When resting on the bottom, this fish often takes on a mottled pattern. The **Longspine Grouper** (*Epinephelus longispinus*) (**Kner, 1865**) is a similar species that occurs from East Africa to Indonesia, north to the Laccadive and Andaman Islands. It attains a maximum length of 55 cm (21.5 in.). The Longspine Grouper differs from *E. maculatus* in having dark blotches on the dorsal fin—adult *E. maculatus* have a white saddle at the origin of the dorsal fin and a white saddle toward the middle of this fin. The Highfin Grouper is also more heavily spotted. The **Blacksaddle Grouper** (*Epi-*

Epinephelus maculatus, Highfin Grouper (subadult): often rests on bottom.

Epinephelus maculatus, Highfin Grouper (adult): perching predator.

Epinephelus malabaricus, Malabar Grouper (Thailand): formidable size.

nephelus howlandi) (**Gunther, 1873**) is similar to these two species. It has dark saddles on the back and upper part of the tail and pale blotches on the head, body, and fins. It ranges from the South China Sea east to Samoa, north to southern Japan, and south to Northwestern Australia. These species are sold in the aquarium trade as "spotted groupers."

Epinephelus malabaricus (Bloch & Schneider, 1801)
Common Name: Malabar Grouper.
Maximum Length: 100 cm (39 in.), possibly up to 140 cm (55 in.).
Distribution: Red Sea and East Africa to the Western Pacific.
Biology: The Malabar Grouper is found in protected habitats, including river mouths, where juveniles are reported to be especially common. It has been found at depths of 2 to 60 m (6.6 to 197 ft.). This species resides in caves and under ledges from which it will ambush passing prey. It is reported to feed on crustaceans (including crabs, shrimps, lobsters, and mantis shrimps) and fishes in equal amounts. Some of the fishes it consumes include large pufferfishes and small sharks. This grouper will also consume the occasional octopus.
Captive Care: Although hardy, this species gets too large for most home aquariums. For more general information on the husbandry of this species, see the Captive Care section in the tribe account, page 26.
Aquarium Size: 300 gal. **Temperature:** 22 to 27°C (72 to 81°F).
Aquarium Suitability Index: 5.
Remarks: This species is light gray to yellowish brown with five broad, dark brown bars on the body. The head and body are peppered with numerous small black spots and larger pale spots and blotches. There are also small black spots on the fins. This species is similar to the **Orange-spotted Grouper** (*Epinephelus coioides*) (**Hamilton, 1822**), but the latter has brownish orange or reddish brown spots on the head and body and lacks pale spots. The Orange-spotted Grouper ranges from East Africa east to Palau and the Fiji Islands, north to the Ryukyu Islands and south to New South Wales (it is reported to be common in the Arabian Gulf). This species is found in estuaries, on inshore reefs and offshore reefs, at depths up to 100 m (328 ft.). It feeds mainly on fishes (including ponyfishes, goatfishes, threadfin bream) and crustaceans (including crabs, decapod shrimps and mysid shrimps). It occasionally eats cuttlefish. Its major reproductive period in the Persian Gulf is March to June. *Epinephelus coioides* attains a maximum length of 95 cm (37.4 in.).

Epinephelus merra Bloch, 1793
Common Names: Honeycomb Grouper, Dwarf Spotted Grouper.
Maximum Length: 31 cm (12.2 in.).

Distribution: South Africa to the Line and Gambier Islands, north to southern Japan, and south to Lord Howe and Rapa Island. This is the most common grouper in the South Seas.

Biology: The Honeycomb Grouper occurs on bay and shallow-lagoon patch reefs, reef flats, channel walls, and protected reef-face areas, from the intertidal zone to 50 m (164 ft.). In one study on the food habits of this species, 68% of 481 adults from the Society Islands had eaten fishes, including lizardfishes, moray eels, squirrelfishes, pipefishes, cardinalfishes, damselfishes, wrasses, small parrotfishes, gobies, surgeonfishes, rabbitfishes, and even toxic tobies; 29% had eaten crustaceans, including portunid crabs, xanthid crabs, pistol shrimps, and the Banded Coral Shrimp (*Stenopus hispidus*); and 4% had eaten mollusks, including octopuses, a snail, and a small rock oyster. In at least some locations, this species consumes more fishes during the day, and more crabs after dark. *Epinephelus merra* is a protogynous hermaphrodite. Males average 24 cm (9.4 in.), while females average about 19 cm (7.4 in.). Spawning occurs monthly over a three- or four-day period and peaks three or four days before the full moon. The Honeycomb Grouper, like many of its relatives, is fairly site-specific.

Captive Care: This compact grouper is better suited for the home aquarium than most members of this genus. It is a more diminutive species and thus can be housed in a smaller tank and kept with a wider variety of tankmates. Young specimens can grow about 4 cm (1.6 in.) in a year's time. See the Captive Care section in the tribe account, page 26, for more details on its husbandry.

Aquarium Size: 75 gal. **Temperature:** 22 to 27°C (72 to 81°F).

Aquarium Suitability Index: 5.

Remarks: The hexagonal brown spots create a pattern resembling a honeycomb or wire mesh. There are no white dots in the corners of the hexagons, as in the very similar Starspotted Grouper (*Epinephelus hexagonatus*), which also sports a brown patch behind the eye.

Epinephelus morio (Cuvier & Valenciennes, 1828)

Common Name: Red Grouper.

Maximum Length: 90 cm (35.4 in.).

Distribution: Massachusetts and Bermuda south to Brazil. This species is very common in the Gulf of Mexico.

Biology: The Red Grouper is most common on rocky or limestone reefs, where it occurs at a depth range of 5 to 120 m (16 to 394 ft.). In the Florida Keys, it is most abundant on inshore patch reefs. This species usually rests on substrate and rarely strays far from the cave, crevice, or overhang in or under which it shelters. The Red Grouper feeds on octopuses, crustaceans (including many species of crab, shrimps, spiny lobsters, and mantis

Epinephelus coioides, Orange-spotted Grouper: often found in estuaries.

Epinephelus merra, Honeycomb Grouper: nice, compact aquarium species.

shrimps), and fishes (including sea robins, snappers, and porgies). Crustaceans are the most important prey items of the Red Grouper, with most of their prey consisting of benthic and slow-moving species. They apparently ambush most of their prey and may feed during both the day and night.

Although few differences have been found in the diets of juveniles and adults, larger specimens (over 28 cm [11 in.] in total length) do feed more on mantis shrimps than do smaller individuals. This species displays size segregation, with smaller individuals occurring at shallower depths. It is a protogynous hermaphrodite, but it has been shown that not all females transform into males. Most change sex at a standard length of 45 to 65 cm (17.7 to 25.6 in.). This species can live for more than 25 years in the wild.

Captive Care: Although sometimes offered by Florida fish sup-

Epinephelus morio, Red Grouper: big fish showing nonaggressive coloration.

Epinephelus morio, Red Grouper: threat colors displayed toward intruder.

Epinephelus morrhua, Comet Grouper: deep-water fish, rarely collected.

pliers, the Red Grouper gets too large for the majority of home aquariums. However, it readily acclimates to captivity and can be housed in an extra-large tank, complete with suitable hangouts and some open bottom space. It has a ravenous appetite and may tax its owner's fish food budget. It will also eat any motile tankmate that can be swallowed whole, and may even tear the appendages off larger crustaceans.

Aquarium Size: 300 gal. **Temperature:** 22 to 27°C (72 to 81°F).
Aquarium Suitability Index: 5.
Remarks: The Red Grouper is able to assume a number of color variations, including a display of dark bars or blotches that can cause it to resemble the Nassau Grouper (*E. striatus*).

Epinephelus morrhua (Valenciennes, 1833)

Common Name: Comet Grouper.
Maximum Length: 90 cm (35.4 in.).
Distribution: Western Indian Ocean, including the Red Sea, east to the Cook Islands, north to southern Japan, and south to New South Wales, Australia.
Biology: This grouper is usually found on deep rocky reef slopes at depths of 80 to 370 m (262 to 1,214 ft.). The author took the photo in this book at a depth of 20 m (66 ft.) off Osezaki, Japan. *Epinephelus morrhua* is often seen hovering or swimming above the substrate and will rapidly seek shelter if threatened. It is a solitary serranid.
Captive Care: The Comet Grouper is rare in the aquarium trade because of its preference for deep water. Its captive care requirements are similar to other *Epinephelus* spp., although it may acclimate more readily if housed in a dimly lit tank. It should also be kept at cooler water temperatures. Like others in the genus, it will make short work of smaller fishes and ornamental crustaceans. Its large size means it needs an extra-large aquarium.
Aquarium Size: 240 gal. **Temperature:** 19 to 23°C (66 to 73°F).
Aquarium Suitability Index: 5.
Remarks: The adult *E. morrhua* is an attractive serranid that is light brown to yellowish brown with dark brown bands. Juveniles tend to be lighter overall, with more dramatic markings. The **Dot-Dash Grouper** (*Epinephelus poecilonotus*) (**Temminck & Shlegel, 1842**) is a similar species that has a pale ventrum with white and black bands on the dorsal surface as a juvenile, although these markings fade as the fish grows. There seem to be two populations of this species—one ranging from East Africa, Mauritius, Chagos, the Maldives, and Sri Lanka; the other ranging from Japan, Taiwan, South China Sea, Vietnam, and Fiji. Like *E. morrhua*, the Dot-Dash Grouper occurs at moderate to great depths (from 45 to 375 m [148 to 1,230 ft.]). It attains a maximum length of 65 cm (25.6 in.).

Epinephelus ongus, Specklefin Grouper: known to venture into freshwater.

Epinephelus polyphekadion, Camouflage Grouper: note spots on snout.

Epinephelus ongus (Bloch, 1790)

Common Names: Specklefin Grouper, Whitespotted Grouper.
Maximum Length: 30 cm (11.8 in.).
Distribution: East Africa to the Marshall Islands, north to the Ryukyus, south to the Great Barrier Reef and New Caledonia.
Biology: The Specklefin Grouper is a resident of shallow coastal and lagoon reefs, at depths from 5 to 25 m (16 to 82 ft.). I have observed it in areas with rich small-polyped stony coral growth as well as on coastal reefs composed primarily of large-polyped scleractinians, like *Euphyllia ancora* and *E. parancora.* This species will enter brackish water, or even freshwater, in some regions. A cryptic fish, the Specklefin Grouper spends most of its time peering out from reef interstices. It feeds on crustaceans and fishes.
Captive Care: *Epinephelus ongus* is a better choice for the home aquarium than many of its relatives, because of the small size it attains. It can be acclimated to a brackish water aquarium, but it should be kept at a specific gravity of 1.014 or more. The Specklefin Grouper can be kept in a shallow- or deep-water reef aquarium, but it will be a threat to crustaceans and small fishes.
Aquarium Size: 75 gal. **Temperature:** 22 to 27°C (72 to 81°F).
Aquarium Suitability Index: 5.
Remarks: Juveniles of less than about 6 cm (2.4 in.) are brown with round white spots on the head, body, and fins, except for the spinous portion of the dorsal fin, where the spots are elongate. Individuals around 10 cm (3.9 in.) have horizontally elongate spots all over the head and body. Adults are brown overall with white spots that tend to form irregular rows, white blotches (as large or larger than the eye) on the body, and a black streak along the edge of the upper jaw. This species is similar to the allopatric Summan Grouper (*Epinephelus summana*).

Epinephelus polyphekadion (Bleeker, 1849)

Common Names: Camouflage Grouper, Marbled Grouper.
Maximum Length: 75 cm (29.5 in.).
Distribution: Red Sea to Line and Gambier Islands, north to southern Japan, south to Lord Howe and Rapa Islands.
Biology: *Epinephelus polyphekadion* is found in clear water, in lagoons, and on fore-reef slopes, usually in areas with lush coral growth. It occurs at depths of 1 to greater than 50 m (3.3 to 164 ft.), although it is typically found at depths of less than 20 m (66 ft.). This species is reported to be more common around atolls than high islands. The Camouflage Grouper spends much of its time in caves and crevices. It feeds mainly on crustaceans (especially swimming crabs) and fishes, but it eats gastropods and cephalopods on occasion. It is also a known predator of slipper and spiny lobsters.
Captive Care: The Camouflage Grouper grows too large for the typical home aquarium. It is a threat to a large number of potential aquarium tankmates. If you have an extra-large tank and choose to keep *E. polyphekadion,* be sure to provide a cave in which it can take shelter. See the Captive Care section in the tribe account, page 26, for more details on its husbandry.
Aquarium Size: 200 gal. **Temperature:** 22 to 27°C (72 to 81°F).
Aquarium Suitability Index: 5.
Remarks: This species is best recognized by the two black spots present in front of each eye, although these spots may be difficult to see in some larger specimens.

Epinephelus quoyanus, Longfin Grouper: handsome, not-too-large species.

Epinephelus sexfasciatus, Sixbar Grouper: hardy but only sporadically seen.

Epinephelus quoyanus (Valenciennes, 1830)

Common Name: Longfin Grouper.

Maximum Length: 39 cm (15.4 in.).

Distribution: Andaman Islands to Papua New Guinea, north to southern Japan, and south to northwest Australia. Not found around oceanic islands.

Biology: This species is most often seen on silty coastal reefs, often in water of less than 1 m (3.3 ft.) in the intertidal zone, but it has been reported to depths of 30 m (98 ft.). It spends most of the day resting on the seafloor, in the open or in caves and crevices. This grouper feeds on fishes (including cardinalfishes and blennies) and crabs. In one study, it was reported to consume fishes ranging in size from 25 to 87 mm in length (1 to 3.4 in.).

Captive Care: This species can be comfortably housed in a moderately large aquarium. As with others in this genus, it will eat any fish or crustacean that can be swallowed whole. See the Captive Care section in the tribe account, page 26, for more details on its husbandry.

Aquarium Size: 75 gal. **Temperature:** 22 to 27°C (72 to 81°F).

Aquarium Suitability Index: 5.

Remarks: *Epinephelus quoyanus* has two oblique dark brown bands on its thorax or elongate dark blotches linked by narrow bands. It is often misidentified in aquarium and field guides as *E. megachir.*

Epinephelus sexfasciatus (Valenciennes, 1828)

Common Name: Sixbar Grouper.

Maximum Length: 27 cm (10.6 in.).

Distribution: Indonesia, northern Australia, New Guinea, Thailand, Vietnam, and the Philippines.

Biology: This poorly known species is reported from silty sand and mud substrates from a depth range of 21 to 80 m (69 to 262 ft.). Nothing else has been published on the natural history of *E. sexfasciatus.*

Captive Care: I have seen the Sixbar Grouper in the aquarium trade on a number of occasions (these were collected off the Java coast). This very hardy fish is shy when first introduced to the tank. Like others in the genus, it will usually become bolder as time passes. It is a predator that will ingest crustaceans and small fishes.

Aquarium Size: 70 gal. **Temperature:** 22 to 26°C (72 to 79°F).

Aquarium Suitability Index: 5.

Remarks: The Sixbar Grouper is pale brown to gray with five brown bars on the body (the bars are slightly diagonal in orientation). There is also a scattering of pale spots on the body and dark spots on the fins. Juvenile *E. sexfasciatus* have large dark spots inside the body bars, but not in the bar on the nape. The **Convict Grouper** (*Epinephelus septemfasciatus*) (**Thunberg, 1793**) is a banded species that is only known from Japan, Korea, and China. It is brownish gray overall with nine very distinct bands on the head and body (the bars are less distinct in large individuals). The caudal peduncle of young individuals is black. The **Eightbar Grouper** (*Epinephelus octofasciatus*) (**Griffin, 1926**) occurs from east Africa to Polynesia. It is light brownish gray with eight dark brown bars (the bars are much thicker than the light spaces between the bars, as is also true in *E. septemfasciatus*). This is a deep-water species reported from depths of 40 to 350 m (131 to 1,148 ft.).

Epinephelus summana (Forsskål, 1775)

Common Name: Summan Grouper.

Maximum Length: 52 cm (20.5 in.).

Distribution: Red Sea and Gulf of Aden.

Epinephelus summana, Summan Grouper: big fish with a big appetite.

Biology: The Summan Grouper occurs in lagoons and on protected reefs at depths of 1 to 20 m (3.3 to 66 ft.) and will also enter brackish water in some regions. It is reported to feed on crabs, shrimps, and squids.

Captive Care: This species should only be kept by aquarists with an extra-large aquarium. Provide *E. summana* with plenty of room to rest on the aquarium bottom and a cave or crevice to hide in. It is a gluttonous predator that will snap up smaller fish and crustacean tankmates. See the Captive Care section in the tribe account, page 26, for more details on its husbandry.

Aquarium Size: 180 gal. **Temperature:** 22 to 27°C (72 to 81°F).

Aquarium Suitability Index: 5.

Remarks: *Epinephelus summana* is closely related and similar in appearance to the Specklefin Grouper (*E. ongus*). The allopatric *E. ongus* has longer pectoral fins, longer pelvic fins, the posterior nostril not enlarged or vertically elongate, and a narrow white margin and broad dark submargin on the median fins. Larger *E. ongus* also have wavy lines on the posterior portion of the body.

Epinephelus striatus (Bloch, 1792)

Common Name: Nassau Grouper.

Maximum Length: 1.2 m (3.9 ft.).

Distribution: North Carolina and Bermuda to Brazil.

Biology: The Nassau Grouper is an icon among Caribbean reef fishes and much is known about its natural history. It is found on coral reefs and in seagrass beds at depths of 1 to 35 m (3.3 to 115 ft.). It has an extensive bill of fare, feeding mostly on fishes and crustaceans, with larger specimens eating more of the former. The fishes eaten by *E. striatus* include morays, lizardfishes, squirrelfishes, other groupers, bigeyes, goatfishes, grunts, snappers, damselfishes, wrasses, parrotfishes, filefishes, and trunkfishes.

Nassau Groupers will eat fish prey items of varying size. For example, *E. striatus* as long as 40 cm (15.7 in.) have been reported to feed on juvenile fishes that have just settled out of the plankton, while a 58-cm (22.8-in.) specimen contained a 64-cm (25-in.) moray. Their crustacean prey include crabs (e.g., calappid, majid, porcellanid, portunid, and xanthid crabs), mantis shrimps, decapod shrimps (e.g., alpheid, caridean, and penaeid shrimps), spiny lobsters, and hermit crabs. Other less frequently fed upon prey items include octopuses, squids, conchs, and small pelecypods. This species has been observed trying to catch a Yellowhead Jawfish (*Opistognathus aurifrons*) by disturbing the entrance to its burrow and the surrounding substrate. The grouper does this by lying on its side with its tail positioned over the burrow entrance. It beats its tail from side to side five or six times, then turns upright and points its head toward the now-disturbed burrow opening. A grouper may engage in as many as 10 to 15 episodes of tail-beating, lasting up to 15 minutes. Although groupers have never been observed capturing a jawfish by employing this behavior, apparently they sometimes do succeed in excavating one or capturing it emerging from its collapsed burrow. One individual *E. striatus* was observed waiting near a burrow for a full hour before abandoning its efforts. This species has been reported to consume 3.6% of its total body weight in food per day. It regularly has parasitic isopods lodged in its nostrils.

The Nassau Grouper was once thought to be a protogynous hermaphrodite, but this is now being questioned. In this grouper, juveniles do go through a phase where they possess immature ovaries and testes (a bisexual phase). As they approach sexual maturity, the organs of one sex will develop, while those of the opposite gender will be lost (although remnants of these sex organs may remain). Sexually maturity is attained at, or before, a total length of 48 cm (18.9 in.). Adults migrate to traditional spawning sites and form large aggregations that can number in the tens of thousands. For example, an estimated 30,000 individuals were observed at one spawning site near Bimini. Spawning has been reported from late December to early February (with most activity occurring in December and January around the time of the full moon), when the water temperature is 25 to 26°C (77 to 79°F). Aggregations usually form about two days before the full moon. The fish aggregate at the spawning site for several days, with a ratio of three to five females for every one male. Courtship begins in the late afternoon, while spawning usually occurs just around sunset. Individuals in these spawning assemblages can exhibit four distinct color patterns: barred phase, white-belly phase, bicolor phase, and dark phase. The color patterns are used by individuals to communicate with other mem-

Epinephelus striatus, Nassau Grouper (South Caicos, British West Indies, Caribbean Sea): an elegant icon among Caribbean species, but for larger systems only.

bers of the group, with chromatic changes often occurring in a matter of seconds. The barred phase is a common ("normal") color pattern seen in this species during the nonreproductive phase. The white-belly phase is the same as the barred phase, but with a very pale abdomen. Females heavy with eggs often assume this color phase early in the day. In the bicolor pattern, most of the body is dark, but there is white on the belly, the underside of the head and jaws, and all the fins except the dorsal fin. There is also a white eye bar. The bicolor phase is assumed by submissive males and females. In spawning aggregations, most fish exhibit the bicolor phase as sunset approaches. The dark phase consists of the body and fins being dark gray to black overall, with the barred pattern being inconspicuous beneath the darker pigment. Dark-phase fish often lead groups of bicolor individuals in courtship and spawning. This has led one researcher to suggest that the dark-phase females are ready to spawn. In the late afternoon, bicolored fish begin following presumed females. They will also circle barred or dark-phase fish. As spawning approaches, the group begins moving higher in the water column, with more members of the assemblage adopting the bicolor phase. Just prior to spawning, the bicolor fish begin circling the dark-phase fish and following them more closely. Spawning occurs when the lead fish (presumably the female)

rapidly swims forward (usually up into the water column, but sometimes parallel to the substrate). This results in small subgroups of males (usually 3 to 25) dashing after the accelerating fish. In some cases, individuals engage in vertical spiraling as they make their spawning ascent. Gamete release typically occurs from 2 to 15 m (6.6 to 49 ft.) above the seafloor. The eggs are about 1 mm in diameter and hatch in about 24 hours (incubation is, of course, temperature-dependent). When they hatch, these groupers are positively buoyant for 2 to 3 days and feed within 60 hours of hatching. They spend 35 to 40 days in the plankton. Newly settled *E. striatus* are often found in shallow mangrove bays hiding among finger coral (*Porites porites*) and macroalgae. This species will live up to 28 years in the wild.

Captive Care: The Nassau Grouper is a large predator that will outgrow the vast majority of home aquariums. It will consume any fish tankmates that it can swallow and many types of motile invertebrates. Excluding these limitations, *E. striatus* is a hardy fish that will acclimate readily to captivity. See the Captive Care section in the tribe account, page 26, for more details on its husbandry.

Aquarium Size: 400 gal. **Temperature:** 22 to 27°C (72 to 81°F).
Aquarium Suitability Index: 5.
Remarks: This species has a black spot on the top of the caudal pe-

duncle. Commercial fishing has significantly reduced the population of this once-common species in many parts of its range. Concentrated exploitation of spawning aggregations has been especially harmful to *E. striatus* populations.

Epinephelus tauvina (Forsskål, 1775)

Common Name: Greasy Grouper.
Maximum Length: 75 cm (29.5 in.).
Distribution: Red Sea to the Marquesas and Ducie Islands, north to southern Japan, and south to New Caledonia and Rapa Islands.
Biology: The Greasy Grouper inhabits coral-rich areas of clear-water lagoons and fore-reef slopes, at depths from 1 to 52 m (3.3 to 171 ft.). Juveniles, and occasionally adults, are found on reef flats and in tidepools, in water as little as 30 cm (11.8 in.) deep. This species feeds mainly on fishes, including squirrelfishes, goatfishes, and damselfishes, but also eats crustaceans (especially crabs) and squids.
Captive Care: This large grouper will need to be housed in an extra-large aquarium. See the Captive Care section in the tribe account, page 26, for more details on its husbandry.
Aquarium Size: 200 gal. **Temperature:** 22 to 27°C (72 to 81°F).
Aquarium Suitability Index: 5.
Remarks: As with many groupers, certain localized populations may accumulate ciguatera toxin in their flesh, making them unfit for human consumption.

Epinephelus tukula Morgans, 1959

Common Names: Potato Grouper, Potato Cod.
Maximum Length: 2 m (6.6 ft.), to at least 100 kg (220 lbs.).
Distribution: East Africa and the Red Sea, east to the Great Barrier Reef, north to southern Japan.
Biology: The Potato Grouper is found on the reef face and fore-reef slope at depths of 1 to 150 m (3.3 to 492 ft.). This species feeds almost exclusively on a variety of bony fishes, but on occasion they will consume skates, crabs, spiny lobsters, and cephalopods. It is thought to use an ambush strategy to capture its prey. This is a solitary fish believed to be territorial. During the mating period (spring and summer in South Africa), they form pairs. Sexual maturity is believed to occur at about 90 cm (35.4 in.). Females were more common than males in one population study.
Captive Care: This species grows much too large for the home aquarium and should be avoided. See the Captive Care section in the tribe account, page 26, for more details on its husbandry.
Aquarium Size: 1,000 gal. **Temperature:** 22 to 27°C (72 to 81°F).
Aquarium Suitability Index: 1.

Epinephelus tauvina, Greasy Grouper (adult): may carry ciguatera toxin.

Epinephelus tukula, Potato Grouper (Great Barrier Reef, Australia): bold giant.

Remarks: Divers hand-feed this bold species at certain sites. There is one report of a drowning in which a diver was thumped in the chest by a large *Epinephelus tukula*. There are reports of this species swallowing divers' appendages, then spitting them out.

Epinephelus undulosus, Wavy-lined Grouper: predatory and voracious.

Gracila albomarginata, Whitemargin Grouper: adult color variant.

Gracila albomarginata, Whitemargin Grouper: spectacular juvenile colors.

Gracila albomarginata, Whitemargin Grouper (subadult): bold, active species.

Epinephelus undulosus (Quoy & Gaimard, 1824)

Common Name: Wavy-lined Grouper.

Maximum Length: 75 cm (29.5 in.).

Distribution: East Africa east to the Solomon Islands, north to China, south to Papua New Guinea.

Biology: The Wavy-lined Grouper is usually found over sand or mud flats and slopes. It sometimes refuges near benthic debris, like waterlogged tree branches, or rocky or coral outcroppings. I have observed it to depths of 30 m (98 ft.) in Milne Bay, Papua New Guinea. This is a voracious predator that is reported to feed heavily on fishes (including eels, lizardfishes, anthias, fusiliers, and sweepers) and crustaceans (including stomatopods and shrimps). They occasionally ingest pelagic tunicates. It is a solitary species.

Captive Care: This species is not often seen in the aquarium trade. It seems to prefer moderate water depths, which makes it less likely to be a target of collectors, unless they can command a high price for it. Its husbandry requirements are probably similar to that of other medium-sized serranids.

Aquarium Size: 240 gal. **Temperature:**23 to 27°C (73 to 82°F).

Aquarium Suitability: 5.

Remarks: This handsome grouper is purplish to brownish gray overall with spots on the head and wavy lines on the body (these lines are indistinct in larger individuals). It is unique within the grouper family in that it has more gill-rakers than any other serranid.

Genus *Gracila* (Whitemargin Grouper)

This is a monotypic genus that contains just one beautiful fish, the Whitemargin Grouper. This species is not common in the aquarium trade, but makes a stunning display animal.

Gracila albomarginata (Fowler & Bean, 1930)

Common Names: Whitemargin Grouper, Masked Grouper, Slenderspine Grouper.

Maximum Length: 38 cm (15 in.) (a report of a specimen 50 cm [19.7 in.] in length may be erroneous).

Distribution: East Africa to the Marquesas, north to the Ryukyus, and south to New Caledonia.

Biology: The Whitemargin Grouper is most common on steep outer-reef dropoffs, having been recorded at depths from 5 to 120 m (16 to 394 ft.). However, it is most common below 15 m (49 ft.). Unlike many groupers, which spend much of their time in repose on the seafloor or hiding in crevices, *G. albomarginata* swims, or hovers, well above the bottom (1 m [3.3 ft.] or more) most of the time. When threatened, it does not hide; instead, it swims away. *G. albomarginata* roams over large areas of the reef and feeds on fishes. It sometimes associates with foraging octopuses, feeding on fishes and crustaceans that the cephalopod flushes from cover.

Captive Care: This is an attractive, bold display animal. It may be reclusive when first introduced to the aquarium, but after adjusting to its new environment and its caretaker, it will begin spending much of its time swimming in open areas. The Whitemargin Grouper should be housed in an extra-large tank with plenty of swimming space and provided with two or three "bolt holes" in which to dash if threatened. It is a zealous predator that will eat any fish small enough to be swallowed whole. Although not commonly collected, adolescent specimens do show up in aquarium stores on occasion. It can be kept in large shallow- and deep-water reef aquariums if provided with enough swimming space. This is a good grouper for the aggressive reef tank, because it will spend more time than most in full view. Do remember that it will eat some ornamental crustaceans and smaller fish tankmates.

Aquarium Size: 180 gal. **Temperature:** 22 to 27°C (72 to 81°F).

Aquarium Suitability Index: 5.

Remarks: Juvenile *G. albomarginata* are spectacular; they are purplish pink or brown overall with orangish red lines on the margins of the dorsal and anal fins and upper and lower lobes of the caudal fin. Some adults have a large white patch on the middle of the body, under the dorsal fin base, and a white area on the caudal peduncle.

Genus *Mycteroperca* (Slender Groupers)

The 13 species recognized in the genus *Mycteroperca* are more slender in build and are distributed in tropical and subtropical waters of the Atlantic (8 species) and Eastern Pacific (5 species). Juvenile *Mycteroperca* species are most often found on inshore

Gonioplectrus hispanus, Spanish Flag: deep-water treasure.

A Sought-After Beauty

A number of smaller seabasses live in deeper reef communities and occasionally find their way into the tanks of rare-fish collectors. One of the most beautiful of these is the Spanish Flag (*Gonioplectrus hispanus*) (Cuvier, 1828). Through the efforts of some adventurous marine-fish collectors, this little-known deep-water seabass has recently become available in the marine aquarium trade. Using mixed-gas, rather than compressed air, the divers that collect the Spanish Flag descend to depths of 91 m (299 ft.). This is not only dangerous, it is time consuming and expensive; therefore, these fish command a very high price. But for the reef-fish aficionado with a few thousand dollars to spare, it is an exquisite addition to a species aquarium of 30 gallons or more, or a moderately aggressive community tank.

The Spanish Flag ranges from Texas to the Bahamas, throughout the Caribbean, south to at least Curaçao. It attains a maximum length of 30 cm (11.8 in.). *Gonioplectrus hispanus* is found on rocky reefs at depths from 60 to 365 m (197 to 1,197 ft.) and is most common where there is an abundance of caves, holes, and overhangs, and it is often seen swimming upside down with its belly directed toward the roof. It is quite reclusive, hiding among sessile invertebrates and in crevices.

This is a very hardy aquarium fish that will thrive in a tank with plenty of hiding places. It will spend more time in the open if the tank is dimly lit, and it prefers cooler water temperatures of 12.5 to 22°C (55 to 72°F). It is aggressive toward members of its own species, related forms, and passive fishes. Therefore, it is best to house it on its own or with moderately aggressive or larger tankmates, like squirrelfishes, soldierfishes, larger Roughtongue Bass (*Holanthias martinicensis*), larger Red Barbier (*Hemanthias vivanus*), angelfishes, and large butterflyfishes. They will also eat any fish or crustacean that can be swallowed whole.

Mycteroperca acutirostris, Comb Grouper: a large "slender" grouper.

Mycteroperca bonaci, Black Grouper: food-fish species, sometimes toxic.

reefs, in estuaries, or in seagrass beds. Adults are most often found hovering just above or cruising over coral reefs. These groupers range over large areas of the reef and most are almost exclusively piscivorous as adults. (There are three species from the Atlantic that feed heavily on macrozooplankton). The majority of *Mycteroperca* species will eat a wide array of fish prey, including sharks (one *M. jordani* stomach was reported to contain a juvenile Scalloped Hammerhead [*Sphyrna lewini*]). The slender body shape may enable them to swim faster, at least over short distances, and capture fast-moving fishes. These fishes may live for more than 25 years.

Because of the large sizes that these fishes attain, and their active lifestyles, these species are generally not well suited for the home aquarium. Juveniles of all members of the genus do adapt well to aquarium confines, but they grow quickly. Unless an extra-large home aquarium is available, most will get too big for this captive venue. They are also dedicated predators, with a special dietary predilection for any fish tankmates that they can swallow whole. The slender groupers should be fed a variety of meaty foods of marine origin. Fresh seafoods, like shrimp and marine fish flesh, and some of the frozen prepared foods for carnivores are good staples. (Limit the number of freshwater feeder fish in their diets.) Feed these fishes until the belly is slightly distended several times a week. Like other serranids, these fishes will consume any fishes or crustacean tankmates that they can ingest.

Mycteroperca acutirostris (Valenciennes, 1828)
Common Name: Comb Grouper.
Maximum Length: 80 cm (31.5 in.), maximum weight about 4 kg (8.8 lbs.).
Distribution: Texas, Bermuda, and Greater Antilles to Brazil.

Biology: The Comb Grouper is found at depths of 3 to 40 m (9.8 to 131 ft.). Juveniles are usually found in lagoons, often among mangrove roots, in seagrass beds, and on shallow reefs among gorgonians and stony corals. Adults of this species occur in high-relief habitats, whether rocky or coral, and are usually observed drifting above the substrate. This species may be a zooplankton feeder, although food consumption data is lacking.
Captive Care: This large, active grouper is not suitable for the majority of home aquariums. See genus account, above.
Aquarium Size: 240 gal. **Temperature:** 22 to 27°C (72 to 81°F).
Aquarium Suitability Index: 5.
Remarks: The head and body of this species is grayish brown with irregular white spots and blotches. Small juveniles (less then 15 cm [5.9 in.]) have a black saddle on the caudal peduncle, while larger adults are mainly a uniform gray.

Mycteroperca bonaci (Poey, 1860)
Common Name: Black Grouper.
Maximum Length: 1.3 m (4.3 ft.), weight of 65 kg (143 lbs.).
Distribution: Massachusetts, Bermuda, and the Gulf of Mexico, south to Brazil.
Biology: The Black Grouper is found on reef faces, fore-reef slopes, or walls at depths of 6 to 33 m (20 to 108 ft.). In the Florida Keys, it is most abundant on inshore patch reefs. It often drifts above the substrate, sometimes high into the water column. Adults feed almost entirely on fishes, while juveniles eat more crustaceans. This species is a protogynous hermaphrodite. In the Gulf of Mexico, ripe females have been reported at lengths of 50 to 100 cm (19.7 to 39 in.), while mature males were 96 to 116 cm (37.8 to 45.7 in.) total length. In some areas, this species is reported to spawn in July and August.

Mycteroperca interstitialis, Yellowmouth Grouper: bright juvenile colors.

Mycteroperca interstitialis, Yellowmouth Grouper: typical adult coloration.

Captive Care: This large, active grouper is not suitable for the majority of home aquariums. See genus account, above.
Aquarium Size: 400 gal. **Temperature:** 22 to 27°C (72 to 81°F).
Aquarium Suitability Index: 5.
Remarks: *Mycteroperca bonaci* is not particularly attractive, with a gray or brown dorsum and sides, and a paler ventrum. It has brassy spots on the head and the lower part of the body, while the side of the body has rectangular, dark gray blotches. Think twice before eating your Black Grouper; the flesh of this species has been known to cause ciguatera poisoning.

Mycteroperca interstitialis (Poey, 1860)
Common Name: Yellowmouth Grouper.
Maximum Length: 76 cm (29.9 in.).
Distribution: Florida and Bermuda, south to Brazil.
Biology: *Mycteroperca interstitialis* is found on coral and rocky reefs to depths of 3 to 150 m (9.8 to 492 ft.). In certain areas (notably the Gulf of Mexico), it is most abundant at depths in excess of 30 m (98 ft.). On coral reefs, it typically occurs on the reef face and fore-reef slopes, often in areas with rich coral growth. In the Gulf of Mexico, it is found on the algal-sponge zone of bank reefs. Adult Yellowmouth Groupers drift above the substrate, while juveniles usually move just over the reef or hide in reef crevices. All age classes feed almost exclusively on bony fishes. In one study, *Chromis* species (damselfishes) constituted 40% of the diet of 25 *M. interstitialis* with food in their stomachs. It also feeds on lizardfishes, silversides, cardinalfishes, grunts, jacks, other damselfishes, parrotfishes, and gobies. The Yellowmouth Grouper is often found near goby cleaning stations. This is a protogynous hermaphrodite: in one study, all fish less than 50 cm (19.7 in.) in total length and younger than 4 years were fe-

males, while fish larger than 75 cm (29.5 in.) and older than 17 years were males. There is some data that indicates some females never change sex. Female Yellowmouth Groupers mature at a total length between 40 to 45 cm (15.7 to 17.7 in.), and 2 to 4 years of age, while males mature at about 50 to 55 cm (19.7 to 21.7 in.) at an age of 4 years. Spawning takes place all through the year; they probably do not form massive aggregations. This fish can live to at least 28 years of age. The growth rate of this species is accelerated for about 2 years, after which it grows very slowly.
Captive Care: The Yellowmouth Grouper is large, active, and not suitable for the majority of home aquariums. See genus account, page 69, and tribe account, page 26, for more information on the husbandry of members of this genus.
Aquarium Size: 240 gal. **Temperature:** 22 to 27°C (72 to 81°F).
Aquarium Suitability Index: 5.
Remarks: Juvenile *M. interstitialis* are bicolored, with a brown dorsum and a white ventrum. Young fish also have yellow on the anterior portion of the dorsal fin. Adults are tan or brown above and pale below, with small, dark, closely set spots on the head and body. The corners of the inside of the mouth are yellow.

Mycteroperca rosacea (Streets, 1877)
Common Names: Leopard Grouper, Leopard Cabrilla, Golden Grouper
Maximum Length: 100 cm (39 in.).
Distribution: Baja, entire Gulf of California, and south to Puerto Vallarta, Mexico. (This is the most common grouper in the central and southern Gulf of California.)
Biology: This grouper is found on inshore rocky and coral reefs at depths of 2 to at least 50 m (6.6 to 164 ft.). Most individuals remain in a fairly limited home range. The diet and behavior of

Mycteroperca rosacea, Leopard Grouper: common Baja California species.

Mycteroperca tigris, Tiger Grouper: cute juvenile may grow to 100 cm (39 in.).

this species differs between small (under 30 cm [11.8 in.]) and large individuals. Smaller Leopard Groupers feed at dawn, dusk, and during the day (occasionally after dark). Their diet consists mainly of crustaceans and benthic fishes (including damselfishes, wrasses, triplefins, clinids, and blennies). Members of this size class regularly follow other fishes, especially the Mexican Hogfish (*Bodianus diplotaenia*). Small individuals occur singly or in groups of 2 to 10 fish. They do not aggregate at specific locations on the reef, but are usually scattered about.

Large Leopard Groupers are crepuscular, doing most of their hunting during the dusk and dawn hours. They feed primarily on schooling fishes, especially herring, sardines, goatfishes, jacks, grunts, and croakers. The grouper's diet varies from one season to the next and is dependent on the abundance of the various schooling species. For example, during certain times of the year,

Flatiron Herring (*Harengula thrissina*) make up almost the entire diet of large individuals. When these schools are present, adult Leopard Groupers will aggregate at the offshore edge of rocky reefs in midday. They are relatively inactive at this time, hovering in tight groups in the midwater. As the sun begins to set, these groupers begin to move into the shallows and position themselves among rocks below the herring schools. They will rest on the bottom so their body is aimed at the schools above. The hungry Leopard Groupers occasionally dash from the substrate to strike at the herring and then return to their ambush sites on the seafloor. Feeding reaches a fevered pitch, with some groupers catapulting themselves out of the water (sometimes as many as 20 individuals leap from the water simultaneously). While most of these groupers eat about five prey fish per evening, one 50-cm (19.7-in.) individual in a feeding study ingested 19 Flatiron Herring. At night, the herring schools move offshore to feed. Many of the groupers follow them for a short distance. When the herring return at dusk, many of the Leopard Groupers follow the schools back into the shallows and resume their feeding activity. Shortly after the sun rises, most individuals gradually move back to their daytime refuging sites. To a lesser extent, adults feed on soldierfishes, damselfishes, wrasses, and surgeonfishes. Crustaceans are rarely eaten. The Serrate Cornetfish (*Fistularia petimba*) will swim alongside adult Leopard Groupers, using them as a moving blind to approach small, benthic fishes.

Captive Care: The Leopard Grouper is a large, active species that is not suitable for the majority of home aquariums. For more information, see the genus account, page 69.

Aquarium Size: 300 gal. **Temperature:** 22 to 27°C (72 to 81°F).

Aquarium Suitability Index: 5.

Remarks: The most common Leopard Grouper color pattern is the spotted phase. It is greenish to gray brown overall, with numerous small reddish brown spots. Approximately 1% of the Leopard Grouper population undergoes a radical transformation when they are still juveniles. They change from the spotted phase to the golden phase. (Some individuals retain small patches of their original pigment.) The function of this transformation is not known. In other fishes (e.g., cichlids), it has been suggested that the color change increases mating success. The **Gulf Grouper** (*Mycteroperca jordani*) (**Jenkins & Evermann, 1889**) is a similar species that ranges from LaJolla, California, south to Mazatlan, and throughout the Gulf of California (it is the most common large grouper in the upper Gulf). Adult *M. jordani* are gray overall, but smaller individuals are grayish brown with dark blotches on the body. There are also lines radiating from the eyes. The **Island Grouper** (*Mycteroperca olfax*) (**Jenyns, 1842**) is known from the Galapagos,

Cocos and Malpelo Islands, and northern Peru. It has also been reported from the Gulf of California. This species exhibits three distinct color phases: a greenish brown phase, an all-brown phase, and a golden phase (about 5% of the population are gold). The first two phases have spots, especially younger individuals.

Mycteroperca tigris (Valenciennes, 1833)
Common Name: Tiger Grouper.
Maximum Length: 100 cm (39 in.).
Distribution: Southern Florida and Bermuda, Gulf of Mexico, and Bay of Campeche to Brazil.
Biology: The Tiger Grouper occurs on coral and rocky reefs and is most common on reef faces and fore-reef slopes (it also occurs on reef flats). It is found at depths of 3 to 40 m (9.8 to 131 ft.). Adult *M. tigris* are often seen hanging near sponges, gorgonians, and coral heads, often in the vicinity of goby and/or wrasse cleaning stations. It can also be found hanging over sand bottoms in reef grooves or slopes. Juveniles occur in areas with rich coral growth and tend to swim away when approached, rather than retreating into the reef. *Mycteroperca tigris* feeds almost entirely on bony fishes, including surgeonfishes, croakers, silversides, filefishes, grunts, blennies, damselfishes, and parrotfishes. It will also eat cephalopods. This species is often cleaned by cleaner fishes and shrimps. When they are cleaned, they often assume their darker (red) color phase. Juvenile Tiger Groupers are very different in color from the adults and are thought to be aggressive mimics of the initial phase of the Bluehead Wrasse (*Thalassoma bifasciatum*). Both juveniles and adults usually occur singly. *Mycteroperca tigris* is a protogynous hermaphrodite. During the spawning period, large individuals (thought to be males) exhibit a yellowish head with a white patch on the posterior portion of the body. At dusk, these individuals form territories from which they aggressively evict consexuals (a leklike mating system). Then they rise off the seafloor and wait for females to visit their breeding territory. When a female arrives, the pair will make a short, vertical spawning ascent, rising less than 1 m (3.3 ft.) into the water column. Some males engage in a different reproductive strategy known as "streaking." They will rush in and join a pair of Tiger Groupers during their spawning ascent and release sperm simultaneously with the paired fishes' gamete discharges.
Captive Care: The Tiger Grouper is a large, active species that is not suitable for the majority of home aquariums. For more information, see the genus account, page 69.
Aquarium Size: 300 gal. **Temperature:** 22 to 27°C (72 to 81°F).
Aquarium Suitability Index: 5.
Remarks: Adult *M. tigris* are greenish brown, brownish gray, or

Mycteroperca venenosa, Yellowfin Grouper: best observed in the wild.

reddish brown. (A rare specimen may have hexagonal spots that are bright orange-red in color). They can lighten or darken very quickly. They also have from 9 to 11 diagonal pale stripes on the body, and the pectoral fins are pale yellow distally. Juveniles are yellow with a dark brown lateral stripe.

Mycteroperca venenosa (Linnaeus, 1758)
Common Name: Yellowfin Grouper.
Maximum Length: 90 cm (35.4 in.).
Distribution: Florida, Bermuda, and southern Gulf of Mexico, south to Brazil.
Biology: The adult Yellowfin Grouper is a resident of reef tops, walls, and fore-reef slopes, occurring at a depth range of 3 to 137 m (9.8 to 449 ft.). Juveniles are also found in seagrass meadows as shallow as 2 m (6.6 ft.). It is observed either hanging just above the reef or resting on the floor of caves. This species feeds on a variety of reef fishes, including benthic and fast-moving open-water forms, including lizardfishes, silversides, squirrelfishes, trumpetfishes, other groupers, jacks, grunts, damselfishes, wrasses, parrotfishes, and surgeonfishes. It also eats Caribbean Reef Squid (*Sepioteuthis sepioidea*) and smaller specimens will feed on shrimps. This species regularly has parasitic isopods lodged in its nostrils. The Yellowfin Grouper is a protogynous hermaphrodite. It can live up to at least 15 years in the wild.
Captive Care: This large, active grouper is not suitable for the majority of home aquariums. See genus account, page 69.

Paranthias furcifer, Creolefish (juvenile): Western Atlantic/Caribbean species.

Paranthias colonus, Pacific Creolefish: juvenile of Pacific sister species.

Paranthias colonus, Pacific Creolefish (adult): hardy aquarium species.

Aquarium Size: 200 gal. **Temperature:** 22 to 27°C (72 to 81°F). **Aquarium Suitability Index:** 5.

Remarks: This species has yellow edges on the margin of the pectoral fins, and there is a dark posterior margin on the caudal fin. The overall body color is a function of the depth where the fish occurs: those from deeper water are red overall; those from lesser depths are olive, with a lighter ventrum.

Genus *Paranthias* (Creolefish)

This genus is comprised of two very similar species that make their living by picking zooplankton out of the water column. Like many zooplanktivores that feed high in the water column, the *Paranthias* have a fusiform body, with stiffened body and forked-tail for propulsion, a small mouth, small teeth, and numerous gill-rakers. These fish spawn in aggregations, well above the bottom.

Paranthias furcifer (Valenciennes, 1828)

Common Name: Creolefish.

Maximum Length: 35 cm (13.8 in.), usually less than 20 cm (7.9 in.).

Distribution: North Carolina and Bermuda to Brazil, east to St. Helena Island and the Gulf of Guinea.

Biology: The Creolefish lives on fore-reef slopes at a depth range of 8 to 100 m (26 to 328 ft.). This species often occurs in schools that swim high in the water column to capture passing zooplankton. These schools can be composed of very few individuals, or they can number into the hundreds. This fish feeds primarily on copepods, but also consumes salps (pelagic tunicates), shrimps larvae, mysids, fish larvae, and fish eggs. Individual Creolefish are often observed sitting on their pectoral fins on sand patches on fore-reef slopes or hiding among the corals. In certain areas, Creolefish are often parasitized by gnathiid isopods. An individual will often have an isopod adhering to each side of its lower jaw. The limited data available on this species indicate it may be gonochoristic (having lifelong determined sexes).

Captive Care: The Creolefish is a durable aquarium species that will eat most aquarium foods, from flakes to live feeder fish. Although they school in nature, they are best kept singly except in very large systems. In the confines of the home aquarium, they are often aggressive toward conspecifics. They will also pester smaller, passive fish species and are best matched with moderately aggressive tankmates like squirrelfishes, angelfishes, banana wrasses (genus *Thalassoma*), damselfishes, and surgeonfishes.

Aquarium Size: 75 gal. **Temperature:** 22 to 27°C (72 to 81°F).

Aquarium Suitability Index: 5.

Paranthias colonus, Pacific Creolefish: wild schools may be small or number in the hundreds, cruising the water column searching for zooplankton targets.

Remarks: The color of the Creolefish can vary from reddish brown to olive brown. The ventral surface is lighter than the dorsum, and there is a row of spots along the back. The **Pacific Creolefish** (*Paranthias colonus*) (**Valenciennes, 1855**) is the sister species to *P. furcifer*, and some ichthyologists consider them to be synonymous. The Pacific Creolefish ranges from the central Gulf of California to Peru. Although adult Pacific Creolefish are similar in color to their Atlantic relatives, the young specimens are bright yellow with blue spots running along the back and a red spot edged in blue at the base of the pectoral fin.

Genus *Plectropomus* (Coral Groupers)

This genus—sometimes called coral trout for their resemblance to certain members of the Subfamily Salmoninae—contains seven species, all of which occur in the Indian and/or the Western and South Pacific oceans. All members of the genus have eight dorsal spines, large canines on each side of the lower jaw, and an angular head. These fishes are accomplished predators that feed heavily on other fishes, although they will also eat cephalopods and crustaceans. The coral groupers employ a number of different feeding strategies. They often hang in the water column, sometimes in the midst of shoaling or aggregating species. When their potential prey becomes accustomed to their seemingly harmless presence, and a feeding opportunity presents itself, the coral grouper launches its explosive attack. I once saw a large coral grouper employ this strategy to strike at an aggregation of goatfish lying on a sandy bottom. The goatfish scattered and the coral grouper selected a particular goatfish and chased it until the potential prey fish shot under a piece of protective debris.

Coral groupers are some of the largest members of the grouper family regularly available in aquarium stores. Not only do these fishes attain hefty sizes, they are also very active and therefore should be housed in spacious, uncluttered aquariums. Although swimming space is of prime importance, a suitable refuge site is also necessary to ensure acclimation. When first acquired, a coral grouper tends to be flighty and will dash for cover if there is any sudden movement outside the aquarium. For this

Plectropomus areolatus, Squaretail Coral Grouper (Maldives): being cleaned.

reason, it is important to provide several holes in which it can make a hasty retreat. When working in or around the aquarium, approach the tank very slowly and give the fish a chance to slip into a favorite hiding place. If startled, these fishes will often dash about the tank recklessly and may harm themselves on aquarium decor. I have had specimens that were injured by sharp decor or tankmates, but their wounds healed quickly.

These are solitary fishes, so members of the same species or similarly marked species should not be placed in the aquarium together. However, the coral trout can be kept with other groupers of similar size with distinctly different color patterns. It is best to introduce all these groupers to the aquarium simultaneously or add the smaller specimens first. The *Plectropomus* species will eat any fishes that they can swallow whole—including other groupers. Don't underestimate the size of their mouths, as they can expand greatly to accommodate surprisingly large prey items.

The coral groupers can be kept in a shallow- or deep-water reef aquarium if enough swimming space is provided. However, they will eat ornamental crustaceans, although cleaner shrimps will sometimes avoid being consumed if they are added to the tank before the grouper. The coral groupers are not above eating the occasional cleaner wrasse.

Plectropomus areolatus (Rüppell, 1830)
Common Name: Squaretail Coral Grouper.
Maximum Length: 73 cm (28.7 in.).
Distribution: Red Sea to the Phoenix Islands and Samoa, north to the Ryukyus and Marshall Islands, south to the Great Barrier Reef.

Biology: The Squaretail Coral Grouper is most common in channels and on fore-reef slopes, but also occurs on lagoon patch reefs. It is most often found in areas of rich coral growth, at depths from 1 to 20 m (3.3 to 66 ft.). This species feeds primarily on fishes. Squaretail Coral Groupers form large spawning groups at specific times and places. In the Solomon Islands, these groups gather in reef passes from February to June (with the largest groups occurring March through May). The males, which are larger than the females, begin congregating in these locations first and hang in the water column, up to 3 m (9.8 ft.) over the seafloor, or erratically move about the area. Females eventually begin to aggregate in the same area. The resulting heterosexual gatherings consist of 3 to 10 females with 1 to 3 males. In observed events, one male, which always exhibited the banded color pattern, would regularly chase consexuals in the group (the chased fish usually exhibited a uniform dark-color phase), especially when the females initially began infiltrating the male groups. The banded (dominant) male would also chase females on occasion. Most spawning occurred during the last seven days of the lunar month. The actual spawning act is done in pairs. The aggregations disperse after the new moon. It has been suggested that this species is a protogynous hermaphrodite. In one study, males ranged in size from 43 to 51 cm (16.9 to 20 in.), while females were 29 to 33 cm (11.4 to 13 in.) in total length.
Captive Care: See genus account, page 75.
Aquarium Size: 200 gal. **Temperature:** 22 to 27°C (72 to 81°F).
Aquarium Suitability Index: 5.
Remarks: This species is gray, brown, or reddish brown overall, with blue spots on the head, body, and lower abdomen that are round to slightly oblong and have dark edges. The tail of the Squaretail Coral Grouper is truncate to slightly emarginate, and the median fins have narrow white posterior margins.

Plectropomus laevis (Lacépède, 1801)
Common Names: Blacksaddle Coral Grouper, Footballer Trout.
Maximum Length: 110 cm (42.3 in.).
Distribution: South Africa to Mangareva, north to the Ryukyus, and south to New Caledonia and Rapa Island.
Biology: The Blacksaddle Coral Grouper occurs in lagoon patch reefs, back reefs, the reef face, and fore-reef slopes, typically in areas with lush coral growth. It can be found at depths from 4 to 90 m (13 to 295 ft.). This grouper usually swims in open water just above the reef and feeds almost exclusively on fishes. The young of this species may mimic the coloration of the toxic Saddled Toby (*Canthigaster valentini*), which would deter some pis-

Plectropomus laevis, Blacksaddle Coral Grouper (juvenile): future tank buster.

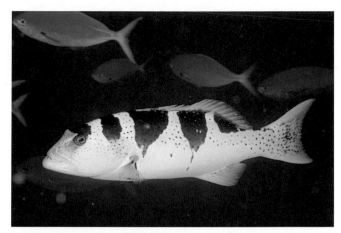
Plectropomus laevis, Blacksaddle Coral Grouper: typical five-bar color form.

civores from attempting to eat them.

Captive Care: The juveniles of this species are the most highly prized members of the genus. However, like most *Plectropomus* species, these manageable juveniles turn into tank-busting giants. Any aquarist entertaining the notion of keeping one of these fish should have both the space and budget to house, feed, and maintain a large adult.

Aquarium Size: 500 gal. **Temperature:** 22 to 27°C (72 to 81°F).

Aquarium Suitability Index: 5.

Remarks: This species displays two distinct color phases. One is white or pale yellow with five dark brown or black bars and numerous dark-edged blue spots that are located primarily on the posterior portions of the body. The second color phase is red, olivaceous, or black overall with or without five dark bars, many dark-edged blue spots on the head, body, and tail, and dark pectoral fins.

Plectropomus leopardus (Lacépède, 1802)

Common Names: Leopard Coral Grouper, Leopard Coral Trout.

Maximum Length: 70 cm (27.6 in.).

Distribution: Indochina and Bali to Fiji, north to southern Japan and south to the Great Barrier Reef and New Caledonia.

Biology: The Leopard Coral Grouper is found on the back of barrier reefs, in channels, and on fore-reef slopes, although they tend to be most common in the latter habitat. Smaller and medium-sized individuals (under 44 cm SL [standard length] [17.3 in.]) occur in lagoons, while larger fish restrict their movements to the fore-reef slope. This grouper occurs at a depth range of 3 to 100 m (9.8 to 328 ft.). It feeds predominantly on fishes. For example, in one study, 87% of 249 individuals whose stomachs were examined had eaten only fishes. The types most fre-

Plectropomus leopardus, Leopard Coral Grouper (juvenile): colors will fade.

quently consumed were cardinalfishes, wrasses, parrotfishes, damselfishes, and blennies, but it also eats conger eels, other groupers, lizardfishes, sand perches, gobies, and filefishes. Large individuals (over 30 cm SL [11.8 in.]) were observed to rise high in the water column to attack small, schooling, pelagic fishes like anchovies, smelt, and herring. Occasionally this species will also consume decapod shrimps, mantis shrimps, and squids. Most prey items eaten by *P. leopardus* are between 1 and 29 cm (0.4 to 11.4 in.) in total length. This species has a ravenous appetite. For example, as many as four fish were found in the stomach of a *P. leopardus* that was only 12 cm (4.7 in.) in total length, while a 59-cm (23-in.) individual had eaten seven fish. Smaller *P. leopardus* (under 6 cm [2.4 in.] in total length) have been observed to attack prey once every 3 to 5 minutes and spend 18 to 37% of their daily time budget hunting. Adult specimens have

Plectropomus leopardus, Leopard Coral Grouper (Great Barrier Reef): old fish.

Plectropomus leopardus, Leopard Coral Grouper: unusual orange color form.

Plectropomus leopardus, Leopard Coral Grouper: aberrant koi-like color form.

Plectropomus maculatus, Spotted Coral Grouper: distinctive blue spots.

been observed using schools of rabbitfishes and snappers to approach unsuspecting prey. It may also rely on habituation to lull prey species into a false sense of security. When the prey species drop their guard, the grouper attacks.

Plectropomus leopardus is active during the day and is usually found associating with three or four specific sites (these are usually shelter sites, feeding sites, or cleaning stations) within its extensive home range. The home range of the Leopard Coral Grouper ranges from about 10,000 to 18,000 m^2 (109,000 to 196,200 ft.^{2}), depending on the reef type (e.g., patch reef vs. fringing reef) that the individual inhabits. There is apparently no correlation between the size of the individual and the home range area in adults of this species. There are also no differences between male and female home range sizes. The mean daily distance moved by *P. leopardus* during one study was about 192 m

(630 ft.), while the maximum distance moved in the home range was 1,121 m (3,678 ft.). They often refuge in the same crevice or cave, night after night. The Leopard Coral Grouper forms spawning aggregations: in October, its densities on the Great Barrier Reef increase by a factor of 12. The increase begins on the full moon and peaks during the new moon, after which time the numbers begin to drop. These fish exhibit a leklike mating system, where males set up temporary spawning territories that are visited by females. The fish then spawn in pairs just around sunset. Postlarval *P. leopardus* settle out of the plankton, onto coral rubble bottoms, at a length of about 2 cm (0.8 in.).

Captive Care: See genus account, page 75.

Aquarium Size: 200 gal. **Temperature:** 22 to 27°C (72 to 81°F).

Aquarium Suitability Index: 5.

Remarks: The overall coloration of this fish varies from olive

Plectropomus punctatus, Marbled Coral Grouper: juvenile from Indian Ocean.

Plectropomus punctatus, Marbled Coral Grouper: large adult form.

Plectropomus oligocanthus, Vermiculate Coral Grouper: large juvenile.

Plectropomus oligocanthus, Vermiculate Coral Grouper: adult specimen.

brown to red. It has very small blue spots on the head, body, median fins, and the base of the pectoral fins, and a blue ring around the eye. The caudal fin has a narrow white margin on the middle of its posterior edge, often preceded by a dark band.

Plectropomus maculatus (Bloch, 1790)

Common Name: Spotted Coral Grouper.
Maximum Length: 70 cm (27.6 in.).
Distribution: Thailand to the Solomon Islands, north to the Philippines, and south to Western Australia and the Great Barrier Reef.
Biology: The Spotted Coral Grouper prefers coastal reefs over clear offshore reefs. It feeds almost entirely on fishes. For example, of 95 specimens examined from around the Great Barrier Reef, 97% of all prey items ingested were bony fishes, 2% were shrimps, and 1% were cephalopods.

Captive Care: See genus account, page 75.
Aquarium Size: 200 gal. **Temperature:** 22 to 27°C (72 to 81°F).
Aquarium Suitability Index: 5.
Remarks: This species has relatively large blue spots, with some more elongate than round, especially those on the head, and a white margin on the edge of the tail. The **Marbled Coral Grouper** (*Plectropomus punctatus*) (**Quoy & Gaimard, 1824**) is a resident of the east coast of Africa and many of the offshore islands (e.g., Seychelles, Mauritius, Chagos, Aldabra). There is one record from Oman. Juveniles of this species are brown with white spots and dashes. Adults are purplish brown to reddish brown with lighter marbling. It is a roving coral and rocky-reef predator that feeds heavily on bony fishes (including squirrelfishes, wrasses, parrotfishes, juvenile barracudas, surgeonfishes, and triggerfishes). The largest known individual was 96 cm (37.8

Plectropomus pessuliferus, Roving Coral Grouper: color form from Red Sea.

in.). It is most common at depths of 10 m (33 ft.) or less. Spawning has been reported from December to February.

Plectropomus oligocanthus (Bleeker, 1854)

Common Names: Vermiculate Coral Grouper, Highfin Coral Grouper.

Maximum Length: 61 cm (24 in.).

Distribution: East Java to the Solomon Islands, north to the Philippines, Caroline, and Marshall Islands, south to northwestern Australia and the northern Barrier Reefs.

Biology: The Vermiculate Coral Grouper is usually observed on fore-reef dropoffs and in steep channels, at a depth range of 5 to 35 m (16 to 115 ft.). It is typically found singly, but adults are also seen in pairs. The juveniles of this species apparently mimic the Celebes Maori Wrasse (*Cheilinus celebicus*). It is similar in color, shape, and behavior. Although both species feed on small fishes and crustaceans, *P. oligocanthus* has a more capacious maw and is thus able to ingest larger prey items than the wrasse. Prey species that would be too large for *C. celebicus* to feed upon would be vulnerable to attacks by the grouper, which is also much less common than the wrasse.

Captive Care: Juveniles of this species are occasionally seen in the aquarium trade. They are beautiful fish and highly desirable display animals. Shy when initially introduced to the aquarium, they will hide among the reef decor and often rest on the bottom for days before they begin exploring their new home. Ag-

gressive toward members of their own species and toward related groupers, they are also voracious predators that will snap up any fish or crustacean that can be swallowed.

Aquarium Size: 200 gal. **Temperature:** 22 to 27°C (72 to 81°F).

Aquarium Suitability Index: 5.

Remarks: The adults vary from light lavender and reddish brown to red with blue lines on the front of the body and the head. There are numerous blue spots on the body and on the fins. The nocturnal coloration is often more red. Juveniles lack the lines, but sport blue spots.

Plectropomus pessuliferus (Fowler, 1904)

Common Name: Roving Coral Grouper.

Maximum Length: 90 cm (35.4 in.). (According to some sources, maximum length only 60 cm [23.4 in.].)

Distribution: East Africa, including Red Sea, Maldives, Sri Lanka, Similan Islands, Sumatra, and Fijian Islands.

Biology: The Roving Coral Grouper is found on shallow lagoon reefs and on fore-reef slopes, at depths of 10 to 147 m (33 to 482 ft.). This species is often found on or near shipwrecks and has also been reported from seagrass beds. Debelius (1984) reported seeing this species attacking garden eels. I have seen a large adult attempting to suck a moribund moray out of a reef crevice. The Roving Coral Grouper is often seen being cleaned by Bluestreak Cleaner Wrasses (*Labroides dimidiatus*). Although it usually occurs singly, in the Red Sea *P. pessuliferus* forms large spawning groups on offshore reefs in May.

Captive Care: This is a large, active, predatory species that requires a big aquarium and appropriately sized tankmates and filtration equipment. See genus account, page 75.

Aquarium Size: 300 gal. **Temperature:** 22 to 27°C (72 to 81°F).

Aquarium Suitability Index: 5.

Remarks: There are two subspecies of *P. pessuliferus*; one of these, *P. p. marisrubri*, is limited in distribution to the Red Sea, while the other, *P. p. pessuliferus*, is found over the remainder of the range. The Red Sea form has numerous blue dots on the cheek, it may have short blue lines on the snout, and usually lacks the white posterior margin on the caudal fin. *Plectropomus pessuliferus pessuliferus* has blue dots widely scattered on the head.

Genus *Variola* (Lyretail Grouper)

This genus contains two of the most elegant of the grouper species. Both regularly haunt the tanks of aquarium retail stores, but are only suitable for those hobbyists willing to set up very large aquariums. These fishes are brightly colored and have lunate (lyre-shaped) tails, hence the common name. They are carnivores with huge appetites and should be provided with appropriate

Variola albimarginata, Whitemargin Lyretail Grouper (large adult): smaller and less common than its fellow genus member, *V. louti*, is a spectacular sight.

tankmates and plenty of swimming room.

Variola albimarginata Baissac, 1952

Common Name: Whitemargin Lyretail Grouper.

Maximum Length: 55 cm (21.7 in.).

Distribution: East Africa to Samoa, north to southern Japan, and south to the Great Barrier Reef.

Biology: The Whitemargin Lyretail Grouper inhabits coastal reefs, reef faces, and fore-reef slopes at depths of 3 to 91 m (9.8 to 299 ft.). It is sometimes observed on patch reefs, which serve as cleaning stations, on sand or mud slopes. This species feeds on fishes, including moray eels. It will follow foraging octopuses, eating small fishes and crustaceans flushed by the cephalopod's hunting activities. It is not as common as its only congener, the Lyretail Grouper (*V. louti*), in most regions.

Captive Care: The overall husbandry of this species is similar to that of the Lyretail Grouper (see below). However, there is one advantage to keeping this fish over *V. louti*—it does not get as large. Nonetheless, full-grown individuals will still have to be housed in a very large aquarium.

Aquarium Size: 200 gal. **Temperature:** 22 to 27°C (72 to 81°F).

Aquarium Suitability Index: 5.

Remarks: Juvenile Whitemargin Lyretail Groupers are similar in color to the adults, but they have fewer large, pale blue spots that are edged in red. The center of the adult's caudal fin margin has a white line, bordered by a black line. The dorsal, anal, and pelvic fins do not have distinct yellow margins as they do in the Lyretail Grouper (*V. louti*).

Variola louti (Forsskål, 1775)

Common Names: Lyretail Grouper, Coronation Grouper.

Maximum Length: 90 cm (35.4 in.).

Distribution: Red Sea to the Marquesas and Pitcairn Group, north to southern Japan, and south to Lord Howe and Rapa Islands.

Biology: The Lyretail Grouper is most common in clear water around oceanic islands or offshore reefs. It prefers coral-rich

Variola albimarginata, Whitemargin Lyretail Grouper: small juvenile.

Variola albimarginata, Whitemargin Lyretail Grouper: large juvenile.

Variola louti, Lyretail Grouper: juvenile of a widespread Indo-Pacific species.

Variola louti, Lyretail Grouper: larger juvenile displays intermediate color form.

areas of lagoon patch reefs, back reefs, reef faces, and fore-reef slopes. In some areas, it is most often found in caves and channels. It occurs at depths of 1 to 240 m (3.3 to 787 ft.), but is usually most abundant at depths greater than 15 m (49 ft.). This is an active fish that is often seen cruising 1 m (3.3 ft.) or more above the reef. As a diurnal predator, it is often spotted hunting along reef ledges. The bulk of its diet consists of fishes, including moray eels, other groupers, goatfishes, fusiliers, damselfishes, wrasses, parrotfishes, surgeonfishes, filefishes, and triggerfishes. In some areas, it apparently prefers nocturnal species, such as squirrelfishes, soldierfishes, cardinalfishes, and bigeyes. It has also been reported to feed on venomous and toxic fish species, including scorpionfishes and tobies. Although of secondary importance in the diet, shrimps, crabs, mantis shrimps, and cephalopods will also be taken by *V. louti*. In the

Red Sea, this species will occasionally associate with the Gray Moray (*Siderea grisea*) or the Common Octopus (*Octopus cyaneus*) as they forage among rubble and reef crevices. In the Fijian Islands, I also observed them following Slingjaw Wrasses (*Epibulus insidiator*) as they fed. In both areas, the Lyretail Groupers prey upon animals flushed out by the activities of the associated species. These groupers are probably territorial—I have seen larger Lyretail Groupers chasing smaller individuals from one hole to another in the wild.

Captive Care: Juveniles are commonly sold in the aquarium trade and will do well in moderate-sized tanks. However, this fish grows quite large and will inevitably have to be moved to a very large aquarium. It should be provided with plenty of swimming room, as well as several holes or crevices in which to shelter. It tends to be less shy than many of the other large grouper species

Variola louti, Lyretail Grouper: variant adult illustrates the scale and appeal of a grouper that can be the centerpiece show species in spacious aquarium settings.

(e.g., *Plectropomus* spp.), and therefore makes a better display animal. It will eat any fish tankmate that it can ingest, including moray eels that measure over half its total body length. Small individuals can be kept in shallow- or deep-water reef aquariums, although adolescents and adults need more swimming room than is usually available in a tank packed with live rock. Be aware, though, that the Lyretail Grouper will not hesitate to eat desirable crustaceans.

Aquarium Size: 300 gal. **Temperature:** 22 to 27°C (72 to 81°F).
Aquarium Suitability Index: 5.
Remarks: Juveniles of this species have a black stripe on the side and a large black spot at the base of the caudal fin.

References

Aguilar-Perera & Aguilar-Davila (1996), Beukers & Jones (1998), Böhlke & Chaplin (1968), Brulé & Rodriguez Canche (1993), Brulé et al. (1994), Bullock et al. (1992), Choat (1968), Colin et al. (1987), DeLoach (1999), Diamant & Shpigel (1985), Donaldson (1989a, 1995a, 1995b), Dubin (1982), Eggleston et al. (1998), Ferreira (1993), Ferreira & Russ (1993), García-Moliner Basora(1986), Goeden (1978), Grover et al. (1998), Harmelin-Vivien & Bouchon (1976), Heemstra & Randall (1986, 1993), Hiatt & Stratsburg (1960), Hobson (1965, 1968), Humann (1993), Johannes (1988), Kingsford (1992), Kuiter (1995), Kuiter & Debelius (1994), Leong & Wong (1988), Lieske & Myers (1994), Manooch (1987), Montgomery (1975), Myers (1999), Nagelkerken (1981), Nemtzov et al. (1993), Ormond (1980), Parrish (1987), Potts & Manooch (1995), Randall (1967), Randall & Brock (1960), Randall & Heemstra (1991), Randall & Hoese (1986), Randall & Kuiter (1989), Randall & Satapoomin (2000), Randall et al. (1997), Rigby & Dufour (1996), Sadovy & Eklund (1999), Sadovy et al. (1994), Samoilys & Squire (1994), Samoilys (1997), Sano et al. (1984), Shapiro et al. (1993, 1994), Shpigel & Fishelson (1989a, 1989b, 1991), Sluka et al. (1998), Sluka & Reichenbach (1996), St. John (1999), Snyder (1999), Snyder et al. (2001), Thompson & Munro (1978), Thurmon (1982), Tucker (1994), Van Der Elst (1985), Zeller (1997, 1998).

Pogonoperca punctata, Leaflip Soapfish: a young fish represents the most sought-after species within this fascinating but toxin-bearing genus.

THE COMMON NAMES ASCRIBED TO REEF FISHES VARY in their degree of appropriateness. Some—marine angelfishes and squirrelfishes come to mind—have obscure origins and no obvious explanations. Many others, however, are appropriate and quite descriptive. For example, there are the hawkfishes, piscine predators that perch on reef substrates; the cowfishes, which have horns and big sad eyes; hogfishes with their piggish appetites; lionfishes with elongate fin filaments reminiscent of the mane of their feline namesakes; and, of course, the venomous stonefishes, which can perfectly mimic a piece of rock. Then there are the soapfishes, which have the unique ability to lather up like a bar of soap. Almost all of the soapfishes exude a toxic skin mucus when distressed, and a soaplike lather is formed when the skin is stroked. This substance, known as grammistin, is bitter-tasting and an effective deterrent against potential soapfish predators. Within the confines of a shipping container or aquarium, it is also capable of killing the soapfish itself, along with other fishes and organisms—a consideration for any aquarist who would attempt to keep one of these unusual fishes.

Classification and Biology

The Tribes Diploprionini and Grammistini include 10 genera and 27 species (3 genera and 5 species in Diploprionini, and 7 genera and 22 species in Grammistini). In these two tribes, collectively known as soapfishes, the base of the inner pelvic ray is attached to the abdomen by a membrane, the soft portions of the dorsal, anal, and caudal fins are rounded, the opercle has 2 to 3 distinct spines, the preopercle margin has 1 to 4 spines or is coarsely serrated, and there are either ctenoid scales or embedded cycloid scales. Members of the Tribe Grammistini often have a dermal appendage on the chin.

Of the 10 genera of soapfishes, representatives from four are regularly seen in the aquarium trade, while members of three others are encountered on rare occasions. Some of the most divergent are the members of the genus *Diploprion* (Tribe Diploprionini). This genus contains two species, with laterally compressed, deeper bodies than all of the other soapfishes and very long pelvic fins that extend back beyond the front of the anal fin. Unlike most other soapfishes, these two species are active during the day, spending much of the diurnal hours cruising just above the substrate or hanging under ledges or in caves. When they hunt, they adopt a head-down posture to inspect the seafloor. One of the *Diploprion* species increases its hunting success by swimming alongside larger fishes, using them as a mobile blind to sneak up on prey. The members of this genus are thought to be sexually dimorphic, with males attaining a larger size than females. Although very different in form, the monotypic (one species only) genus *Belonoperca* is also a member of the Tribe Diploprionini. Unlike the *Diploprion* species, this fish, *Belonoperca chabanaudi*, has an elongate body and a narrow, sharply pointed head. It is a nocturnal species that spends its days under overhangs and in caves. This species is occasionally encountered by divers, but rarely enters the aquarium trade.

The genus *Grammistes* (Tribe Grammistini) is another taxon commonly encountered by aquarists and divers. The Sixline Soapfish (*Grammistes sexlineatus*) is a heavy-bodied species that looks more like the stereotypical grouper than most of the other members of the soapfish tribe. The genus *Pogonoperca* (Tribe Grammistini) contains two species, one of which occasionally appears in the aquarium trade. This species, the Leaflip Soapfish (*Pogonoperca punctata*), is the most sought-after soapfish. It is pleasingly marked and has a leaflike appendage extending from the lower jaw. Both the Sixline and Leaflip Soapfishes spend their days tucked away in crevices and caves and more actively hunt after dark. Both species employ an unusual mode of capturing their prey. When closing the distance between themselves and their potential victims, they turn on their sides and begin an exaggerated swimming behavior. Both of these species also exhibit a dramatic ontogenetic color transformation.

The genus *Pseudogramma* (Tribe Grammistini) is comprised of smaller, more secretive species that are typically only encoun-

Grammistes sexlineatus, Sixline Soapfish (Indonesia): a durable aquarium fish, but one with a gluttonous appetite. Note post-feeding belly distension.

tered by ichthyologists using poisons to sample cryptic fish populations. Only one of these, a Western Atlantic species known as the Reef Bass (*Pseudogramma gregoryi*), is seen in the aquarium trade, although several members of this genus and closely related genera (e.g., *Aporops, Grammistops,* and *Suttonia*), are very common on reefs in the Indo-Pacific. (These fishes are very secretive and thus rarely seen by divers.) All these fishes were once placed in their own family, the Pseudogrammidae. Most of these diminutive fishes live deep in reef crevices, among coral branches or rubble. Some of them are also found in more turbulent areas of the outer-reef flat and reef crest. They rarely, if ever, leave their hiding places but prey on sympatric cryptic crustaceans. Unlike the rest of the soapfishes, most of the fishes in these genera (excluding *Grammistops*) do not produce the skin toxin grammistin. At least one member of the genus *Pseudogramma* (i.e., *P. polyacanthum*) is known to be sexually dichromatic and to produce large red eggs, which are probably demersal. This same species also apparently occurs in heterosexual pairs, with numerous pairs occupying the same large rubble mound. One member of the *Suttonia* is seen in the aquarium trade on rare occasions. Like the Reef Bass, this, too, is a very secretive fish that spends its entire life deep in reef crevices. Little else is known about its biology.

The genus *Rypticus* (Tribe Grammistini) is only represented in the Atlantic and Eastern Pacific. The nine species that make up this group are quite different from the other soapfishes. Like members of *Diploprion*, they are laterally compressed, but they are more elongate, with long heads, and eyes that can be rotated in their sockets so that they have binocular vision when they look forward. When threatening a rival, they often adopt a head-down posture and spread their opercula or gill covers. The *Rypticus* species move in a more serpentine fashion than their cousins and spend more time slinking around or sitting on the substrate. Most of these fishes spend their days wedged in reef crevices, the interstices between or under rocks, empty conch shells, and among the sessile invertebrates on pier pilings. Young of some species are common in estuaries and mangrove areas. Randall's Soapfish (*Rypticus randalli*) has been reported in estuaries and up rivers at salinity levels of 13.5 to 30.6 ppm. Some members of *Rypticus* have been reported to bury just under the surface of the sand or mud, but I have never seen them engage in this behavior in captivity. *Rypticus* species leave their diurnal shelter sites at dusk and hunt in the same habitat where they spend the more quiescent daytime hours. They typically feed on fishes and crustaceans, including small crabs and shrimps, and may ingest several prey items in a single hunting foray. For example, Hobson (1968) reported that the Pacific Soapfish (*Rypticus bicolor*) would eat as many as four shrimps in a single night of hunting. Like their relatives, the members of this genus have a peculiar way of stalking. When approaching potential prey, they adopt a head-down posture and quiver until within striking range, at which time they dash forward to grab their victim. Members of this genus are protogynous hermaphrodites.

One word of caution from a preeminent reef fish biologist: never put a soapfish into your pants. According to Dr. John E. Randall, who once actually placed a soapfish that he had speared into his swim trunks to carry it, considerable irritation to human skin can result.

Captive Care

The soapfishes are durable aquarium inhabitants, but few are highly regarded by hobbyists because of their subdued color patterns and secretive tendencies. This is unfortunate, because all the soapfishes exhibit interesting behaviors and will usually warm up to their keepers over time. The size of the tank used to house a soapfish will depend on the species in question. Some of the smaller members of the group will do fine in tanks as small as a standard 20-gallon, while others should be kept in nothing less than 55-to-75-gallon aquariums.

Most soapfishes spend the majority of the daylight hours hiding among the aquarium decor, occasionally slinking from one crevice to another. Therefore, it is very important to provide them with plenty of suitable shelter sites. After being in the tank for a while, most soapfishes will learn to recognize the aquarist as a source of food and become quite tame. Although it may be necessary to induce feeding by offering these fishes live food, such as feeder fish and grass shrimp, most are easily trained to accept bite-sized pieces of fresh or frozen seafood, frozen preparations, and frozen mysid and brine shrimp. When they feed, some soapfishes simply dart out from their lair, grab the prey item, then dash back to cover. Others approach their prey slowly and perform unusual swimming motions as they make the final approach.

Although most soapfishes behave aggressively toward conspecifics or congeners, they are rarely hostile toward unrelated fish species. They are, however, very predatory and can ingest surprisingly large prey. One of the biggest gluttons in the clan is the Sixline Soapfish (*Grammistes sexlineatus*). I have seen more than one of these gorgers swimming around its aquarium for hours with the head or tail of a prey fish that it could not swallow sticking out of its mouth until it was gradually swallowed. The Sixline Soapfish and others in the group are able to eat prey items as long as themselves and will consume food until their stomachs look as if they might burst.

The biggest downside to soapfish ownership is the potential risk to tankmates posed by their toxic body slime. If a soapfish is being harassed by another fish, by the aquarist, or if it is ill, it may secrete copious amounts of grammistin, which could result in the death of the soapfish itself and any other fish in the tank. Fortunately, this happens very rarely in the home aquarium. The only time I have seen this occur is when a *Rypticus* sp. was handled and then placed back into the tank. If you do notice fishes kept with a soapfish breathing heavily or behaving abnormally, remove them to another tank immediately. When capturing a soapfish use a specimen container, rather than a net, as this is less stressful to the fish. The spines on the preopercle and opercle are susceptible to tangling in aquarium nets.

SOAPFISH SPECIES

Genus *Aulacocephalus*

Aulacocephalus temmincki Bleeker, 1854
Common Name: Golden Ribbon Soapfish.
Maximum Length: 40 cm (15.6 in.).
Distribution: Red Sea, South Africa, Mascarenes, Japan, New Zealand, Kermadec Islands (where it is common), Rapa Island (a single individual).

Aulacocephalus temmincki, Golden Ribbon Soapfish (Norfolk Island): a flashy and highly prized subtropical species very rarely seen by divers—or aquarists.

Biology: This gorgeous soapfish is primarily subtropical. It is found on rocky reefs, typically at depths of 20 to 120 m (66 to 394 ft.), usually along steep walls. This fish resides under ledges, overhangs, and in caves. Like many other soapfishes, it is a nocturnal predator, leaving its hiding places at night to hunt.

Captive Care: *Aulacocephalus temmincki* is rare in the aquarium trade. It is a highly prized soapfish because of its beautiful coloration. It should be provided with a suitable cave or overhang that it can use as a sanctuary. Keeping it in a dimly lit aquarium (possibly one where only actinic lighting is used), will aid it in acclimating. Also, it should be kept at a lower water temperature (a chiller will probably be required).

Aquarium Size: 75 gal. **Temperature:** 19 to 23°C (66 to 74°F).
Aquarium Suitability Index: 4.
Remarks: This attractive soapfish is bright blue with a yellow stripe from the snout along the back. It is very thin (laterally compressed).

Genus *Belonoperca* (Arrowhead Soapfishes)

Belonoperca chabanaudi Fowler & Bean, 1930
Common Names: Arrowhead Soapfish, Chabanaud's Soapfish.
Maximum Length: 15 cm (5.9 in.).

Distribution: East Africa to Samoa, north to the Ryukyus, and south to New Caledonia.

Biology: The Arrowhead Soapfish is found on the reef face, fore-reef slopes and dropoffs, usually in areas with rich coral growth. It occurs at a depth range of 4 to 50 m (13 to 164 ft.). *Belonoperca chabanaudi* is a solitary species that hovers in caves or under ledges during the day. At dusk, it usually vacates its daytime sanctuary to hunt small fishes and crustaceans.

Captive Care: This interesting soapfish is only rarely available to home aquarists. Although it seldom displays interspecific aggression, it is a lethal predator that will eat any fish or shrimp small enough to fit into its mouth. It slowly approaches its prey by undulating its dorsal and anal fins and then, with incredible speed, swoops down to capture its quarry. The Arrowhead Soapfish will consume feeder fish and live grass shrimp, but unfortunately it is not easy to switch it over to nonliving foods. In the aquarium, it is very reclusive. It is best to provide *B. chabanaudi* with a sizeable arch, overhang, or cave under which to hover. Otherwise it will spend much of its time resting on its pelvic fins on the bottom, behind aquarium decor. Only one should be kept per tank, but it can be kept with related forms (i.e., other soapfishes, groupers). It can be kept in a shallow- or deep-water reef aquarium, but it may spend more time in the

Belonoperca chabanaudi, Arrowhead Soapfish: seldom-seen cave dweller.

Diploprion bifasciatum, Two-banded Soapfish: attractive juvenile specimen.

Diploprion drachi, Yellowface Soapfish: expert at hunting by subterfuge.

open in a more dimly lit environment.
Aquarium Size: 40 gal. **Temperature:** 22 to 27°C (72 to 81°F).
Aquarium Suitability Index: 4.

Genus *Diploprion* (Deep-bodied Soapfishes)

Diploprion bifasciatum (Cuvier, 1828)
Common Names: Two-banded Soapfish, Barred Soapfish, Yellow Emperor.
Maximum Length: 25 cm (9.8 in.).
Distribution: India to Papua New Guinea, north to southern Japan, and south to the Maldives and Lord Howe Island.
Biology: The Two-banded Soapfish is most common on coastal reefs, in calm lagoons, on protected reef faces and fore-reef slopes. It can be found at depths of 1 to 25 m (3.3 to 82 ft.). On rare occasions, it will also enter estuaries. *Diploprion bifasciatum* is a solitary fish. During the day, it is usually observed hanging in caves or under overhangs or moving from one crevice to another. It feeds on crustaceans and small fishes. The Two-banded Soapfish spawns at dusk, with males forming temporary breeding territories on the edge of the reef. When a female approaches a male, he will begin to swim in a quick, exaggerated fashion in front of her. If the female is in spawning condition, the male moves above her with his head angled upward slightly. The pair will then rise up into the water column until they are from 7 to 14 m (23 to 46 ft.) above the substrate, at which time they will rapidly turn, release their gametes, and dash back toward the ocean floor.
Captive Care: The Two-banded Soapfish is well suited to captivity. It may hide when initially introduced to its new home, but will usually start swimming around the tank within a few hours. This species will eat finely chopped fresh seafood, frozen brine shrimp, frozen mysid shrimp, frozen preparations, and even flake food. Occasionally live guppies are necessary to induce a feeding response. The Two-banded Soapfish is not aggressive toward other fishes, but it will eat any tankmate it can swallow whole. Conspecifics can be kept together, rarely behaving aggressively toward each other. They may release grammistin, a toxic substance exuded from the skin, when stressed or frightened. This can kill both the soapfish and any other fishes kept with it.
Aquarium Size: 75 gal. **Temperature:** 22 to 27°C (72 to 81°F).
Aquarium Suitability Index: 4.
Remarks: Most Two-banded Soapfish are pale to bright yellow, with a thin black band on the head that runs through the eye and a thick black band in the middle of the body. Some individuals are black overall, with yellow on the median fins and yellow margins on the pelvic fins. I have seen the black color

morph only around Heron Island on the Great Barrier Reef; it may be that this is an aggressive mimic of the common Queensland Yellowtail Angelfish (*Chaetodontoplus meredithi*—often referred to incorrectly by hobbyists as the Personifer Angelfish [*Chaetodontoplus personifer*]), which is restricted in distribution to northwestern Australia. The shape and coloration of the black morph of *D. bifasciatum* and *C. meredithi* are similar overall. The angelfish feeds on sessile invertebrates and fish eggs, while the soapfish eats small fishes and crustaceans. On the southern Barrier Reef, the proposed model (the angelfish) is much more common than the mimic. For example, of eight *D. bifasciatum* I observed around Heron Island, only two exhibited the black color pattern. During this same observation period, I noted 22 *C. meredithi*. Rudie Kuiter, a longtime reef fish observer and author, reports that in Java the juveniles of *D. bifasciatum* are gray with a black head. He suggests that the juveniles may be Batesian mimics of a sympatric poison fang blenny (*Meiacanthus* sp.).

Diploprion drachi Estève, 1955
Common Name: Yellowface Soapfish.
Maximum Length: 14 cm (5.5 in.).
Distribution: Red Sea and Gulf of Aden.
Biology: The Yellowface Soapfish is found on the reef face, fore-reef slopes, and dropoffs, at depths from 4 to 40 m (13 to 131 ft.). It feeds on crustaceans, fish larvae, and small fishes and is crepuscular, increasing its hunting efforts a few hours after sunrise and before sunset. This fish will often adopt a head-down position over reef interstices, waiting for prey items to emerge. *Diploprion drachi* will often "hunt by riding," following another fish species closely, especially medium-sized predators or nonpredatory species, using them as a mobile blind. In one 202-minute observation period, individual *D. drachi* were observed to engage in hunting by riding 32 times (about 4% of the time), with the mean length of each bout lasting 15 seconds and the longest single bout lasting 133 seconds. In this study, they were observed to follow alongside or just behind the Peacock Hind (*Cephalopholis argus*), the Sohal Surgeonfish (*Acanthurus sohal*), the Striped Bristletooth (*Ctenochaetus striatus*), the Purple Tang (*Zebrasoma xanthurum*), the Indian Ocean Sailfin Tang (*Z. desjardinii*), the Indian Ocean Longnose Parrotfish (*Hipposcarus harid*), and the Slingjaw Wrasse (*Epibulus insidiator*). I have also seen it swimming alongside the Red Sea Bannerfish (*Heniochus intermedius*). It has been described as moving so close alongside the "ridden" fish that "it appears as an extra fin of the larger fish." When the larger fish moves past a potential prey item, the Yellowface Soapfish launches its attack.

Captive Care: *Diploprion drachi* is seldom imported for the aquarium trade, but with the increase in collecting in the Red Sea, there is a greater chance of it showing up from time to time. The husbandry of this species is similar to that of *D. bifasciatum*, above. In a spacious biotope aquarium with larger herbivores (such as some of the fishes listed in the Biology section, above), it will occasionally engage in hunting by riding if offered live grass shrimp.
Aquarium Size: 55 gal. **Temperature:** 22 to 27°C (72 to 81°F).
Aquarium Suitability Index: 4.

Genus *Grammistes*

Grammistes sexlineatus (Thünberg, 1792)
Common Names: Sixline Soapfish, Sixstripe Soapfish, Goldstriped Soapfish, Skunk Fish.
Maximum Length: 30 cm (11.7 in.).
Distribution: Red Sea to the Marquesas and Mangareva, north to southern Japan, and south to New Caledonia.
Biology: The Sixline Soapfish is found on lagoon patch reefs, reef flats, fore-reef slopes, near outcroppings on muddy slopes, and, on occasion, in estuaries. It has been reported at a depth range from 1 to 130 m (3.3 to 426 ft.), and demonstrates some degree of size-related depth segregation, with juveniles occurring more frequently in shallow water and large adults moving to greater depths. The Sixline Soapfish is a solitary species that lives in holes, crevices, and under ledges. It usually stays within or very near to a hiding place during the day, but at dusk it will travel farther afield to hunt. It feeds heavily on crustaceans, including crabs, juvenile crayfishes, and shrimps, but also eats small fishes. When the Sixline Soapfish approaches a potential prey item, it will roll on its side, presenting its quarry with a view of its back only. This gives the impression that the soapfish is not as large as it would appear from the side. The soapfish approaches its prey slowly and may rapidly shake its head from side to side right before the final strike. Aquarists have reported seeing fishes approach a newly introduced Sixline Soapfish to be "cleaned," possibly mistaking the white longitudinal stripes of this fish for that of a cleaner species.

Smaller Sixline Soapfish may mimic several of the more common cardinalfish species (e.g., *Apogon novemfasciatus* and *A. nigrofasciatus*). The soapfish is not only similar in appearance to these fishes, but it is also found in the same habitat and may even associate with them. If a mimetic relationship does exist between these species, it is probably a form of aggressive mimicry, where the soapfish is able to approach prey items that are not threatened by the less aggressive cardinalfishes.

Grammistes sexlineatus, Sixline Soapfish: attractive but very predatory fish.

Pogonoperca punctata, Leaflip Soapfish: large specimen with adult coloration.

Pogonoperca ocellata, Ocellated Soapfish (Weh Island): Indian Ocean native.

Captive Care: The Sixline Soapfish is a durable aquarium fish but one with an incredible appetite. It will eat any tankmate, either fish or crustacean, that will fit into its capacious mouth, including prey items almost as large as itself. It has even been known to eat other groupers and members of its own species. The Sixline Soapfish will eagerly suck up live feeder fish and live grass shrimp and can usually be coaxed into accepting chunks of fresh seafood, krill, or cubes of frozen preparations.

Aquarium Size: 55 gal. **Temperature:** 22 to 27°C (72 to 81°F).

Aquarium Suitability Index: 4.

Remarks: The coloration of this species varies greatly throughout its life. Individuals of less than 1.7 cm (0.7 in.) standard length have a coal black body with whitish yellow spots and look very similar to a noxious sea slug in the genus *Phyllidia*. This color pattern, which possibly serves to warn predators of the soapfish's distasteful body slime, is very conspicuous in the low-light conditions that occur under ledges and in caves. In individuals between 5 and 8 cm (2 to 3.1 in.) standard length, there are three yellowish white, longitudinal stripes, while those over 8 cm (3.1 in.) standard length have six white stripes. In large adults (over 14 cm [5.5 in.] standard length) the stripes are even more numerous, but they are broken up into dashes.

Genus *Pogonoperca*

Pogonoperca punctata (Valenciennes, 1830)

Common Names: Leaflip Soapfish, Spotted Soapfish, Snowflake Soapfish, Leaflip Grouper.

Maximum Length: 35 cm (13.7 in.).

Distribution: Comoros to the Marquesas and Society Islands, north to southern Japan, and south to New Caledonia.

Biology: The Leaflip Soapfish is most abundant on outer-reef slopes in areas with rich coral growth exposed to moderate or strong currents. It lives under ledges and in caves, usually over sand substrate, at depths from 15 to 150 m (49 to 492 ft.). This species probably feeds on crustaceans and small fishes.

Captive Care: This hardy aquarium fish makes an interesting display animal. Although young specimens can be quite secretive, with time they will become bolder and spend more time in the open. *Pogonoperca punctata* is a ravenous predator that will eat any fish or crustacean that it can swallow whole, and will even eat poisonous fishes (e.g., tobies [*Canthigaster* spp.]). While only one Leaflip Soapfish should be kept per aquarium, they can be housed with other groupers and even other soapfish species. However, be sure that any tankmates, including related species, are too large for them to swallow whole.

Aquarium Size: 75 gal. **Temperature:** 22 to 27°C (72 to 81°F).

Aquarium Suitability Index: 4.

Remarks: Juvenile *P. punctata* have several large white circles on the belly that are filled with smaller white spots, and yellowish tan saddles on the back with white spots. As the juvenile grows, it develops black saddles on its back and small white spots all over its body and head. The **Ocellated Soapfish (*Pogonoperca ocellata*) Günther, 1859** is a closely related form that is found only in the Indian Ocean (it has been reported from East Africa, the Seychelles, Mauritius, the Maldives, and western Indonesia). *Pogonoperca ocellata* attains a maximum length of 23 cm (9 in.) and is dark brown overall, with black blotches and numerous small white spots. It occurs on reef slopes and around small patch reefs and coral heads, usually at depths in excess of 30 m (98 ft.).

Genus *Pseudogramma* (False Grammas)

Pseudogramma gregoryi (Breder, 1927)

Common Names: Reef Bass, Foureye Basslet.

Maximum Length: 7.6 cm (3 in.).

Distribution: Bermuda and south Florida, south to northern South America.

Biology: The Reef Bass is an extremely secretive species that is rarely seen by divers. It is found on the reef flat, reef face, and fore-reef slope, often in areas with live stony corals or coral rubble. *Pseudogramma gregoryi* occurs among branching corals or in the interstices of mound-shaped scleractinians or stony corals. This species is also abundant among the rubble that composes Sand Tilefish (*Malacanthus plumieri*) nests. It feeds on cryptic crustaceans that share its rubble interstices. The Reef Bass will also refuge in empty conch shells. It occurs at a depth range of less than 1 to 45 m (3.3 to 148 ft.). When threatened, this species flares open its gill covers to expose its large, bold, false eyespots to an approaching rival. The Reef Bass is a sequential hermaphrodite, changing sex as it grows. Along with other members of this genus, it does not produce toxic skin mucus.

Captive Care: *Pseudogramma gregoryi* is not a highly suitable aquarium species because it is so secretive. If kept in a tank with live rock and live sand, it will prey on associated invertebrate life. It is a difficult fish to feed because of its reclusiveness, so in a more sterile tank it will probably starve. If it does see small food items, such as brine shrimp, floating past its diurnal hiding place, it will dash out from cover to capture them. It is best kept in a smaller species tank with a scattering of coral rubble, live sand, and few pieces of live rock. It is also more likely to spend time in the open in a dimly lit tank, but if placed in a typical reef tank, it will rarely, if ever, be seen. *Pseudogramma gregoryi*

Pseudogramma gregoryi, Reef Bass: secretive W. Atlantic and Caribbean fish.

can be kept in pairs or small groups if there are enough hiding places. Because these fish lack toxic mucus, they are not dangerous to their tankmates. This species is usually collected with drugs such as quinaldine.

Aquarium Size: 20 gal. **Temperature:** 22 to 27°C (72 to 81°F).

Aquarium Suitability Index: 2.

Remarks: The Reef Bass has an interrupted lateral line, a small tentacle over each eye, the head and anterior part of the body is brown or greenish brown, and the rear portion of the body is reddish brown. The body often has pale blotches with a large, pale-edged eyespot on each gill cover.

Genus *Rypticus* (American Soapfishes)

Rypticus bistrispinus (Mitchill, 1818)

Common Name: Freckled Soapfish.

Maximum Length: 15 cm (5.9 in.).

Distribution: South Carolina and the Bahamas to southeastern Brazil. Also reported from the West African coast, but this record is doubtful. Most common around islands.

Biology: *Rypticus bistrispinus* is usually found on sandy bottoms near the edge of the reef. It hides under scattered rocks and rubble or refuges in empty conch shells. While in some areas it is said to emerge at night to feed, in Brazil it is reported to be more active during the day and at dusk (they are rarely seen after dark here). This species is usually found at depths of less than 5.4 m (18 ft.).

Captive Care: The Freckled Soapfish is a durable aquarium species that should be kept in a tank with several suitable hiding places. Although it is often secretive, peering out from a cave or crevices, this species will quickly learn to associate the aquarist with food.

Rypticus bistrispinus, Freckled Soapfish: shy, smallish W. Atlantic species.

Rypticus maculatus, Whitespotted Soapfish: becomes bolder with time.

Like all soapfishes this species is a threat to any fish or crustacean that can be swallowed whole. Fortunately, its smaller size means that it is less of a threat to a broader range of tankmates. I once had a *R. bistrispinus* release its toxin after being transferred from one tank to another.

Aquarium Size: 30 gal. **Temperature:** 22 to 27°C (72 to 81°F).

Aquarium Suitability Index: 4.

Remarks: The Freckled Soapfish differs from the Spotted Soapfish (*Rypticus subbifrenatus*) in having small dark spots close together on the body and two, rather than three or four, dorsal spines.

Rypticus maculatus Holbrook, 1855

Common Name: Whitespotted Soapfish.

Maximum Length: 20 cm (7.8 in.).

Distribution: North Carolina south to Palm Beach, Florida, and the northern Gulf of Mexico. Stragglers have been reported from Rhode Island.

Biology: *Rypticus maculatus* occurs on coral reefs, rock jetties, pier pilings, and near oil platforms. It is a secretive, nocturnal species, often seen lying on the substrate. It has been observed cleaning the Goliath Grouper (*Epinephelus itajara*).

Captive Care: This hardy species is sporadically collected for the aquarium trade. It is a reclusive fish that becomes bolder over time. Because of its smaller size, the Whitespotted Soapfish can be housed with a broader range of tankmates. For more information on the husbandry of this species, see the Captive Care account for the soapfish tribes, page 86.

Aquarium Size: 30 gal. **Temperature:** 22 to 27°C (72 to 81°F).

Aquarium Suitability Index: 4.

Remarks: The Whitespotted Soapfish has a dark brown body with black-bordered white spots on its back.

Rypticus saponaceus (Bloch & Schneider, 1801)

Common Name: Greater Soapfish.

Maximum Length: 33 cm (13 in.).

Distribution: South Florida and Bermuda to Brazil, east to St. Paul's Rocks, St. Helena, and the Eastern Atlantic (from Mauritania south to Angola).

Biology: The Greater Soapfish resides on sand substrates, eroded limestone escarpments, the reef flat, or among live stony and soft corals on the reef face, fore-reef slopes, and reef dropoffs. (It has been reported to live in tidepools along with *Rypticus subbifrenatus*.) It occurs at a depth range of less than 1 to 60 m (3.3 to 197 ft.), but is most common in water less than 6 m (20 ft.) deep. It occurs in both silty and clear water. While the Greater Soapfish is most often found near or on the seafloor, it sometimes enters the water column. *Rypticus saponaceous* is a solitary species that is occasionally seen lying in the open, on sand, or on hard reef substrate. However, it typically spends much of the daylight hours in reef crevices or near cave entrances, emerging at night to hunt. It feeds mainly on small fishes (like cardinalfishes, wrasses, and gobies) and decapod shrimps, but also consumes crabs and mantis shrimps. The Greater Soapfish will ambush prey items that swim past its diurnal refuge or will stalk its prey. I have seen these fish shove their heads into holes and crevices in search of food and closely follow Sharptail Snake Eels (*Myrichthys breviceps*) as they probe coral rubble interstices. At dusk, *R. saponaceus* individuals form pairs and spawn.

Captive Care: *Rypticus saponaceus* is a secretive aquarium species that will spend much of the daylight hours hiding among the decor when initially added to the aquarium. However, after becoming accustomed to its new home, it may become quite bold, sometimes begging for food. It will eat any live foods offered, including feeder fish and grass shrimp, and can usually be enticed into taking nonliving foods, like chopped seafoods, frozen preparations, krill, and mysid shrimp. The Greater Soapfish often adopts strange postures, including lying on its side, shoving its head into a crevice with its body and tail sticking straight up in the water column, and perching on the side of a coral head with its head down and tail up. It will eat smaller fishes and crustaceans housed with it and may behave aggressively toward members of its own species or closely related forms. The only real drawback to keeping this species is its ability to kill both itself and its tankmates by exuding a toxic skin mucus if it is stressed or, possibly, dying.

Aquarium Size: 75 gal. **Temperature:** 20 to 27°C (68 to 81°F).

Aquarium Suitability Index: 4.

Remarks: The Greater Soapfish has the ability to lighten or darken its color to better match the substrate it is lying on. Juvenile *R. saponaceus* have a white stripe running down the head and back (lacking in adults). This species is very closely related to the **Mottled Soapfish** (*Rypticus bicolor*) **Valenciennes, 1846,** which ranges from Baja California to Peru, including the Galapagos and other offshore islands, and **Courtenay's Soapfish** (*Rypticus courtenayi*) **McCarthy, 1979,** which is only known from the Revillagigedo Islands.

Rypticus subbifrenatus Gill, 1861

Common Name: Spotted Soapfish.

Maximum Length: 18 cm (7 in.).

Distribution: South Florida and the Bahamas to Venezuela. In the Eastern Atlantic it occurs from Senegal south to Angola (including Cape Verde to Annobón).

Biology: The Spotted Soapfish occurs on rocky and coral substrates near shorelines and on open reefs, at depths from less than 1 to 21 m (3.3 to 69 ft.). It is sometimes found in tidepools. Occasionally specimens also occur in tidal creeks and among the sessile invertebrates on pier pilings. This is a very secretive species. Juveniles are more often found in turbid water than adults.

Captive Care: The Spotted Soapfish is an engaging aquarium species and frequently available to aquarists. Like its relatives, it has a propensity to remain hidden most of the time. When food is introduced, it will dash out to capture a morsel and then shoot back to its original hiding place. Its smaller size means it can be kept with a broader range of tankmates. Like others in its genus, it can exude toxic mucus and should be handled with care.

Aquarium Size: 75 gal. **Temperature:** 22 to 27°C (72 to 81°F).

Aquarium Suitability Index: 4.

Remarks: This species is pale olive to reddish brown overall with widely separated dark spots. The **Largespotted Soapfish** (*Rypticus bornoi*) **Beebe and Tee Van, 1928** is another spotted species that is known from the Bahamas and the Atlantic coast of Panama. The latter species lacks pale rings around the spots on the head and body (seen in *R. subbifrenatus*) and *R. macrostigmus* has two dorsal spines (*R. subbifrenatus* has three or four). The Largespotted Soapfish occurs at a depth range of 11 to 32 m (36 to 105 ft.), where it occurs on silty bottoms among dead corals or on living reefs in clear water.

References

Böhlke & Chaplin (1968), Büttner (1996), Chlupaty (1985), Courtenay (1967), Diamant & Golani (1984), Kuiter & Debelius (1994), McCarthy (1979), Myers (1999), Randall (1967), Thresher (1984), Van Der Elst (1985).

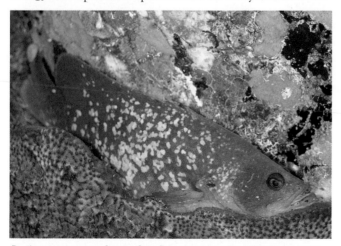

Rypticus saponaceus, Greater Soapfish: chameleon-like color-change artist.

Rypticus subbifrenatus, Spotted Soapfish: engaging and often collected.

TRIBE LIOPROPOMINI
REEF BASSLETS

Liopropoma carmabi, Candy Basslet: an exquisite fish for a deep-water reef aquarium, this species is challenging to collect and always fetches premium prices.

AS REEF AQUARIUMS HAVE GAINED POPULARITY WITH an ever-growing guild of marine aquarists, demand has increased for brightly colored fishes that will not harm sessile invertebrates, especially stony and soft corals. One group that has emerged as a new favorite of those seeking "reef-safe" species is the genus *Liopropoma,* commonly known as reef basslets. These exquisite fishes are colorful, disease-resistant, and, with the possible exception of ornamental crustaceans, they do not bother the more desirable invertebrates. While these fishes were often considered difficult to keep in conventional fish-only systems, the reef basslets can thrive in the reef aquarium, with its abundance of caves and crevices to hide in, its usual lack of larger, more aggressive tankmates, and, often, its sources of live microfauna to supplement their diets. The fact that these fishes tend to be secretive, expensive, and far from common in the retail aquarium trade seems to add to their mystique among reef keepers.

Classification and Biology

Although many of the *Liopropoma* species are abundant in certain parts of their range, relatively little is known about them due to their secretive nature. Not only is their way of life somewhat of a mystery, their taxonomic status was also an enigma for many years. Although not all ichthyologists agree, Nelson

(1994) classifies the genus *Liopropoma* within the grouper family, Serranidae, the Subfamily Epinephelinae, and the Tribe Liopropomini. The reef basslets share this tribe with the genera *Bathyanthias* and *Rainfordia*. Certain morphological, life history, and behavioral characteristics suggest that these fishes are more closely allied with the soapfishes (Tribe Grammistini) than the rest of the groupers. Five species of *Liopropoma* occur in the tropical Western Atlantic, while 18 species are known from the tropical Pacific and Indian Oceans. Unfortunately, few of the Indo-Pacific forms make it to the North American aquarium fish trade. All of these basslets are rarely seen in open water, but instead reside in caves and crevices and are sometimes observed dashing from one hiding place to another or skulking in the back of deep caves. These fishes live as solitary individuals or form pairs. Dusk spawning has been observed in the Swissguard Basslet (*L. rubre*). This consisted of a pair dashing off the bottom, shedding their gametes, and retreating back to the reef. Studies suggest that unlike many of the seabasses, these fishes are secondary gonochorists, which means they develop into one gender or the other and do not change sex. There is no known sexual dimorphism in any of the *Liopropoma* species although one would expect females to be more rotund than males, especially during the mating period.

Little information exists on the food habits of *Liopropoma*, but the smaller species are thought to feed mainly on crustaceans, like swarming mysid shrimp, while larger species also consume small fishes. Their large jaws enable them to consume relatively large prey items. Reef basslets are not always the hunters, they are sometimes the hunted; for example, they have been found in the stomachs of moray eels and emperor snappers.

Captive Care

For the most part, reef basslets make outstanding aquarium residents. They are especially well suited to the minireef system, where they take full advantage of the numerous caves and crevices to hide in and under. The smaller *Liopropoma* species will not bother most ornamental invertebrates, but they may consume smaller shrimps. Although some specimens may lose their color over time, most are relatively colorfast if given a varied diet. These fishes will eat almost anything, with shaved table shrimp, frozen preparations for carnivores, and frozen mysid shrimp being good staples. They will eat most prepared foods as well and will feed on small crustaceans (e.g., amphipods, copepods) that live in and among the live rocks of the reef aquarium. If housed in an established reef tank with good populations of microfauna, they should be fed two or three times a week. In a tank without live rock, they should be fed daily.

Liopropoma rubre, Swissguard Basslet (juvenile): typical native habitat for this genus of small fishes, with a rocky cave or crevice always close by.

When initially introduced, the *Liopropoma* species may hide for several days or even as long as a fortnight before coming out to inspect their new surroundings. Although they may never become as bold as a butterflyfish or clownfish, they will gradually become a more conspicuous part of the fish community. For example, a Ridgeback Basslet (*Liopropoma mowbrayi*) I kept in a reef tank was extremely secretive for just over a day before it began to make brief excursions into the open to feed or to investigate its surroundings. However, it spent most of its time moving under ledges and among the reef structure. One thing that will prevent their successful acclimation is aggressive tankmates. If these basslets are kept with large, competitive fishes, they often hide constantly and will not eat.

One of the most appealing attributes of the smaller *Liopropoma* species is that they are rarely aggressive to other fishes. For example, I kept a Swissguard Basslet (*Liopropoma rubre*) in a 15-gallon reef tank with a much smaller Yellow Assessor (*Assessor flavissimus*) that it never bothered. A Ridgeback Basslet (*L. mowbrayi*) I housed in a 30-gallon reef tank was indifferent to two smaller Blackcap Basslets (*Gramma melacara*) and a Dusky Gramma (*G. linki*). Two *Liopropoma* basslets of different species can be kept in the same aquarium if they are introduced simultaneously and if plenty of hiding places are provided. But members of the same species should not be kept together except in a large aquarium (e.g., with a surface area of at least 11,614 cm^2

Liopropoma africanum, African Basslet: secretive Indian Ocean species.

Liopropoma aurora, Aurora Basslet: a relatively large deep-water species.

Liopropoma latifasciatum, Blackstriped Basslet: found off Japan and Korea.

[1,800 in.^{2}]) with lots of hiding places. If a mated pair is acquired, they may settle into a smaller space, but even then a larger, more dominant individual may harass a subordinate when they cross paths. Fighting between conspecifics can be violent, often involving vicious jaw-locking behavior, and can lead to the death of subordinate individuals. Reef basslets will occasionally skirmish over a hiding place with other basslets or other cryptic fish species (e.g., cardinalfishes), but this can be prevented by providing numerous crevices and caves. Those species typically found on vertical dropoffs will appreciate a steep wall of rock in their aquarium home.

It has been reported that the *Liopropoma* species are hypersensitive to poor water quality and decreased oxygen levels, and they have been known to succumb to dinoflagellate and protozoan infections, although they are not overly susceptible to them. Several authors have suggested that these fishes are difficult to keep in aquariums, stating that they often refuse to eat. This may be the case in a more belligerent fish-only tank, but I (and others) have found them to be hardy in reef aquariums if provided with plenty of hiding places and kept with nonaggressive tankmates.

At least two species of reef basslets have spawned in captivity. These are the Wrasse Bass (*Liopropoma eukrines*) and the Swissguard Basslet (*L. rubre*). Although getting them to reproduce in aquarium confines can be quite easy, raising the larvae is another matter altogether. The larvae are quite spectacular, sporting two extremely elongate dorsal spines at the front of the dorsal fin that extend back about another body length behind the tail.

REEF BASSLET SPECIES

Liopropoma africanum (Smith, 1954)

Common Name: African Basslet.

Maximum Length: 8.8 cm (3.4 in.).

Distribution: East Africa north to Djibouti, east to the Maldives and Chagos Islands.

Biology: The African Basslet is found on inshore reef faces and fore-reef slopes, often on steep walls that have an abundance of caves. It occurs at depths from 8 to 48 m (26 to 157 ft.) and is often found in the back of caves, moving in and between crevices.

Captive Care: The husbandry of this species is like other smaller members of the genus. For more information, see the Captive Care section in the tribe account, above.

Aquarium Size: 20 gal. **Temperature:** 22 to 27°C (72 to 81°F).
Aquarium Suitability Index: 4.

Liopropoma aurora (Jordan & Evermann, 1903)
Common Names: Aurora Basslet, Sunset Basslet, Yellowmargin Basslet.
Maximum Length: 20 cm (7.8 in.).
Distribution: Hawaiian Islands.
Biology: The Aurora Basslet is typically found in deep water, usually at depths greater than 50 m (164 ft.) and has been reported in water as deep as 85 m (279 ft.). Lisa Privitera (1991) reported that at the depths where this basslet occurs, it is very similar in appearance to a brown cardinalfish (*Apogon* sp.) that lives in the same habitat. She and Richard Pyle collected this species among a patch of coral rubble at 60 m (197 ft.). This species has been taken from the stomach of Berndt's Moray (*Gymnothorax berndti*).
Captive Care: The Aurora Basslet attains a larger maximum length than most members of the genus and therefore is a greater threat to small fishes and crustaceans. It can be kept in a shallow- or deep-water aquarium, but will spend more time in the open in a dimly lit tank.
Aquarium Size: 30 gal. **Temperature:** 21 to 27°C (70 to 81°F).
Aquarium Suitability Index: 5.
Remarks: This species was once placed in the genus *Pikea*, now considered a synonym of the genus *Liopropoma*. The **Black-striped Basslet (*Liopropoma latifasciatum*) Tanaka, 1922** is a resident of rocky reefs off Japan, Korea, and Palau. It is a larger basslet, like *L. aurora*, attaining a maximum length of 20 cm (7.8 in.). It is usually found at depths of 50 m (164 ft.) or more.

Liopropoma carmabi (Randall, 1963)
Common Name: Candy Basslet.
Maximum Length: 6 cm (2.3 in.) (larger around Ascension Island).
Distribution: Florida Keys, Bahamas, Puerto Rico, Barbados, Curaçao, and Bonaire. Also Ascension Island in the Eastern Atlantic.
Biology: The Candy Basslet occurs at depths of 15 to 70 m (49 to 230 ft.), but is most abundant at depths greater than 24 m (79 ft.). It is usually observed among hard corals and in reef recesses on dropoffs, but it also occurs on gently sloping rubble bottoms. This species has been estimated to use a home range of about 9 m² (100 ft.²), which includes the infrastructure of the reef. It is apparently quite site-attached, with individuals having been observed inhabiting the same reef crevice for as long as 16 months.
Captive Care: Unfortunately for aquarists, *Liopropoma carmabi* is

Liopropoma carmabi, Candy Basslet: a beauty that may shun bright lights.

not easily collected because of its preference for deep water and its reclusive nature. The majority of individuals that make it into the U.S. aquarium trade command a formidable price. Nevertheless, it is an exquisite display animal that has been reported to live at least two years in captivity. It will hide among the reef decor when first introduced to the aquarium, but after acclimation it will spend more time in full view, usually near the entrance to a hole or crevice. This is especially true if the tank is not brightly illuminated. (It is best kept in a deep-water reef aquarium.) The captive Candy Basslet has been reported to be more active at night.
Aquarium Size: 20 gal. **Temperature:** 22 to 27°C (72 to 81°F).
Aquarium Suitability Index: 4.
Remarks: Both the Candy and Swissguard Basslet (*L. rubre*) have alternating stripes running from the nose to the tail. *Liopropoma carmabi* has pale blue edges around the spot on the dorsal and caudal fins, lacks a spot on the anal fin, and its stripes are orange and lavender, while those of the Swissguard are reddish brown and pinkish tan. The Candy Basslet is definitely the more stunning of these two fishes. Juvenile Swissguard Basslets (see photo, page 95) possess characteristics similar to those of *L. carmabi*. For example, they often lack the spot on the anal fin, and the two spots on the caudal fin are not contiguous as in adult *L. rubre*. However, the overall color of the two species is very distinct.

Liopropoma eukrines (Starck & Courtenay, 1962)
Common Names: Wrasse Bass, Wrasse Basslet.

Liopropoma eukrines, Wrasse Bass: captive spawnings reported.

Liopropoma fasciatum, Rainbow Basslet: found in the Galapagos Islands.

Maximum Length: 13 cm (5.1 in.).
Distribution: North Carolina to the Florida Keys.
Biology: In Florida waters, the Wrasse Bass occurs on rock patches, coral heads, and under ledges in water 30 to 116 m (98 to 380 ft.) deep. It is often observed with the Orangeback Bass (*Serranus annularis*) and the Chalk Bass (*S. tortugarum*). Although they are secretive, Wrasse Basses occasionally fall prey to larger piscivores. For example, one specimen was recovered from

the stomach of a grouper. This species is usually seen singly or in pairs, but in areas of suitable habitat they may occur in very loose aggregations. The Wrasse Bass eats crustaceans in the wild and is said to be particularly fond of the Golden Coral Shrimp (*Stenopus scutellatus*).
Captive Care: The larger size of the Wrasse Bass makes it a greater threat to smaller fishes, but it prefers to feed on targets that are considerably smaller than itself. One aquarist with a larger specimen reported that it ate at least one and maybe more small fairy wrasses (*Cirrhilabrus* spp.). It will also eat ornamental crustaceans, including shrimp in the genus *Stenopus*, like the Banded Coral Shrimp (*S. hispidus*). More than one Wrasse Bass can be kept in a larger aquarium, but they will often fight before settling down and beginning to tolerate each other. To keep more than one specimen, choose individuals that are slightly different in size and introduce them to the tank simultaneously. *Liopropoma eukrines* will reproduce in captivity and has been reported to spawn almost every night in the tanks of an experienced aquaculturist.
Aquarium Size: 30 gal. **Temperature:** 19.5 to 26°C (67 to 79°F).
Aquarium Suitability Index: 5.
Remarks: The Wrasse Bass has a single black stripe down the flank that becomes broader toward the posterior end and is bordered on the top and bottom by a narrower yellow stripe. Larger individuals tend to be more colorful than smaller specimens.

Liopropoma fasciatum Bussing, 1980
Common Names: Rainbow Basslet, Wrasse-ass Bass.
Maximum Length: 25 cm (9.8 in.).
Distribution: Central Sea of Cortez to the Galapagos Islands.
Biology: The Rainbow Basslet is most abundant below the thermocline, at depths of 25 to 240 m (82 to 787 ft.), and is most common below 33 m (108 ft.). It is usually observed hanging at the entrance to caves, in reef crevices, or under overhangs.
Captive Care: Because it attains a greater maximum length than most of its congeners, *L. fasciatum* is a greater threat to small fishes and crustaceans. I have seen them kept in pairs in larger tanks (e.g., surface area greater than 11,614 cm^2 [1,800 in.^{2}]). It should be housed in a dimly lit tank with plenty of holes and crevices in which it can refuge.
Aquarium Size: 30 gal. **Temperature:** 20 to 23°C (68 to 73°F).
Aquarium Suitability Index: 5.
Remarks: This species is closely related to the Wrasse Bass. It has a dark flank stripe almost equal in width over its entire length. Aquarium observations suggest that this species may be sexually dimorphic, with males attaining a greater length than females.

Liopropoma mowbrayi, Ridgeback Basslet: a rarely collected deep-water fish.

Liopropoma multilineatum, Many-lined Basslet: excellent, reef-safe species.

Liopropoma mowbrayi Woods & Kanazawa, 1951

Common Names: Ridgeback Basslet, Cave Basslet.

Maximum Length: 9 cm (3.5 in.).

Distribution: South Florida, Bermuda and the Bahamas, south to Venezuela.

Biology: The Ridgeback Basslet inhabits caves and crevices near reef dropoffs or on vertical reef walls, at depths of 15 to at least 85 m (49 to 279 ft.). This species is reported to prefer smaller reef interstices. In certain areas *L. mowbrayi* is common under plate or sheet corals (*Agaricia* spp.) at depths between 75 and 85 m (246 and 279 ft.). It is usually found in pairs.

Captive Care: The Ridgeback Basslet is a secretive fish that should be housed with nonaggressive species in a tank with plenty of hiding places. More than one *L. mowbrayi* can be kept in a larger aquarium (e.g., more than 7,742 cm^2 [1,200 in.^{2}] surface area), and it can also be housed with congeners. It is a pricey rarity because it is most common at depths where only limited collecting occurs and it is difficult to decompress when brought to the surface.

Aquarium Size: 20 gal. **Temperature:** 21 to 26°C (70 to 79°F).

Aquarium Suitability Index: 4.

Remarks: *Liopropoma mowbrayi* was originally described in 1951 from a specimen that washed up on a beach during a storm. It has a pinkish or reddish gray body with a yellow stripe running from the tip of the snout to the eye, a blue-ringed black spot on the dorsal and anal fin, and both a black band and white band on the caudal fin margin. In some specimens, the black tail band may be broken up into three spots. This species was named for the prominent ridge between the two dorsal fins. The body is more compressed and has a more pointed operculum than its sympatric congeners.

Liopropoma multilineatum Randall & Taylor, 1988

Common Names: Many-lined Basslet, Yellow Basslet.

Maximum Length: 8 cm (3.1 in.).

Distribution: Northwestern Australia east to Fiji, north to the Philippines, and south to the Coral Sea.

Biology: This species is found on reef faces and fore-reef slopes, often on sheer dropoffs with abundant caves or at the base of the reef. It is seen at depths from 25 to 46 m (82 to 151 ft.) and usually lives deep in large caves and reef recesses. This species has been taken from the stomach of the Orangefin Emperor (*Lethrinus kallopterus*).

Captive Care: The husbandry of this species is like other smaller members of the genus. It is an excellent reef-aquarium species, most comfortable in a complex live-rock aquascape. For more information, see the Captive Care section in the tribe account, page 95.

Aquarium Size: 20 gal. **Temperature:** 22 to 27°C (72 to 81°F).

Aquarium Suitability Index: 4.

Remarks: This attractive basslet has a white stripe running through the middle of the caudal peduncle, to about the middle of the dorsal fin, with bright red stripes above and below it. *Liopropoma multilineatum* has a reddish head and a yellow body. It also has many red stripes on the sides and back.

This species is closely related to the **Redstriped Reef Basslet** (*Liopropoma tonstrinum*) **Randall & Taylor, 1988**. Although the overall coloration of the two species is similar, *L. tonstrinum* lacks the fine pinstripes on the sides of the body that are present in *L. multilineatum*. The Redstriped Reef Basslet is known from Christmas Island in the Indian Ocean, Micronesia, Fiji, and Samoa. It is a cave dweller that occurs on fore-reef dropoffs at depths of 11 to 50 m (36 to 164 ft.).

Liopropoma rubre, Swissguard Basslet: esteemed reef-aquarium fish.

Liopropoma susumi, Pinstripe Reef Basslet: widespread Indo-Pacific species.

Liopropoma mitratum, Headband Reef Basslet: note yellow-striped head.

Liopropoma rubre Poey, 1861

Common Names: Swissguard Basslet, Peppermint Basslet.

Maximum Length: 8 cm (3.1 in.).

Distribution: South Florida to Yucatan, south to Venezuela.

Biology: The Swissguard Basslet is often found in water as shallow as 5 m (16 ft.), but has been collected to depths of 40 m (131 ft.). It is rarely observed during the day, when it spends its time deep in coral crevices. When encountered by divers, it is usually observed hanging near the entrance of its refuge and if approached will retreat into the reef. It will often hover near the interstices formed by overlapping colonies of plate or sheet corals (*Agaricia* spp.). Dekker (1987) reports that *L. rubre* is often observed hanging upside down under ledges on the reef, much like the *Gramma* species and will even adopt this posture under leather corals in the aquarium. Most often, the Swissguard Basslet is observed singly or in pairs but has been reported to form small groups. DeLoach (1999) observed a pair of these fish spawning. The two fish swam alongside each other so that their heads were in contact and directed upward. (Their bodies were held at an angle of about 45° to each other.) From this position, the pair dashed up into the water column in an apparent spawning ascent.

Captive Care: Because it is hard to approach, let alone capture, the Swissguard Basslet is not common in aquarium stores and when available it comes at a high price. It is, however, the most readily available member of the genus. The Swissguard Basslet should be housed with nonaggressive species. More than one *L. rubre* can be kept in the same aquarium if the tank is large enough. The dominant fish may intimidate and behave aggressively toward the subordinate individual, however, so be prepared to remove one if this should occur. Overt aggression may not be witnessed, but if one specimen starts to hide all the time, there is a strong likelihood it is being picked on. I have also had subordinate specimens jump into overflow boxes to get away from an aggressive conspecific. This species has spawned in aquarium confines.

Aquarium Size: 20 gal. **Temperature:** 20 to 27°C (68 to 81°F).

Aquarium Suitability Index: 5.

Remarks: For comments on the similarities between this species and *L. carmabi*, see the *L. carmabi* species account, above.

Liopropoma susumi (Jordan & Seale, 1906)

Common Names: Pinstripe Reef Basslet, Meteor Reef Basslet.

Maximum Length: 9.2 cm (3.6 in.).

Distribution: Red Sea east to Samoa, south to New Caledonia, and north to southern Japan.

Biology: The Pinstripe Reef Basslet is found around lagoon patch reefs as well as deep dropoffs in crevices and caves. It occurs at depths of 2 to 34 m (6.6 to 112 ft.) and is considered the most abundant species of its genus in the Indo-Pacific.

Captive Care: Husbandry requirements for this species are identical to those of other smaller members of the genus. For more information see the Captive Care section in the tribe account, page 95.

Aquarium Size: 20 gal. **Temperature:** 22 to 27°C (72 to 81°F).

Aquarium Suitability Index: 5.

Remarks: There are several other reef basslets with longitudinal stripes on the body. One that is very similar to *L. susumi* is **Collette's Reef Basslet** (*Liopropoma collettei*) **Randall & Taylor, 1988.** This species is pale red overall, with four dark brown stripes on the body (*L. susumi* usually has eight). *Liopropoma collettei* is known from Papua New Guinea, the Philippines, and the Hawaiian Islands. It has been collected on coral reefs at depths of 6 to 34 m (20 to 112 ft.) among stony corals like *Porites compressa*. This species attains a maximum length of 8 cm (3.1 in.).

The **Headband Reef Basslet** (*Liopropoma mitratum*) **Lubbock & Randall, 1978,** is another species with fine stripes. This species is reddish brown with a yellowish caudal peduncle and tail and numerous fine stripes on the body. It also has several yellow bands on the head. It has been reported from numerous locations in the Indo-Pacific, where it occurs at depths from 3 to 46 m (9.8 to 151 ft.). The Headband Reef Basslet attains a maximum length of 8.6 cm (3.4 in.).

Liopropoma swalesi (Fowler & Bean, 1930)

Common Name: Swalesi Reef Basslet.

Maximum Length: 6.4 cm (2.5 in.).

Distribution: Indonesia (including Sulawesi and the Moluccas) and New Britain (probably the Philippines as well).

Biology: This little known reef basslet is apparently very secretive. As a result, virtually nothing is known about its biology. A 4.6 cm (1.8 in.) female was reported to be sexually mature.

Captive Care: This is a secretive but stunning aquarium fish. Provide it with plenty of small caves and crevices in which to hide. It will accept a variety of aquarium foods, but may not get enough to eat if placed in a tank with fish tankmates that are "overzealous" feeders. If kept in a fish community tank, make sure you place food in areas where this fish is likely to get its fair share. Keep one per tank unless your aquarium is larger (135 gallons or more) with lots of rock work, or you acquire a heterosexual pair (this species is known to be sexually dimorphic). It may jump out of an open aquarium.

Aquarium Size: 20 gal. **Temperature:** 23 to 28°C (74 to 82°F).

Liopropoma swalesi, Swalesi Reef Basslet: stunning but reclusive.

Aquarium Suitability Index: 4.

Remarks: As of 1988, the Swalesi Reef Basslet was known to science from only four specimens. In the last few years, this species has began to show up in the aquarium trade with great regularity. Unfortunately, most of these individuals are no doubt captured using chemicals (e.g., cyanide). This does not appear to have long-term, deleterious effects on the individuals that make it to North American aquarium stores, but these chemicals can cause microhabitat destruction. *Liopropoma swalesi* is very similar in color to the Candy Basslet (*L. carmabi*) and the Swissguard Basslet (*L. rubre*)—both of these species occur in the Atlantic Ocean. The Swalesi Reef Basslet, however, has no markings on the caudal fin. *Liopropoma swalesi* is unique in having 26 or 27 gill rakers (only two of which are rudimentary). Other basslets have 23 gill rakers or fewer, with at least 6 of these being rudiments.

References

Bussing (1980), Campbell (1979), Colin (1974, 1976), Dekker (1987), Delbeek (1991), Freeman & Alevizon (1983), Klocek & Kolman (1976), R. Kuiter (personal communication), Kuiter & Debelius (1994), Moe (1992), Myers (1999), Privitera (1991), Randall (1963b, 1968), Randall et al. (1997), B. Rice (personal communication), Smith (1971), Starck & Courtenay (1962), Thresher (1980, 1984), F. Young (personal communication), Wilkie (1986).

FAMILY PSEUDOCHROMIDAE
DOTTYBACKS

THE CORAL REEF IS HOME TO MYRIAD SMALL, BRIGHTLY colored fishes. Unfortunately, many are overlooked by those divers, snorkelers, and underwater photographers who have eyes only for the big and the bold. One family of smaller, grouper-like fishes regularly missed by such divers is the dottybacks. For chromatic attire, some rival the flashiest of reef fishes, such as the angels and butterflyfishes. Because most dottybacks are diminutive and will quickly retreat into reef crevices when ap-proached, most underwater observers usually catch only fleeting glimpses of them and very few take the time to "wait them out."

Aquarists, on the other hand, are very familiar with the dot-tybacks. They are often recommended for their durability, small size, vivid colors, and food habits—they are easily fed and most will not eat desirable invertebrates. But these fishes do have some traits that can't be ignored. For example, many of them have belligerent dispositions and will wreak havoc in a peaceful com-munity tank. Some are also prone to disappointing color loss, changing from dramatic to dull.

Classification and Biology
Most of the dottybacks of interest to aquarists belong to the Subfamily Pseudochrominae. Currently, this subfamily contains a total of about 70 species, but there are more yet to be described, including two deep-water forms that have been observed from a submersible off Enewetak Atoll. (One of these was purple with a red dorsal fin, the other was yellow with a red lateral stripe. Rare-fish lovers are awaiting their collection with great anticipa-tion.)

All the dottybacks are limited in distribution to the Indo-Pacific and Red Sea, reaching their apex of diversity in the West-ern Pacific, and all species occur on coral or rocky reefs. Several characters distinguish the dottybacks from their near relatives—the most conspicuous of these being eyes with pear-shaped pupils. They also have scales on their heads, a continuous dorsal fin with one to three spines, and a disjunct lateral line. Most members of this subfamily are small: the largest species attains 20 cm (7.8 in.) in total length.

The majority of dottybacks feed on small benthic inverte-

Labracinus cyclophthalmus, Red Dottyback: displays both the allure and the pugnacious nature that characterize many members of this genus.

brates, such as small crustaceans, polychaete worms, and zoo-plankton. A few larger species also consume larger shrimps, crabs, and small fishes. All of the dottybacks are diurnal preda-tors, feeding by day and slumbering in reef holes and interstices at night.

Most dottybacks are shy and never stray far from a crevice or hole. Their relatively small size and lack of anatomical defenses make them palatable to many fish predators, and they must de-pend on elusiveness and constant vigilance to avoid being picked off by the myriad piscivores that hunt over the reef. In a reef-type aquarium, without the constant presence of large preda-tory enemies, they tend to become less reclusive and can put on a very interesting display of behaviors.

Dottyback Mimicry
Several dottybacks appear to mimic unrelated species, possibly to reduce the risk of predation. For example, it has been suggested that the Midnight Dottyback (*Pseudochromis paranox*) mimics the Midnight Angelfish (*Centropyge nox*). The dottyback not only has a color pattern similar to that of the angelfish, but it com-monly associates with and swims like it. This vulnerable black dottyback may mimic the spiny, less palatable *C. nox* so that smaller predators avoid ingesting it. It has also been suggested that the closely related Splendid Dottyback (*Pseudochromis splen-dens*) may mimic the Vermiculated Angelfish (*Chaetodontoplus mesoleucus*) for similar reasons.

Off Oman in the Arabian Sea, there is also an unusual mimetic relationship between a dottyback and a blenny. The dot-tyback is *Pseudochromis leucorhynchus*, the Whitelip Dottyback. The blenny is *Oman ypsilon*, the Oman Blenny. These two fishes are close in color (they share similar markings on the head) and shape, but why one would mimic the other is not yet known. Many fishes mimic blennies of the genus *Meiacanthus* because they have large, venomous fangs. Although it has not been de-termined if it is venomous or not, the Oman Blenny has two large canines in its lower jaw that it may use to bite predators that threaten it. If this is the case, then the Whitelip Dottyback may be avoided by those piscivores that have had a bad experience with the Oman Blenny. (For more on dottybacks and mimicry see the account describing *Pseudochromis springeri*, the Springer's Dottyback, page 137.)

Manonichthys polynemus, Longfin Dottyback: ready to dart.

Observing and Photographing Dottybacks in the Wild

While the dottybacks are fairly common on reefs in the Indo-west Pacific, many divers overlook them because of their small sizes and secretive behaviors. They are usually seen darting from one hiding place to another or hovering in front of a hole or crevice. The first step in successfully observing or photographing dottybacks is to find suitable pseudochromid habitat. Caves, overhangs, and areas with rich sponge growth are all habitats that seem to attract these fishes (see the species accounts that follow for more about the habitat preferences of individual species).

When you find likely habitat, take a position off the reef face or fore-reef slope and remain still for five minutes or more. Keep a close lookout for dottybacks darting between hiding places. You can also swim along the reef to try to catch a fleeting glimpse of a dottyback as it ducks for cover. These fishes often move in fairly predictable paths. Once you have found a dottyback, all you have to do is concentrate on that area and wait patiently.

To photograph the dottyback, focus on the edge of the hole or crevice where it disappeared and keep your eye close to the viewfinder. The dottyback will usually pop out for several seconds before it dashes back into its refuge or moves to another. In the case of the more aggressive dottybacks, try using a small mirror to draw them out into the open. Just position the mirror near the dottyback's hideout so that it can see its reflection when it emerges and wait to see what happens—the dottyback may forget you are there as it comes out to attack the apparent "intruder."

Social Behavior and Reproduction

Most dottybacks are territorial, chasing away members of their own kind as well as certain other species. However, a few dottybacks are regularly observed in loose groups. For example, Sankey's Dottyback (*Pseudochromis sankeyi*) occasionally occurs in groups numbering more than 60 individuals, while the Orchid (*P. fridmani*) and Diadem Dottyback (*P. diadema*) are reported to form smaller groups.

When a territory-holding dottyback encounters an intruding conspecific, it will raise all of its median fins and swim quickly around its adversary. If the intruder flees, the aggressor will often chase it out of its territory. If the interloper stands its ground, tail-beating (where one dottyback moves next to the other and pummels it with its tail), biting, or jaw-locking (where the two fish grasp each other by the jaws) can ensue. The latter two behaviors can result in severe injuries to the combatants. As far as other species are concerned, many dottybacks are especially intolerant of wrasses. This is probably due to the fact that wrasses eat fish eggs, and dottybacks, which demonstrate parental care of their demersal spawn, learn, or are genetically programmed, to attack egg predators that approach their nests.

Dottybacks change sex, and at least those have been studied to date exhibit protogynous (female to male) hermaphroditism. However, captive observations suggest that they may be capable of sex changes in both directions. Courtship and spawning commence when a female's eggs become hydrated and her abdomen swells. The male begins to approach her and attempts to lure her back to a hole, crevice, or burrow to lay her eggs. He does this by engaging in an undulating swimming performance or "leading" display. A short bout of chasing by the male may precede his courtship display. It may take the male a couple of hours to entice the female into his lair and up to an hour before the eggs are actually deposited once the pair finally enters the nest. Eggs are produced in a mass called an egg ball, and the male fertilizes it and then usually chases the female away from the nest. The male defends the egg ball from predators and aerates it by fanning the eggs with its fins until they hatch. The egg ball, which is not affixed to the substrate, often rolls around the nest as the dottyback agitates it with its fins and body.

Dottyback eggs are held together in a spherical cluster by thin, sticky threads. There are inconspicuous channels between the eggs that allow water to circulate through the egg mass. The egg ball can be from about 2 to 3.5 cm (0.8 to 1.4 in.) in diameter and can be comprised of approximately 500 to more than 1,000 eggs. Dottyback eggs range in size from 1 to 1.3 mm. Hatching occurs about five or six days after the eggs are deposited and often occurs at night. (The incubation period is, of course,

Pseudochromis springeri, Springer's Dottyback: cleaner mimic?   *Larabicus quadrilineatus*, Red Sea Cleaner Wrasse: cleaner species.

Dottybacks as Cleaners

Although dottybacks have not been reported to clean other fishes in the wild, they have been observed to do so in the aquarium. For example, an adult Arabian Bluelined Dottyback (*Pseudochromis aldabraensis*) was regularly seen cleaning a Purple Tang (*Zebrasoma xanthurum*), which would seek out the dottyback and pose as the dottyback picked at its flanks and fins. I have observed the Bluelined Dottyback (*Pseudochromis cyanotaenia*) pick at the body and fins of a posing Copperband Butterflyfish (*Chelmon rostratus*) on 12 different occasions. A Merten's (*Chaetodon mertensii*) and Raccoon Butterflyfish (*C. lunula*) were also "cleaned" by this same fish several times. Finally, I once kept a juvenile Springer's Dottyback (*Pseudochromis springeri*) that would clean a female Whitley's Boxfish (*Ostracion whitleyi*). The boxfish remained stationary as the dottyback picked at its sides. It is hard to say if dottybacks serve as facultative cleaners in the wild, or whether this behavior is an artifact of captivity. But one cannot help but speculate that the color pattern of these dottybacks (e.g., the blue longitudinal line), which is similar to many other cleaner fishes, may act to signal their cleaning services to potential hosts and make them less vulnerable to predators.

temperature-dependent.) The larvae are from 2.5 mm to about 4 mm when they hatch. They use up the yolk in their stomachs during the first night and begin to feed the next morning.

Captive Care

The dottybacks are hardy aquarium fishes that ship well and readily adapt to captivity. One real advantage is their small size. It is possible to house them in tanks as small as 10 gallons. However, behavioral problems may result if you attempt to stock other fishes in a small tank with a dottyback (see below). Although it is a good idea to maintain optimal water quality in any marine aquarium, these fishes can withstand less-than-ideal conditions (high nitrates, high dissolved organics). They vary in their tolerance of low oxygen levels. Some of the species that regularly inhabit tidepools can withstand oxygen-impoverished conditions, but those from deep fore-reef slopes are less tolerant.

Dottybacks are not highly susceptible to the common aquarium diseases and parasites, but can contract velvet (*Amyloodinium ocellatum*), ich (*Cryptocaryon irritans*), and *Uronema marinum*. They are fairly tolerant of the treatment protocols used

to eliminate these parasites. Although it is rare, dottybacks can suffer from head and lateral line erosion. A dottyback may occasionally leap out of an open aquarium. This usually occurs when it is suddenly disturbed, as when the lights are abruptly turned on or off or when it is being chased by a larger fish or a net. If you do not have a top on your aquarium, make sure the lights turn off gradually and that your dottyback is not being picked on by its tankmates. Smaller dottyback species are also susceptible to being eaten by certain piscivores, notably the lizardfishes, frogfishes, scorpionfishes, flatheads, groupers, and snappers.

Compatibility

One of the biggest dottyback husbandry challenges is to control the malevolent temperament of some species. When I worked at an aquarium store, I regularly had customers return dottybacks because of aggression problems. The dottyback species do vary in their desire to attack their tankmates, but most can cause problems if afforded the opportunity or not given enough space. While the small species may constantly pester vulnerable tankmates or newly added fishes, the larger dottybacks can inflict

Pseudochromis fridmani, Orchid Dottyback: a glorious Red Sea species with relatively mild manners, graceful swimming movements, and vivid coloration.

lethal damage. Therefore, research the dottybacks carefully before you purchase one, and select their tankmates carefully.

One of the best ways to prevent dottybacks from inflicting harm on their tankmates is to house them in a large—the bigger the better—tank loaded with nooks, crannies, and crevices. In this way, those fishes that the dottyback selects to harass have an easier time avoiding their tormentor. I have seen some amazing fish-community tanks that contained several different dottyback species (in some cases male-female pairs) and an assortment of other fishes. But these were spacious reefs tanks (over 200 gallons), with plenty of live rock and live corals. The dottybacks would occasionally chase one of their tankmates, but there was enough room for the target fish to get away. Most pseudochromid disposition problems occur in small aquariums.

If you are attracted to one of the larger, more notorious dottybacks (e.g., *Labracinus* spp., *Ogilbyina* spp., larger *Pseudochromis* spp.), it is essential to keep it with other belligerent species or with fishes that are large enough that their size alone will intimidate the pseudochromid. Larger hawkfishes (*Cirrhitus,*

Paracirrhites), snappers, damsels (*Dascyllus, Neoglyphidodon, Plectroglyphidodon, Premnas, Stegastes*), angelfishes (*Holacanthus, Pomacanthus*), surgeonfishes, rabbitfishes, triggerfishes, and puffers (*Arothron*) are good choices for a tank that contains one of the larger dottybacks. Be sure you add a feisty dottyback to the aquarium after its less aggressive tankmates have fully acclimated.

Although risky in many aquarium venues, it is possible to keep more than one dottyback in the same aquarium. (The section on Captive Spawning, below, explains how to acquire a pair of conspecifics.) Once again, the secret is to have a big tank with lots of hiding places. Also, it is always prudent to introduce the dottyback species from least to most aggressive.

Dottybacks in Reef Aquariums
There was a direct correlation between the popularity and availability of dottybacks in the ornamental marine fish trade and the tremendous growth of interest in reef aquariums. These fishes are well-suited to the reef tank because they do not harm sessile invertebrates. They also tend to be small and nimble, and thus do

not require lots of room to maneuver. While they can be a threat to ornamental crustaceans (especially the larger dottybacks), they will also prey on undesirable invertebrates that are inadvertently introduced into an aquarium with live rock. They are especially fond of bristleworms, including the noxious Fireworm (*Hermodice carunculata*). Because they are microcarnivores, they tend to be able to find enough minute fare living on the live rock to make them relatively self-reliant in a well-established reef aquarium.

Some hobbyists have suggested that it is actually detrimental to keep dottybacks, as well as other microcarnivores, in a reef aquarium. They claim that these fishes deplete the number of small, invertebrate herbivores (e.g., amphipods, copepods) that aid in keeping filamentous algae in check. However, the degree to which dottybacks contribute to microalgae growth in the reef tank is still open to debate. I have had and seen many reef tanks where microalgae was not a problem despite the presence of one or more dottybacks. The pseudochromids may compete for natural prey with some of the less agile microcarnivores, such as seahorses, pipefishes, and dragonets. Therefore, you may not want to keep dottybacks with fishes that depend on the food stocks of the live substrate for most of their nutrition.

Captive Spawning
Many members of this group hold great promise for captive-breeding programs because of their small adult size and hardiness. A number of species have spawned in captivity and some captive raised stock are now available in the U.S. marine trade (e.g., Australian Dottyback, Arabian Bluelined Dottyback, Orchid Dottyback, Sunrise Dottyback).

The obvious first step in dottyback breeding is to obtain a heterosexual pair. Unfortunately, this can be difficult. Some pseudochromoids exhibit color and morphological differences between the sexes, which makes obtaining a pair easier in those species. But even if you do get a male and female, the aggressive nature of these fishes can still cause problems. The more pugnacious partner, usually the male, may harass its mate to death. This means keeping a close eye on any dottyback pair. One critical factor is having enough space for both fish. Numerous hiding places will enable the subordinate fish to avoid unwanted attention.

As mentioned above, the dottybacks are protogynous hermaphrodites, and at least some species apparently can reverse their sex (male back to female) in certain social contexts. The fact that they are hermaphrodites works to the potential dottyback breeder's advantage. One way to increase the chances that you end up with a male-female pair is by acquiring two smaller individuals. The more dominant of the two will eventually change into a male, while the subordinate fish will be the female. The dottybacks attain maturity very quickly (some in as little as four months with good feeding), so you will not have to wait long before they are of spawning size. Another pairing method used by some dottyback breeders is to acquire two fish that differ significantly in size. In protogynous hermaphrodites, there is a good chance that the larger individual will be a male and the smaller fish will be a female or an immature fish. (If it is still immature, it should develop into a female.) The problem with this pairing method is that the larger fish may harass or kill the smaller conspecific. If you do acquire two individuals that differ in size, you may be able to reduce the likelihood that fighting will occur by keeping them separated at first, using a glass divider. In this way, they can see each other and may become habituated before they are allowed to intermingle.

Once you get a pair that lives in relative harmony, there are several things that will facilitate spawning and successful propagation of the young. First, provide the adults with larger quantities of high-quality food (e.g., chopped fresh seafoods, mysid shrimp, krill, enriched live adult brine shrimp, high-quality dry foods). Reproduction is energetically expensive, especially for the females, so be sure to feed them heavily. Dottyback breeders have found that the diet will impact the health of the eggs and larvae. Water quality is also an important consideration. Poor water quality can cause egg and larval mortality. To maintain optimal abiotic conditions, you should employ a protein skimmer, chemical filtration (e.g., carbon), and small water changes.

What about egg and larval care? Studies have shown that egg mortality is usually reduced if the eggs are left with the male. However, some breeders will separate the egg ball from the parents so that it is easier to deal with the larvae when they hatch. The egg ball is placed in a smaller container within the rearing tank and agitated by introducing an airstone. If you decide to keep the eggs with the tending male until they hatch, you will have to fish out as many of the larvae as you can (or want to) as soon as the eggs hatch. Fortunately, the larvae are phototactic (attracted to light), which will facilitate their capture. Just place a point-source of light (flashlight) over the top of the otherwise dark aquarium and they will gather around it. You can then draw them out of the tank with a plastic specimen container. The larvae will need to be fed on the first day after hatching. Enriched rotifers are a suitable first food.

If fed well and given enough space, these fishes will grow very quickly. Depending on the species, adult size can be attained in 5 to 12 months. Aggression often becomes a problem when trying to "grow out" the young fish. The size at which casualties begin to take their toll because of agonistic interactions varies

Congrogadus subducens, Carpet Eel Blenny: green color form.

Congrogadus subducens, Carpet Eel Blenny: brown color form.

What's in a Name?

Congrogadus subducens (Richardson, 1843) is a fish with an identity crisis. In ichthyological guides, its preferred common name fish is the Carpet Eel Blenny. In the aquarium trade it's often the Green Wolf Eel. I have also seen it referred to as the Mud Blenny and the Green Wolf Blenny. So what is this beast? Is it an eel? A blenny? A wolf? This unusual fish is actually a member of the Family Pseudochromidae—the dottyback family. It is one of at least a dozen species in the Subfamily Congrogadinae. All the species in this group are eel-like; many are referred to as snakelets. Most are cryptic, hiding in crevices and tidepools. At least one species in known to live among the spines of sea urchins. Only *C. subducens* is encountered in the aquarium trade with any regularity.

The Carpet Eel Blenny ranges from Nicobar Island in the Indian Ocean east to Papua New Guinea, south to northwestern Australia and north to the Ryukyus. It occurs in lagoon seagrass beds and lagoon and tidal rubble flats and has also been reported from sand, mud, and rubble substrates. Preferring shallow water, it is usually found at depths of less than 1 m (3.3 ft.). It has even been observed with most of its body out of the water as it squirms from one tidepool to another. It spends most of its time wriggling into interstices among rubble or among rocks and benthic debris. The color can be brown or green overall with varying degrees of lighter mottling and blotches. It can change its color to better match its background or when threatened. It can become very pale overall, a color pattern often adopted at night. Some have suggested that *C. subducens* is sexually dichromatic, but this does not appear to be the case, although there is some evidence that males are usually larger than females.

Congrogadus subducens is an interesting aquarium pet. It is also extremely hardy, making it a suitable choice for the neophyte fishkeeper. It should be housed in a tank with numerous hiding places and a secure top, as the fish is prone to leaping out. This voracious predator will eat small fishes and ornamental crustaceans, so tankmate selection is of paramount concern. It will do best with larger fishes, like squirrelfishes, soldierfishes, angelfishes, butterflyfishes, surgeonfishes, and rabbitfishes. It can also be kept with more placid morays, although larger species (e.g., *Gymnothorax favagineus, G. moringa*) will eat *C. subducens*. It is prudent to keep only one *C. subducens* per tank, unless you can acquire a known heterosexual pair.

The Carpet Eel Blenny should be fed fresh crustacean and marine fish flesh. This fish is especially fond of crayfish. Live food may be required to get some individuals to feed initially. Once *C. subducens* has adjusted to its captive home it will learn to recognize its keeper as a source of food and will leave the substrate when he or she moves toward the tank. It should be fed to satiation (several large food items) at least every other day. If fed daily, it will grow very quickly. Young fish or subadults will double their size in six months. If you are attempting to breed these fish, feed them frequently. The Carpet Eel Blenny grows to 45 cm (17.6 inches) in length and can be housed in species tanks as small as 20 gallons. It should be kept at water temperatures of 23 to 27°C (73 to 81°F). If you are not concerned about keeping crustaceans, it can be housed in a reef tank.

The Carpet Eel Blenny will readily spawn in captivity. The key is to acquire a male and female, which can be difficult. Conspecifics will fight and have been known to bite and chase each other until one of the combatants is killed. It has been suggested that they may be hermaphrodites, so selecting individuals that differ in size may increase the chances of getting a heterosexual pair. Changes of salinity and/or temperature may catalyze reproductive activity. The female builds and guards a nest with a mass of pink or purplish eggs numbering from about 50 to 100, and the male should be excluded at this point. The young are relatively large at hatching and not difficult to raise. They are reported to take enriched baby brine shrimp.

from one species to the next. There are two schools of thought when it comes to diffusing juvenile aggression. The first is that by keeping fish densities high, no one individual becomes the recipient of enough aggression to cause serious problems. The other is that densities should be reduced as aggression becomes a problem, so that individuals have enough space and hideouts. The success rates of the techniques employed may be partially dependent on the species in question. For example, Moe (1997) suggests that the young of *Pseudochromis fridmani* (a less aggressive species) do best at high densities. In contrast, Brons (1996) indicates that juvenile *Pseudochromis flavivertex*, which are more pugnacious than *P. fridmani*, need to be thinned out in the grow-out tank (to about 20 fish per 50 liters) at a size of about 5 cm (2 in.).

DOTTYBACK SPECIES

SUBFAMILY PSEUDOCHROMINAE (DOTTYBACKS)

This subfamily is comprised of 85 species and includes the fishes that are most familiar to divers and aquarists.

Genus *Cypho* (Oblique-lined Dottybacks)

Cypho purpurascens (De Vis, 1884)

Common Name: Oblique-lined Dottyback.
Maximum Length: 7.5 cm (2.9 in.).
Distribution: New Guinea, south to the Great Barrier Reef, and east to Fiji.
Biology: The Oblique-lined Dottyback occurs in shallow tidepools to depths of nearly 41 m (134 ft.). I have observed it most frequently at depths of 5 to 14 m (16 to 46 ft.), hiding among stony corals near the edge of the reef face, in caves, or amid coral rubble on the reef slope. In Papua New Guinea, I frequently saw this species sharing its habitat with the Twolined Dottyback (*Pseudochromis bitaeniatus*). During courtship, the color of the male is often brighter than normal, and the dark line on the edge of the anal fin distal margin becomes more pronounced. The male performs a leading display to entice the female into his nest. The male will also nudge the female's abdomen with his snout during courtship.
Captive Care: In the aquarium, *C. purpurascens* can be aggressive, attacking smaller, more docile fishes. I have successfully housed it with damselfishes, larger wrasses, and shrimp gobies in capacious reef aquariums loaded with live rock. But it can be lethal to smaller fishes in a more confined setting. To keep it successfully with less aggressive tankmates, place it in a large tank with

Cypho purpurascens, Oblique-lined Dottyback (male): gorgeous but a terror.

C. purpurascens, Oblique-lined Dottyback (female): vulnerable to male attack.

C. purpurascens, Oblique-lined Dottyback (female): variant color form.

C. purpurascens, Oblique-lined Dottyback: variant lacking eyespots.

Cypho zaps, Zap's Dottyback (male): note blue head spots and eye ring.

plenty of hiding places, add it to the aquarium last, and avoid keeping it with any other red fishes (e.g., Redfin Fairy Wrasse, *Cirrhilabrus rubripinnis*), similarly shaped species, or other dottybacks. (It can, however, be kept with other dottybacks in extra-large reef aquariums). *Cypho purpurascens* can be kept in pairs, but only in a spacious tank (100 gallons or larger). If you can succeed in acquiring a pair, there is a good chance they will spawn—provided the male doesn't first kill the female. I have seen this species attack and bite the legs off a mantis shrimp that was 3 cm (1.2 in.) long. It is obviously a threat to ornamental shrimps. I once had an Oblique-lined Dottyback change from male to female coloration when it was shifted to a small system that contained no other fishes, suggesting that it may be a protandric hermaphrodite, or that without a social catalyst (i.e., other dot-

tybacks) males revert back to females. This transformation occurred over a period of about two months.

Aquarium Size: 20 gal. **Temperature:** 22 to 27°C (72 to 81°F).

Aquarium Suitability Index: 5.

Remarks: This genus contains two species, both of which can be encountered by aquarists. The Oblique-lined Dottyback is often referred to as *Pseudochromis mccullochi* and is erroneously sold in the trade as McCulloch's Dottyback. Male *C. purpurascens* are bright red overall, with black on the posterior edge of the scales, a blue ring that partially encircles the eyes, and one to three black ocelli (eyespots) on the dorsal fin. Females are gray anteriorly, with an area of orange in the middle of the body and yellow toward the tail.

The second species in the *Cypho* genus is **Zap's Dottyback** (*Cypho zaps*) Gill, 2003. The male is reddish pink posteriorly and orange anteriorly, with blue trim on the scales, tiny blue spots on the head, a blue ring partially encircling the eye, and no ocelli on the dorsal fin. This species has been recorded in northern Indonesia, the Philippines, Taiwan, and the Ryukyu Islands. It is similar in its husbandry to *C. purpurascens*.

Genus *Labracinus* (Lined Dottybacks)

Labracinus cyclophthalmus (Müller & Troschel, 1849)

Common Names: Red Dottyback, Dampiera, Firetail Devil, Red Grouper.

Maximum Length: 20 cm (7.8 in.).

Distribution: Philippines and Japan, south to Papua New Guinea and Indonesia.

Biology: The Red Dottyback lives on coastal and outer reefs, in tidepools, in channels on the reef flat and crest, and on the reef face. It is often found in areas exposed to surge and tidal currents, where it lives under ledges and between dead coral rock. This is a solitary, territorial species and is one of the more aggressive pseudochromoids. The territory of this species can cover an area measuring from 9 to 41 m^2 (97 to 441 ft.^{2}).

Labracinus cyclophthalmus feeds mainly on crabs, snails, peanut worms, and small fishes (including gobies), but also consumes shrimps, mantis shrimps, mysids, chitons, isopods, small urchins, serpent stars, and polychaete worms. Its preferred foraging strategy is to ambush passing prey, remaining at an ambush site for approximately 20 to 30 seconds before moving to another location.

Captive Care: Aggressiveness, coupled with its larger size, makes this a potentially destructive aquarium inhabitant. Therefore, it should not be kept with smaller, passive fishes, but with eels, large squirrelfishes, groupers, snappers, larger angelfishes, large hawk-

Labracinus cyclophthalmus, Red Dottyback (male): highly variable colors.

L. cyclophthalmus, Red Dottyback (female): red belly during breeding season.

Labracinus cyclophthalmus, Red Dottyback: male with bright blue lines.

fishes, and triggerfishes. It can be kept in male-female pairs if the aquarium is large enough (i.e., over 135 gallons) and if the pair is introduced simultaneously. One effective way to introduce a potential pair (and keep them from fighting) is to divide the aquarium with a pane of glass or acrylic and let them habituate to each other for several days before pulling it out.

Lange and Kaiser (1988) reported on the spawning of *L. cyclophthalmus* at the Berlin Aquarium. Spawning took place once every three weeks. During these events, the female deposited a ball of eggs on a stone on the bottom of a cave, which the male preceded to fertilize. After spawning was complete, the male chased the female from the cave and guarded and fanned the egg mass. The eggs hatched in about three days and were fed a varied diet of plankton and commercially available fry food 10 to 15 times a day. After one week, the larvae left the burrow and entered the plankton. There were problems raising the young due to aggressive interactions that occurred between them after 40 days of development. (In the wild, this belligerent behavior serves to disperse the young.) After 4 months the offspring were just over 3 cm (1.2 in.).

This dottyback is a voracious predator that will eat almost anything, including frozen prepared foods, chopped seafoods, live and frozen brine shrimps, and even "pinky" baby mice (not that I recommend this as normal fare). In the wild and in the aquarium, *L. cyclophthalmus* eat smaller fishes. If the prey is too large to swallow whole, the Red Dottyback will break it into pieces by bashing it against a rock or piece of coral. It will also consume ornamental shrimps with gusto.

Aquarium Size: 30 gal. **Temperature:** 22 to 27°C (72 to 81°F).

Aquarium Suitability Index: 5.

Remarks: The color of *L. cyclophthalmus* is highly variable, with the overall body color ranging from red to black. An individual's color is apparently a function of its sex and age. For example, males usually have elongate spots on the dorsal fin and a red tail, while females have a large red area over and in front of the anal fin origin, which is especially conspicuous during the breeding season. The females also have comma-shaped black markings on the posterior part of the dorsal fin. Most males have a dark head and some have bright blue lines on the body. During aggressive encounters or when alarmed, they develop light bands. According to Dr. Gill, *Labracinus melanotaenia* (Bleeker, 1852) is now thought to be synonymous with this species. A fourth species, the **Blackbarred Dottyback** (*L. atrofasciatus*) (**Herre, 1933**), is known from a single specimen from the Philippines and rarely makes it into the marine trade.

Labracinus lineatus, Lined Dottyback: Western Australia species.

Manonichthys alleni, Red-dot Dottyback: note blood-red spot on pelvic fin.

Manonichthys cf. alleni, Red-dot Dottyback: probable new species.

Labracinus lineatus (Castelnau, 1875)
Common Name: Lined Dottyback.
Maximum Length: 25 cm (9.8 in.).
Distribution: Western Australia.
Biology: The Lined Dottyback occurs on shallow reefs and inhabits crevices among rocks and live stony corals. It is reported from depths of 5 to 15 m (16 to 49 ft.). Like other members of the genus, it probably feeds on crustaceans and small fishes.
Captive Care: This species gets slightly larger than the Red Dottyback, making it even more dangerous to its tankmates. The Lined Dottyback should only be housed with more aggressive fishes, such as groupers, snappers, triggerfishes, and porcupinefishes. It will eat smaller fishes and ornamental crustaceans, including smaller mantis shrimps.
Aquarium Size: 40 gal. **Temperature:** 22 to 27°C (72 to 81°F).
Aquarium Suitability Index: 5.
Remarks: It has been reported that male *L. lineatus* have blue dots on the body, while those of the female are brown.

Genus *Manonichthys* (Bigfinned Dottybacks)
This group includes five species characterized by their relatively deep bodies and large pelvic and median fins. At least one is thought to mimic a pygmy angelfish. These medium-sized dottybacks can be quite scrappy in the home aquarium.

Manonichthys alleni Gill, 2003
Common Names: Red-dot Dottyback, Allen's Dottyback, Borneo Dottyback.
Maximum Length: 12 cm (4.7 in.).
Distribution: Sabah and Borneo.
Biology: The Red-dot Dottyback is found in clear water on coastal fringing reefs. It occurs on reef faces and fore-reef slopes from depths of 6 to 30 m (20 to 98 ft.). It often favors habitats with rich sponge growth and refuges in the lumens of large sponges. This dottyback usually occurs singly.
Captive Care: This interesting dottyback has only recently been seen with any regularity in the aquarium trade. Its husbandry requirements are probably similar to the closely related *M. splendens* and *M. polynemus*. It has been known to pick on smaller fish tankmates and does best in a large community aquarium. Keep only one per tank, unless you can acquire a pair—perhaps by adding two juveniles to a tank and hoping that they pair up.
Aquarium Size: 30 gal. **Temperature:** 22 to 27°C (72 to 81°F).
Aquarium Suitability Index: 5.
Remarks: This dottyback is closely related to *M. splendens* and *M. polynemus*. Unlike these species, the Red-dot Dottyback has a red spot near the base of each pelvic fin. There are two color

Manonichthys paranox, Midnight Dottyback: pygmy angelfish mimic.

Manonichthys polynemus, Longfin Dottyback: associates with sponges.

phases. One is yellow on the lower part of the body, yellow on the pelvic fins, and often has a yellow caudal fin. The other is gray overall, with white pelvic fins and a white caudal fin (in some individuals the caudal peduncle is also white)—this latter form is most common in the aquarium trade. Both variants have rows of yellow dots along the body and on the dorsal fin. The yellow form is found in Malaysia, while the white form occurs in the more eastern part of the fish's range (curiously, both occur around Derawan, Kalimantan). These two color forms probably represent two distinct species.

Manonichthys paranox (Lubbock & Goldman, 1976)

Common Name: Midnight Dottyback.

Maximum Length: 7 cm (2.7 in.).

Distribution: Solomon Islands, Papua New Guinea, and the Great Barrier Reef.

Biology: This species is found in channels, on reef faces, and fore-reef slopes at depths to at least 20 m (66 ft.). It is found among branching corals, in coral crevices, and in small caves. In Milne Bay, Papua New Guinea, where it is not uncommon, it is found on sheltered fringing reefs and steep reef faces at depths of 6 to 18 m (20 to 59 ft.). It occurs in the same habitat as the Oblique-lined Dottyback (*Cypho purpurascens*) and the Twolined Dottyback (*Pseudochromis bitaeniatus*). It is a solitary species that will hover in the open for a few seconds and then dash under cover. In contrast to many of the pseudochromids I have observed, the Midnight Dottyback will move over a larger open area. Lubbock and Goldman (1976) report that *M. paranox*, "was only observed in association with the pomacanthid *Centropyge nox*; the former swam with a dancing motion (very unusual for a pseudochromid) similar to that of the *Centropyge*." They suggest that the Midnight

Dottyback mimics the pygmy angelfish, just as the juvenile Chocolate Surgeonfish (*Acanthurus pyroferus*) and the Indian Ocean Mimic Surgeonfish (*A. tristis*) mimic *Centropyge* spp.

Captive Care: The Midnight Dottyback is not common in the aquarium trade. As a result, little information is available on its captive behavior or care. Keeping this dottyback and the Midnight Angelfish in the same aquarium would make an interesting and educational display. However, you will need to make sure you have a large enough tank so that aggression between the two fishes will not cause problems.

Aquarium Size: 20 gal. **Temperature:** 22 to 27°C (72 to 81°F).

Aquarium Suitability Index: 5.

Remarks: This elegant fish has relatively long pectoral and pelvic fins. (Its larger fins increase the similarity to a *Centropyge*.) The caudal fin is rounded. It is the only dottyback that is dark brown or black with black pelvic fins.

Manonichthys polynemus (Fowler, 1931)

Common Name: Longfin Dottyback.

Maximum Length: 12 cm (4.7 in.).

Distribution: North eastern Indonesia and Palau.

Biology: The Longfin Dottyback inhabits coastal reefs and fore-reef slopes at depths from 2 to 50 m (6.6 to 164 ft.). It is most common in areas with prolific growths of long, gray tube sponges, in which it often seeks shelter. However, it also moves among the branches of soft corals (e.g., *Sinularia*) and stony corals. I once observed an individual on a coastal patch reef as it moved over an area of approximately 4.5 m² (48 ft.²) in one hour and was in the same location when I returned to the patch reef on several consecutive days. I also observed a *Pseudochromis steenei* on this same patch reef. I watched a smaller individual for about

Manonichthys splendens, Splendid Dottyback: now being bred in captivity.

30 minutes and never saw it behave aggressively toward any of the numerous anthias, cardinalfishes, damselfishes, blennies, gobies, etc. that inhabited the same patch reef.

Captive Care: This dottyback is a very durable aquarium inhabitant. Like its relatives, it does have a tendency to bully smaller tankmates; however, it is not as aggressive as some. Refrain from keeping it in a tank with other dottybacks, especially more aggressive species (e.g., Australian Dottyback, Steene's Dottyback).

Aquarium Size: 30 gal. **Temperature:** 22 to 27°C (72 to 82°F).

Aquarium Suitability Index: 5.

Remarks: *Manonichthys polynemus* is very closely related to an undescribed species known as the Red-dot Dottyback (*Manonichthys alleni*). The Longfin Dottyback has yellow to yellowish orange markings on the pelvic fins and a tearlike marking under the eye. The overall color can be light gray to dark greenish gray. *Manonichthys polynemus* is very similar in general appearance to the Ambon Chromis (*Chromis amboinensis*), which is much more common than the dottyback and shares similar habitat preferences. It is not clear whether some type of mimetic relationship exists between these two fishes.

Manonichthys splendens Fowler, 1931

Common Name: Splendid Dottyback.

Maximum Length: 13 cm (5.1 in.).

Distribution: Flores and the Banda Sea, Indonesia.

Biology: The Splendid Dottyback is a resident of coastal reefs and outer-reef faces and fore-reef slopes. It is typically found among rich coral and sponge growth, at depths of 3 to 40 m (9.8 to 131 ft.). Juveniles are sometimes observed in small aggregations among elongate, bushy yellow sponges, while adults are usually solitary and often live in large yellow tube sponges or among staghorn corals. I've observed three *M. splendens* of varying sizes residing on a coastal patch reef composed of coral rock, sparse stony coral growth (including *Goniopora* spp.), and purple tube sponge. These three dottybacks spent most of their time in an area of 1.1 m^2 (12 ft.^{2}) and were not observed to engage in any overt aggression; however, the smaller individual did avoid the larger conspecifics. I have never seen this species behaving agonistically toward any of the other fishes. Instead, they spend most of their time darting from one crevice to another.

Captive Care: Although it is not known to be overly aggressive, its large size alone makes the Splendid Dottyback a potentially dangerous introduction to a community tank containing passive or smaller fish species. It is best kept with larger fishes. Although it will do well in the reef aquarium, it is inclined to eat ornamental shrimps. This species has also been reported to eat fireworms. Although *M. splendens* is not uncommon in certain parts of Indonesia, it is rarely collected for the marine aquarium trade. Fortunately, captive-spawned juveniles are now showing up on the market.

Aquarium Size: 30 gal. **Temperature:** 22 to 27°C (72 to 81°F).

Aquarium Suitability Index: 5.

Remarks: Juvenile *M. splendens* usually have more yellow on the body and the fins than the adults. This species is most similar morphologically to the Longfin Dottyback (*M. polynemus*) and the Red-dot Dottyback (*M. alleni*).

Genus *Ogilbyina* (Australian Dottybacks)

This genus is only represented on coral reefs in Queensland. They are fairly large dottybacks and are most common in shallow water on the reef flat or reef face. The Australian dottybacks are some of the most aggressive members of the Subfamily Pseudochrominae. Because they attain larger sizes than many other dottybacks, they are also better equipped to inflict damage to their tankmates. They will make short work of any ornamental shrimps in your aquarium, but will also consume small mantis shrimps. A more positive trait is that they are extremely durable fishes and often survive when others in the tank succumb to poor water quality or disease. All of these dottybacks are sexually dichromatic, with sexes sporting distinctive color forms.

Ogilbyina novaehollandiae (Steindachner, 1879)

Common Names: Australian Dottyback, Multicolored Dottyback.

Maximum Length: 10 cm (3.9 in.).

Distribution: Southern Great Barrier Reef.

Biology: The Australian Dottyback is found on fringing and inner reefs along the Great Barrier Reef. It is found in tidepools on the reef flat and on the reef face. It occurs at depths of less than 30 cm to at least 18 m (1 to 59 ft.). It is secretive, often hiding out under ledges and in crevices. There is no information available on the food habits of *O. novaehollandiae*, but it probably feeds on worms, crustaceans, and small fishes.

Captive Care: The Australian Dottyback is one of the more aggressive members of the subfamily. Its large size makes it a greater threat than its smaller congeners. Debelius and Baensch (1994) state that "this is an amiable fish that is an appropriate addition to the community tank." Do not believe it. This fish will attack almost anything that enters its domain, even if the intruding species is larger. For example, an individual that I kept in a reef aquarium would persistently beat up a larger Comet (*Calloplesiops altivelis*). This species should not be housed with placid species (e.g., grammas, assessors, juvenile sweetlips, butterflyfishes, sand tilefishes, gobies) or other dottybacks. It is best kept with squirrelfishes, larger angelfishes, hawkfishes, surgeonfishes, and triggerfishes. Even placing a male and a female together is risky, as they tend to tear each other up. The Australian Dottyback can be housed in a reef aquarium, if you do not include smaller, docile fishes, and crustaceans. It spends most of its time moving through tunnels and crevices, occasionally darting from one crevice to another or coming out to feed. It will dig holes under pieces of coral by carrying coral rubble away in its mouth. One of its most appealing traits is its hardiness. It eats almost anything, does not lose its magnificent coloration, and is disease resistant. One Aussie aquarist told me that "you could hit it with a stick" and still do it no harm (I do not advise testing this theory). This species will also eat pestilent species in the reef aquarium, including bristleworms and small mantis shrimps. I have seen a larger Australian Dottyback grasp a 3 cm (1.2 in.) mantis shrimp by the tail and bash it against the substrate until it was broken into smaller species. Like most Australian endemics, it is fairly expensive and is only sporadically available. This species has been bred in captivity by C-Quest of Puerto Rico.

Aquarium Size: 30 gal. **Temperature:** 21 to 27°C (70 to 81°F).

Aquarium Suitability Index: 5.

Remarks: The Australian Dottyback has no less than five color forms, seemingly related to the age and possibly to the gender of the fish. For example, medium-sized females are usually orange, pinkish, or yellow overall with short reddish bars below the posterior part of the dorsal fin, while larger females are often dark gray to black with a red belly. Male *O. novaehollandiae* are

Ogilbyina novaehollandiae, Australian Dottyback: one of five color forms.

Ogilbyina novaehollandiae, Australian Dottyback: battered black variant.

gray or black overall, with an orange head and a yellow tail. Juveniles are pale pink with a yellow head and anterior dorsal fin. All the color varieties have blue median fin margins and a light blue line under and around the back of the eye.

Ogilbyina queenslandiae (Saville-Kent, 1893)

Common Name: Queensland Dottyback.

Maximum Length: 15 cm (5.9 in.).

Distribution: Great Barrier Reef.

Biology: The Queensland Dottyback occurs in tidepools, on lagoon patch reefs, and on the fore reef. It can be found in 1 m (3.3 ft.) to depths of over 33 m (108 ft.).

Captive Care: This dottyback is as aggressive as *O. novaehollandiae.* Therefore, it is a hazardous choice for the reef aquarium or passive community tank. It has been reported to spawn in cap-

Ogilbyina queenslandiae, Queensland Dottyback: female with orange body.

Oxycercichthys velifera, Sailfin Dottyback: male with dorsal spot.

tivity, laying eggs once every two weeks over several months' time.
Aquarium Size: 30 gal. **Temperature:** 22 to 27°C (72 to 81°F).
Aquarium Suitability Index: 5.
Remarks: The best way to tell *O. queenslandiae* and *O. novaehollandiae* apart is by their coloration. Female Queensland Dottybacks sport a grayish head, yellowish orange above the anal fin, five or six brown bars on the upper part of the back, and reddish fins. The males are reddish anteriorly, with a purplish or gray posterior region and bluish fins, except for a reddish area on the anterior portion of the dorsal fin.

Genus *Oxycercichthys* (Sailfin Dottyback)

Oxycercichthys velifera (Lubbock, 1980)
Common Name: Sailfin Dottyback.
Maximum Length: 12 cm (4.7 in.).
Distribution: Great Barrier Reef and western Coral Sea.
Biology: This species is found on fringing reefs and in lagoons along the Great Barrier Reef. It is often seen in coral rubble areas or around patch reefs at depths of 15 to 48 m (49 to 157 ft.). The Sailfin Dottyback will retreat into crevices and under ledges when threatened. It usually occurs singly.
Captive Care: *Oxycercichthys velifera* is large and aggressive. Much care should be taken when selecting suitable tankmates for this fish. It is a beautiful addition to the reef aquarium, but *O. velifera* will pick on smaller fishes, ornamental shrimps, and porcelain crabs. I have seen the Sailfin Dottyback living with relatively peaceful fishes in large reef tanks, but in one such situation it was responsible for the deaths of several sleeper gobies. In that case, the dottyback attacked the gobies and caused them to leap out of the aquarium. Even in a larger aquarium, any fish that enters its preferred shelter sites will be punished.
Aquarium Size: 30 gal. **Temperature:** 22 to 27°C (72 to 81°F).
Aquarium Suitability Index: 5.
Remarks: Juvenile and female *O. velifera* are pinkish overall, with yellow on the top of the head and on front of the dorsal fin. Males are typically pink with a bluish head and dorsal fin, a dark spot on the front of the dorsal fin, and yellow pectoral, anal, and caudal fins. A captive specimen was reported to change from the female to male color form in about two weeks, suggesting both-direction sex change.

Genus *Pholidochromis* (Scaly Dottyback)

Pholidochromis sp.
Common Name: Cherry Dottyback.
Maximum Length: 8 cm (3.1 in.).
Distribution: Philippines and Indonesia
Biology: Nothing is yet known about the biology of this species.
Captive Care: The individuals I kept were not especially aggressive; in fact, they were picked on by a slightly smaller Bluelined Dottyback (*Pseudochromis cyanotaenia*). However, Japanese aquarists report that as it grows larger it does get more aggressive and that adults can be quite belligerent. It tends to spend a considerable amount of time in the open.
Aquarium Size: 20 gal. **Temperature:** 22 to 27°C (72 to 81°F).
Aquarium Suitability Index: 5.
Remarks: Juveniles and females are pinkish to bluish gray overall with orange spots on the back and caudal peduncle. The body of this species is deeper than most of their relatives. This genus also includes the **Margined Dottyback** (*Pholidochromis marginatus*) (**Lubbock, 1980**). This species is known from Indone-

Pholidochromis sp., Cherry Dottyback: female with characteristic spots.

Pictichromis diadema, Diadem Dottyback: pretty fish prone to troublemaking.

sia and Papua New Guinea, where it was collected from shallow water in habitats with rich stony and soft coral growth. The Margined Dottyback has a dark, submarginal stripe on the dorsal, caudal, and anal fin.

Genus *Pictichromis* (Magenta Dottybacks)

There are six species of dottybacks in this genus. They are most readily separated on the basis of their coloration, which can even vary slightly within a species. All the members of this group have relatively large heads, and a lower number of soft dorsal and anal rays than most other dottybacks. They vary somewhat in their captive husbandry, but they tend to be hardy and aggressive.

Pictichromis diadema Lubbock & Randall, 1978

Common Name: Diadem Dottyback.
Maximum Length: 6 cm (2.3 in.).
Distribution: Malaysia Peninsula and Sabah to the western Philippines.
Biology: *Pictichromis diadema* is usually encountered on reef slopes and at the base of dropoffs, in coral crevices, or hiding among rocks on the sandy ocean floor, in water from 5 to 25 m (16 to 82 ft.) in depth. It feeds on planktonic and small bottom-dwelling crustaceans. The Diadem Dottyback is found singly, in pairs, or often in small groups. However, trying to duplicate the latter social structure in the home aquarium usually leads to disaster for subordinate individuals.
Captive Care: The Diadem Dottyback can be kept in small groups in a large aquarium (greater than 6,452 cm^2 [1,000 in.^{2}] in surface area), packed with coral to provide adequate hiding places. It can be very aggressive toward other fish species, terrorizing tankmates that are smaller or of similar size. They will attack dam-

selfishes, fire gobies, gobies, grammas, anthias, and juveniles of larger species; they will even attack cleaner shrimps. When kept with larger fish (e.g., tangs, angels, butterflies) they are much less belligerent. This is a moderately hardy dottyback, but is prone to radical color loss (the magenta stripe often fades). It is fairly resistant to the common saltwater parasites, but I have seen several die from *Uronema marinum*, a ciliated protozoan that is difficult to treat. This infection takes the form of red, abrasion-like sores on the body.
Aquarium Size: 10 gal. **Temperature:** 22 to 27°C (72 to 81°F).
Aquarium Suitability Index: 5.
Remarks: *Pictichromis diadema* is one of the most common members of this family in the aquarium trade. The coloration can vary slightly between individuals. In some individuals, the magenta stripe has a white border. In others, the purple dorsal stripe extends onto the lower jaw. It has been suggested that some of these color differences may be related to the individual's sex. Some individuals observed around the island of Sipadan, South China Sea, have been described as having a magenta area that covers the anterior part of the body. In these individuals, the line of demarcation between the magenta and the yellow runs diagonally from behind the eyes to the middle of the dorsal fin.

Pictichromis paccagnellae Axelrod, 1973

Common Name: Royal Dottyback.
Maximum Length: 5 cm (2 in.) in the wild; reported to 8 cm (3.1 in.) in captivity.
Distribution: Indonesia to northern Australia, east to Papua New Guinea and the Solomon Islands.
Biology: This pseudochromid is usually found on steep reef slopes or dropoffs at depths from less than 1 to 70 m (3.3 to 230 ft.).

Pictichromis paccagnellae, Royal Dottyback: gram-for-gram, notorious terror.

Pictichromis paccagnellae, Royal Dottyback: variant with white vertical line.

Pictichromis coralensis, Bicolor Dottyback: Great Barrier Reef species.

However, it is rarely found at depths of less than 10 m (33 ft.). The Royal Dottyback is usually found living in cracks and crevices in vertical reef substrate. It moves in and out of its hiding places, spending a small amount of time in the open before darting back into shelter. Individual *P. paccagnellae* are scattered over reef walls and are almost always observed singly, although individuals may be seen within 2 m (6.6 ft.) of one another. This fish probably feeds on planktonic and benthic crustaceans.

Captive Care: The Royal Dottyback is a durable aquarium fish, the only drawback being its agonistic nature and tendency to lose some of its chromatic brilliance. Gram for gram, it is one of the most aggressive dottybacks. I have seen this fish viciously attack other pugnacious fishes three times its size. For example, I introduced an individual into a 58-gallon aquarium that housed a full-grown Blue Devil (*Chrysiptera cyanea*). Initially, the belligerent damselfish chased, nipped, and subdued the newly introduced dottyback. But within 12 hours the tables had turned—the damsel was hiding in the corner of the aquarium with shredded fins, while the dottyback was victoriously darting from one hole to the next. I frequently had customers who purchased Royal Dottybacks return them because of their aggressive tendencies. It is highly inadvisable to keep this fish with inoffensive species (e.g., gobies, dart gobies, fire gobies, small wrasses) unless you have a large aquarium with lots of hiding places. It will even attack cleaner fishes, like neon gobies and cleaner wrasses. In the wild, they usually stay at least several meters apart, so keeping more than one in anything but a very large home aquarium would be foolhardy. They are not particularly susceptible to bacterial and parasitic infections, but they do occasionally contract common saltwater parasites.

Aquarium Size: 10 gal. **Temperature:** 22 to 27°C (72 to 81°F).

Aquarium Suitability Index: 5.

Remarks: In some areas, the Royal Dottyback has a white line dividing the two colors, which may be related to the fish's gender (further study is needed to confirm this). Larger specimens may have filaments extending from the upper and lower edges of the caudal fin. The Royal Dottyback is almost identical to the **Bicolor Dottyback** (*Pictichromis coralensis*) (**Gill, 2003**) from the Great Barrier Reef and New Caledonia. There are slight differences in the coloration and in the fin spine counts. On the northern Great Barrier Reef, I observed many Bicolor Dottybacks, in water deeper than 15 m (49 ft.). They often hang upside down beneath overhangs or in caves. In one cave, I counted as many as four Bicolor Dottybacks, separated by about 1 m (3.3 ft.).

The **Yellowsaddle Dottyback** (*Pictichromis ephippiata*) **Gill et al., 1996** is another close relative that was collected in

Milne Bay and the D'Entrecasteaux Islands, Papua New Guinea. This species is magenta overall, with a yellow saddle that extends from the front of the dorsal fin to the top of the caudal fin. The ventral surface of the caudal peduncle and the posterior part of the body are also yellow. It has been observed at depths of 30 to 50 m (98 to 164 ft.) on sandy slopes, vertical-reef walls, and undercuts. It has been recorded in the same habitat as *P. paccagnellae*.

Pictichromis porphyrea Lubbock & Goldman, 1974

Common Names: Magenta Dottyback , Purple Dottyback , Strawberry Dottyback.
Maximum Length: 6 cm (2.3 in.).
Distribution: Samoa to Indonesia, and from the Ryukyu Islands of southern Japan to Fiji.
Biology: The Magenta Dottyback is most abundant at modest depths over much of its range and usually occurs on dropoffs where it resides in crevices, small holes, or under ledges. It is occasionally seen in coral rubble areas at the base of fore-reef slopes or over mud near coral heads on coastal reefs. It occurs at depths from 6 to 65 m (20 to 213 ft.), but in most areas it is most abundant between 20 to 35 m (66 to 115 ft.). This fish feeds on zooplankton. It is a very nervous fish, never straying far from a hiding place. It is also a solitary species that maintains at least 61 to 100 cm (24 to 39 in.) between individuals.
Captive Care: Magenta Dottybacks are moderately hardy and will accept most fresh or prepared foods. In captivity they tend to lose their brilliance as their color gradually fades. Feeding them a varied diet will help to prevent this fading. Like its cousins, *P. porphyrea* does best when not housed with conspecifics, unless you have a very large tank with lots of hiding places. It is possible to keep a male-female pair in a medium-sized tank (e.g., 75 gallons). Although it can be a behavioral problem in the passive community tank, it is less aggressive than many members of the genus. It has been known to harass grammas, small wrasses, dart gobies, and other small, mild-mannered reef fishes, especially in smaller aquariums.
Aquarium Size: 10 gal. **Temperature:** 22 to 27°C (72 to 81°F).
Aquarium Suitability Index: 5.
Remarks: *Pictichromis porphyrea* is an intense shade of magenta overall, with no black markings on its head or body (as in *P. fridmani*). At the depths that this fish usually occurs, it is very conspicuous because it glows like a neon blue light. Larger individuals often have filaments extending from the upper and lower edges of the caudal fin. It is most similar to the **Goldcrown Dottyback** (*Pictichromis aurifrons*) **Lubbock, 1980**. This species differs from *P. porphyrea* in having yellow on the snout

Pictichromis porphyrea, Magenta Dottyback: at depth, glows like a neon light.

Pictichromis aurifrons, Goldcrown Dottyback: note characteristic yellow snout.

and anterior part of the head, which sometimes extends back along the dorsal fin. The body is magenta or bright pink. Some individuals also have a line separating the yellow and magenta portions of the body.

The Goldcrown Dottyback is a rare species that has been collected in Papua New Guinea and photographed off Irian Jaya, Indonesia. It occurs at depths from 21 to 48 m (69 to 157 ft.) among small patch reefs scattered on a sandy reef slope.

Pseudochromis aldabraensis, Arabian Bluelined Dottyback: strikingly hued.

Pseudochromis dutoiti, African Bluelined Dottyback: note green body color.

Genus *Pseudochromis* (Common Dottybacks)

This is the largest genus in the family, with approximately 60 species. Members of this genus are the most commonly encountered of the pseudochromids both on the reef and in the aquarium trade. This genus also includes some of the most colorful fishes in the sea. Most of the *Pseudochromis* spp. are smaller dottybacks. Even so, ounce-for-ounce, some species can be as aggressive as the aforementioned genera. Fortunately, their small size precludes them from being as destructive. While the *Pseudochromis* spp. are very hardy, their brilliant colors often become muted if they are not given a varied diet.

Pseudochromis aldabraensis Bauchot-Boutin, 1958

Common Names: Arabian Bluelined Dottyback, Neon Dottyback.

Maximum Length: 8.5 cm (3.3 in.).

Distribution: Arabian Gulf, east to Pakistan. It may also occur in Sri Lanka. It is the most abundant dottyback in the Gulf of Oman.

Biology: The Arabian Bluelined Dottyback is found in a variety of habitats: in bays among rocky rubble and on fringing reefs among coralline algae, rubble, boulders, and live stony corals. It is also found in tidepools. It has even been reported under oil rigs, living in soft drink and beer cans on the muddy substrate. It can be found in water as deep as 40 m (131 ft.), but is usually found in shallow-water habitats. Off Kuwait, it is most common at depths between 1 to 3 m (3.3 to 9.8 ft.). No information exists on the feeding habits of this species in the wild, but it probably feeds on larger planktonic and benthic crustaceans and polychaete worms. *Pseudochromis aldabraensis* is bolder than its fellow dottybacks and will spend much of its time in the open. Adults are usually found in pairs, occupying a territory of approximately 1 m (3.3 ft.) in diameter. The focal point of the territory is usually a crevice where the pair spend much of their time.

Captive Care: The Arabian Bluelined Dottyback is very aggressive on the reef and in the aquarium. As a result, it is a threat to many of its tankmates; I have even had them disembowel tankmates of smaller or equal size. They are best kept with larger, more aggressive species (e.g., large angelfishes, surgeonfishes, large damselfishes, and hawkfishes). If you are determined to keep one of these beauties in a less aggressive community tank, be sure that it is a smaller individual and that it is the last fish introduced. Like its belligerent cousins, it is less of a threat in an extra-large aquarium replete with hiding places. One study noted that wrasses were not present in areas where *P. aldabraensis* was common, and it was suggested that this fish is intolerant of labrids. Therefore, it is best not to keep them with these fishes in the aquarium (at least not in small tanks).

This durable dottyback is well suited to the moderately aggressive community tank. It will eat a wide variety of frozen, prepared, and fresh foods, including small fishes, brine shrimps, mysid shrimps, krill, and flake foods. It retains its color well if fed a varied diet. In the reef aquarium, it will consume small tube worms and your prized ornamental shrimps (e.g., camel shrimps, peppermint shrimps). It will also feed heavily on fireworms, including larger individuals. (I have observed one dottyback swimming around the tank with a fireworm sticking out of its mouth that was too large for it to swallow whole.) This species has spawned in captivity, laying demersal eggs in large shells, but, unfortunately, the sexes are not readily separable. Currently, the Arabian Bluelined Dottyback is being bred commercially by C-Quest in Puerto Rico. Courtship in wild-caught pairs is often

Pseudochromis bitaeniatus, Twolined Dottyback: hardy, feisty little fish.

Pseudochromis sp., Togean Dottyback: note orange marking under eye.

Unidentified species photographed by author: Milne Bay, Papua New Guinea.

brutal, with the male biting the abdomen of the female to elicit her to deposit her eggs. Injuries resulting from the mating act are often lethal to the female. However, in captive-born-and-raised individuals, courtship is not nearly as aggressive.

Aquarium Size: 20 gal. **Temperature:** 22 to 27°C (72 to 81°F).
Aquarium Suitability Index: 5.
Remarks: This is one of the most striking reef fish available to the marine aquarist. The body is yellowish orange, with one iridescent blue stripe running from the snout to the caudal fin, another from the upper jaw to the gill cover, and two on the iris. It also has blue accents on its tail, dorsal fin, opercula, preopercula, and the median fins are sometimes tinged with red. This species is closely related to, and often misidentified as, the **African Bluelined Dottyback (*Pseudochromis dutoiti*) Smith 1955,** which occurs from Kenya to South Africa. *Pseudochromis dutoiti* differs from *P. aldabraensis* in having a pair of blue lines on the top and bottom of the tail, and is olive green overall, rather than orange. *Pseudochromis dutoiti* is found among rocks and stony corals on fringing reefs. It is reported to be common in Sodwana Bay, South Africa but is an aquarium rarity.

Pseudochromis bitaeniatus (Fowler, 1931)

Common Name: Twolined Dottyback.
Maximum Length: 7 cm (2.7 in.).
Distribution: Indonesia and the Great Barrier Reef, north to the Philippines.
Biology: The Twolined Dottyback is found on coastal and outer reefs, at depths of 2 to 38 m (6.6 to 125 ft.). It is found on the reef face, fore-reef slope, or steep-reef dropoffs. This fish lives among stony corals, sponges, and macroalgae, and usually does not stray far from cover. On several occasions I observed this

species living among ramose stony corals, along with the Oblique-lined Dottyback (*Cypho purpurascens*), in Papua New Guinea. (It would be dangerous to place these fishes together in the same aquarium, unless it was quite large [e.g., 6,452 cm^2 [1,000 in.^{2}] or larger). It has been suggested that this species may mimic the Striped Eel Catfish (*Plotosus lineatus*), which has toxic spines. This seems unlikely, as the two species tend to occupy different habitats.

Captive Care: Although very hardy, *P. bitaeniatus* can be an aggressive little fish. It has been known to attack and kill smaller fishes and eat ornamental shrimps. For this reason, it is best housed in a larger aquarium if the tank is to contain smaller or similarly sized fishes, or kept with equally aggressive species. If placed in a larger tank with plenty of hiding places, it will often ignore its tankmates, unless they venture too close to its preferred hiding places. Although not common, *P. bitaeniatus* occasionally can be found in aquarium stores and is inexpensive.

Aquarium Size: 10 gal. **Temperature:** 22 to 27°C (72 to 81°F).

Aquarium Suitability Index: 5.

Remarks: In juvenile *P. bitaeniatus*, the black lines on the body are even more distinct and the head is not yellow. Kuiter (2001) reports that an undescribed species that is closely related to this fish has been found in Tomini Bay, Togean Island (Indonesia). According to Kuiter, this fish (which he calls the **Togean Dottyback,** *Pseudochromis* **sp.**) occurs in caves at depths in excess of 30 m (98 ft.). It is easily recognized by the orangish red marking under that eye and its lyretail. In Milne Bay, I have photographed a pseudochromid similar to Kuiter's Togean Dottyback. It has an orange marking under the eye, a blue marking behind it, and the larger individuals have a lyretail. The head is dark gray, the body is brownish with a light yellow wash, and it lacks dark stripes. The caudal fin can be bluish, as can the edges of the median fins. This dottyback is not uncommon on sheltered fringing reefs and on reef faces in Milne Bay. It occurs in caves, in crevices, and under overhangs at depths of 6 to 12 m (20 to 39 ft.). One adult individual was observed to move over an area of approximately 2 m² (22 ft.²). It shared this area with a small Twolined Dottyback and several Oblique-lined Dottybacks (*C. purpurascens*) and an Elongate Dottyback (*P. elongatus*).

Pseudochromis caudalis Boulenger, 1898

Common Name: Bandtail Dottyback.

Maximum Length: 11 cm (4.3 in.).

Distribution: Sri Lanka east to the west coast of India and Pakistan, north to Oman.

Biology: This dottyback lives in tidepools, on rock/rubble areas, sand flats, and slopes. On sand bottoms, *P. caudalis* is reported to live in burrows under isolated rocks or in under heads of *Porites*. It occurs at depths of 12 to 30 m (39 to 98 ft.). Adults are found singly or in pairs and will defend a hiding place from conspecific intrusion, although occupants are sometimes expelled. Lubbock (1975) reports seeing as many as four or five *P. caudalis* around a boulder that covered an area of about 10 m² (111 ft.²). It is sometimes found living in the same habitat as the Arabian Bluelined Dottyback (*Pseudochromis aldabraensis*).

Captive Care: The Bandtail Dottyback is not regularly encountered in the aquarium trade. However, this could change if brood stock could be obtained by some of the more successful ornamental marine fish breeders. Because of their scarcity in the hobby, information on its aquarium care is limited. Like most of the fishes in this genus, it is a durable aquarium species. Its larger size means that *P. caudalis* tankmates should be selected with care. It is also a threat to ornamental crustaceans.

Aquarium Size: 20 gal. **Temperature:** 22 to 27°C (72 to 81°F).

Aquarium Suitability Index: 5.

Remarks: *Pseudochromis caudalis* is yellow to brownish yellow overall, with a dark spot in the center of each of the upper body scales. There is a bright blue spot, edged with black, behind each eye, and light blue lines under the eye and on the gill cover. Adults have black bands.

Pseudochromis coccinicauda (Tickell, 1888)

Common Name: Orangetail Dottyback.

Maximum Length: 6 cm (2.3 in.).

Distribution: Laccadine Islands to central Indonesia.

Biology: Little information is available on the biology of this species. However, it is not uncommon around Java.

Pseudochromis caudalis, Bandtail Dottyback: potential for captive breeding.

Pseudochromis coccinicauda, Orangetail Dottyback: male with yellow patch.

Captive Care: In the aquarium, this species moves only short distances from shelter or darts from one hiding place to another. If kept with larger fish, *P. coccinicauda* may spend most of its time hiding and may not get enough to eat. It is not as aggressive as many of its congeners and has been successfully housed with more peaceful species in larger aquariums. However, be aware that larger males may terrorize small passive species (e.g., gobies, dartfishes) in smaller tanks. I have also had larger individuals beat up other dottybacks that were of similar size.

Aquarium Size: 10 gal. **Temperature:** 22 to 27°C (72 to 81°F).

Aquarium Suitability Index: 5.

Remarks: The Orangetail Dottyback is sexually dichromatic. Males are bluish gray to black overall. The lower part of the head and body, in front of the center of the anal fin, are yellowish brown to bright yellow. There are often blue spots and bars on the caudal peduncle. Juveniles and females are brown, with a slightly lighter ventrum. The caudal peduncle and caudal fin are yellowish brown to orange. The females of this species and the Bluelined Dottyback (*Pseudochromis cyanotaenia*) are almost identical, while the males of the two species exhibit some similarities. **Ransonnet's Dottyback (*Pseudochromis ransonneti*) Steindachner, 1870** is another small species, but it is less colorful and is not as highly sought after by aquarists as *P. coccinicauda*. It is usually gray with a light ventrum (either cream-colored or pale yellow).

Pseudochromis cyanotaenia Bleeker, 1857

Common Names: Bluelined Dottyback, Bluebarred Dottyback, Bluestriped Dottyback, Surge Dottyback.

Maximum Length: 6 cm (2.4 in.).

Distribution: Indonesia to the Gilbert Islands, north to the Ryukyus, south to the Great Barrier Reef.

Biology: The Bluelined Dottyback is most commonly found in tidepools on the reef flat and among rocks and coral on the reef face. It occurs to a depth of 30 m (98 ft.), but it is most common in less than 4 m (13 ft.) of water. It is often found in areas with lots of surge, like exposed outer-reef flats and reef-crest margins. *Pseudochromis cyanotaenia* feeds on small crabs, isopods, and copepods. It is very secretive, spending much of its time hiding in crevices and holes. This dottyback is often observed in male-female pairs.

Captive Care: In the aquarium, *P. cyanotaenia* moves only short distances from shelter or darts from one hiding place to another. If kept with larger fish, the Bluelined Dottyback tends to spend more time hiding and may not get enough to eat. It is not as aggressive as many of its congeners and can be successfully housed with more peaceful species in larger aquariums. However, it should be one of the last additions to a community tank con-

Pseudochromis coccinicauda, Orangetail Dottyback: typical brown female.

Pseudochromis cyanotaenia, Bluelined Dottyback: male with blue stripes.

Pseudochromis cyanotaenia, Bluelined Dottyback: relatively drab female.

Pseudochromis dilectus, Esteemed Dottyback: durable but belligerent.

Pseudochromis dilectus, Esteemed Dottyback: blue variant.

taining more docile species. I have kept it with anthias, gobies, anemonefishes, other damsels, pygmy angels, and dragonets with limited aggression problems. It may bully smaller wrasses and other dottybacks of equal or smaller size. Conspecifics of the same sex should not be kept together, but a male and female may tolerate each other in the same tank. However, I have had male Bluelined Dottybacks attack and kill females housed with them in smaller aquariums (i.e., less than 55 gallons). Therefore, make sure there are plenty of hiding places in case intersexual aggression does occur. As far as invertebrates are concerned, it may attack ornamental shrimps, especially if they are introduced after the dottyback. I have seen this species grasp the opercula of upended *Astraea* snails and attempt to rip them from their shells, generally without success unless the dottyback is very large. This species has been reported to spawn in captivity

and is an excellent candidate for captive breeding because of its small size, aquarium adaptability, and sexual dichromatism. I have seen individuals displaying male colors transform into the female color after being in an aquarium without other dottybacks. It may be a protandric hermaphrodite, but is more likely to engage in sex reversal when it lacks contact with conspecifics.

Aquarium Size: 10 gal. **Temperature:** 22 to 27°C (72 to 81°F).
Aquarium Suitability Index: 5.
Remarks: *Pseudochromis cyanotaenia* is regularly seen in aquarium stores. Males are yellow or yellow-green anteriorly, which merges with a dark blue posterior section. There is a yellow line on each side under the dorsal fin and bright blue stripes on the flanks. The fins are bright blue and are occasionally tinged with pink distally. The female color phase has a brown body with an orange or yellow-orange caudal fin, and orange along the base and posterior portion of the dorsal fin and sometimes on the posterior edge of the anal fin. Occasionally (e.g., during agonistic encounters), females display light stripes on the sides of the body. The female is often confused with several other species of dottybacks that display a similar female coloration. This species is very similar to the Orangetail Dottyback (*P. coccinicauda*), which is restricted in distribution to the Indian Ocean. Myers (1999) reports that there is a similar, undescribed species around Fiji and Tonga.

Pseudochromis dilectus Lubbock, 1976
Common Names: Esteemed Dottyback, Sri Lankan Dottyback.
Maximum Length: 9 cm (3.5 in.).
Distribution: Sri Lanka.
Biology: The Esteemed Dottyback has been reported from areas of coral rock with sparse stony and soft coral growth from depths of 8 to 15 m (26 to 49 ft.).
Captive Care: *Pseudochromis dilectus* is a very durable aquarium species, but like many of its relatives, it will behave belligerently towards smaller, more peaceful tankmates. It should not be kept with other dottybacks, unless you have a very large aquarium and should not be housed with members of its own species, unless a compatible pair is acquired. Even then, the pair should have plenty of room and there should be a plethora of hiding places. The Esteemed Dottyback does well in the reef aquarium, but may feed on ornamental shrimps.
Aquarium Size: 20 gal. **Temperature:** 22 to 27°C (72 to 81°F).
Aquarium Suitability Index: 5.
Remarks: This species exhibits two primary chromatic forms. One has a greenish yellow to orange head, while the other has a brown head. All individuals have wavy gold lines on the opercula. These color differences do not appear to be related to gender.

Pseudochromis dixurus Lubbock, 1975

Common Name: Forktail Dottyback.

Maximum Length: 9 cm (3.5 in.).

Distribution: Red Sea.

Biology: This dottyback occurs in harbors and reef slopes at depths of 5 to 60 m (16 to 197 ft.) in caves and around isolated rocks and coral colonies, often inhabiting silt-covered areas. It is not common at depths of less than 50 m (164 ft.). Juvenile *P. dixurus* are found singly, while adults are usually found in pairs.

Captive Care: This handsome dottyback is not common in aquarium stores, but may be one day if broodstock can be acquired by some of the more proficient dottyback breeders. It can be aggressive, therefore you should select potential tankmates carefully. Stay away from smaller, more docile fishes, unless you keep it in an extra-large aquarium. Keep one per tank, or keep it in male-female pairs. It is great selection for the deep-water reef aquarium.

Aquarium Size: 20 gal. **Temperature:** 22 to 27°C (72 to 81°F).

Aquarium Suitability Index: 5.

Remarks: The juvenile and adults of *P. dixurus* exhibit different color patterns. The juvenile has a stripe from the snout to the upper portion of the caudal peduncle. Near the head the stripe is black, but it turns yellow toward the tail. There is also a stripe under the eye that ends on the lower part of the caudal peduncle. This stripe is red in small specimens and the tail is yellow. The transformation from juvenile to adult color occurs at a standard length of 5 to 6 cm (2 to 2.3 in.).

Pseudochromis elongatus Lubbock, 1980

Common Names: Elongate Dottyback, Floppytail Dottyback.

Maximum Length: 6.5 cm (2.5 in.).

Distribution: Sulawesi and the Moluccas, Indonesia.

Biology: *Pseudochromis elongatus* is found on the edge of the reef flat, on fore-reef slopes, and dropoffs. It has been reported around small coral heads on sandy slopes and among coral rubble at depths from less than 1 to at least 15 m (3.3 to 49 ft.).

Captive Care: The Elongate Dottyback is an attractive little fish that occasionally shows up in the aquarium trade. Although small, it is a fairly brazen species that will frequently dart out into the open to explore its surroundings. While its small size makes it less of a threat than some of its larger relatives, it can be aggressive toward smaller fishes in cramped quarters. Keep only one per tank, unless the aquarium is large (i.e., 75 gallons or more). The Elongate Dottyback is a minimal threat to crustaceans or other ornamental invertebrates. Therefore, it is a great fish for the reef tank.

Aquarium Size: 10 gal. **Temperature:** 22 to 27°C (72 to 81°F).

Aquarium Suitability Index: 5.

Pseudochromis dixurus, Forktail Dottyback: handsome Red Sea species.

Pseudochromis elongatus, Elongated Dottyback: excellent reef tank choice.

Remarks: The head of *P. elongatus* may be orange or yellow. Those individuals with an orange head may have orange on the dorsal fin as well (some have suggested that this color form represents the female).

Pseudochromis flammicauda Lubbock & Goldman, 1976

Common Names: Firetail Dottyback, Orangetail Dottyback.

Maximum Length: 5.5 cm (2.2 in.).

Distribution: Great Barrier Reef, Australia.

Biology: This dottyback is found in inner lagoon reefs at depths of 3 to 10 m (9.8 to 33 ft.). It is a shy fish that will dash between branching corals or holes in the reef.

Captive Care: *Pseudochromis flammicauda* is a wonderful aquarium fish. It is small and less aggressive (or at least less able to inflict injury) than most of the other pseudochromids. Unfortu-

Pseudochromis flammicauda, Firetail Dottyback: wonderful aquarium fish.

Pseudochromis flavivertex, Sunrise Dottyback: blue beauty from the Red Sea.

nately, even though it is common in parts of Australia, it is rarely collected. Provide it with plenty of hiding places and avoid housing it with more aggressive dottybacks. More than one can be kept in the same tank (heterosexual pairs are preferred). It is a good candidate for captive breeding.

Aquarium Size: 10 gal. **Temperature:** 23 to 28°C (74 to 82°F).

Aquarium Suitability Index: 5.

Remarks: Kuiter (1996) suggests this species is sexually dichromatic, with both sexes being mainly gray to black, but the male has an orange head, red eye, and an orange caudal fin with red at its base. The head of the female is the same color as the body, the eye is white, and the caudal fin is a pale yellow.

Pseudochromis flavivertex Rüppell, 1835

Common Name: Sunrise Dottyback.

Maximum Length: 8 cm (3.1 in.).

Distribution: Red Sea and the Gulf of Aden.

Biology: The Sunrise Dottyback is found on reef faces and fore-reef slopes, often near the base of isolated coral heads or near rocks on sandy bottoms. It has been recorded at depths of 2 to 31 m (6.6 to 102 ft.), but is more abundant at depths in excess of 15 m (49 ft.). It is usually seen dashing from one crevice to another and often remains hidden deep in reef interstices for extended periods of time. *Pseudochromis flavivertex* is found singly or in pairs. Even when in pairs, individuals do not occupy the same hole or burrow (Brons [1996] report that males and females often reside about 2 m [6.6 ft.] apart.) Other sources suggest that the territory of an adult may cover approximately an area of approximately 1 m^2 (11 ft.^{2}).

Captive Care: *Pseudochromis flavivertex* is an undemanding aquarium fish that is becoming more abundant in aquarium stores

due to increased collecting in the Red Sea and captive-breeding programs. It has been reported that *P. flavivertex* will not do well in an aquarium with larger fishes, due to its shyness. It will hide constantly and, as a result, may starve to death. This may happen in some cases, but if there is live rock in the tank, it can usually find enough small worms and crustaceans associated with the rock to feed on. It's best to feed this fish a varied diet that includes some color-enhancing foods. Although it is not subject to extreme color loss like some of the other dottybacks, *P. flavivertex* may become dull if an adequate diet is not provided.

Pseudochromis flavivertex is a moderately aggressive dottyback. In larger tanks, it can be housed with other dottybacks or a conspecific individual of the opposite sex. If you keep a pair, be attentive to the condition of the subordinate individual (the female). The male may persistently chase and bite her, especially during the reproductive period. If housed in a smaller tank, the male may kill his female tankmate. The Sunrise Dottyback is a worthy addition to the reef aquarium and can assist in controlling certain invertebrate pests. For example, larger *P. flavivertex* have been observed to capture and feed on small mantis shrimps and fireworms. Unfortunately this species has also been known to attack cleaner shrimps (*Lysmata* spp.). The courtship and mating behavior of *P. flavivertex* has been studied in captivity. The male will either dig a hole under a piece of coral or use a hole or interstice in a piece of live rock as a nest. Once the male lures the female into the nest, he will remain there until spawning is over. When the female enters the nest to spawn, she will flip upside down. The male moves alongside her and places his abdomen against hers. The pair then release their gametes over the next two or three hours. The egg ball is 2 to 3 cm (about 1 in.)

in diameter and is comprised of about 500 eggs. The male, after violently evicting the female from his shelter, guards and fans the egg mass, which hatches in five or six days. Spawning can occur at least as often as every two weeks.

Aquarium Size: 20 gal. **Temperature:** 22 to 27°C (72 to 81°F). **Aquarium Suitability Index:** 5.

Remarks: Baensch and Debelius (1992) report that this species is sexually dichromatic. They suggest that males are sky blue over the back and flanks, with a light ventrum and a yellow stripe running down the back from the nose to the tip of the tail, while females are grayish blue dorsally, with rows of dark spots, a white ventrum, and a yellow tail. However, after observing numerous pairs of spawning *P. flavivertex,* Brons (1996) reports that there are no differences in color between the sexes. (He suggests that this color form may represent a juvenile color variation.) Brons suggests that males are more robust and larger than females, while females tend to have a more rounded abdomen.

Pseudochromis fridmani Klausewitz, 1968

Common Names: Orchid Dottyback, Fridman's Dottyback, King Solomon's Dottyback.

Maximum Length: 7 cm (2.7 in.).

Distribution: Northern Red Sea.

Biology: This beautiful fish is abundant in the wild on steep fore-reef areas or dropoffs. They usually hide among soft corals (e.g., *Dendronephthya* spp.) or associate with large sea fans. Dozens of these fish can be found swimming over the latticed structure of these immense sea fans; in fact, every sea fan I observed in the Straits of Tiran had numerous *P. fridmani* associated with it. It can be found at depths of 1 to 60 m (3.3 to 197 ft.), but is most common shallower than 35 m (115 ft.). The Orchid Dottyback feeds on small crustaceans, both benthic and planktonic forms, and polychaete worms. It is often found in loose groups, with as many as eight individuals occurring in an area of 1 m^2 (11 ft.^{2}).

Captive Care: *Pseudochromis fridmani* is one of the most highly prized aquarium species. It is extremely hardy and adapts well to an aquarium that contains smaller, less aggressive fishes. Initially, it can be quite shy, but it will become more bold as it adjusts to its captive surroundings—unless housed with larger, more aggressive species. In the latter situation, it will hide more and may not get enough to eat. This is one of the most sociable of all the dottybacks. That said, there are always exceptions to the rule. For example, Greg Scheimer, a master aquarist who keeps numerous dottybacks, had one *P. fridmani* that was more belligerent than any of its congeners. However, in most cases the Orchid Dottyback is less pugnacious than the majority of its

Pseudochromis fridmani, Orchid Dottyback: hardy favorite of reef aquarists.

relatives. It can even be kept in small groups if you have a large enough aquarium that has plenty of hiding places. When attempting to keep more than one individual in an aquarium, make sure you introduce them all at the same time or introduce the smaller individual(s) first. In some cases, one individual may "stalk" and attack its conspecific tankmate(s). If this occurs persistently, you will probably have to remove the subordinate individual(s). Although *P. fridmani* is one of the least aggressive members of the genus, an occasional individual will pester smaller, more passive species (e.g., smaller wrasses, fire gobies, gobies). It will also defend its shelter sites from intrusion. The Orchid Dottyback will accept a wide variety of live and prepared foods. Provide it with a variety of meaty foods, including frozen preparations for carnivores, mysid shrimps, and flake foods. Another positive *P. fridmani* characteristic is that it maintains its brilliant color better than most of its congeners. It is ideally suited to the mini-reef aquarium and will usually not bother any ornamental invertebrates, with the possible exception of delicate shrimps (e.g., *Periclimenes*) or small fanworms. This species will jump out of open aquariums.

Aquarium Size: 10 gal. **Temperature:** 22 to 27°C (72 to 81°F). **Aquarium Suitability Index:** 5.

Remarks: *Pseudochromis fridmani* is magenta with a black stripe running from the lip, through the eye, and terminating at the edge of the operculum. At the posterior edge of most of the scales there is a darker spot which gives the body a cross-hatched appearance. A dark blue spot is present on the gill cover. The Ma-

Pseudochromis fuscus, Dusky Dottyback: yellow morph of a bold species.

Pseudochromis fuscus, Dusky Dottyback: gray variant with yellow shading.

Pseudochromis fuscus, Dusky Dottyback: dark variant with horizontal lines.

genta Dottyback (*Pictichromus porphyrea*) lacks the black "face" stripe and the body markings. Like *P. porphyrea*, this species glows like a neon blue light at depth. Lubbock (1975) was the first to suggest that this species was sexually dichromatic and dimorphic. He stated that the males have a magenta anal fin and the caudal fin tends to be longer than that of the female. But these characteristics are apparently not reliable for separating the sexes. Brons (1996) suggests that females are smaller and have a plumper abdomen, while males are thinner and more elongate.

Pseudochromis fuscus Müller & Troschel, 1849
Common Names: Dusky Dottyback, Yellow Dottyback.
Maximum Length: 10 cm (3.9 in.).
Distribution: Sri Lanka east to Vanuatu, north to the Philippines, south to Queensland, Australia.
Biology: The Dusky Dottyback is common on lagoon patch reefs, in tidepools on the reef flat, and in coral crevices on fringing reefs and the fore-reef slopes. It is most common in relatively shallow water, but occurs over a depth range of less than 1 to 30 m (3.3 to 98 ft.). On Lizard Island, Great Barrier Reef, studies indicate that one or two *P. fuscus* live per patch reef. Unlike most of its close relatives, the Yellow Dottyback feeds heavily on small fishes, including damselfishes that have just recently settled out of the plankton. They make frequent, often unsuccessful strikes at small fishes in complex stony coral habitat. *Pseudochromis fuscus* also eats large zooplankters and small benthic crustaceans.

The reproductive behavior of this species has been observed in the wild. The male swims ahead of the female with his tail angled slightly upward, body quivering, and then circles her. After the male executes this display, the receptive female will enter the male's hiding place and lay an egg mass, which the male fertilizes. The female will spend up to 50 minutes in the nest before the male chases her away and proceeds to guard and aerate the eggs (by fanning them with his fins and prodding them with his jaws). The male chases away any fish that approaches the site and is especially intolerant of wrasses.
Captive Care: The Dusky Dottyback is one of the bolder members of the genus, spending a considerable amount of time in the open. In the aquarium, it may hide initially, but will soon begin to spend more time in view. This species is territorial, but its disposition varies greatly between individuals. In most cases it should not be trusted with small or inoffensive fishes. It should not be kept with members of its own kind, unless a sexual pair can be acquired. If you do get a boisterous individual, beware that this species' larger size makes it a greater threat than its smaller cousins. *Pseudochromis fuscus* is a good candidate for the reef

Pseudochromis fuscus, Dusky Dottyback: blue-shaded color variant.

Pseudochromis marshallensis, Yellowspeckled Dottyback: small, secretive.

aquarium, although it is more of a threat to ornamental crustaceans than the smaller dottybacks.

Aquarium Size: 30 gal. **Temperature:** 22 to 27°C (72 to 81°F).
Aquarium Suitability Index: 5.

Remarks: The Dusky Dottyback is a stocky, medium-sized pseudochromid that is highly variable in color. It can be a canary-yellow (this morph was once called *Pseudochromis aureus*), gray, or brown overall. One color form that has been reported from Bali and Flores, Indonesia, is lighter gray overall with yellow on the dorsal fin and along the back. In other localities, individuals have yellow trim on the edge of the caudal fin. All color morphs have dark spots in the center of each scale, which form subtle lines running down the body. Kuiter (2001) recognizes a similar species that he calls the **Bluetail Dottyback**. He states that individuals range in color from blackish brown to yellow, but does not give any identifying characteristics. From the photos he includes with the species account, it appears that the Bluetail Dottyback differs from *P. fuscus* in having a black line at the base of the pectoral fins and the caudal fin can be metallic blue (but not in all cases). The tail also appears to be more round than that of *P. fuscus*. Kuiter states that this species is widespread in the Western Pacific. In any case, more research is required to determine if this is one highly variable species or whether a number of species are now being classified as *P. fuscus*. In a private communication, dottyback expert Dr. Anthony Gill said that after having looked at hundreds of specimens, he is not ready to separate these various color forms of *P. fuscus* into distinct species.

Pseudochromis marshallensis (Schultz, 1953)
Common Name: Yellowspeckled Dottyback.
Maximum Length: 6 cm (2.3 in.).

Distribution: Philippines and Taiwan to Vanuatu, north to the Bonin Islands, south to New Caledonia.

Biology: *Pseudochromis marshallensis* is found on coastal reefs, lagoon patch reefs, and on the outer-reef flat and face at depths of 0.5 to 10 m (1.6 to 33 ft.). It is quite secretive, often hiding among the branches of stony corals or under mushroom corals (*Fungia* spp.). It spends little time in the open, but darts quickly from one shelter site to another.

Captive Care: This diminutive dottyback is not a common species in the aquarium trade, due to its very secretive habits, as well as its somewhat subdued coloration. It will spend much of its time hiding among aquarium decor, but will race out to snatch passing food. The Yellow Speckled Dottyback is not as aggressive as some of its relatives, but it will defend its preferred hiding places and may cause problems with passive species in smaller tanks.

Aquarium Size: 10 gal. **Temperature:** 22 to 27°C (72 to 81°F).
Aquarium Suitability Index: 5.

Remarks: The Yellowspeckled Dottyback is brown overall with a series of yellow spots on the body scales that form stripes; the tail is yellow.

Pseudochromis moorei Fowler, 1931
Common Name: Jaguar Dottyback.
Maximum Length: 12 cm (4.7 in.).
Distribution: Philippines.

Biology: The Jaguar Dottyback occurs over silty bottoms, around isolated coral heads and rocks, at depths of 15 to 20 m (49 to 66 ft.). It has a nasty disposition and has been reported to attack and bite divers.

Captive Care: This is a large, aggressive dottyback and should only be kept with larger fishes that can take care of themselves. This in-

Pseudochromis moorei, Jaguar Dottyback (male): with fierce looks and a potentially lethal disposition, this is an attractive fish that lives up to its name.

cludes large angelfishes, surgeonfishes, and triggerfishes. It will attack and kill smaller fishes and ornamental crustaceans. (For more on the husbandry of this fish, see the Captive Care notes for the similar Steene's Dottyback [*Pseudochromis steenei*].)

Aquarium Size: 30 gal. **Temperature:** 22 to 27°C (72 to 81°F).
Aquarium Suitability Index: 5.
Remarks: Male *P. moorei* are orange overall with rows of small black spots on the upper part of the back and head, and a larger black spot on the opercula. Like Steene's Dottyback, the females are gray.

Pseudochromis nigrovittatus Boulenger, 1897

Common Names: Blackstripe Dottyback, Darkline Dottyback.
Maximum Length: 9 cm (3.5 in.).
Distribution: Iran, Gulf of Oman, Arabian Gulf, south Oman and Djibouti.
Biology: *Pseudochromis nigrovittatus* is found on fringing reefs living in tidepools, around boulders, and on rocky and coral reefs. It occurs at depths of 1 to 12 m (3.3 to 39 ft.). This dottyback will sometimes refuge among the spines of *Diadema* sea urchins.

Gill and Mee (1993) report that the striped color phase of *P. nigrovittatus* resembles the bicolor phase of the Gulf Blenny (*Ecsenius pulcher*). They also suggest more research is needed to determine if a mimetic relationship exists between these two species.

Captive Care: The Blackstripe Dottyback is not found in the aquarium trade. Therefore, little information exists on its captive biology. It is reported to be a secretive species that will spend much of its time in interstices and crevices. As with most dottybacks, you should select its tankmates carefully.

Aquarium Size: 20 gal. **Temperature:** 22 to 27°C (72 to 81°F).
Aquarium Suitability Index: 5.
Remarks: There are two color forms of *P. nigrovittatus*—a striped phase and a dark phase. The striped phase has a black stripe down the center of the body onto the caudal fin. The dark phase is light gray overall and lacks the distinct dark stripe. Both color forms have small blue spots scattered on the body and a blue spot on the rear edge of the gill cover. Individuals in an intermediate color phase have been observed. This species is similar to the Persian Dottyback (*Pseudochromis persicus*).

Pseudochromis nigrovittatus, Blackstripe Dottyback: rare fish, light phase.

Pseudochromis olivaceus, Olive Dottyback: spawns readily in the aquarium.

Pseudochromis olivaceus Rüppell, 1835

Common Name: Olive Dottyback.

Maximum Length: 9 cm (3.5 in.).

Distribution: Red Sea.

Biology: The Olive Dottyback inhabits shallow fringing reefs with rich stony coral growth. It occurs at depths of less than 1 to 20 m (3.3 to 66 ft.), but is most often found at depths of less than 10 m (33 ft.). *Pseudochromis olivaceous* is a cryptic dottyback, spending much of its time sheltering between the branches of corals (especially *Acropora* and *Pocillopora* spp.). The juveniles are especially secretive, spending most of their time deep within coral colonies, while adult *P. olivaceous* occur within *Acropora* coral thickets as well as among coral boulders. Adults often occur in pairs.

Captive Care: This fish is a durable aquarium inhabitant. It will dig holes under pieces of coral or live rock or hide among branching corals. The Olive Dottyback can be aggressive toward smaller or more peaceful fishes, including docile anthias, grammas, assessors, small sweetlips, small wrasses, fanged blennies, gobies, and dart gobies. A male and female can be kept together, but only in large aquariums. This species spawns readily in captivity.

Aquarium Size: 20 gal. **Temperature:** 22 to 27°C (72 to 81°F).

Aquarium Suitability Index: 5.

Remarks: This dottyback is olive to black overall (the black color phase is sometimes erroneously sold as the Black Dottyback [*Pseudochromis melas*]), with crescent-shaped blue spots on many of the scales, and a dark blue spot with gold edging on the operculum. The overall coloration, the number of blue spots, and the color of the fins can vary from one geographical location to the next. I have had dark individuals transform into the lighter color phase after several months in the aquarium. The margins of the tail and median fins are often yellow. This species is very similar to **Linda's Dottyback (*Pseudochromis linda*) Randall & Stanaland, 1989**, which is known from the Arabian Gulf, Oman, and Somalia. The Olive Dottyback differs in having an emarginate caudal fin, a tail with a limited amount of yellow, and many elongate dark blue spots.

Pseudochromis persicus Murray, 1887

Common Names: Persian Dottyback, Bluespotted Dottyback.

Maximum Length: 15.4 cm (6 in.).

Distribution: Arabian Gulf to Pakistan.

Biology: This dottyback is found on fringing reefs, where it can be observed darting among rocks, coral rubble, and live stony coral. It typically occurs on silt-covered reefs in shallow water, usually at depths of 1 to 2 m (3.3 to 6.6 ft.). However, it has been recorded at depths of 25 m (82 ft.). *Pseudochromis persicus* is reported to feed primarily on porcelain crabs. They wrest these crustaceans from crevices and from under rocks. Relyea et al. (1979) and Gill and Mee (1993) suggest that this species may mimic the Gulf Blenny (*Ecsenius pulcher*). This sympatric blenny exhibits three color forms, two of which may be mimicked by *P. persicus*. However, it might be that the blenny mimics this highly aggressive dottyback so that its potential competitors will steer clear of its territory. More study is required to verify if a mimetic relationship actually exists between this blenny and a dottyback (also see the Biology section of *Pseudochromis nigrovittatus*).

Captive Care: The Persian Dottyback is often shy when first introduced into the aquarium, spending most of its time peeking out from its lair and occasionally darting out for passing morsels of food. However, it will fervently defend its territory, the focal point of which is usually a favored hole or crevice. Its aggressive

Pseudochromis persicus, Persian Dottyback: rugged and aggressive.

Pseudochromis persicus, Persian Dottyback: light-colored variant.

Pseudochromis perspicillatus, Onestripe Dottyback: a true terror.

nature is no doubt the reason for its being reported as the most dominant fish on near-shore reefs in Kuwait. Conspecifics should never be kept together in captivity, unless you can obtain a male and a female and can house them in a very large aquarium. Great care must be taken when selecting potential tankmates for this fish. They are very aggressive and are best housed with snappers, large angelfishes, surgeonfishes, and triggerfishes. Also remember to give it plenty of hiding places. This is not a popular species with aquarists because of its subtle colors and high price. But true dottyback enthusiasts will tend to look past its modest chromatic highlights and its feisty behavioral characteristics. It is almost indestructible, colorfast, and adapts well to captivity. It should not be kept in a reef aquarium with docile fish or with your valued crustaceans (e.g., shrimps, small crabs), which it will eagerly consume.

Aquarium Size: 30 gal. **Temperature:** 22 to 27°C (72 to 81°F).
Aquarium Suitability Index: 5.
Remarks: *Pseudochromis persicus* has an elongate body, with bright spots on its sides, opercula, and caudal fin. These spots are in rows at the base of the dorsal and anal fins. The Persian Dottyback displays two distinct color phases. In one phase, the body and median fins are dark gray with iridescent blue spots. In the other, the body is cream or white overall, with blue spots and a dark stripe running from the snout to the tail. The dark phase is most commonly adopted by larger fishes, while juveniles usually display the lighter color. In both phases, each operculum has a black eyespot that is trimmed in blue, and the red eyes have two blue lines running through them. There are also faint orange and blue markings under the eyes. This species is most similar to the Blackstripe Dottyback (*Pseudochromis nigrovittatus*).

Pseudochromis perspicillatus Günther, 1862
Common Names: Onestripe Dottyback, Blackstripe Dottyback.
Maximum Length: 12 cm (4.7 in.).
Distribution: Philippines, south to Bali, Indonesia, east to Komodo.
Biology: The Onestripe Dottyback occurs singly, in turbid water, often around coral heads or rocks with algae, sponges and gorgonians. It is found over sand, rubble, or mud bottoms and lives at depths from 3 to 40 m (3.9 to 131 ft.). Information is not available on its food habits, but it probably feeds on worms and crustaceans.
Captive Care: The more muted coloration and malevolent disposition of *P. perspicillatus* are drawbacks for aquarists. It is most similar in temperament to the Australian dottybacks (*Ogilbyina* spp.) or members of the *moorei*-complex—that is, very aggressive. It is also a larger species that is not only eager to inflict damage,

Pseudochromis perspicillatus, Onestripe Dottyback: variant with yellow wash.

Pseudochromis pesi, Pale Dottyback: usually found in deeper waters.

Pseudochromis punctatus, Blackback Dottyback: seldom-seen species.

but has the bulk to do so. One specimen I kept attacked and disemboweled a larger cardinalfish and tore up the fins of a Red-cheek Anthias (*Pseudanthias huchtii*) before being relegated to a tank with more aggressive fishes. Even in this aquarium, it was the boss, chasing and nipping larger damselfishes, a Harlequin Tuskfish (*Choerodon fasciatus*) and a Bird Wrasse (*Gomphosus varius*), all of which were introduced before it. For this reason, it is best to keep this beast with larger squirrelfishes, snappers, aggressive hawkfishes (e.g., *Paracirrhites* spp.), large surgeonfishes, and triggerfishes.

Aquarium Size: 30 gal. **Temperature:** 22 to 27°C (72 to 81°F).

Aquarium Suitability Index: 5.

Remarks: The color of *P. perspicillatus* can be somewhat variable. Most individuals are white overall, with fine yellow lines on the body, and a black line running from the upper jaw, through the eye, to the end of the dorsal fin. There are silver scales along a portion of the lateral line. Some individuals have a yellow, pink, or salmon-colored wash over portions of the body or tail. The dorsal surface of the head, above the black line, is also black rather than gray in some individuals.

Pseudochromis pesi Lubbock, 1975

Common Name: Pale Dottyback.

Maximum Length: 10 cm (3.9 in.).

Distribution: Red Sea to South Africa.

Biology: This dottyback is found on reef faces and reef slopes at depths of 10 to 45 m (33 to 148 ft.), but most often in excess of 20 m (66 ft.). The Pale Dottyback is usually found hiding under, or hovering above, isolated rocks or coral colonies on sandy slopes. Adults occur singly or in pairs.

Captive Care: *Pseudochromis pesi* is another Red Sea/Indian Ocean species that has yet to show up in the aquarium trade with any regularity. It is a large, potentially aggressive species, so select tankmates carefully. It will pester smaller or more passive fish species and may ingest ornamental crustaceans. Keep only one individual per tank, unless you can acquire a pair.

Aquarium Size: 30 gal. **Temperature:** 22 to 27°C (72 to 81°F).

Aquarium Suitability Index: 5.

Remarks: The Pale Dottyback is dark gray dorsally and lighter ventrally with a yellow tail and yellow anal fin. The dorsal fin has scattered black spots. On the upper edge of the gill cover, there is a dark blue, oblong spot (ocellus) that is trimmed in gold. The pelvic fins of this species are long and elegant. This species is somewhat similar to the **Blackback Dottyback** (*Pseudochromis punctatus*) **Kotthaus, 1970,** which is only known from Somalia and the Gulf of Oman. This dottyback has a dark gray to black

Pseudochromis pictus, Painted Dottyback: small, virtually unknown species.

Pseudochromis sp., Rinca Dottyback: still-undescribed species.

Pseudochromis pylei, Pyle's Dottyback: very rare fish from deep water.

Pseudochromis flavopuctatus, Yellowspotted Dottyback: Komodo Island fish.

dorsal surface and is yellow, pale pink, or white ventrally. There are black dots on the dorsal fin and on the anal fin of larger individuals. *Pseudochromis punctatus* has been reported from a depth range of 17 to 65 m (56 to 213 ft.).

Pseudochromis pictus Gill & Randall, 1998
Common Name: Painted Dottyback.
Maximum Length: 7 cm (2.7 in.).
Distribution: Alor Island, Indonesia.
Biology: The Painted Dottyback occurs around isolated coral heads and rocks on fore-reef slopes. It is reported from depths of 28 to 36 m (92 to 118 ft.).
Captive Care: Although virtually unknown in the marine trade, this is probably a durable aquarium fish. Its small size means it would be suitable for a wide range of community tanks.

Aquarium Size: 10 gal. **Temperature:** 22 to 27°C (72 to 81°F).
Aquarium Suitability Index: 5.
Remarks: The overall coloration of *P. pictus* is white to pink over most of the body, becoming bluish gray behind the middle of the anal fin. The top of the head and the lips are yellowish. A gray stripe runs from the back of the eye and merges with the darker rear portion of the body and tail. The **Rinca Dottyback** (*Pseudochromis* sp.) is a small species with an orangish head and a gray or grayish blue body. It has been reported from the Komodo region, including Rinca Island.

Pseudochromis pylei Randall & McCosker, 1989
Common Name: Pyle's Dottyback.
Maximum Length: 8 cm (3.1 in.).
Distribution: Indonesia, in Flores and the Banda Sea, also Palau.

Pseudochromis sankeyi, Sankey's Dottyback: a Red Sea fish whose color and behavior suggests a mimickry of the venomous juvenile Striped Eel Catfish.

Biology: Pyle's Dottyback has only been reported from deep water. It is known from steep reef dropoffs and at the base of the fore reef, among coral rock and sand. This fish occurs at a depth range of 40 to 85 m (131 to 279 ft.).

Captive Care: I have yet to see *P. pylei* in the North American aquarium trade, but it has been kept in Japan. It is reported to be a durable species that is not as aggressive as some of its relatives, but I would still avoid keeping it with peaceful tankmates. From the habitat data available for this species, it would appear to be better suited to the lower-light conditions of a deep rather than a shallow reef aquarium.

Aquarium Size: 20 gal. **Temperature:** 22 to 27°C (72 to 81°F).

Aquarium Suitability Index: 5.

Remarks: *Pseudochromis pylei* is gray overall with yellow on the posterior part of the body, the caudal peduncle, and caudal fin. The **Yellowspotted Dottyback** (*Pseudochromis flavopunctatus*) **Gill & Randall, 1998** is similar in form, but markedly different in color.

Both species have a black spot at the pectoral fin axil, but *P. flavopunctatus* has a pale to bright yellow spot at the base of each scale. This species is known only from Komodo Island.

Pseudochromis sankeyi Lubbock, 1975

Common Name: Sankey's Dottyback.

Maximum Length: 8 cm (3.1 in.).

Distribution: Southern Red Sea to the Gulf of Aden.

Biology: Sankey's Dottyback typically occurs on the reef face and fore-reef slopes at depths of 2 to 10 m (6.6 to 33 ft.), living under ledges and in crevices. This dottyback is reported to be a colonial species and sometimes occurs in large groups. For example, Lubbock (1975) reported seeing a colony of 60 to 100 individuals under a ledge in an area 3 to 4 m² (33 to 44 ft.²). Their color and behavior was similar to that of juvenile Striped Eel Catfish (*Plotosus lineatus*), which have venomous spines. It may be that this harmless dottyback mimics the noxious catfish to dissuade predators.

Captive Care: This is a very durable aquarium fish. Although Sankey's Dottyback is apparently a more social species, keeping groups of this fish in captivity can be difficult. They have been kept in small groups in very large aquariums. If you try to reproduce this social structure in a large tank, be sure all of your *P. sankeyi* are introduced to the tank simultaneously. Even so, if one individual becomes overly aggressive, you may have to re-

Pseudochromis sp., Raja Dottyback: possible male of a new species.

Pseudochromis sp., Yellowbelly Dottyback: undescribed species from Java.

Pseudochromis springeri, Springer's Dottyback: hardy, elegant aquarium fish.

move the bully from the aquarium. These dottybacks will definitely fight, even until the weaker fish perishes, if kept in a system that confines them too closely. *Pseudochromis sankeyi* tends to be more aggressive than the closely related Orchid Dottyback (*P. fridmani*) and will be avoided by this species if they are in the same tank. It will also pick on docile fish tankmates in smaller aquariums and will jump out of open aquariums.

Aquarium Size: 20 gal. **Temperature:** 22 to 27°C (72 to 81°F).

Aquarium Suitability Index: 5.

Remarks: *Pseudochromis sankeyi* is almost identical to the Orchid Dottyback (*P. fridmani*) morphologically, but it is radically different in color. Juvenile *P. sankeyi* have a tail that is more truncate, but as it grows the lower lobe becomes pointed. The white coloration may take on a pinkish hue when this fish is stressed.

Pseudochromis sp.

Common Names: Raja Dottyback, Bantanta Dottyback.

Maximum Length: 9 cm (3.5 in.).

Distribution: Northern Irian Jaya and Halmahara, Indonesia.

Biology: This undescribed dottyback is found on fore-reef outcroppings at depths of 15 to 40 m (49 to 131 ft.). It occurs in areas with rich sponge and coral growth.

Captive Care: Husbandry requirements are similar to those of other similarly sized dottybacks.

Aquarium Size: 20 gal. **Temperature:** 22 to 27°C (72 to 81°F).

Aquarium Suitability Index: 5.

Remarks: The Irian Dottyback appears to be closely related to **Cole's Dottyback (*Pseudochromis colei*) Herre, 1933.** The latter species is known from the Philippines and northern Indonesia. The two species differ in coloration. The Raja Dottyback develops long filaments on the upper and lower caudal lobes as it grows.

Pseudochromis sp.

Common Names: Yellowbelly Dottyback, Karimunjawa Dottyback.

Maximum Length: 7 cm (2.7 in.).

Distribution: Northern Java, Indonesia.

Biology: This species has been reported from fore-reef slopes at depths of 20 m (66 ft.).

Captive Care: Its husbandry requirements are probably similar to those of most other smaller dottybacks.

Aquarium Size: 10 gal. **Temperature:** 22 to 27°C (72 to 81°F).

Aquarium Suitability Index: 5.

Remarks: In the Yellowbelly Dottyback, the lower portion of the head and body is yellow, whereas the middle and upper portion of the body is grayish brown.

Pseudochromis springeri Lubbock, 1975

Common Names: Springer's Dottyback.

Maximum Length: 4 cm (1.6 in.).

Distribution: Red Sea.

Biology: Springer's Dottyback lives on the reef face and fore-reef slope of fringing and offshore bank reefs. It is most often found among branching stony corals (e.g., *Acropora* spp., *Pocillopora* spp.) at depths of 2 to 60 m (6.6 to 197 ft.). This fish has been reported from relatively turbid inshore habitats, as well as clear water. The coloration of *P. springeri* may possibly afford it some protection from predators. Its color is similar to that of the sympatric Fourline Wrasse (*Larabicus quadrilineatus*), a species not consumed by most predators because it is a cleaner fish. Springer's Dottyback may occasionally clean other fishes as well, as it has been observed to do in the aquarium. (See "Dottybacks as Cleaners," page 105.) No data exists on the diet of this species, but it probably feeds on small crustaceans and polychaete worms. In the wild, *P. springeri* is often encountered in pairs.

Captive Care: Springer's Dottyback is a hardy, relatively colorfast species that I would highly recommend to any aquarist. It accepts a wide variety of prepared foods and is relatively resistant to disease. It is also moderately aggressive; it will pester anthias, placid wrasses, and dart gobies, especially in more limited confines. Keep only one individual per aquarium, unless you are sure you have a mated pair or you have a large tank (e.g., 10,968 cm^2 [1,700 in.^{2}] of surface area or more). *Pseudochromis springeri* is very active, flitting from one hiding place to another. One advantage to keeping Springer's Dottyback in the reef aquarium is that it will eat small bristleworms.

Aquarium Size: 10 gal. **Temperature:** 22 to 27°C (72 to 81°F).

Aquarium Suitability Index: 5.

Remarks: The overall color of *P. springeri* varies from black to dark gray. Adults tend to be lighter overall than juveniles.

Pseudochromis steenei Gill & Randall, 1992

Common Names: Steene's Dottyback, Lyretail Dottyback.

Maximum Length: 12 cm (4.7 in.).

Distribution: Indonesia (Bali, Komodo, Flores and Sulawesi).

Biology: Steene's Dottyback occurs near coral ridges or isolated rocks on deep black-sand slopes, where it is often found associating with crinoids, sponges, and soft corals. It has been observed at depths of 8 to 50 m (26 to 164 ft.), but is most often found deeper than 30 m (98 ft.). Adult *Pseudochromis steenei* usually occur in male-female pairs.

Captive Care: This dottyback is an extremely aggressive fish on the reef and in the aquarium. It has large canine teeth that can

Pseudochromis steenei, Steene's Dottyback: female of a deadly species.

Pseudochromis steenei, Steene's Dottyback: male with canine teeth showing.

inflict serious damage to its rivals. Divers have reported having their camera housing attacked when they approached too close to one of these fish. In the aquarium, they will attack and kill any fish that is smaller, of similar size, and, in some cases larger than themselves. For example, I had a smaller individual attack and fray the fins of a much larger shrimp goby. I have also had it kill wrasses, blennies, and gobies. Therefore, this dottyback

The Deadly Dottyback

The bright, "cheerful" colors of the male Steene's Dottyback (*Pseudochromis steenei*) belies a not-so-merry temperament. This is one of the most aggressive members of the group, and perhaps, ounce for ounce, the most aggressive fish in the sea. This fish, which only attains a maximum length of around 12 cm (4.7 in.) has a reputation for attacking divers who approach too closely.

We discovered a pair of these fish at a dive site in Lembeh Strait, Sulawesi. They were residing in a debris patch consisting of sponges, some man-made debris (e.g., pipe) and rocks, on a black-sand slope at a depth of about 26 m (85 ft.). I had heard about how aggressive this fish was from diving friends, and had read in Dr. Anthony Gill and Dr. John Randall's report about the voraciousness with which the species was originally described. The authors state:

"*Pseudochromis steenei* and its close relatives appear to be highly territorial and aggressive. The second author's camera housing was bitten while photographing the holotype and a paratype of *P. steenei*, and the late Roger Lubbock's unpublished field notes indicate that he was bitten while attempting to collect a pair of *Pseudochromis moorei*."

I was amazed at how aggressive this fish could be toward creatures hundreds of times larger than itself. While trying to photograph the pair, I lured them out into shooting range by placing my hand near their debris patch. When I fluttered my fingers, both the male and female dashed out to attack. They actually took the end of my glove in their mouths and shook it, then dashed back under cover. Moments later, one or both flew out to try to do more damage. Provoking them in this way turned out to be an efficacious way to get photos. They also attacked the camera ports as I tried to take pictures of creatures sharing their microhabitat.

Pseudochromis steenei, **Steene's Dottyback: displaying a typical aggressive pose before dashing out to attack the author.**

Their underwater oasis was home to a number of interesting organisms, including a small Ornate Ghost Pipefish, an Allied Cowrie, and several beautiful nudibranchs. Because of this diversity, the site was a popular stop for other photographers. My wife, Janine, and I had great fun watching them approach. The dottybacks swam out from cover to face each diver, then retreated to wait for the intruder to come closer.

When the unsuspecting diver rested his or her hand near the patch, it was swiftly attacked. It took a few seconds for most of the divers to figure out what had just bitten them, even though the fish often remained nearby, seemingly "sneering" at its victim.

The next time you are diving in *steenei*-infested waters, watch where you place your hands. If you feel a bite, look around for this fearless pseudochromid.

---

should only be kept with other belligerent species, such as groupers, larger hawkfishes, larger angelfishes, surgeonfishes, and triggerfishes. It is possible to house male and female Steene's Dottybacks together if they are placed in a very large aquarium with plenty of hiding places and if they are introduced simultaneously. But even then, there is still a possibility that the male will attack and injure the female. Habituating them to each other, using the method described for the Red Dottyback (*Labracinus cyclophthalmus*), would also help to curb initial bouts of fighting. *Pseudochromis steenei* will eat crustaceans, including smaller mantis shrimps. Other than a taste for ornamental shrimps and crabs, this dottyback will not harm more desirable invertebrates and can be kept in a shallow- or deep-water reef aquarium.

Aquarium Size: 30 gal. **Temperature:** 22 to 27°C (72 to 81°F). **Aquarium Suitability Index:** 5.

Remarks: Steene's Dottyback is somewhat of a living contradiction. From afar, the bright orange or yellowish head and the contrasting grayish brown body of the male are quite striking. But when you get closer, this beauty turns into a beast. The protruding lower jaw is studded with relatively large teeth which are prominently displayed even when the jaws are shut; it looks like a bicolored bulldog. The female is not quite as remarkable as the male, although still somewhat attractive. She is dark gray, with a blue line behind the eye and a yellow tail. Both sexes have white pelvic fins. Steene's Dottyback is very similar to the Jaguar Dottyback (*P. moorei*) and **Thinstriped Dottyback** (*P. howsoni*) **Allen 1995**, and the **Spotted Dottyback** (*Pseudo-*

chromis quinquedentatus) **McCulloch, 1926.** It is separated from these two species on the basis of color alone. The Spotted Dottyback also has a rounded caudal fin, which is emarginate in the other three species. *Pseudochromis quinquedentatus* is only known from northwestern Australia. Male *P. steenei* differ from male *P. moorei* in being yellow to orange anteriorly and gray posteriorly (*P. moorei's* body is orange overall), and featuring an indistinct black spot on the gill cover (distinct in *P. moorei*), well-defined white markings on the head (diffuse in *P. moorei*), and a gray dorsal and anal fin (*P. moorei* has orange dorsal and anal fins). Because the coloration of *P. steenei* can vary, some have suggested that it is a color variant of *P. moorei*.

Male *P. howsoni* are almost identical in color to male *P. steenei*, but differ in lacking the bluish bar behind the eye, dark margins on the pelvic and anal fins, and orange on the upper and lower margins of the tail. The differences between the females of the two species are similar to those found in the males. Thinstriped Dottyback is known from northwestern Australia and the Timor Sea. In the latter location it was collected near a sponge formation in 23 m (75 ft.) of water. All of these species are members of the *moorei*-complex.

Pseudochromis sp.
Common Names: Tono's Dottyback, Sumatran Dottyback.
Maximum Length: 9 cm (3.5 in.).
Distribution: Only known from the Indonesian island of Sumatra, although probably more wide-ranging in the Andaman Sea.
Biology: Tono's Dottyback was only recently discovered at a depth of 40 m (131 ft.). It seems to be limited in distribution to deep-reef slopes.
Captive Care: To the best of my knowledge, this species has yet to show up in the aquarium trade. Its small size and its sexual dichromatism means that it would be easy to pair up and potentially breed in captivity.
Aquarium Size: 30 gal. **Temperature:** 22 to 27°C (72 to 81°F).
Aquarium Suitability Index: 5.
Remarks: Male and female Tono's are very different in color. The central band along the body of the male is orange with blue dots, while that of the female is dark brown with blue dots.

SUBFAMILY PSEUDOPLESIOPINAE (FALSE PLESIOPS)
This subfamily consists of five genera, with 32 species. They differ from other dottybacks in the morphology of the lateral line (the anterior lateral line on the shoulder has only a single tubed scale rather than a series of tubed scales that extend beneath the dorsal fin). These fishes are found throughout the Indo-Pacific, but rarely observed by divers—with the possible exception of

Pseudochromis howsoni, Thinstriped Dottyback: male with yellow forebody.

Pseudochromis sp., Tono's Dottyback: male with orange central band.

those who inspect the back of large caves. They are very cryptic, often inhabiting deep crevices and caves. The only time they typically move from shelter is when relocating to a different hiding place. These fishes occasionally show up in the aquarium trade. Because they are so cryptic and may be difficult to feed, they will do best in a tank with live rock. They will come out to accept introduced foods if there are no aggressive tankmates and no activity outside the tank, which typically frightens them.

Genus *Chlidichthys*
There are 12 species in this genus of small pseudochromids, several of which have yet to be formally described. These are secretive fishes that are often found moving among crevices in the back of caves or hiding under ledges.

Pseudochromis sp., Tono's Dottyback: female with typical brown central bar. (male, pg. 139.)

Pseudochromis inornatus, Inornate Dottyback: tiny species appropriate for small aquariums.

Lubbockichthys multisquamatus, Finescaled Dottyback: secretive, cave-dwelling species.

Pseudoplesiops collare, Collared Dottyback: rests on its elongate pelvic fins when not swimming.

Pseudoplesiops rosae, Largescaled Dottyback: pretty little species that tends to remain hidden.

Pseudoplesiops typus, Ringeyed Dottyback: cryptic fish that haunts caves and crevices.

Chlidichthys inornatus Lubbock, 1976

Common Names: Inornate Dottyback, Yellow Dottyback.

Maximum Length: 4.5 cm (1.8 in.).

Distribution: Maldives, Chagos, Sri Lanka.

Biology: *Chlidichthys inornatus* is found in lagoons and on reef faces at shallow depths to at least 20 m (66 ft.). Adult males and females can usually be found living close to one another.

Captive Care: Although somewhat secretive, this is a good dottyback for the small aquarium and will do best in a reef tank with numerous caves and crevices. It is likely to be picked on by larger dottybacks or other aggressive piscine tankmates. More than one can be kept in the same tank (heterosexual pairs are preferred). It is a good candidate for captive breeding.

Aquarium Size: 10 gal. **Temperature:** 23 to 28°C (73 to 82°F).

Aquarium Suitability Index: 5.

Remarks: This species is sexually dichromatic. The male is yellow on the head and median fins and the body is greenish gray. The female is gray overall. The **Cerise Dottyback (***Chlidichthys johnvoelckeri***) Smith, 1954** is very similar in appearance to the Magenta Dottyback (*Pictichromis porphyrea*)—it is magenta overall. It is only known from the East African coast (i.e., Pemba,

Natal). It is found at depths of 12 to 75 m (39 to 246 ft.), often on dropoffs where there is rich gorgonian growth. It is fed on by the Redmouth Grouper (*Aethaloperca rogaa*).

Genus *Lubbockichthys* (Lubbock's Dottybacks)

Lubbockichthys multisquamatus Allen, 1987

Common Names: Finescaled Dottyback, Pink Dottyback.

Maximum Length: 6 cm (2.3 in.).

Distribution: West Pacific.

Biology: The Multiscaled Dottyback is found on reef faces and slopes (it is most common on dropoffs) at depths of 12 to 60 m (39 to 197 ft.) and usually inhabits large caves, crevices, and overhangs. *Lubbockichthys multisquamatus* dashes from one hole to another in the back of caves. It probably feeds on small crustaceans.

Captive Care: Like others in the genus, *L. multisquamatus* is very secretive. It is most likely to thrive in an aquarium on its own (species tank). It could be kept with other cryptic or passive species (e.g., mandarinfishes). However if housed with aggressive feeders, it may have difficulty getting enough to eat. Keep only one individual per tank (a male and female could be kept together). **Aquarium Size:** 10 gal. **Temperature:** 22 to 27°C (72 to 81°F). **Aquarium Suitability Index:** 4.

Remarks: *Lubbockichthys multisquamatus* is pink overall, with yellow on the caudal fin. This species was formerly placed in the genus *Pseudoplesiops*.

Genus *Pseudoplesiops* (Secretive Dottybacks)

Pseudoplesiops collare (Gill et al., 1991)
Common Name: Collared Dottyback.
Maximum Length: 3.5 cm (1.4 in.).
Distribution: Philippines, Indonesia to the Solomon Islands.
Biology: *Pseudoplesiops collare* has been observed on the reef edge near sand substrate. It has been reported at depths of 33 to 113 m (108 to 371 ft.). It is very secretive and comes into the open only to move from one hiding place to another and has been observed moving across small sand patches when relocating. This fish rests on its long, erected pelvic fins when not swimming.
Captive Care: While this species is not readily found in the aquarium trade, it is possible that *P. collare* may occasionally be collected and exported from the Philippines and Indonesia. It is a secretive species that is best housed in a small species tank, as it is likely to be picked on or have difficulty competing with bolder or more pugnacious species.
Aquarium Size: 10 gal. **Temperature:** 22 to 27°C (72 to 81°F).
Aquarium Suitability Index: 4.
Remarks: The Collared Dottyback differs from other members of the genus in having two oblique bars on the head and anterior portion of the body; the pelvic fins are very elongated.

Pseudoplesiops rosae Schultz, 1943
Common Name: Largescaled Dottyback.
Maximum Length: 3.5 cm (1.4 in.).
Distribution: East Andaman Sea to Samoa, north to the Yaeyamas, south to northwest Australia and the southern Great Barrier Reef.
Biology: This dottyback is found on reef crests, reef faces, and fore-reef slopes at depths to 10 m (33 ft.). It often occurs in areas exposed to surge, but I have also seen it in very protected habitats. *Pseudoplesiops rosae* lives under ledges, in crevices, and in large caves, where it slinks from one small hole to another. It eats small crustaceans.
Captive Care: Like other members of this group, this is a secretive fish that will spend very little time in full view. You might

occasionally see it darting from one hole to another. The Largescaled Dottyback will spend more time in the open in a dimly lit aquarium. It may be difficult to feed if housed with more pugnacious eaters.
Aquarium Size: 10 gal. **Temperature:** 22 to 27°C (72 to 81°F).
Aquarium Suitability Index: 4.
Remarks: This species has red eyes and a yellow or orange head.

Pseudoplesiops typus Bleeker, 1858
Common Names: Ringeyed Dottyback, Hidden Dottyback.
Maximum Length: 6 cm (2.3 in.).
Distribution: Borneo to the Solomon Islands, north to the Philippines, south to northwest Australia and Queensland.
Biology: The Ringeyed Dottyback is found in lagoons and on reef faces at depths of 6 to 9 m (20 to 30 ft.). It is a very secretive fish that is rarely observed by divers, apparently haunting deep-reef crevices and caves.
Captive Care: The Ringeyed Dottyback is the most common member of the genus in the aquarium trade. It will hide most of the time in the aquarium, but will occasionally dash out from cover to snag pieces of food once fully acclimated. While it is not overly aggressive to unrelated fish tankmates, it may pick on small, passive species in cramped quarters. Keep only one per tank, unless the aquarium is quite large. Their color is prone to fading in the aquarium, especially if not given a varied diet (include a color-enhancing food).
Aquarium Size: 10 gal. **Temperature:** 22 to 27°C (72 to 81°F).
Aquarium Suitability Index: 4.
Remarks: *Pseudoplesiops typus* is pink overall with a black ring around the eye and dark red highlights on the dorsal and anal fins. The dorsal and anal fin tips are light, or there is a light blue line along the margins.

References

B. Addison (personal communication), Allen (1994), Barrall & Gill (1997), Brons (1996), Coleman (1981), Debelius (1986, 1993), Debelius & Baensch (1994), Edwards & Randall (1983), Esterbauer (1990), Gardner (1997), Gill (1993, 2003), Gill & Allen (1996, In Press), Gill & Edwards (2002), Gill & Mee (1993), Gill & Randall (1992, 1998), Gill & Senou (2002), Gill & Tanaka (In Press), Gill & Woodland (1992), Gill et al. (1991, 1995, 1996), A. Gill (personal communication), Grant (1982), Kuiter (1992, 1996, 2001), Lubbock (1975, 1976, 1980), Lubbock & Goldman (1974), Moe (1997), Myers (1999), Randall (1983), Randall et al. (1990), Relyea et al. (1979), Schroeder (1980), H. Tanaka (personal communication), Thresher (1984).

Gramma loreto, Royal Gramma: a vividly colorful species that is part of a small serranid-like family spread around the Caribbean and tropical Western Atlantic.

ANYONE WHO HAS DIVED IN THE CARIBBEAN OR VISITED a marine aquarium shop is highly likely to have encountered a member of the Family Grammatidae. Because of their vivid colors and abundance, at least two of the grammas are frequent targets for both underwater photographers and fish collectors. One of these, the Royal Gramma (*Gramma loreto*), has been a favorite among saltwater aquarists for decades and is a mainstay choice for the reef aquarium. Their popularity is justified: Royal Grammas are colorful, hardy, not overly aggressive, and they do not bother ornamental invertebrates.

However, other species in the family are relative unknowns because of their deep-dwelling habits or their more secretive lifestyles. Although these grammas are less often encountered in fish stores, some are equally well suited for passive fish-only and minireef aquariums, and all are well worth the attention of aquarists.

Classification and Biology

The Family Grammatidae currently consists of 2 genera, which contain 11 species. However, the taxonomic status of the family and some of its members is still uncertain, and some of the genera and species may eventually be placed in the allied Family Serranidae (known commonly as the groupers and seabasses).

The genera in this family, *Gramma* and *Lipogramma*, are comprised of species common to the Bahamas, the Caribbean and the coast of Brazil. Although many of the *Lipogramma* are beautiful and ideally suited for smaller aquariums, they rarely appear in the North American aquarium trade (and when they do a high price is attached). They are also seen less frequently by divers because many are found beyond safe diving limits (at least those depths explored by the average sport diver or collector) or are quite cautious, hiding deep in reef crevices or among coral rubble.

Although there is some overlap in areas where the three Bahamian and Caribbean Gramma species occur together, there is typically a marked difference in their depth distribution. This may in part be due to exclusion of one species by the other. For example, in areas where the Blackcap Basslet (*G. melacara*) and Dusky Gramma (*G. linki*) are not sympatric or do not share the same geographic range, the latter species is found in much shallower water (see species accounts). The members of the genus *Lipogramma* also show species-specific depth "preferences."

Captive Care

All of the grammas readily adapt to captive life and can be housed in small and large aquariums alike. They do appreciate lots of good hiding places, into which they will quickly dart if threatened, and are best kept with passive fishes, rather than with overly antagonistic species (e.g., large damselfishes, some hawkfishes, triggerfishes). If you choose to house them with potentially aggressive fishes, the gramma should be added to the aquarium before the belligerent tankmates. If they are the recipients of harsh treatment from other fishes, they will often hide constantly or cower in an upper corner of the aquarium until they perish. Grammas are good jumpers, so cover your tank accordingly.

These fishes can be kept in small groups in the aquarium if there is enough space to meet their territorial requirements and if they are added simultaneously or if a larger specimen is added last (for more information on this, see the species accounts below). One of the biggest drawbacks in keeping the more resplendent species is that their colors may fade in captivity. They may still be attractive even after this chromatic change, but their captive coloration is often only a shadow of their former brilliance. This is probably the result of dietary deficiency, but bright lighting and low dissolved oxygen levels are also a possible cause. The grammas will eat a variety of flake, frozen, and fresh foods; the more varied the diet, the less rapid or less likely the color loss. Using some of the new color-enhancing marine fish rations may help retain or restore bright pigmentation.

Another potential malady in the deep-water grammas is decompression—swim bladder malfunction resulting from improper collecting techniques. Avoid buying specimens that have

Gramma loreto, Royal Gramma: typical habitat for the grammas, all small fishes that never stray far from the protective cover of caves and crevices.

a difficult time maintaining their position in the water column or that swim in a labored fashion, with the tail higher than the midline of the body. These specimens usually spend most of their time wedged in a crevice to keep from floating to the surface.

The grammas are not a threat to most ornamental invertebrates, with the possible exception of small shrimps. For example, large grammas will occasionally ingest small *Periclimenes* shrimps. As far as invertebrates that feed on grammas are concerned, the species that poses the greatest threat is the Elephant Ear Anemone (*Amplexidiscus fenestrafer*). This species feeds by slowly closing up around prey items that rest on its disc. Grammas are some of

Gramma brasiliensis, Brazilian Gramma: compare to *G. loreto*, opposite page.

Gramma linki, Dusky Gramma (female): deep-dwelling fish prefers dim light.

the fish species that have been observed to fall victim to this large, predatory corallimorpharian. Carpet anemones, large crabs, and piscivorous mantis shrimps (most species found in live rock do not fall into this category) are other invertebrates that may be a threat to a gramma.

GRAMMA SPECIES

Genus *Gramma*

Gramma brasiliensis Sazima, Gasparini & Moura, 1998
Common Name: Brazilian Gramma.
Maximum Length: 10 cm (3.9 in.).
Distribution: Brazil (mainland as well as near offshore islands).
Biology: *Gramma brasiliensis* is a shallow-water species, having been reported from a depth range of 3 to 22 m (9.8 to 72 ft.). Like its close relative, the Royal Gramma (*Gramma loreto*), it is often found under ledges and in caves. It feeds mainly on zooplankton, although it has been reported to clean chromises and grunts.
Captive Care: The disposition of the Brazilian Gramma is different from its northern cousin; this species is more aggressive. It is more risky to keep two *G. brasiliensis* together, unless you have a larger aquarium (standard 75-gallon or larger) or a confirmed male-female pair. They are also more likely to harass smaller, docile species.
Aquarium Size: 20 gal. **Temperature:** 22 to 27°C (72 to 81°F).
Aquarium Suitability Index: 5.
Remarks: This species differs from *G. loreto* in having an upper jaw that extends about one pupil distance beyond the rear margin of the eye and a first dorsal spine that is noticeably shorter than the remainder of the dorsal spines. The color is similar to *G. loreto*, but there are no yellow streaks on the head.

Gramma linki Starck & Colin, 1978
Common Names: Dusky Gramma, Yellowcheek Basslet.
Maximum Length: 7 cm (2.7 in.).
Distribution: Cozumel, Puerto Rico, Bahamas, Jamaica, and British Honduras.
Biology: The Dusky Gramma tends to occur in deeper water than the Royal Gramma (*G. loreto*) or Blackcap Basslet (*G. melacara*), especially in areas where it and the latter two species are sympatric. Here it is most abundant at depths of 69 to 97 m (226 to 318 ft.). But in those locations where it does not occur with *G. melacara* (e.g., Puerto Rico) it can be common at depths as shallow as 27 m (89 ft.). This species prefers vertical reef faces and often lives under overhangs and in caves, usually hanging upside down. This species will form small groups of up to a dozen individuals that hang in the water column, staying within about 15 cm (5.9 in.) of their shelter sites and picking off passing zooplankton, such as amphipods and copepods. Some of these planktonic crustaceans are probably also captured by these fish in reef crevices. The Dusky Gramma is less conspicuous than its relatives, spending much of its time perched in coral cracks, and is quick to retreat at the approach of a diver. Individuals I've had in the aquarium often perched, upside down, between two rocks. They would also swim upside down, usually under ledges, more than any other *Gramma* species I have kept.
Captive Care: This is a hardy aquarium inhabitant that will acclimate to captive life quickly if provided with dim illumination, plenty of hiding places, and no overly aggressive tankmates. If

these criteria are met, your Dusky Gramma should be darting out to catch food items within a day or so of its being placed in the tank. After the Dusky Gramma acclimates, it can be exposed to more intense illumination, like that used on many reef tanks.

Although they are sensitive to being bullied when first introduced, my experiences indicate that they are the most aggressive *Gramma* species once acclimated. For example, a small specimen I kept with two Blackcap Basslets (*G. melacara*), a Ridgeback Basslet (*Liopropoma mowbrayi*), and two blennies, dominated the slightly larger *G. melacara,* even though all the *Gramma* species were introduced at the same time. The Dusky Gramma would chase the Blackcaps from their preferred hiding place and display at them by raising all of its median fins and twisting its head to one side. After several days, it was obvious that the Blackcaps would yield to the Dusky Gramma when it moved out from cover. The individuals I have kept showed relatively little aggression toward noncongener species, with the exception of fishes that dared to approach a favorite hiding hole. As with the other members of the genus, care must be taken when keeping more than one Dusky Gramma at a time. It is important that the tank be at least 75 gallons and have a large number of cracks and crevices to provide refuge for subordinates. When stressed or sleeping, this species displays pale bars on the body; like the Blackcap, it is prone to decompression problems during collection.

Aquarium Size: 20 gal. **Temperature:** 20 to 26°C (68 to 79°F).
Aquarium Suitability Index: 4.
Remarks: This species is less frequently seen in aquarium stores than the other gramma species because of its deep-dwelling habits and its more subdued coloration. *Gramma linki* was formally described in 1978; the first specimens were observed by scientists exploring the deep reef face with manned submersibles. It has since been reported from other areas.

Gramma loreto Poey, 1868
Common Names: Royal Gramma, Fairy Basslet.
Maximum Length: 8 cm (3.1 in.), although this species is reported to grow larger in captivity.
Distribution: Bermuda to the Bahamas, south to the West Indies and Venezuela. A single specimen, probably a "waft" or a specimen released by an aquarist, was also reported from the Florida Keys.
Biology: The Royal Gramma is typically found in shallower water than its congeners. Although it has been reported as deep as 76 m (249 ft.) in some areas, it is most abundant at depths of 1 to 29 m (3.3 to 95 ft.). It occurs near large coral heads, steep ledges, under overhangs, and in caves. The Royal Gramma picks copepods and isopods from the water column and is unique for a zooplankton feeder in having a relatively large mouth. On occasion, individuals will also clean parasitic isopods off other fishes. They have been observed cleaning Yellowtail Snappers (*Ocyurus chrysurus*) and the Nassau Grouper (*Epinephelus striatus*), often along with other facultative cleaners, like the Spanish Hogfish (*Bodianus rufus*) and Neon Goby (*Gobiosoma oceanops*). The Royal Gramma is typically found in small groups, but in the right habitat, like in a cave or under an overhang, they often occur in large aggregations, consisting of more than 100 individuals. They are also found in large numbers on isolated coral heads; for example, in the Bahamas, as many as 116 Royal Grammas have been reported from a single coral head 6 m (20 ft.) in diameter. The Royal Gramma can be found associating with a number of different types of coral species (including *Montastraea,*

Gramma loreto, Royal Gramma: northern form with smaller magenta area.

Gramma loreto, Royal Gramma: southern form with more magenta coverage.

Acropora, and *Diploria*), but is most prevalent in areas where the reef has the greatest vertical relief. This type of topography would give this little planktivore access to a larger area of the water column and food without it having to stray as far from shelter, and it would allow individuals to spread out more, reducing intraspecific competition.

Within most Royal Gramma groups, individuals form small territories from which they often exclude smaller conspecifics. A larger individual will remain in an area of about 832 to 4,994 cm^2 (128 to 774 in.^{2}), but will only defend a portion of its domain. This defended area can be 123 to 3,620 cm^2 (19 to 561 in.^{2}). Although the Royal Gramma mainly concerns itself with members of its own species, it will occasionally chase small zooplankton feeders (e.g., Masked Goby [*Coryphopterus personatus*], juvenile Bluehead Wrasses [*Thalassoma bifasciatum*], and Chromis damselfishes [*Chromis* spp.]), juvenile damselfishes (which compete with it for holes to hide in), and fishes that are predators on its eggs. In extremely large groups, grammas will abandon their territories and form dominance hierarchies, with size determining an individual's position in the pecking order. This species is now thought to be gonochoristic (individuals do not change sex), although some authors in the past have suggested that it is a protogynous hermaphrodite (females transform into males). Males defend a small cylindrical hole or narrow crevice, often on the side of a coral head or under an overhang, which will serve as a nest. The gramma will use pieces of algae, sea urchin spines, and sponge to cover the depression or seal secondary holes that lead to the nest. The male gramma will hover in front of the primary opening or sit in the hole with only its head protruding. If an intruder approaches the hole, the male will defend it by moving toward the intruder with its mouth wide open or contorting its body into an S-shape. The male maintains the nest by adding pieces of algae ripped from the substrate or caught as they float past in the water column, and by removing detritus from the hole. Algae species, such as *Amphiroa fragilissima*, *Jania adhaerens* (both red algae), *Dictyota divaricata* (a brown alga), and *Cladophoropsis* sp. (a green alga), are attached to the wall of the nest and will provide a framework to hold the eggs in the nest. Reproduction occurs between January and February to June. Reproductive activity has also been observed in mid-October.

Captive Care: In the aquarium, Royal Grammas will viciously defend a preferred hiding place from intrusion. They will threaten conspecifics, as well as other fishes, by swimming toward them with their mouths open wide. If aggression escalates between two *Gramma* species, they may lock jaws and head shake, or nip at each other's fins and bodies. If agonistic interactions become frequent or reach this level, it is best to separate the fishes before permanent damage occurs. I have seen individuals severely injure the skeletal elements of their jaws during these ritualized battles.

Creating Basslet Biotope Tanks

To create an authentic reef fish community—a biotope tank—the aquarist must have information about which other species are found in the same geographic area, depth, and habitat of the target species. Following are some of the fishes that naturally occur in the same habitats where the two common *Gramma* species are most abundant.

Blackcap Basslet (*Gramma melacara*)
Habitat Type: deep water 46 to 76 m (151 to 249 ft.), Jamaica.
Sympatric Species:

Ridgeback Basslet	(*Liopropoma mowbrayi*)
Aberrant Basslet	(*Liopropoma aberrans*)
Dusky Gramma	(*Gramma linki*)
Whitestar Cardinalfish	(*Apogon lachneri*)
Jackknife Fish	(*Equetus lanceolatus*)
Caribbean Longnose Butterflyfish	(*Prognathodes aculeatus*)
Spotfin Hogfish	(*Bodianus pulchellus*)
Creole Wrasse	(*Clepticus parrae*)
Yellowhead Wrasse	(*Halichoeres garnoti*)
Purple Chromis	(*Chromis scotti*)
Sunshinefish	(*Chromis insolata*)
Sharpnose Puffer	(*Canthigaster rostrata*)

Royal Gramma (*Gramma loreto*)
Habitat Type: 9 m (30 ft.), Bahamas.
Sympatric Species:

Flamefish	(*Apogon maculatus*)
Spotfin Butterflyfish	(*Chaetodon ocellatus*)
Foureye Butterflyfish	(*Chaetodon capistratus*)
Blue Chromis	(*Chromis cyanea*)
Sergeant Major	(*Abudefduf saxatilis*)
Spanish Hogfish	(*Bodianus rufus*)
Bluehead Wrasse	(*Thalassoma bifasciatum*)
Creole Wrasse	(*Clepticus parrae*)
Neon Goby	(*Gobiosoma oceanops*)
Atlantic Blue Tang	(*Acanthurus coeruleus*)
Diamond Blenny	(*Malacoctenus boehlkei*)
Sharpnose Puffer	(*Canthigaster rostrata*)

A vertical reef wall, whether comprised of live rock or artificial corals, will provide the gramma with a habitat similar to what they prefer in the wild. If you are keeping more than one gramma or other planktivores, the reef wall will also help to increase distances between individuals, which will help to curb aggressive encounters.

Royal Grammas can be kept in groups in the aquarium, but they should not be overcrowded and should include individuals of varying sizes. Although several juveniles can be kept in aquariums as small as the standard 30-gallon, an aggregation containing adult specimens should have no less than a 55-gallon tank. Remember, field studies show that Royal Grammas defend a territory 123 to 3,620 cm² (19 to 561 in.²) in area and a standard 55-gallon has a surface area of 4,338 cm² (672 in.²). Ideally a group will be composed of one medium-sized or large individual and two or more smaller specimens (the latter number depends on how large the aquarium is). If you are keeping more than one large specimen (i.e., male), the tank should have a surface area of over 6,452 cm² (1,000 in.²). The only difference between the sexes is size; on average, males are larger than females and attain a greater length. Therefore, by placing one larger fish and several small fish in an aquarium, you are increasing the chances of having only one male and several females. If you have a smaller aquarium (less than 30 gallons) you should keep only one gramma, or possibly a male-female pair.

It was once thought that the Royal Gramma and its relatives were mouth brooders, that is they incubated the eggs in their mouths like the assessors, jawfishes, and cardinalfishes. But aquarium and field observations of breeding behavior have proven this theory incorrect. The male Royal Gramma will build a nest by lining a hole in or under a rock with filamentous algae and macroalgae, like *Caulerpa*. He will then lead the female into the hole and she will lay from 20 to 100 small eggs, about 1 mm in diameter, on the nest material. The eggs have small threads that enable them to adhere to each other and form a sheet that covers an area of 2 to 25 cm² (0.2 to 4 in.²). In the aquarium, they are reported to hatch in 5 to 7 days, usually after dusk, while in the wild they hatch in 10 to 11 days (the rate of embryonic development is probably temperature-dependent). At hatching, the larvae range from 2.86 to 3.78 mm in length. The male will guard and tend the eggs until they hatch, and the pair will continue to spawn every day, or every other day, for a month or longer. Parental care is very important to egg development. If the male is removed (even in captivity where no egg predators are present), egg mortality is very high. The fry are phototropic: to attract them to a specific portion of the aquarium's surface, all you need to do is to place a light where you want them to ag-

gregate. The fry will eat rotifers and newly hatched brine shrimp and grow quickly. Such spawning events are not rare in home aquariums.

Aquarium Size: 20 gal. **Temperature:** 23 to 27°C (73 to 81°F).
Aquarium Suitability Index: 5.
Remarks: The Royal Gramma is one of the most ubiquitous fishes in the marine aquarium hobby. This fish is two-tone, like the Royal Dottyback (*Pseudochromis paccagnellae*), with magenta or purple on the anterior part of the body and yellow or gold on the posterior section. There is a distinct difference in coloration between the more northern and southern Royal Gramma populations, although they are considered to be the same species. In individuals from Bermuda, the Bahamas, and the northern Caribbean (e.g., Cayman Islands) the magenta coloration only extends back as far as the middle of the pectoral fins, while in the more southern color form, this magenta may diffuse back past the anal fin origin. Individuals throughout the range have a black spot on the anterior portion of the dorsal fin and a diagonal line that bisects the eye. This species also has long, elegant pelvic fins. The Brazilian Gramma (*Gramma brasiliensis*) is a distinct species known only from Brazil (see above listing).

Gramma melacara Böhlke & Randall, 1963
Common Names: Blackcap Basslet, Blackcap Gramma.
Maximum Length: 10 cm (3.9 in.).
Distribution: Bahamas, Jamaica, and Grand Cayman to Central America and the southern Caribbean.

Gramma melacara, Blackcap Basslet: a beauty that thrives in deeper water.

Lipogramma klayi, Bicolor Basslet: lovely little fish needs peaceful tankmates.

Biology: The Blackcap Basslet can be encountered in water as shallow as 12 m (39 ft.), but reaches its apex of abundance in much deeper water. For example, on the fore reef of the Bahamas, the Blackcap Basslet is the most abundant species of fish at depths of 87 and 107 m (285 and 351 ft.), and in Jamaica it is the dominant species (i.e., in number) at a depth range of 48 to 97 m (157 and 318 ft.). The topography of this deep-reef zone consists of overhangs, caves, and ledges, with a few species of sponge and antipatharian coral. But the key characteristic of Blackcap habitat is vertical relief (e.g., walls), so these fish can be found at shallower depths (e.g., 12 m [39 ft.]) in areas where this type of habitat occurs nearer the surface.

Captive Care: *Gramma melacara* (Blackcap) is similar in overall disposition to *Gramma loreto* (Royal); however, I have found that large male *G. melacara* can become quite aggressive once they have become established members of the aquarium community. They are especially fervent about defending their favorite hole or interstice, chasing away any fishes that venture too near. The Blackcap may be slightly shyer than the Royal Gramma initially, and must be kept with less belligerent tankmates if it is to acclimate to its new home. Because they tend to inhabit deeper reef areas, with light levels usually less than 7000 lux, less intense lighting also helps them to adjust more readily.

Like *G. loreto*, they can be kept in groups, but I would recommend a slightly larger aquarium if you want to duplicate their

natural social unit. I would suggest nothing less than a standard 100-gallon (surface area of 6,452 cm^2 [1,000 in.^{2}] or more), with plenty of hiding places. Add one medium-sized Blackcap and two smaller individuals simultaneously, or add the smaller specimens first. If one individual begins to bully the others constantly, they must be separated or mortalities may result. As in the habitat for a Royal Gramma, the rock or coral wall should be as steep as possible.

The Blackcap Basslet can be bred in aquarium confines, but it is more difficult to induce spawning in this species than it is in *G. loreto*. Like the latter species, a pair of these basslets builds a nest in a hole in the reef. Potential nesting material for captive basslets includes algae, yarn, bits of gorgonians, or sponge. The male leads the female into the nest and she lays her eggs. Egg deposition occurs daily, and the eggs hatch in approximately 7 days. From 1 to 250 eggs hatch per day, and the newly hatched young are slightly larger than those of the Royal Gramma, measuring 3 mm. Like the Royal Gramma, the larvae will take rotifers as a first food.

Aquarium Size: 20 gal. **Temperature:** 21 to 27°C (70 to 81°F).
Aquarium Suitability Index: 4.

Genus *Lipogramma* (Deep-water Basslets)

This genus is comprised of 6 species, all but one of which are residents of deep-water reef habitat. The deep-water basslets differ morphologically in having a lateral line that stops halfway down the length of the body, rather than extending all the way to the tail as it does in the other grammas. Most of these basslets are also much more secretive than other family members, hiding in reef holes and crevices. Four of these species are rarely if ever encountered in the aquarium trade. These are the Spotfin Basslet (*Lipogramma anabantoides*), the Banded Basslet (*L. evides*), the Royal Basslet (*L. regia*), and the Rosy Basslet (*L. rosea*). Two of the *Lipogramma* species (listed below) are available in the aquarium trade on rare occasions—and usually at steep prices.

Lipogramma klayi Randall, 1963
Common Names: Bicolor Basslet, Heliotrope Basslet.
Maximum Length: 4 cm (1.6 in.).
Distribution: Bahamas, Puerto Rico, Jamaica, and Central America to Venezuela.
Biology: The Bicolor Basslet is a resident of fore-reef slopes and dropoffs, in areas of mixed sand, rock, and rubble. In some areas, it is most common on steeply sloping rock shelves that are covered with sediment. It occurs at depths greater than 45 m (148 ft.) and is most abundant in water over 60 to 75 m (197 to 246

ft.) deep, depending on the location. For example, in Puerto Rico, *L. klayi* is reported to be a "common element" of the fish community below 60 m (197 ft.), while off Jamaica it is most common at depths from 90 to 125 m (295 to 410 ft.). It is often found in the same habitat as the Royal Basslet (*L. regia*), although the latter is much more cryptic. The Bicolor Basslet hovers less than 30 cm (11.7 in.) above the bottom, over a crevice or a hole in the sand in which it will quickly retreat if threatened.

The Royal Gramma (*Gramma loreto*) is sometimes found in the same habitat as this species, but is usually observed hanging upside down under hard substrate, rather than hovering right side up in the water column like the Bicolor Basslet.

Captive Care: The Bicolor Basslet will usually adjust to aquarium life if it withstands the shipping process. According to Forrest Young, fish collector and biologist, about 50% of the Bicolor Basslets sent out do not survive shipping. This species is best housed on its own. Its small size and peaceful disposition make it especially vulnerable to being bullied. For example, I have had Rusty Gobies (*Priolepis hipoliti*) of similar body size pick on it in smaller aquariums. It can be successfully kept with very docile tankmates in larger tanks. Its home should be dimly lit and outfitted with numerous caves and crevices. Under these conditions, this species will become quite bold after a week or so of acclimation.

These fish will behave aggressively toward one another if placed together in a small aquarium. To house more than one per tank, give them lots of room, provide them with plenty of hiding places, and keep only one large individual. They will eat finely chopped shrimp, brine shrimp, mysid shrimp, and frozen prepared foods.

Aquarium Size: 20 gal. **Temperature:** 22 to 27°C (72 to 81°F).
Aquarium Suitability Index: 3.

Lipogramma trilineata Randall, 1963

Common Name: Threeline Basslet.
Maximum Length: 3.5 cm (1.4 in.).
Distribution: Southeast Florida and the Bahamas, west to Mexico, and south to Curacao.
Biology: The Threeline Basslet is found on fore-reef slopes, at depths from 7.5 to 60 m (25 to 197 ft.), but is most common deeper than 21 m (69 ft.). This species occurs beneath rocky and coral ledges and often shares these haunts with reef basslets (*Liopropoma* spp.). A captive Threeline Basslet was reported to construct a shallow mound out of algae with a tunnel running through it. The basslet would hide in the tunnel and vigorously defend it from potential invaders.

Lipogramma trilineata, Threeline Basslet: secretive and uncommonly seen.

Captive Care: This secretive basslet ships very poorly. Even those specimens transported in large shipping bags, in larger volumes of water, rarely survive the long trip from the collector to an aquarium store. However, those individuals that do not succumb to the various stresses associated with shipping will do well in an aquarium that contains plenty of hiding places and peaceful tankmates or no other fishes at all.

Although this species occurs in relatively shallow water, it is more likely to spend time in the open if the tank is dimly lit. The Threeline Basslet can be kept in a reef tank, but if the tank is large and full of live rock, it may be seen very rarely or not at all. For this reason I recommend keeping this species in a smaller tank, with several suitable hiding places, so that it can be observed more frequently.

Aquarium Size: 20 gal. **Temperature:** 22 to 27°C (72 to 81°F).
Aquarium Suitability Index: 2.

References

Addison (1994), Asoh & Shapiro (1997), Asoh & Yoshikawa (1996), Böhlke & Randall (1963), Colin (1974, 1976), Delbeek (1991), Freeman & Alevizon (1983), Moe (1992), Randall (1963b, 1968), Robins & Colin (1979), Starck & Colin (1978), Thresher (1980, 1984), F. Young (personal communication).

Calloplesiops altivelis, Comet: this elegant species is part of a family that tends to be cryptic in the wild but hardy and endearing to knowledgeable aquarists.

A CORAL REEF IS A CALCAREOUS MAZE, RIDDLED WITH HOLES, interstices and caverns. This subterranean world is home to countless invertebrates and fishes, but many come out from hiding only at night to feed, while others rarely emerge. Because many of the fishes that live in this labyrinth are seldom seen by divers and snorkelers, most would still be unknown to science if it were not for special collecting techniques used by ichthyologists to flush them out. One group whose members make up part of this cryptic fauna is the Family Plesiopidae, commonly referred to as longfins, devilfishes, prettyfins, or roundheads.

Classification and Biology
The Family Plesiopidae is comprised of about 30 species and 11 genera that inhabit tropical and warm temperate waters in the Indo-Pacific. All are characterized by a disjunct lateral line, a short snout, 9 to 15 dorsal fin spines, three anal fin spines and pelvic fins with one to four rays. Members of this family also have unusual eggs, which have adhesive filaments and are deposited on the substrate.

The plesiopids associate with coral or rocky reefs and are solitary, cryptic fishes that hide in caves, crevices, and beneath overhangs. Several species, however, form aggregations during the day. The majority of plesiopids occur in water less than 30 m (98 ft.) deep. Unfortunately for the aquarist, some of the most spectacular members of the family prefer the cooler, temperate waters of New South Wales, Victoria, Southern and Western Australia and are rarely collected for North American hobbyists. But there are at least a half dozen coral-reef-dwelling members of the family that do show up in fish stores on occasion. One of these, the Comet or Marine Betta (*Calloplesiops altivelis*), is extremely popular with hobbyists who maintain reef and fish-only aquariums. All of the members of this family are extremely durable aquarium fish. They do not present any feeding problems and are very resistant to disease. They vary in their aggressiveness, with the assessors (*Assessor* spp.) being the least aggressive and the longfins (*Plesiops* spp.) potentially posing the greatest risk to other tankmates.

Assessor flavissimus, Yellow Assessor: wonderful home aquarium fish.

LONGFIN SPECIES

Genus *Assessor* (Assessors)

This lovely group of fishes is a welcome addition to the reef aquarium or more sedate fish-only tank. The fully scaled head and upper jaw and the forked tail separate the assessors from the other plesiopids.

Assessor flavissimus Whitley, 1935

Common Names: Yellow Assessor, Yellow Devilfish.
Maximum Length: 5.5 cm (2.1 in.)
Distribution: Northern Great Barrier Reef to southern Papua New Guinea and eastern Irian Jaya.
Biology: The Yellow Assessor occurs at depths from 2 to 25 m (6.6 to 82 ft.) in lagoons, reef faces, and fore-reef slopes. It is often found near the top of the surge zone. The Yellow Assessor usually lives in caves, under overhangs, or in large crevices, where it is usually found swimming upside down. In contrast to its close relative, *Assessor macneilli*, this assessor is not always seen in social assemblages, but may be observed singly, in pairs, or in small groups. It feeds on zooplankton (mainly minute crustaceans). This species lays its eggs in a nest in the coral.

Assessor flavissimus, Yellow Assessor: color variant.

Captive Care: The Yellow Assessor is a great fish for the home aquarium. It can be kept on its own, in pairs, or in trios. If you do keep more than one, be sure the tank is large enough and that there are several suitable hideouts in case squabbles occur between individuals. This species often tends to display more intraspecific aggression than the Blue Assessor. *Assessor flavissimus* is rarely aggressive toward other fish tankmates, with the possible exception of congeners. You must be careful not to include them in a tank with overly boisterous species, as they are likely to be the targets of aggression—especially if the display aquarium has a small footprint.

The Yellow Assessor is an ideal fish for the reef aquarium. It

Assessor flavissimus, Yellow Assessor: Papua New Guinea variant.

Assessor macneilli, Blue Assessor: usually found in groups of 3 to 100 fish.

Assessor macneilli, Blue Assessor: abberant color variant.

Assessor randalli, Randall's Assessor: rare species from Japan and Taiwan.

will not bother ornamental invertebrates. It will feel most at home if provided with an overhang or cave refuge.

Aquarium Size: 15 gal. **Temperature:** 22 to 28°C (72 to 82°F).

Aquarium Suitability Index: 5.

Remarks: It has been suggested that the population of *A. flavissimus* found around Papua New Guinea and Irian Jaya may actually represent a distinct species.

Assessor macneilli Allen & Kuiter, 1976

Common Names: Blue Assessor, Blue Devilfish.

Maximum Length: 6 cm (2.3 in.).

Distribution: Great Barrier Reef and New Caledonia.

Biology: The Blue Assessor occurs at a depth range of 2 to 20 m (6.6 to 66 ft.) in lagoons, on reef faces, and fore-reef slopes. It is usually found in groups, numbering from 3 to over 100. This fish is almost always seen swimming upside down, with its ventral surface facing a cave or an overhang ceiling. You can enjoy this behavioral feature in your aquarium by re-creating its natural microhabitat—a large cave or rocky overhang.

This fish is a zooplankton feeder that preys on copepods, ostracods, and amphipods. This assessor is a mouthbrooder; the male holds the egg mass in his mouth for about two weeks until they hatch, at which time the fry enter the plankton. Male Blue Assessors, which are larger on average than the females, apparently outnumber females in aggregations and tend several broods over the duration of the mating period. The males cease feeding during the egg-tending phase and are more quick to seek shelter than nonbrooding individuals.

Captive Care: The Blue Assessor is a wonderful aquarium fish. They can be kept singly, in pairs, or as groups. If you establish a group, ensure that the tank is large enough and contains several suitable hideouts in case squabbles occur between individuals. To achieve the greatest success with an assemblage of these fish, add three smaller individuals and one larger specimen to a tank of 100 gallons or more. All individuals should be added to the tank simultaneously. Larger individuals (which are probably males) have a greater tendency to fight with one another, so it is best to keep only one of these per tank. This species tends to display less intraspecific aggression than *A. flavissimus.* It is of no threat to unrelated fish tankmates, but may pick on smaller congeners. For example, when housed together in a smaller tank , one of my larger *A. macneilli* nipped at an *A. flavissimus.* Do not keep it with belligerent tankmates like larger dottybacks, many of the damselfishes, hawkfishes in the genus *Cirrhitichthys* and *Paracirrhites,* banana wrasses (*Thalassoma* spp.), and larger lined wrasses (*Paracheilinus* spp.). Smaller dottybacks, hawkfishes, and pygmy angelfishes (*Centropyge* spp.) might also harass this fish in smaller aquariums. Of course, their smaller size makes them more vulnerable to a larger range of piscivorous fishes as well. The Blue Assessor is an ideal candidate for reef tanks and aquariums that contain small fishes and crustaceans. If you keep them in a shallow-water reef aquarium, it is vital that the reef be constructed so that there are areas of subdued light where they can shelter during the daylight hours. Large crevices and caves are ideal. In aquariums with reduced lighting, like a deep-water reef tank, they are more likely to spend time in the open. Solitary specimens can be housed in tanks as small as 15 gallons, but if you're interested in keeping a group of these fish, you will need a larger aquarium.

Because of their small size and reproductive mode, they are great candidates for captive breeding. The Blue Assessor has been spawned in the home aquarium. One male was reported to incubate eggs every 14 to 32 days, with the eggs hatching in 14 to 16 days. The fry are small at hatching (about 2 mm) and will require live food, such as ciliates or rotifers.

Aquarium Size: 15 gal. **Temperature:** 22 to 28°C (72 to 82°F).

Aquarium Suitability Index: 5.

Remarks: I once had an unusual-looking assessor that was similar in form to the Blue Assessor, but had yellowish-white on the body and head. It was purchased as a cross between a Blue and a Yellow Assessor, but after time in the tank it became blue overall, like a typical *A. macneilli*.

Randall's Assessor (*Assessor randalli***) Allen & Kuiter, 1976,** is a similar species. It is only known from southern Japan and Taiwan and does not show up in the aquarium trade because limited collecting occurs in these regions. It is very similar in appearance to the Blue Assessor, differing in the number of gill rakers (*randalli* has 23 to 27, while *macneilli* has 33 to 36) and the types of scales present on the cheeks and in the region above the lateral line (in *randalli* the scales in this area are ctenoid, while in *macneilli* they are cycloid).

Genus *Belonepterygion* (Spiny Basslets)

Until recently, this genus was placed in the Family Acanthoclinidae along with three other genera. But after extensive study, Mooi (1993) lowered this family to the subfamily status within the Plesiopidae. Most of the members of the Subfamily Acanthoclininae are residents of the temperate waters around New Zealand. But there are four species, representing two different genera, known to occur on coral reefs. I have encountered one of these, the Banded Spiny Basslet (*Belonepterygion fasciolatum*), in aquarium stores. All of the members of this subfamily are very reclusive and are seldom seen by divers. They are a rare commodity in the marine fish trade.

Belonepterygion fasciolatum, Banded Spiny Basslet: reclusive and rare.

The Banded Spiny Basslet is brown with narrow, dark bars on its body, orange on the lower part of the head and a white stripe from the eye to the pectoral fin. In some specimens, the dorsal and anal fin are bright red or orange. This species is known from Australia to southern Japan and attains a maximum length of 5 cm (2 in.). It is an extremely cryptic species that is not suitable for most aquariums because of its secretive nature. For example, I placed two Banded Spiny Basslets in different aquariums, both of which were medium-sized and contained numerous pieces of live rock. I never saw one of them again, while I located the other one by accident when I removed a piece of live rock in which it was hiding. It was in good condition and had apparently been feeding on small creatures associated with the live rock. If you do find one of these attractive little fish and decide to purchase it, you should place it in a smaller (e.g., 10 gallon) species tank (i.e., a tank devoted only to this fish) with several smaller pieces of live rock for it to hide among. Place a red incandescent bulb or low wattage "moon light" over the tank at night, when all the other lights are off, and you may be able to observe it slinking around the tank decor. You may even see it dart out to snatch a passing morsel at feeding time.

Genus *Calloplesiops* (Comet)

The Comet (*Calloplesiops altivelis*) is currently the only species recognized in this genus. This is a handsome, unmistakable fish. It is brown overall, with white spots on the head, body, and fins. There is also an ocellus (false eyespot) on the posterior portion of the dorsal fin. It tends to be secretive and is not common in most areas. For this reason, it is rarely observed by divers. Fortunately, it tends to frequent the same sites, and once a specimen is spotted, it can usually be seen in the same area for months or years.

Calloplesiops altivelis, Comet: a true survivor, much beloved by aquarists.

Calloplesiops altivelis, Comet: small juvenile specimen displays larger spots.

Calloplesiops argus, Finespotted Comet: author considers it a valid species.

"You get what you pay for," certainly applies to captive *C. altivelis*. This is not an inexpensive aquarium fish, but one with visual appeal, interesting behavior, and unrivaled hardiness. The Comet is a worthy acquisition for the beginning and advanced hobbyist alike.

Calloplesiops altivelis (Steindachner, 1903)

Common Names: Comet, Marine Betta, Sea Betta.
Maximum Length: 20 cm (7.8 in.).
Distribution: Red Sea, east to the Line Islands, north to southern Japan, and south to the Great Barrier Reef and Tonga.
Biology: The Comet occurs on lagoon patch reefs and pinnacles, on the reef face, and fore-reef slopes at depths from 3 to 45 m (9.8 to 148 ft.). In its natural habitat, the Comet is an elusive fish that spends most of the daylight hours in caves and crevices. It occurs singly, in pairs, or in small aggregations. For example, Kuiter and Debelius (1984) report finding three individuals in an area of 1 m² (9 ft.²). At night, they move from cover to stalk shrimps, crabs, and small fishes. Sometimes, it shares caves and crevices with shrimps (e.g., *Stenopus hispidus*), the Spotfin Lionfish (*Pterois antennata*), and pygmy angelfishes.

This fish exhibits a series of unique motor patterns when it stalks its prey. When hunting benthic prey, it tips its body forward, erects its huge pelvic fins, and curls its tail to one side. It then propels itself toward its potential victim by undulating the pectoral fins. This hunting behavior appears awkward and conspicuous to the human observer, but it may be that this exaggerated approach distracts the Comet's victim, and the extended pelvics and laterally directed tail form a barrier to impede the prey's escape (similar in function to the lionfish's enlarged pectoral fins). Whatever the function, the Comet often succeeds in closing the distance between itself and its prey, and when within striking range it lunges forward to ingest the food item.

Captive Care: The Comet is incredibly hardy. I have had several specimens survive otherwise total tank wipe-outs caused by parasitic infections, and have yet to see a specimen with a severe case of saltwater ich (*Cryptocaryon irritans*), even in aquariums where every other fish was covered with cysts. During attempts to extract several of these fish from aquariums, I have watched them tear their fins up and scrape their scales off in order to wedge themselves between pieces of live rock. These wounds healed quickly without any signs of bacterial infection. On rare occasions, a Comet may suffer from lateral line and fin erosion, but this can typically be prevented or possibly even treated by feeding a varied diet and soaking the fish's food in a fatty acid supplement, such as Selco.

Comet-keeping is not always without drawbacks. When initially introduced into an aquarium, these fish are very shy (especially in brightly-lit tanks). Your new Comet may hide for a week or more before you even catch a fleeting glimpse of it. Their timid nature can present a problem when feeding time rolls around, especially when included in a tank with more aggressive tankmates, and without live rock. When first acquired, they will usually eat only live food, so try adding small feeder fish (preferably a species that can live in saltwater like mollies or guppies) or live brine shrimp. If this does not elicit a feeding response, try dimming the lights. This fish will often spend more time in the open in tanks with dim lighting, or when light levels are reduced. - Acquaint yourself with your Comet's preferred hideouts and present the food near these areas. Although these fish may only accept live food at first, it is usually not difficult to wean them onto frozen preparations, such as frozen mysid shrimp and chopped seafoods, once they are fully acclimated. One way to dupe your Comet into accepting these substitutes is to place the food in the current produced by a water pump. With time and conditioning, your Comet will spend more time in view. Some specimens will beg for food when you approach the aquarium. But do not expect your Comet to constantly swim about at the front of the aquarium—this is not the nature of this elegant fish.

Adults of this species may be housed in tanks as small as 30 gallons, although an aquarium of 55 gallons or larger would be preferable. *Calloplesiops altivelis* is a good candidate for the reef aquarium. However, beware—your Comet may thin out your crustacean community. Although Comets may ignore resident crustaceans, newly introduced shrimp often become the targets of their hunting efforts. For instance, I once watched as a large *C. altivelis* snapped up three newly acquired Peppermint Shrimp (*Lysmata wurdemanni*). Because a newly released shrimp is most vulnerable to attack when it is drifting in open water, the best way to prevent it from being eaten is to transport the shrimp to the security of the reef structure with your hand or a net.

Usually Comets are of little danger to established residents, but small fishes may be at some risk when introduced to a resident Comet. I had a large individual that persistently stalked a new Bluelined Dottyback (*Pseudochromis cyanotaenia*) and small

Gymnothorax meleagris, Whitemouth Moray: typical threatening appearance with head exposed and body concealed in the reef.

Calloplesiops argus, Finespotted Comet: broad tail fin and ocellus (eyespot) looks similar to the head and eye of the aggressive moray.

A Moray Mimic

Batesian Mimicry is defined as a relationship in which a harmless animal resembles another with dangerous characteristics. It serves as a defensive strategy. By appearing to be something threatening, the mimic is often ignored by experienced predators.

There appears to be a mimetic relationship between the comets (*Calloplesiops* spp.) and the Whitemouth Moray (*Gymnothorax meleagris*). When threatened, a comet will raise all of its median fins and swim head-first into a hole or crevice. But rather than disappearing completely, it will usually stop in the entrance of its sanctuary and leave the posterior part of its body exposed. With its large ocelli and white-spotted body, the comet's back end is similar in appearance to the head of *G. meleagris*.

By mimicking this aggressive moray, comets may intimidate or scare off would-be predators. Comets regularly perform this display in the aquarium. Sometimes they will lower one pelvic fin, spread the dorsal and anal fins, and swim backward toward the observer.

A similar type of mimicry exists in certain butterflies. Some of these vulnerable insects have ocelli on their wings that when viewed from the right vantage point look like the eyes of an owl.

The comet's eyespots might also serve another protective function. Because many predators go for the head in order to incapacitate their prey, the eyespots on the posterior part of the comet's body may serve to deflect such attacks to the less vulnerable tail region.

Trachinops caudimaculatus (Southern Hulafish)

Trachinops noarlungae (Yellowheaded Hulafish)

Hulafish—Piscine Oddities from Down Under

The genus *Trachinops* contains four species that are distributed around the coast of southern Australia. These fish are of slender build, have a pointed tail fin, and move by undulating their bodies from side to side. This locomotory style has given rise to their common name, hulafish. They are small fishes, the largest species attaining a maximum length of around 10 cm (3.9 in.), that live in aggregations, beneath overhangs, in crevices, or in mid-water.

The species that make up this genus are: the Bluelined Hulafish (*Trachinops brauni*), Southern Hulafish (*T. caudimaculatus*), Yellowheaded Hulafish (*T. noarlungae*), and Eastern Hulafish (*T. taeniatus*). The Bluelined (black with bright blue lines) and Eastern Hulafish are the two most colorful members of the genus and are great candidates for the temperate-water aquarium.

Unfortunately, these fishes are not readily available in North America. But if you like to catch your own fish, the Eastern Hulafish is particularly common around southern New South Wales in water 30 to 70 m (98 to 230 ft.) deep, while its Bluelined relative is abundant on the reefs of southwest Australia. According to Australian aquarists, the *Trachinops* spp. are hardy aquarium fish that should be kept in small aggregations and at a water temperature of less than 21°C (70°F).

Wheeler's Shrimp Goby (*Amblyeleotris wheeleri*). Fortunately, it never succeeded in capturing either of these diminutive tankmates. Aggression between Comets is not common, and they are not combative toward heterospecific tankmates. (It is a good idea to have a larger aquarium with plenty of hiding places if you plan on keeping two Comets together.) In contrast, the passive *C. altivelis* may be harassed and physically damaged by larger, more aggressive fishes, like large dottybacks, certain hawkfishes, and triggerfishes. It may also have some difficulty competing for food with aggressive species in an aquarium that lacks live rock.

It is unnecessary to feed Comets frequently in a thriving, well-established reef aquarium; they apparently feed on organisms, like worms and small crustaceans, on live rock. I once had a Comet that I thought had died survive while hiding in a tank with only live rock, unfed for at least 4 months. This fish is still alive (at the Henry Doorly Zoo, Omaha, Nebraska) after being in captivity for more than eight years.

Aquarium Size: 55 gal. **Temperature:** 22 to 27°C (72 to 81°F).
Aquarium Suitability Index: 5.

Remarks: Although it was once thought that there were two distinct species in this genus, only *C. altivelis* is recognized as valid by many authors. I believe that there is a second species, known scientifically as the **Finespotted Comet** (*Calloplesiops argus*) **Fowler & Bean, 1930.** It can be distinguished from its congener by the presence of more numerous, smaller spots on the body, lines rather than spots on the median fins, and a larger white patch at the end of the tail. The pelvic fins are also longer (when folded down, they extend back to about the middle of the anal fin). It has been suggested that *C. altivelis* changes to the *C. argus* form as it grows larger. But I have seen *C. argus* as small as 7 cm (2.7 in.) in total length and have yet to see a *C. altivelis* change to the *C. argus* form in the aquarium. The Finespotted Comet is relatively rarely seen in the aquarium trade and in nature. It has been reported from Indonesia and the Philippines and acquires a total length of about 18 cm (7 in.). Even more than *C. altivelis*, it tends to engage in the exaggerated swimming behavior during hunting as described in the Biology section for species *C. altivelis* (page 154).

Comet Reproduction

The Comet is a beautiful but reclusive fish that is rarely seen by scuba divers. As a result, very little is known about its biology. Most of the information available about the Comet comes from aquarium observations. On a recent trip to Lembeh Strait, northern Sulawesi, I was fortunate enough to witness some Comet reproductive behavior (thanks to the keen observation skills of John Hoover). In a large crack in a stone wall there was a Comet with a mass of eggs attached to the top of a small cave within the larger crevice. The cave was located in about 11 m (36 ft.) of water. The egg mass appeared to be about 5 cm (2 in.) long and about one-third as wide. A single adult Comet was tending the eggs. Even when we approached the fish to take its photograph, it refused to retreat—which is rare for this normally shy fish. When a human came near, the fish would position its body perpendicular to the observer and cover the eggs with its dorsal fin. It would also engage in the common "tail-first" display, where it is thought to be mimicking the head of a Whitemouth Moray (*Gymnothorax meleagris*). At one time, the Comet appeared so agitated by our presence that it attacked and bit a File Shell (*Lima* sp.) that shared its cave. The Comet also appeared to fan the eggs with its dorsal fin.

***Calloplesiops altivelis,* Comet: with eggs (above, on cave top).**

Two days later we returned to the same location. The Comet was there, but the eggs were gone. Six days after that visit, we went to the site again and the Comet was guarding another batch of eggs. Author and photographer Ned DeLoach visited the same Comet soon after we left Lembeh. He told me that the eggs were present for at least five days.

All that is reported on Comet reproduction in the literature is the result of aquarium spawnings. For the most part, the observations detailed in aquarium studies match what we observed in the wild. Actual courtship behavior has not been described, because it occurs in the caves and crevices in which the adult Comets hide. Males are reported to be more secretive than the females, which are often found hanging near the entrance of their nesting site. It is not uncommon for one of the individuals, apparently the female, to have torn fins as a result of mating activity.

A captive female will lay a golden brown egg mass on the cave or crevice wall that is about 2.5 cm (1 in.) long and 0.5 mm (0.2 in.) in thickness. This egg mass is comprised of 300 to 500 eggs that measure about 1 mm in diameter. The eggs are attached together and to the substrate by sticky threads. The male Comet ceases to feed and guards the eggs, spreading its fins and shielding them with its body. The male will even chase its partner away from the nesting site if it gets too close. Wassink (1990) reports a latency period of 10 days or longer between spawnings, while Baez (1998) reports they are not predictable, cyclic spawners like other fish species that they raise. Our limited observations of the wild Comet suggest that spawning may occur slightly more frequently than every 10 days (e.g., after an eight-day period of rest). We have dived at the site many times over a five-year period and have only seen the Comet with eggs during this one period of time (October and November, 2000).

Captive studies have shown that at a water temperature of 26°C (79°F), the eggs hatch in about five or six days. (The incubation period seems to correspond with the limited data we have from the field.) Most of the eggs hatch at dusk or after dark, although they will also hatch during the day. The fry are about 3 to 4 mm (0.12 to 0.16 in.) long when they emerge. They are remarkably well developed and feed immediately. They double in length in the first 14 days, and on the 16th day the dark-colored youngsters develop a white spot on each side of the body due to a loss of pigmentation in this area. The pigment cells continue to disappear until the body is white overall. At the same time, the free-swimming fry begin to lead a more reclusive lifestyle, hiding in reef crevices. As night falls, the fry come out of hiding to feed. At two months of age, the spots begin to appear on the head, but the sides remain white until they are about seven months old.

The Comet is a great candidate for captive-breeding programs. In fact, at least one ornamental marine fish hatchery (Sea Quest Hatcheries, Puerto Rico) has sold captive-raised stock. Of course, getting a pair is always easier if you can tell the sexes apart. In the case of the Comets, differentiating the fish is apparently difficult to do. One reference suggested that the only possible difference between the sexes appears to be the size of the spots—those on males are reported to be smaller than those on females. But this seems to be more a function of the size than the sex. (It may be that the males tend to be larger than the females and therefore they usually have smaller spots.)

Paraplesiops meleagris (Western Blue Devilfish): one a group of hardy, magnificent fishes seldom collected for export from their native Australia.

Genus *Paraplesiops* spp. (Devilfishes)

The five members of this genus are only found on coral and rocky reefs off the Australian coast. They are secretive, cave-dwelling species, some of which are spectacularly colored. Unfortunately, the "chromatically challenged" **Bluetip Devilfish (*Paraplesiops poweri*) Ogilby, 1908** is the only genus member that makes it into the North American aquarium trade, and then only on rare occasions. This species is brown overall, with narrow dark bars on its side, blue spots on its face, a blue spot on each operculum and blue trim on the edge of the dorsal fin. It ranges from northern New South Wales to the southern Great Barrier Reef. It is similar in its husbandry to the *Plesiops* spp. (see below), except that it attains a larger size (i.e., 18 cm [7 in.]), which makes it a threat to a greater range of tankmates. This species should be kept at water temperatures from 18 to 24°C (64 to 75°F), but is otherwise a very durable aquarium fish. I once kept an individual that had its abdomen ripped open and a pelvic fin removed by a Lined Dottyback (*Labracinus lineatus*). Its wounds healed and it thrived in its captive home.

The more colorful members of the genus occur on warm, temperate, rocky reefs. These include **Alison's Blue Devilfish (*Paraplesiops alisonae*) Hoese and Kuiter, 1984**, the **Eastern Blue Devilfish (*Paraplesiops bleekeri*) (Günther, 1861)** and the **Western Blue Devilfish (*Paraplesiops meleagris*) (Peters, 1869)**. Alison's Devilfish is brownish-green to orangish-brown, with blue spots on the head and blue lines on the median fins. Adult Eastern Blue Devilfish are pale gray to black overall (most individuals are dark blue) with neon blue spots on the body, while their eastern counterpart has a dark head with blue spots, light and dark bands on the body, and yellow pectoral fins and tail. These magnificent fish are kept by some local Australian aquarists and are said to be quite hardy, but the Eastern Blue Devilfish is protected by law and can only be collected if a permit is obtained.

Genus *Plesiops* spp. (Longfins)

This is the largest genus, containing 10 species (see Table 1. for a list of those species most likely to be encountered by hobbyists). Most members of this genus are small (less than 8 cm [3.1 in.]), occur in tropical waters, and inhabit coral reef habitats. The majority of longfins are found in relatively shallow water on the reef flat and upper fore reef and hide in reef crevices, between coral branches, and under rocks during the day. At night they cruise around the reef, hunting small fishes, polychaete worms, gastropods, shrimps, small crabs, amphipods, and copepods. They may also ambush prey items that venture past during the day. The *Plesiops* have long pelvic fins (thus the common name), which they rest upon while in repose on the reef surface.

Longfins that make it into aquarium stores can be kept in tanks as small as 15 gallons. However, they are more likely to cause behavioral problems in small quarters. Provide your longfin with numerous hiding places to ensure acclimation. They do particularly well in reef aquariums, because these tanks tend to have numerous hiding places. You will rarely see your longfin in the open, but if you patiently watch the tank, you will occasionally see them perched in reef interstices. They will rest on their extended, elongate pelvic rays and move quickly from one crevice to another. They will occasionally erect the dorsal spines against a ledge in order to brace themselves. Their feeding behavior is quite spectacular. They will emerge from and return to their hiding place with amazing velocity to capture food as it floats past. Although they do most of their hunting at night, they will feed during the daytime as they become fully acclimated to aquarium life.

The longfins can be aggressive, especially toward fishes that invade their favorite hiding places, are closely related, or are introduced into the aquarium after the longfins have become established. For example, I had a Redtipped Longfin (*Plesiops coeruleolineatus*) attack a yellow brotulid, a fairy wrasse, a similar-sized Dusky Dottyback (*Pseudochromis fuscus*) and dominate an Orchid Dottyback (*P. fridmani*), that were introduced to the aquarium well before the longfin. Longfins will also fight among themselves, so it is advisable to add only one member of the genus per aquarium, unless you can acquire a mated pair. I had one specimen that would charge the tank wall and bite at its reflection in the glass with such vigor there was an audible pop when the fish hit the side of the tank.

When longfins display at a rival, they lower the skin fold under the bottom jaw, erect their fins, undulate their body with the head up and tail down, and intensify in color. For example, in Redtipped Longfins, the color is usually a dull tan or gray with orange and blue on the median fins. When performing an agonistic display, the overall color changes to a more rust-orange. Longfins will also slap opponents with their tail fin. Larger specimens are a threat to ornamental shrimps, small snails, and possibly feather duster worms, but will not harm other invertebrates.

References

Baez (1998), Debelius & Baensch (1994), K. Gaines (personal communication), Hiatt & Stratsburg (1960), Hoese & Kuiter (1984), Kuiter (1992), Kuiter & Debelius (1994), Mooi (1995), Mooi & Randall (1991), Myers (1999), Randall et al. (1997), Thresher (1984), Wassink (1990).

Paraplesiops alisonae, Alison's Blue Devilfish: rare beauty from Down Under.

Paraplesiops bleekeri, Eastern Blue Devilfish: protected species.

Plesiops coeruleolineatus, Redtipped Longfin: aggressive, tail-slapping fish.

Some of the Longfin Species (*Plesiops* spp.).

Species	Identifying Characteristics	Size	Distribution	Habitat
Longfin (*P. cephalotaenia*)	Similar to *P. oxycephalus*, but no yellow marking on gill cover or tail; three black stripes on gill cover; pelvic fins dark in color; deep-bodied form with steep head profile.	6 cm (2.3 in.)	Southern Japan to New Guinea.	
Redtipped Longfin (*P. coeruleolineatus*)	Body brown to black with orangish-red dorsal fin spine tips; faint orange band on edge of caudal fin; blue lines on dorsal and anal fins.	8 cm (3.1 in.)	Red Sea to Samoa, north to Japan, south to Great Barrier Reef.	Outer-reef flats and slopes in less than 23 m. Feeds on crabs, hermits, shrimps, sm. fishes, gastropods. Prefers strong wave action; hides under live coral.
Bluegill Longfin (*P. corallicola*)	Small bluish or white spots on body; fins with blue ocelli on the gill covers; tail black, sometimes with light margin. Juveniles with more elongate body.	8 cm (3.1 in.)	Madagascar to Line Islands, north to Japan, south to Great Barrier Reef.	On reef flats, often in small tidepools, under coral boulders and small rocks. Feeds on crabs, hermit crabs, copepods, fishes (incl. damsels and cardinals).
Cheekveil Longfin (*P. genaricus*)	Lacks spots and lines; some specimens with dark spot on base of pectoral fin; 22-25 pectoral rays, some free of the membrane, forming a fringe; narrow band of cheek scales that do not reach maxilla.	9 cm (3.5 in.)	Great Barrier Reef.	In tide pools on reef flats, usually in water less than 5 m.
Slenderfin Longfin (*P. gracilis*)	Nine pale stripes on body; cheek and gill cover pale yellow, tail with pale central band; head slender and long; pelvic fins long and slender, tips extend past middle of anal fin.	8 cm (3.1 in.)	Palau to New Guinea and Western Australia.	Down to 16 m, but most in water less than 8 m.
New Caledonian Longfin (*P. insularis*)	No spots or lines; head wide and round; 21 to 24 pectoral rays; gill cover with scales in kidney-shaped patch that reaches maxilla.	11 cm (4.3 in.)	New Caledonia and Lord Howe Island.	Common on outer reef in 2 to 25 m.
Whitespotted Longfin (*P. nigricans*)	Small white or bluish spots on body and fins; no ocelli on gill cover; caudal fin black.	14 cm (5.5 in.)	Red Sea.	Reef flat and fore-reef from 5 to 30m.
African Longfin (*P. multisquamatus*)	Small blue spots on body and fins; some have ocelli over gill cover; caudal fin black.	25 cm (9.8 in.)	South Africa.	
Yellowtailed Longfin (*P. oxycephalus*)	Most similar to *P. gracilis*; has spots on body, some individuals with six to eight bands on body; gill cover often yellow; tail with two crescent-shaped yellow bands; deep-bodied form with steep head profile.	6 cm (2.3 in.)	Southern Japan to New Hebrides.	Lives among corals in lagoons.

Opistognathus aurifrons, Yellowhead Jawfish (Bahama color phase): a fascinating sand-dwelling genus in which the males incubate egg masses in their mouths.

WHILE A CORAL REEF TEEMS WITH FISHES THAT THRIVE IN its protective complexity, the adjacent sandy bottoms and mud habitats are structurally impoverished by comparison. The animals that have adapted to this relatively stark environment often exhibit special anatomical features and/or behaviors that enable them to find food and sanctuary where obvious hiding places are few and far between.

One family of sand-dwelling fishes that beguiles divers and aquarists alike is the jawfishes (Family Opistognathidae). These comical-looking fishes are a delight to observe as they burrow in the substrate, emerging to put on displays for their conspecifics or for fishes that would dare to invade their territories. They also engage in a unique reproductive strategy, incubating over-

sized eggs in their mouths. As far as marine aquarists are concerned, all of the jawfishes are fascinating and unusual aquarium inhabitants that will provide an ongoing show of behaviors that range from amusing to astonishing. And all are relatively hardy if a few simple requirements are met.

Classification and Biology

The Family Opistognathidae is comprised of about 60 described species in three genera, with most members of the family belonging to the genus *Opistognathus.* (At this writing there are nearly 40 additional species that still await formal description and certainly more still undiscovered.) The jawfishes have elongate bodies, with large, blunt heads and big mouths, and they usu-

Opistognathus dendriticus, Dendritic Jawfish: typical jawfish repose, ensconced in the substrate and appearing to blend into the seafloor. Note shrimp on head.

ally have large, protruding eyes. The dorsal fin is long and continuous. Most members of the genus do not exceed 13 cm (5.1 in.). The behemoth of the family is the Giant Jawfish (*Opistognathus rhomaleus*), which attains a maximum length of 51 cm (20 in.). Many of the jawfishes occur over relatively small geographic ranges. For example, a handful are endemic to northern and western Australia. There are also species found only in the tropical Eastern Pacific (many of these occur from the Gulf of California to Panama). In the Western Pacific, there are a couple of species that have been found only in Indonesia. The only regions where jawfishes are not known to occur are the Eastern Atlantic and Central Pacific.

Most of the jawfishes display various earth-tone colors to facilitate their blending with the seafloor. Many sport blotches, spots, or speckles. A number of species possess ocelli, or false eyespots, on the anterior portion of the dorsal fin, which would be a visible warning sign to approaching predators. A few species are brightly colored, and the males of several species are known to exhibit showy pigmentation during the spawning period.

The jawfishes occur at depths of less than 0.3 m down to 375 m (1 to 1,230 ft.). Most are found on sand or sand/rubble flats and slopes near rocky and coral reefs. Many jawfishes occur in quiet, shallow back-reef habitats or on outer-reef faces and slopes. They tend to avoid areas of strong water turbulence, as these conditions will destroy their burrows. While many occur in relatively shallow water, some species are limited in distribution to deep habitats. Unfortunately, a few of the most colorful species inhabit deep water, where they are seldom collected. One of these is *Opistognathus leprocarus,* the Roughcheek Jawfish, which is found at depths in excess of 165 m (541 ft.). This species is bright yellow overall, with three broken, blue-lavender stripes on the body, and bright yellow blotches and blue-lavender bands on the dorsum. The caudal fin is mainly blue and the pelvic fins are white. Another deep-water species, the Megamouth Jawfish (*Opistognathus melachasme*), is mainly red and lavender. This species is found at a depth range of 146 to 275 m (479 to 902 ft.).

One of the most interesting jawfish behaviors is a lifelong dedication to burrowing. All the jawfishes studied thus far dig burrows in mud, sand, or sand/rubble bottoms, and all live in burrows that they create. They thrust their tails in the substrate and rapidly undulate them, creating an initial depression. Then they turn, take substrate in their mouths, and spit it out of the depression. They continue this process of tail-wagging and mouth-scooping until they have created a tunnel that they can retreat into if threatened. Some species use empty sea shells, rubble, and rocks to shore up the entrance of their burrows. In some cases, neighboring jawfishes may steal these bits and pieces from each other. Even the smaller jawfish species have been known to dig burrows as deep as 50 cm (20 in.). At night, some of the jawfishes pull a shell or piece of rubble over the entrance of their burrow to create a lid. There are jawfishes that have been observed to share their tunnels with other organisms. For example, the Variable Jawfish (*Opistognathus* sp.) and the Goldspecs Jawfish (*Opistognathus* sp.) will sometimes accept shrimps in the genus *Palaemonella* into their hiding places. There are also jawfishes that allow microdesmids (i.e., wormfishes) to enter and share their subterranean homes.

When it comes to feeding, jawfishes can be classified into two groups. Some are plankton-pickers that feed in the water column, others are macrocarnivores that feed heavily off or near the seafloor. The zooplankton-feeders often hover in the water column over their burrows and maintain a vertical orientation. From this position, they pick off individual plankters as they float past. Often groups of these zooplanktivores will hover in the water simultaneously. If they detect a threat, they will back into their burrows tailfirst or, if facing serious danger, they rapidly dart into the opening headfirst. The macrocarnivorous jawfishes ambush crustaceans and small fishes that move along the seafloor or that swim by their burrows. Most members of this later group ambush their prey during the daylight hours. But there is at least one species that is known to hunt motile invertebrates after dark. Many of the jawfishes have large eyes that are located on the top or on the front of their heads. Based on these characteristics, it would appear that the jawfishes have good binocular vision, which would facilitate prey detection and capture.

Social structure in jawfishes can vary between and, to some extent, within the different species. They do exhibit several general trends in social organization. Some individuals occur singly, keeping a considerable distance between conspecifics. Other species live in heterosexual pairs, building burrows in close proximity to one another. There are also species that live in colonies. In some cases, individuals will form heterosexual pairs within these larger groups. In other cases, pair-forming does not occur within the colonies. The social system of some species depends on the age of the individual(s) and the abundance of the species in a particular area.

A number of jawfishes are sexually dimorphic and a few are sexually dichromatic, with clear differences between the sexes. In the dimorphic species, the males are often larger. Males may also have larger mouths than females of similar size. This is an apparent adaptation to their mouthbrooding habits (i.e., the larger mouth increases gas exchange and the rate of larval development). In some species, the male has a long flange on the upper

Opistognathus aurifrons, Yellowhead Jawfish: spawning behavior among these fishes in Florida tends to be seen in the months from spring to late fall.

jaw bone (the maxilla). Several species exhibit color differences between the sexes (e.g., Yellow Jawfish [*Opistognathus gilberti*]). In one group of jawfishes (the *Opistognathus macrognathus* group) individuals can be sexed by the markings on the maxilla. Males of these species often sport one or two brown stripes on the inner maxilla surface, while females have a single stripe or lack these markings all together.

The spawning season occurs year-round in some species, while in other jawfishes (or at least in some regions) spawning occurs during the warmer months of the year (e.g., spring to late autumn in Florida). Some species exhibit lunar periodicity in spawning, with a peak in spawning activity on the day of the full moon, while others do not. Relatively little is known about the courtship and reproductive behavior of jawfishes. Some jawfishes do exhibit extraordinary courtship displays. In those that feed on zooplankton, males regularly engage in courtship displays above their burrows. For example, male Bluespotted Jawfish (*Opistognathus rosenblatti*) engage in "flashing," in which the fish hovers in the water for a few seconds and then dashes into its burrow, changing color as it does. The male may do this for hours or until he entices the female back to his burrow to spawn.

Male opistognathids orally incubate their eggs. After the eggs are laid by the female and fertilized, the male picks them up in his mouth. The eggs remain in the male's mouth during most of the incubation period (which can range from 5 to 9 days in the species studied to date). Food-consumption rates fall consider-

Opistognathus rosenblatti, Bluespotted Jawfish: classic,industrious jawfish behavior—excavating and spitting sand from a nest hole (Sea of Cortez, Baja Mexico).

ably during this time, but the males occasionally manage to eat. In the Yellowhead Jawfish (*Opistognathus aurifrons*), food consumption rates in males holding eggs can decrease by as much as 86%. When males do feed, they will deposit the eggs in the burrow, but only briefly. It has been suggested that males may require a recuperation period after brooding a clutch before they are able to spawn again, in order to restore energy reserves. Males aerate the eggs by spitting the egg mass out and then quickly sucking it back in. It has been documented that those species with a clutch size that is smaller relative to the size of the mouth have eggs that develop more rapidly than those with a clutch that completely fills the mouth. The mortality rate of clutches is apparently very low. If the eggs are not fertile or unhealthy, the male may eat them. When the eggs are ready to hatch, the male remains at the entrance of the burrow and spits the hatching larvae into the water column (this often occurs at dusk). The larvae swim up into the water column and enter the plankton. They develop quickly, and at least some species are known to settle out of the plankton in 15 to 28 days after hatching. The tiny jawfish immediately begin digging burrows after settling from the plankton. These refuges are usually short tubes (5 to 7.5 cm [2 to 3 in.]) that lack a terminal chamber.

The number of clutches brooded by the jawfishes studied to date is usually one to two, and rarely three to four, per month. In most species, the mouth of a brooding male will contain eggs that are all the same age, suggesting that males rarely take clutches from more than one female at a time. However, there are some species (and situations) where a male may brood the clutches of up to three different females simultaneously. While in some species females are "true" to a single male during the reproductive period (e.g., *O. aurifrons*), there are others that exhibit less mate fidelity. For example, in some situations, Banded Jawfish (*O. macrognathus*) females will alternate, spawning with one male and then another. This species typically exhibits a nonmonogamous mating system (members usually live in "clumps" of one or two males and two to four females). The Dusky Jawfish (*Opistognathus whitehurstii*) is reported to exhibit a promiscuous mating system.

Captive Care

Members of the jawfish family can make amusing, fascinating aquarium inhabitants. Most are relatively easy to keep, as long as their special requirements are understood and met. The more diminutive forms can be kept in tanks as small as 10 or 20 gallons. The larger species, which are rarer in the trade, will require more substantial accommodations (e.g., 75 gallons). All of the jawfishes do extremely well in reef aquariums as long as the husbandry conditions mentioned below are met.

One of the keys to successful jawfish husbandry is to select the right kind and right amount of bottom substrate. Because these fishes are industrious diggers, it is important to give them appropriate building supplies. In most species, this means a heterogeneous blend of coral sand, shells or bits of shells, and other natural bits of reef rubble. With this mix of materials they can create more stable burrows. It is also important that the layer of substrate be deep enough to allow them to create a useable burrow where they can feel secure. Of course the depth depends on the maximum length of the species or individual in question, but for most of the smaller aquarium species, 8 to 10 cm (3.1 or 3.9 in.) of substrate should suffice. A few flat pieces of live rock placed on the substrate may be appreciated. Jawfishes will often dig under such rocks, which can serve as a roof for their burrow chambers.

An aquarium that will contain jawfish ought to have plenty of open sandy bottom. If live rock or corals extend from the back of the tank to the front, it will give the jawfish very little room to burrow. Some public aquariums place jawfish colonies into tanks with a thick sand bed and no other decor, which can make for a fantastic display.

Fortunately, jawfishes are fairly disease-resistant. The leading cause of captive jawfish death is leaping out of aquariums. They seem to have an uncanny ability to find small holes in the aquarium cover from which to propel themselves. Additionally, they are notorious for engaging in this suicidal practice when the aquarium lights are turned off. This is especially true when the fish has recently been placed in the tank and has yet to find a suitable shelter. This is not surprising. Most jawfishes refuge in their burrows at night and may even seal the entrance. When we place them in a tank and turn off the lights before they have a chance to find a place to refuge, they are easily startled by sudden movements. Even snapping off the lights can initiate a jumping spree. Therefore it is best to let them find some shelter, perhaps under a piece of rock, or allow them to build a burrow before you turn the lights off. A small night light over the tank will also help prevent them from jumping.

Jawfishes will also leap when they are being harassed by aggressive tankmates. To prevent this from happening, the tank must have a cover. If you're worried about gas exchange, use fiberglass mesh, eggcrate, or your ingenuity to create a barrier to prevent jawfish jumping. One do-it-yourself approach is to build a frame of PVC pipe and then string it with monofilament line. The line is tied around opposite ends, spaced to create a monofilament grid or a sort of aquatic tennis racquet to bounce

Opistognathus sp.: Goldspecs Jawfish: mouthbrooding eggs. The male jawfish eates very little during the 5-to-9-day incubation period.

the jawfish back into bounds.

When first added to the tank. jawfishes often engage in something Thresher (1984) calls "gulping." This is where the fish swims along the surface of the water and appears to gulp air. (During this period jawfishes are very prone to jumping.) They will usually stop engaging in this behavior once they find a suitable place to begin digging a burrow. It they are harried by tankmates, they may continue this behavior and even remain in the corners of the tank. This must be remedied (i.e., remove the jawfish or the aggressors) or the fish will die.

It is important to keep jawfishes (at least the smaller varieties) with passive fish species. This is especially the case when keeping them in a smaller tank. Aquarium bad actors, such as dottybacks, some of the pygmy angelfishes, larger sand perches, triggerfishes, and others will pester jawfishes, causing them either to cower in the upper corners of the tank, to hide all the time and not feed, or to leap out of the aquarium. Eels, frogfishes, groupers, and snappers are jawfish predators that will sooner or later cause your jawfish to disappear.

At least some of the jawfishes do very well in colonies. These species will live in harmony, unless crowded to the point where there is not enough space for all. In such a case, the most subordinate (usually the smallest) individuals will end up hiding in the corners of the tank. Some species are very aggressive toward one another. For example, the Bluespotted Jawfish is a more aggressive species. Unless you can acquire a pair of these lovely fish, or you have a tank with a relatively vast surface area (say a standard 180-gallon), I would only keep one per tank. Jawfishes are rarely aggressive to fish tankmates, unless they attempt to enter their burrows. They will display at intruders and push them from their homes with their open mouths or spit sand at them. Some of the larger jawfishes will eat small fishes.

Jawfishes can be kept in reef aquariums that have sufficient open sand/rubble substrate for them to burrow in. They may, however, cover corals that are situated near the bottom of the aquarium when they dig their burrows. Be sure that stony corals kept near jawfish burrows are those that readily shed sediment. Do not place soft corals in an area where they can be buried. It is also possible that a larger jawfish could cause the reef structure to cave in as a result of their digging activities. Be sure rockwork is stable by setting up the bulk of the rockwork before you add sand to the aquarium. This will ensure that the jawfish cannot undermine the reef structure, causing it to collapse. It must be noted that some jawfish species may eat ornamental crustaceans and other motile invertebrates (e.g., worms, serpent stars) to the dismay—and education—of the aquarist.

Some jawfishes may regularly spawn in captivity. This is especially true for those species that form colonies in the wild (e.g., *O. aurifrons*). If you keep these species in groups, they will typically pair up on their own. (To ensure getting a heterosexual pair, it is best to obtain individuals that are different in size.) Once the eggs hatch, the real challenge begins. The larvae are phototropic (attracted to light) and can be removed from the broodstock tank by holding a light at the water's surface. Remove the larvae by dipping them up in a plastic container or by gently siphoning them out of the tank. If you use a net, you will cause damage to the young fish, resulting in high mortality rates. The size of a normal Yellowhead Jawfish hatch can be more than 1,000 larvae, so you should be prepared to raise them in an aquarium of at least 20 gallons and preferably larger. Feeding will begin about 8 to 12 hours after hatching, and the aquarist will need to be ready to provide live rotifers. Walch (1994) suggests feeding the rotifers microalgae (e.g., *Nannochloropsis*)—this is often sold as "green water"—for 10 to 12 hours before adding them to the rearing tank. Rotifer density in the rearing tank should be about 20 rotifers per ml of tank water. Walch suggests adding microalgae (from water that has been pH adjusted to 7.9) to the larval-rearing tank as well. The trick to all this is keeping the density of well-fed rotifers high enough to be sure that the larvae have enough to eat. If rotifer densities get too high or crash, it can cause pollution or oxygen depletion problems. The young jawfishes are ready to eat brine shrimp nauplii at an age of about 10 days. Begin introducing the baby *Artemia* into the rearing tank, along with the rotifers and "green water." Make sure you do not add too many *Artemia,* as they will grow and begin eating the rotifers (Walch recommends adding no more *Artemia* nauplii than the larvae can eat in a day). By day 15, all the larvae should be able to consume the young brine shrimp. At this time, rotifers should be removed and "green water" additions stopped. Enriched two-day-old brine shrimp can then be fed until metamorphosis, at which time the young can be weaned onto other nutritious foods. Water changes can also begin at this time, although changes in their environment should occur very gradually. Walch recommends doing water exchanges "drop by drop," as sudden changes can kill the newly settled jawfishes. Finally, the young fishes should be moved to grow-out tanks that have a rubble/sand substrate.

JAWFISH SPECIES

Jawfishes present special identification challenges, especially as there are still many questions that need to be answered regarding their taxonomy. I have identified the photographs to the best of my ability, using many of the latest field guides that include opistognathids. The identification of jawfishes from photographs (especially when in many cases you only see the head of the fish) is often a dubious practice. Adding to the complexity is the fact that many Indo-Pacific forms have yet to be formally described and named.

Genus *Lonchopisthus*

The genus *Lonchopisthus* contains at least five species, with all but one species occurring in the Western Atlantic. On the Pacific side of Central America, one species is found in the Gulf of California. Some of these fishes have a long, pointed caudal fin, while others are chunky, with a shorter tail. The *Lonchopisthus* spp. tend to occur in fairly deep water (many at depths of 100 m [328 ft.]). One species occasionally shows up in the aquarium trade.

Lonchopisthus micrognathus (Poey, 1860)
Common Name: Swordtail Jawfish.
Maximum Length: 17.8 cm (6.9 in.).
Distribution: Florida Keys and the Gulf of Mexico to northern coast of South America, including the Greater Antilles.

Biology: The Swordtail Jawfish is typically found on the quieter, leeward side of islands, usually on sandy-mud slopes and flats. According to Colin and Arneson (1978), the substrate where this species builds its burrows is homogeneous in nature, consisting of a "slightly granular mix of mud and fine sand." This type of sediment is more common in back-reef lagoon habitats. The habitat where this jawfish is typically found is relatively barren, but can be covered with an algal mat or sparse seagrass growth. It is found at depths of 12 to 40 m (39 to 131 ft.) where it occupies a burrow of its own construction. When digging, it enters the tunnel headfirst, then takes mouthfuls of sediment and spits them out at the edge of the burrow entrance. Unlike some of its relatives, this species will perform two exhalations when spitting out sediment. The first puff expels most of the material, while the second, less vigorous exhalation is employed to clear fine sediment from the mouth and gill chambers. The depth of *L. micrognathus* burrows typically range from 17 to 35 cm (6.6 to 13.7 in.) below the substrate surface, but may be as deep as 50 cm (19.5 in.) on occasion. The tunnel is narrowest in the central portion, expanding somewhat near the terminal end. The narrowest point of the burrow usually measures 2.5 to 5 cm (1 to 2 in.) in diameter. There are no shells, stones, or rubble lining the burrow as is the case with many other jawfishes. The sediment this species is usually found in is very cohesive, so these larger pieces of super structure are not needed. There are also accessory tunnels that travel horizontally and then upward until they reach the surface. In some cases there is more than one accessory opening. The secondary openings are smaller than the primary opening, and these side entrances are rarely used. A small crab, *Chasmocarcinus cylindricus*, sometimes lives commensally with *L. micrognathus* and constructs small accessory tunnels of its own off the jawfish's main burrow. Other fishes that occur in the same habitat with the Swordtail Jawfish include the White-eye Goby (*Bollmania boqueronensis*), Orangespotted Goby (*Nes longus*), Signate Goby (*Microgobius signatus*), Dash Goby (*Gobionellus saepepallens*), mojarras, sand perches (*Diplectrum* spp.), and Lane Snapper (*Lutjanus synagris*).

The Swordtail Jawfish never strays far from its refuge—rarely moving farther than 1 m (3.3 ft.) from the burrow (they are more often found within 0.5 m [1.6 ft.] of the entrance). During the day, they hover, tail-down, in the water column over their burrow entrances. They orient themselves into the current, using the pectoral fins and tail to maintain position. This species can also use its pectoral fins to move backward. If a larger predator approaches, it dives into the burrow headfirst. While hovering in the water column, *L. micrognathus* has been observed to curl the posterior portion of its body upward and insert its elongate tail

Lonchopisthus micrognathus, Swordtail Jawfish: colonial fish, one per burrow.

into the gill opening. The fish then moves the tail forward and backward for several seconds. In some cases the mouth is opened when the tail is inserted and the end of the caudal fin actually protrudes from the mouth. It is thought that this behavior serves to clean sediment from the gill rakers, gill arches, and the mouth. *Lonchopisthus micrognathus* feeds on zooplankton, targeting and ingesting specific prey items from the water column. Stomach-content analysis indicates that it feeds mainly on veliger larvae and copepods. It feeds on other larvae as well, including those of polychaete worms, shrimps, crabs, barnacles, and gastropods. Eggs, diatoms, and foraminiferans complete the diet. There is some indication that it will also eat coral mucus that drifts past.

Lonchopisthus micrognathus lives in colonies, with just one individual per burrow in most cases. Individuals usually remain in the same burrow, although on rare occasions they have been observed changing burrows. At night, this jawfish retreats deep into its tunnel, but, unlike the Yellowhead Jawfish (*Opistognathus aurifrons*), this species does not cover its burrow entrance at night. When a conspecific intruder approaches its shelter, *L. micrognathus* swims toward the interloper with its mouth greatly expanded and its gill covers flared. It will also spread its fins and shake its head. This species does not segregate by size, and small juveniles are often found living adjacent to adults. The eggs are orally incubated and are occasionally spit out and sucked back into the mouth. The egg mass is about 10 mm in diameter and contains about 1,000 spherical eggs that are 0.8 to 0.9 mm in diameter. Reproduction appears to occur year-round. Colin and

Arneson (1978) report seeing brooding males during the months of February, March, July, August, October, November, and December. Upon settling out of the plankton, juveniles immediately burrow. Individuals as small as 14 mm have been observed in small burrows.

Captive Care: The Swordtail Jawfish is an unusual aquarium inhabitant that requires special care if it is going to thrive in captivity. It does best if housed on its own or with conspecifics. (More than one *L. micrognathus* can be housed in the same aquarium if the tank is large enough.) Any other fishes in the aquarium must be peaceful species (e.g., some of the small, sympatric gobies). If your Swordtail Jawfish is picked on by its tankmates or kept with aggressive feeders, it may simply skulk in its burrow and slowly starve. The substrate should consist of a layer of approximately 10 cm (3.9 in.) of fine coral sand. Put a few smaller, flat pieces of live rock on the bottom or add no decor at all. When there is complex aquascaping in the aquarium, this fish may build its burrow behind or within the reef structure, out of view of the aquarist. This species is a skilled jumper, and the aquarium must be covered. In most cases they will accept frozen mysid shrimp or frozen brine shrimp. However, an occasional individual may require live brine shrimp or tiny feeder guppies to catalyze a feeding response. It should be fed a varied diet that includes finely chopped fresh seafoods and some of the nutritionally complete frozen preparations.

Aquarium Size: 20 gal. **Temperature:** 22 to 28°C (72 to 82°F).

Aquarium Suitability Index: 3.

Remarks: This is a unique jawfish that is readily distinguished from its confamilials. No sexual dimorphism has been reported in *L. micrognathus.*

Genus *Opistognathus*

Opistognathus aurifrons (Jordan & Thompson, 1905)
Common Names: Yellowhead Jawfish, Pearly Jawfish.

Maximum Length: 10 cm (3.9 in.).

Distribution: South Florida and Bahamas to Barbados and northern South America.

Biology: The Yellowhead Jawfish is found at depths of 3 to 50 m (9.8 to 164 ft.). It is found in lagoons and on fore-reef sand slopes. Because this species digs burrows in the substrate, its distribution on the reef is limited by the type of substrate present. It needs substrate that is heterogeneous in consistency. For example, rubble is an important component. The varied materials utilized by Yellowhead Jawfish consist of broken coral branches, pieces of coral limestone, bivalve and snail shells, and assorted pieces of hard reef debris ranging in size from 5 to 10 mm in size. Dr. Patrick Colin, one of the world's leading authorities on jawfishes, reports: "It is probably impossible for this species to construct a burrow in fine, homogeneous sand." Sand depth, as well as sand type, also limits the distribution of this jawfish. The Yellowhead Jawfish builds several different types of burrows. One type is constructed adjacent to a large rock so that the terminal chamber can be hidden securely under the rock. It may also build an open-chambered burrow where the terminal chamber is lined with rock and rubble but is not roofed by a rock. This jawfish sometimes constructs a rock chamber burrow where the end chamber actually occurs in an erosion hole or fracture in a larger buried rock, but this type of burrow is the least common. Burrows range in depth from 11 to at least 22 cm (4.3 to 8.6 in.). The burrow chamber can be as long as 24 cm (9.4 in.) long, as wide as 23 cm (9 in.) wide, and up to 6 cm (2.3 in.) high. In some cases there are two chambers with a connecting tunnel. The burrow entrance is usually surrounded by flattened rocks from 1.4 to 2 cm (0.5 to 0.8 in.) in diameter. The floor of the chamber is comprised of fine sand or small rocks. An individual Yellowhead Jawfish may stay in the same burrow or area for long periods of time, perhaps for its entire life. It may build new burrows on occasion, but typically does so in close proximity (1 m [3.3 ft.]) to its original home. As a result, the dynamics of a Yellowhead Jawfish population does not change much, although older individuals will occasionally disappear and new recruits will join the group.

This species will hang a maximum height of 1.5 m (4.9 ft.) over the burrow entrance. If in the water column, it will slowly back into its burrow when approached. If the risk is greater, it will dive headfirst into its burrow. It has been demonstrated that larger piscivores produce the most dramatic flight response, while larger non fish-eating species produce a mild response. They will behave aggressively toward smaller fishes. At night, the jawfish will retreat into its burrow and cover the entrance with a rock or piece of rubble.

The Nassau Grouper (*Epinephelus striatus*) has been observed to bury Yellowhead Jawfish burrows and then position itself nearby for up to several hours. The grouper lies on its side with its tail over the jawfish hole. Then it beats its tail, causing the burrow entrance to collapse. A patient grouper may engage in this behavior for as long as 15 minutes. The grouper may occasionally turn to face the site of the buried burrow entrance and blow water out of its mouth at the substrate in what appears to be an attempt to excavate the jawfish. These groupers have also been observed to sit on the bottom, sometimes for long periods of time, with their mouths positioned near jawfish burrow entrances. The groupers have never actually been observed to cap-

Opistognathus aurifrons, Yellowhead Jawfish: subtle beauty in a peaceful fish.

Opistognathus aurifrons, Yellowhead Jawfish: Bonaire color variant.

ture a jawfish successfully.

Yellowheads interact with many of the fishes that share their environment. They react aggressively toward some species and ignore others. In some cases they may avoid or retreat from heterospecifics. For example, smaller Sand Tilefish (*Malacanthus plumieri*) are often chased by Yellowhead Jawfish. But a larger tilefish can evoke a flight response. Larger Sand Tilefish may eat jawfishes and have been observed chasing them and shoving their heads into burrow entrances. The tilefish also steal rocks and rubble from the margins of jawfish burrows. Some wrasses, like the Yellowhead Wrasse (*Halichoeres garnoti*) and Slippery Dick Wrasse (*H. bivittatus*), will dash at Yellowhead Jawfish or enter their burrows. The Yellowhead Wrasse will even remove the stones covering the burrow entrance and enter it.

The Yellowhead Jawfish will usually chase fishes that are smaller than itself or similar in size, from a radius of about 20 to 25 cm (7.8 to 9.8 in.) around its burrow entrance. They will also spit mouthfuls of sand at larger fish intruding in their territories. They have been observed behaving aggressively toward small lizardfishes, Tobacco Fish (*Serranus tabacarius*), Harlequin Bass (*Serranus tigrinus*), Spotted Goatfish (*Pseudupeneus maculatus*), Slippery Dick, Yellowhead Wrasse and Atlantic Sharpnose Puffer (*Canthigaster rostrata*). Besides the species mentioned above, other fishes observed in the same habitat as the Yellowhead Jawfish include the Brown Garden Eel (*Heteroconger longissimus*), Bridled Goby (*Coryphopterus glaucofraenum*), Blue Goby (*Ptereleotris calliurus*), and the Hovering Goby (*P. helenae*). These species usually skirted around Yellowhead territories.

The Yellowhead feeds on plankton, 85% of the diet being copepods, 9.4% shrimp larvae, and small percentages of fish eggs, siphonophores, barnacle larvae, and polychaetes (Randall, 1967). It spends about 90% of the daytime hours feeding. This species

has a teardrop-shaped pupil, and the eye anatomy may be an adaptation to its plankton-feeding lifestyle. Randall (1967) states: "The antero-ventral lobe is oriented so that the fish probably has binocular vision along a plane parallel to the horizontal while maintaining a near vertical position."

The Yellowhead Jawfish occurs in small to large aggregations. According to Colin (1973) the mean distance between adjacent burrows was 27 cm (11 in.) in a colony consisting of three fish, 83 cm (33 in.) in a colony of eight fish, and 115 cm (45 in.) in a colony of 115 jawfish. The edges of the colonies were usually within 20 cm (7.8 in.) of some rocky or coralline structure. Adults in an *O. aurifrons* colony are typically spatially paired, with the nearest neighbors almost always being a male and female. These pairs behave differently toward each other than they do toward other nearby neighbors. Pair members may exchange burrows or occupy the same burrow for short periods of time (e.g., during the reproductive period). This species appears to be monogamous, forming long-term pair bonds.

When courting, the male orients himself alongside the female and displays. He arches his body, spreads his fins and gill covers, and opens his mouth wide. If she is receptive, she will follow the male to a burrow. Spawning takes place in the burrow. Most courtship and spawning occurs at dusk and day, although some reproductive activity appears to occur throughout the day. These jawfish reproduce from spring to late autumn. The majority of egg clutches are laid during the full and new moon, with most pairs producing from zero to two clutches per month (on rare occasions, a pair may produce up to three egg clutches). The eggs are about 0.8 to 0.9 mm in diameter. The eggs hatch in 7 to 9 days at a temperature of 25 to 26°C (77 to 79°F). On the night of the hatch, the male will enter his burrow, but will not cover the opening as he usually does. He will remain at the entrance of

Opistognathus aurifrons, Yellowhead Jawfish: Florida color variant.

Opistognathus castelnaui, Blackcapped Jawfish: possible import from Java.

Opistognathus gilberti, Yellow Jawfish: most common in deep-water habitats.

the burrow, open his mouth, and the eggs will hatch. Hatching usually takes about 30 minutes. The larvae swim up into the water column. The larvae are about 4 mm long at hatching and look like tiny adults about 9 days after hatching. The larvae settle out of the plankton in 21 to 28 days. The young fish begin digging burrows immediately, usually among colonies of adults.

Captive Care: The Yellowhead Jawfish is the most popular member of the family in the aquarium trade. It is very affordable (at least in U.S. fish stores) and readily acclimates if the prerequisites listed above are met. When first added it may engage in "gulping" (described above) and is prone to leaping from the tank. Be sure you wait to turn off the lights until the fish finds a place to hide, and keep a night light on to prevent jumping—most leap out of the aquarium the first night. This fish will often dig burrows behind aquarium aquascaping or facing the back of the aquarium. However, if they are fed at the front of the tank, they will usually relocate to the place where the most food moves past. Colonies of these beautiful fishes make an incredible display. It is best to add all the individuals at once, first being sure that the tank's biological filter is ready to take a full load. Alternatively, you might add the smaller individuals to the tank first. There is no tested formula to figure out how many can be kept in one tank, but a good rule of thumb is approximately one jawfish per 13 to 16 cm^2 (2 to 2.5 in.^{2}) of tank surface area. (Remember that in the wild, individual burrows are from 15 to 114 cm [5.9 to 44 in.] apart.) If you have too many individuals crowded together, the subordinate fish will be forced to hide in the upper corners of the aquarium. These fish should be removed or they will perish. *Opistognathus aurifrons* does best if housed in a species tank or with other peaceful fish species. It will chase smaller fishes away from its burrow, like dwarf seabass, goatfishes, small wrasses, and Sharpnose Puffers. Feed this fish mysid shrimp, vitamin-enriched brine shrimp, finely chopped table shrimp, or frozen preparations for carnivores. Studies have demonstrated that below a temperature of 20°C (68°F) this species becomes inactive and feeds sparingly. Temperatures lower than 17°C (63°F) are lethal. This species regularly spawns in captivity.

Aquarium Size: 20 gal. **Temperature:** 21 to 28°C (70 to 82°F).

Aquarium Suitability Index: 4.

Remarks: Unlike some of the jawfishes, *O. aurifrons* does not display sexual differences in the size of the jaws. It has recurved canine teeth in the lower jaw that, while not important for feeding, may enable the fish to carry large rocks. In specimens under 20 mm, the yellow is centralized on the top of the head just behind the eyes, the body is not blue, and there are often black spots on the side extending from the origin to the end of the anal fin. In larger individuals, the head and nape are pale yellow, while the rest of the body and fins are grayish blue. There is also a dark blue line along the dorsal fin margin. The color of individuals differs from Florida and the Caribbean. Those individuals from Florida almost always lack black spots on the "chin," while Yellowhead Jawfish from the Caribbean may or may not have black spots. Bahamian specimens usually have black spots on the chin, black under the gill membrane at the isthmus, and a dark, curved line beneath the maxillary and the preopercle. Some Bahamian individuals also possess an eye bar—a faint line that runs between the eyes and extends to the edge of the lower jaw. Individuals from the Bahamas are paler blue than those specimens from Florida, but the head tends to be more yellow. In Florida, most specimens lack the black markings. Specimens from other locations in the Caribbean vary in whether or not they have these various black markings. The yellow of specimens from Florida often fades in captivity and can disappear completely in several weeks' time. There is a very similar jawfish that is known from the southeastern Caribbean and Brazil that appears to be a distinct species. It has a blue line running from behind the eye onto the nape and is sometimes called the Bluebar Jawfish.

Opistognathus castelnaui Bleeker, 1859
Common Names: Blackcapped Jawfish, Bluespotted Jawfish.
Maximum Length: 12 cm (4.7 in.).
Distribution: Andaman Sea, Singapore, and western Java.
Biology: Kuiter (2001) reports that this species is found at depths of 20 to 25 m (66 to 82 ft.) on sand and rubble slopes. It is often seen singly.
Captive Care: I have never seen this species in the trade, but it is possible it could be exported from the west coast of Java.
Aquarium Size: 20 gal. **Temperature:** 23 to 28°C (73 to 82°F).
Aquarium Suitability Index: 4.
Remarks: This species usually sports a black head, with blue spots on the gill cover and blue markings on the body. Kuiter identifies the accompanying photograph as *O. castelnaui* and provides most of the details listed above. In his treatise on the species, he suggests that the name *O. castelnaui* has also been erroneously applied to a larger, deep-water species from Japan. As with much of jawfish taxonomy, more research is needed.

Opistognathus gilberti Böhlke, 1967
Common Names: Yellow Jawfish, Gilbert's Jawfish.
Maximum Length: 11 cm (4.3 in.).
Distribution: Bahamas and western Caribbean Sea.
Biology: The Yellow Jawfish is found on sand slopes and ledges near reef walls. It is usually seen in deep water—rarely at depths of less than 30 m (98 ft.)—and is not common in water less than 45 m (148 ft.) deep. *Opistognathus gilberti* feeds on zooplankton. It forms colonies or clusters.
Captive Care: This species is rare in the aquarium trade because of its preference for deep water. However, with more divers using mixed gases or rebreathers to collect deep-water fish in the Caribbean, the Yellow Jawfish may become more accessible to aquarists. Its behavior and husbandry requirements are probably similar to that of the Yellowhead Jawfish (*Opistognathus aurifrons*). Unlike the Yellowhead, male and female Yellow Jawfish can be readily separated by their color patterns (see the Remarks section below).
Aquarium Size: 20 gal. **Temperature:** 21 to 28°C (70 to 82°F).
Aquarium Suitability Index: 4.
Remarks: This species is sexually dichromatic. Females are gray on the sides and dorsum, but paler below, with a thin golden stripe on the dorsal and anal fins, and a large yellow area on the caudal fin. The male is reddish gray on the head and body. Toward the tail, it becomes black. The belly is white, as are the dorsal, pelvic, and anal fins. In males, there is also a spot between the fifth and sixth dorsal spines and one on the caudal fin. The **Moustache Jawfish** (*Opistognathus lonchurus*) **Jordan & Gilbert, 1882** is another deep-water species that is seen in the aquarium trade on rare occasions. It is sometimes collected by divers using mixed gases or rebreathers to explore very deep reef habitats. It usually occurs on sand and mud slopes at depths of 15 to over 60 m (49 to 197 ft.). It ranges from Southeastern Florida and northeastern Gulf of Mexico to Suriname. The Moustache Jawfish grows to 10 cm (3.9 in.) long and is attractively colored.

Opistognathus rosenblatti Allen & Robertson, 1991
Common Name: Bluespotted Jawfish.
Maximum Length: 10 cm (3.9 in.).
Distribution: Gulf of California.
Biology: Bluespotted Jawfish are typically encountered near offshore islands, usually near the base of cliffs and rocky outcroppings. They build their burrows in mixed shell fragments and pebbles, covering the entrance to their burrows at night and rebuilding the entrances in the morning. While adult individuals are usually found at depths of 18 to 24 m (59 to 79 ft.), juveniles are sometimes found as shallow as 4.6 m (15 ft.). This species lives in colonies, with individuals spaced about 1 to 3 m (3.3 to 9.8 ft.) apart. These colonies can number up to several hundred individuals. The males of this species engage in a spectacular courtship display. The male will dash up into the water column and hover there for one to three seconds with its fins fully erected. It will then quickly turn around and dart back to its

Opistognathus rosenblatti, Bluespotted Jawfish: spectacular aquarium fish.

Opistognathus sp., Variegated Jawfish: note metallic green color.

Opistognathus sp., Variegated Jawfish: yellow variant, possibly female.

burrow. During this display, the posterior half of the male's body is black, while the anterior portion is whitish. This pre-mating ritual may carry on for hours, with the male dashing out of its burrow and displaying every 3 to 5 minutes. The male's courtship display ends when a female leaves her burrow and enters his.

Captive Care: At one time, this jawfish was affordable and not uncommon. But a strong market for this species in Japan drove the price up, and very few individuals entered the North American market for a period of years. Recently, this species has again become more available to U.S. aquarists. This is a magnificent aquarium fish that never fails to provoke wonder. Its husbandry is similar to that of the other small members of the family, except it tends to be more aggressive toward members of its own kind. Keep more than one individual only if you have a larger tank. It is also risky to keep it with other jawfish species, although it can be done in a spacious system. Like others in the family, it is a very effective jumper that seems able to find the smallest of holes in the aquarium top to leap through.

Aquarium Size: 20 gal. **Temperature:** 21 to 28°C (70 to 82°F).

Aquarium Suitability Index: 4.

Remarks: This jawfish is not easy to overlook, as it is the most spectacular member of the family. It is beige to yellowish brown overall with blue spots on the head and the body. Juveniles are yellow with or without spots. The **Panamanian Jawfish (*Opistognathus panamaensis*) Allen & Robertson, 1991** is a very similar species, but differs in having a higher number of pectoral fin rays, gill rakers, and lateral line pores. The color is similar, but the blue spots on the body of the Panamanian Jawfish sometimes coalesce to form stripes. This species has been reported from Cocos and Malpelo Islands and from Panama. Its biology is very similar to that of the Bluespotted Jawfish.

Opistognathus sp.

Common Name: Variegated Jawfish.

Maximum Length: 10 cm (3.9 in.).

Distribution: Bali to the Moluccas and the southern Philippines (possibly from the Maldives to Vanuatu, north to Taiwan).

Biology: This lovely jawfish occurs at depths of 0.5 to 35 m (1.6 to 115 ft.). It lives on sand/rubble flats and slopes, sometimes in small colonies, but also singly. The Variegated Jawfish feeds on zooplankton that passes by its burrow entrance. Metallic blue specimens, thought to be males, will hover high above their burrows in what appears to be courtship behavior.

Captive Care: This species is rarely available in the aquarium trade (although it can be quite common in some areas where fish collecting occurs). It is a fairly hardy fish that should be provided with a varied diet. Small groups can be kept together if the tank

Opistognathus sp., Variegated Jawfish: magnificent displaying male.

is large enough. Start by providing approximately 16 cm^2 (2.5 in.^{2}) of tank surface for each individual jawfish; if they fight, be prepared to separate them.

Aquarium Size: 20 gal. **Temperature:** 23 to 28°C (73 to 82°F).

Aquarium Suitability Index: 4.

Remarks: The Variegated Jawfish is usually brown or metallic green overall. Some individuals have a spot on the anterior portion of the dorsal fin. There appear to be two distinct courtship colors. Sexually mature males are believed to exhibit a metallic blue coloration, while bright yellowish orange individuals are apparently females—although more study is required to confirm this. There may be more than one similar species.

Opistognathus sp.

Common Name: Goldspecs Jawfish.

Maximum Length: 10 cm (3.9 in.).

Distribution: Indonesia.

Biology: This common jawfish is found on mixed rubble and sand flats and slopes. It occurs on back-reef faces, outer-reef faces, and outer slopes at depths of 6 to 20 m (20 to 66 ft.). It is most common on coastal reefs. This species is usually found singly or in small groups. Usually its nearest neighbors are not too close, usually about 1 to 2 m [3.3 to 7 ft.] away. If one individual attempts to enter the burrow occupied by a conspecific, the resident fish will bite the intruder and chase it from the area. It is apparently a zooplankton feeder. The Goldspecs Jawfish will hover over the opening of its burrow, but does not swim high in the water column like some of its relatives (e.g., *O. aurifrons*).

Captive Care: The Goldspecs Jawfish is an attractive species that will do well in certain aquarium venues. It should be kept in a tank with at least 7.5 cm (2.9 in.) of mixed substrate that includes sand of varying grades and small pieces of shell and/or calcareous rubble so that it can construct a burrow. A flat rock laid on the sand can also provide a roof for a potential burrow. It is a notorious jumper that will leap from an open tank if frightened. Turn off the aquarium lights gradually to prevent jumping. It is also less likely to jump after it has constructed its burrow (most leap out of the aquarium the first night). Keep with docile tankmates. It will only behave aggressively toward fishes that try to enter its burrow. The Goldspecs Jawfish can be kept singly or in pairs. In the wild it is usually not found close to conspecifics, so it is probably best not kept in colonies. I have had a pair of these fish adopt an artificial PVC burrow, although usually a burrow will be occupied by a single fish. It may take a while before the Goldspecs Jawfish finds and takes over an artificial burrow.

Aquarium Size: 20 gal. **Temperature:** 23 to 28°C (73 to 82°F).

Aquarium Suitability Index: 4.

Remarks: This species is not yet described and not assigned a binomial name, but is easily identified by its dark head and the orange or gold color at the top of the eye (this gold color is not always present in smaller individuals).

Opistognathus sp.

Common Names: Ringeye Jawfish, Wass' Jawfish.

Maximum Length: 13 cm (5.1 in.).

Distribution: Great Barrier Reef to Fiji, north to the Philippines.

Biology: This little-known species is most common at depths of 10 to 45 m (33 to 149 ft.) or more on coarse rubble slopes in reef channels. It is a solitary species.

Captive Care: Although I have never encountered this species in the North American aquarium trade, I am sure it shows up on occasion, as it is quite common in areas where fishes are regularly collected. Its captive care requirements are probably similar to those of the Goldspecs Jawfish.

Aquarium Size: 20 gal. **Temperature:** 23 to 28°C (73 to 82°F).

Aquarium Suitability Index: 4(?).

Remarks: This species has a very distinct white iris and an eyespot on the anterior dorsal fin.

Opistognathus sp., Goldspecs Jawfish: note dark head, gold rim at eye top.

Opistognathus sp., Ringeye Jawfish: note distinctive white iris.

Opistognathus macrognathus, Banded Jawfish: large, hard-working burrower.

"Dusky" Jawfish Species Group

This is a group of approximately seven jawfishes that are found in the tropical Western Atlantic. (There are "sister species" in the tropical Eastern Pacific that share the same characteristics.) They have shorter bodies and large heads with bulbous eyes. They sport muted, cryptic colors that include brown and gray mottling and/or bands. Some of these species grow quite large and feed on small fishes and a variety of motile invertebrates. They are most often found in shallow-water habitats.

Opistognathus macrognathus Poey, 1860

Common Name: Banded Jawfish.

Maximum Length: 20 cm (7.8 in.).

Distribution: Florida, Gulf of Mexico and the Bahamas to northern South America.

Biology: The Banded Jawfish is most often found in sandy areas near submerged reefs. This species has been reported from depths of 0.5 to 44 m (1.6 to 144 ft.), but is commonly observed at depths of 8 to 10 m (26 to 33 ft.). It feeds mainly on benthic animals or planktonic forms that stay near the seafloor (e.g., mysid shrimps). Primary components of the diet include shrimps, isopods, and fishes. It also eats polychaete worms, mysid shrimps, and copepods. It does not hover in the water column, but sits in a burrow with its head protruding. It builds its tunnel in fine sand, with bits of shell and rubble used to support the burrow. It is reported to regularly share its shelter with hovering gobies (*Ptereleotris* spp.). This species is fairly site-attached, although they may build new burrows near old ones. Pairs, clumps, and isolated individuals have been reported. Only males whose nearest neighbor is a female hold egg clutches. Males may relocate their burrows to get closer to a female, which often results in their receiving a clutch of eggs. According to Hess (1993), spawning occurred in all months (observed April to September), with a peak of spawning activity on the day of the full moon. She also reported that males may receive clutches sequentially from up to three different females. Some females spawn with a single male, others appear to spawn alternately with two different males. Males isolated from a clump of individuals never receive clutches. Within a group, egg-laying is not synchronous. The eggs develop in about 5 days. The young fish settle out of the plankton in about 18 days and immediately begin burrowing.

Captive Care: This large jawfish can make a very interesting aquarium inhabitant. Just watching it construct and maintain its burrow is fascinating. You should provide a sand bed (consisting of sand, rubble, shells, and rocks of varying size) at least 13 cm (5.1 in.) deep for this species (and maybe deeper for large adults). Be sure to include some shells and rubble of varying sizes to fa-

Opistognathus maxillosus, Mottled Jawfish: builds elaborate tunnels.

Opistognathus robinsi, Spotfin Jawfish: hefty, larger species with muted color.

cilitate burrow construction. Its larger size and piscivorous feeding habits means that you have to select fish tankmates more carefully. It will eat fishes and crustaceans that can fit into its mouth. If your tank has enough surface area (100 gallons or larger), you could keep more than one in the same aquarium. Like others in the genus, this species is prone to jumping, especially until it finds a suitable hiding place. Keep some lights on over the tank until it has settled in.

Aquarium Size: 40 gal. **Temperature:** 22 to 28°C (72 to 82°F).

Aquarium Suitability Index: 4.

Remarks: This species is tan overall with four to five pairs of dark brown blotches (which are sometimes joined) on the base of the dorsal fin and the sides. Between the sixth and ninth dorsal spine there is a dark blotch. Males have two bands on the underside of the maxilla, which are conspicuous when the fish displays. Males are also larger than females. Males and females of similar size have a similar mouth volume. Males do have a longer maxilla that extends past the eye.

Opistognathus maxillosus Poey, 1860

Common Name: Mottled Jawfish.

Maximum Length: 13 cm (5.1 in.).

Distribution: Southern Florida and Bahamas, most of the Caribbean to Panama and Tobago.

Biology: *Opistognathus maxillosus* is a shallow-water species that is usually found at depths of 2 m (7 ft.) or less, although it has been reported to at least 12 m (39 ft.). It is usually found on the protected side of coral reefs, where it inhabits areas of sand, coral rubble, and seagrass. This species builds an elaborate burrow around 30 cm (11.7 in.) deep with a terminal chamber and a vertical shaft lined with coral and shell fragments. The Mottled Jawfish lives in pairs, with the male and female living in close

proximity. The next nearest neighbor of the pair usually lives far away. This species is highly site-attached and rarely relocates or builds a new burrow. Reproductive activity shows two annual peaks—one in November and December, another during April and May. Spawning in *O. maxillosus* is synchronous, with most spawning events occurring on the day before the new moon. Most males incubate a single clutch every month (eggs develop in 7 to 8 days), but an occasional individual may incubate a second clutch.

Captive Care: Like others in this subgroup of jawfishes, *O. maxillosus* is a durable aquarium fish that makes an interesting pet. Although not as colorful as some members of the family, its comical appearance and interesting behavior makes up for some of its chromatic shortcomings. Select its tankmates carefully. It has a very large mouth and may prey on ornamental crustaceans and small fishes. It can be kept in pairs (try to acquire a heterosexual pair by selecting individuals that differ in size). Like others in the family, it is prone to leaping from open tanks, at least until it settles into its new tank.

Aquarium Size: 30 gal. **Temperature:** 22 to 28°C (72 to 82°F).

Aquarium Suitability Index: 4.

Remarks: When comparing heterosexual pairs of *O. maxillosus*, Hess (1993) found that the male was always larger than the female. Males also have a larger mouth volume than females of the same size. There is a black spot on the dorsal fin in the lower half of the fin, usually located between the sixth and ninth spines. There is some brown pigment at the corner of the mouth, but no black and white bands inside the maxilla.

Opistognathus robinsi Smith-Vaniz, 1997

Common Name: Spotfin Jawfish.

Maximum Length: 15 cm (5.9 in.).

Opistognathus whitehurstii, Dusky Jawfish: male mouthbroods a clutch of eggs while well-protected in his burrow. A good jawfish for community aquarium settings.

Distribution: South Carolina to Florida (a single straggler collected in the Bahamas), also the Gulf of Mexico.

Biology: This species occurs in estuaries and lagoons at depths of less than 1 m to at least 46 m (3.3 to 151 ft.). Most of those collected were taken at depths of less than 20 m (66 ft.). Although food-habit data is lacking for this species, like similar species it probably feeds mostly on crustaceans and small fishes. It is eaten by other fishes, including the Black Seabass (*Centropristis striata*).

Captive Care: This hefty jawfish is regularly collected by Florida fish dealers. It is a durable species that is not as highly sought after because of its muted color pattern, but it does make an interesting aquarium fish. Provide it with 13 cm (5.1 in.) of heterogeneous substrate (including empty shells, rocks, pebbles and rubble). It will eat motile invertebrates (especially crustaceans) and small fishes. Keep one per tank, unless you can acquire a heterosexual pair. A pair should be kept in a tank with a volume of 70 gallons or larger.

Aquarium Size: 30 gal. **Temperature:** 22 to 28°C (72 to 82°F).

Aquarium Suitability Index: 4.

Remarks: The overall color of the head and body of this species is light brown to almost black, and there are pale blotches and white spots. There are also dark reticulations and speckles on the head and the nape, and a distinct ocellus with a white ring between the sixth and ninth dorsal spines. The males have a black inner maxillary stripe, and the inside of the mouth is jet black with white adjacent areas. This species is sexually dimorphic, with the male having a thin, flexible flange that extends beyond the rear edge of the operculum. Males also have a distinct black stripe on the inner lining of the maxilla and the surrounding membranes (this is less pronounced in females). There is also a dark area surrounding the esophageal opening.

Opistognathus whitehurstii (Longley, 1927)

Common Name: Dusky Jawfish.

Maximum Length: 10 cm (3.9 in.).

Distribution: South Florida and the Bahamas to northern South America.

Biology: *Opistognathus whitehurstii* is a resident of shallow water

Opistognathus whitehurstii, Dusky Jawfish: promiscuous mating practices.

Stalix histrio?, Black Marbled Jawfish: one of a rare, little-studied genus.

(often less than 2 m [6.6 ft.]) on the protected side of reefs. It lives on sandy bottoms, often in areas with some coral rubble and seagrass. The Dusky Jawfish feeds on invertebrates and fishes that live near the seafloor, with shrimps providing the most important dietary component, followed by fishes and isopods. It feeds on serpent stars and small crabs to a much lesser degree. Groups of these jawfish are usually scattered over suitable habitats. Individuals are also known to vacate their burrows, regularly relocating and building new burrows up to 10 m (33 ft.) from their original burrow site. In some cases, they may even leave the group all together. The nearest neighbor of a male Dusky Jawfish could be a consexual or a female—they do not seem to form pairs within the groups in which they live. They practice a promiscuous mating system. According to Hess (1993), spawning did not occur in November or October, but did every other month between April and September. She found no lunar periodicity in spawning. A male *O. whitehurstii* will tend from zero to four clutches per month.

Captive Care: Its aquarium requirements are similar to those of the other jawfishes. Of all the species sold under the common name of "dusky" jawfish, this is the best species for a community aquarium with smaller fishes and crustaceans because of its smaller maximum length (it only gets about 3 inches long). This fish often occurs at fairly high densities in the wild. It is also possible to keep more than one *O. whitehurstii* in the same aquarium. A good rule of thumb is to add one individual Dusky Jawfish for every 26 cm² [4 in.²] of bottom surface area. Keep this fish with docile tankmates. Although it does not tend to be overly aggressive, it may display at and nip at fishes that try to enter its burrow. This species will spawn in captivity.

Aquarium Size: 20 gal. **Temperature:** 22 to 28°C (72 to 82°F). **Aquarium Suitability Index:** 4.

Remarks: The Dusky Jawfish is mostly dark brown with some lighter mottling. There is a dark spot (sometimes bluish in color) on the dorsal fin between the second and fourth dorsal spines (the spot is often obscured by the black dorsal margin). Some individuals have light yellow on the dorsal and anal fin. The Dusky Jawfish is sexually dimorphic, with males tending to be slightly larger than females. The males also have a significantly larger mouth volume than females of similar size.

Genus *Stalix*

This genus contains approximately 11 described species and possibly a number of undescribed forms (much work is still needed on the systematics of the genus). Many occur at moderate water depths (greater than 50 m [164 ft.]). The fish photographed here has tentatively been identified as the **Blackmarbled Jawfish** (*Stalix histrio*) **Jordan & Snyder, 1902** by Kuiter (2001). This species is reported from Red Sea to Indonesia, north to Japan. (Its distribution is poorly known.) The Red Sea population may represent a distinct species. It may show up in the aquarium trade on rare occasions. No information exists on its husbandry.

References

Allen & Robertson (1991), Böhlke & Thomas (1961), Colin (1971, 1972, 1973), Colin & Arneson (1978), DeLoach (1999), Hess (1993), Humann & DeLoach (2002), Kerstitch (1979, 1988), Kuiter (2001), Randall (1967), Shinohara (1999), Smith-Vaniz (1989, 1997), Thresher (1980, 1984), Walch (1994), Young (1982).

FAMILY PRIACANTHIDAE
BIGEYES

Cookeolus japonicus, Bulleye: a rarely photographed species near Ambon, Indonesia, displays the huge eyes and appealing looks of an unusual genus.

DUBBED GOGGLE-EYES, CATALUFAS, GLASSEYE SNAPPERS and bigeyes, members of this family have garnered a range of common names that focus on one of their most noteworthy features—extremely large eyes that display incredible eyeshine. This phenomenon is explained by a layer of brightly reflective cells, known as the *tapetum lucidum,* which covers the retina. This structure gives their eyes greater sensitivity and enables them to function more effectively under low-light conditions. Other shared characteristics include deep bodies, rough scales, and muscles attached to the inside body wall and swim bladder that can produce a "knocking" sound when the body wall is vibrated. Sound production occurs more frequently at dusk, dawn, and during the night. Most of the bigeyes are deep red overall during the day, while at night they often become mottled, barred, or silver. The bigeyes can also change their coloration in a matter of seconds when stressed, threatened, or communicating with conspecifics—especially during aggression and courtship.

Their size makes them inappropriate for the modestly sized home marine system, but bigeyes do make very appealing, unusual specimens in larger tanks and spacious biotope displays.

Classification and Biology
Although their appearance is suggestive of the squirrelfishes and soldierfishes, the bigeyes have smaller scales, distinctive, upturned

mouths, and are somewhat distant from them in classification schemes. There are 18 species of bigeyes, with the majority occurring in the tropical Indo-Pacific. Two species are known from the Atlantic and four from the tropical Eastern Pacific. Most priacanthids associate with rocky or coral reefs, living in crevices, caves, or under ledges during the day, often sharing a lair with squirrelfishes, sweepers, and cardinalfishes. The majority of bigeyes leave their hiding places and enter the water column at night to feed on larger zooplankters. But some also occur in the open and feed during the day. These fishes are found at water depths between 3 and at least 400 m (9.8 and 1,312 ft.). Sexual dimorphism is nonexistent in all but one species, which displays differences in caudal fin length between males and females. Although most bigeyes are thought to be gonochoristic, at least one species may occasionally exhibit hermaphroditism. The bigeyes release pelagic eggs into the water column, and the larvae have a protracted, pelagic stage, thus explaining the broad distribution of many of these species. The young of some of the deep-water priacanthids are found associating with flotsam at the water's surface or in shallow inshore waters during the spring and summer.

Captive Care

Bigeyes are relatively hardy, but need to be housed in a larger tank—100 gallons or more. This is especially true for members of the genus *Priacanthus*. The *Pristigenys* species are less active than their cousins and can be housed in aquariums as small as 75 gallons. The tank should have one or two suitable hiding places, but should not be crammed full of rocks or coral. The *Priacanthus* species should also be provided with a cave or ledge to hide in or under. Because these fishes are more active when light levels are low, they will make better display animals and more readily acclimate if housed in tanks that are dimly lit. (It has been suggested that if they are exposed to bright lights for extended periods of time, their vision may be impaired.)

Bigeyes will usually accept chopped seafoods (like squid, shrimp, and fish), frozen *Mysis* shrimp, and other frozen meaty preparations after they have acclimated to their new home, but live feeder fish (e.g., guppies) may be necessary to elicit a feeding response. Dimming the aquarium lights may also facilitate the feeding of a finicky bigeye. Although many bigeyes do most of their feeding at night in the wild, they can be trained to take food when the lights are on. Installing one or more "moonlight" bulbs, which cast a delicate blue light into the water, will greatly enhance evening viewing of these fishes.

Bigeyes sometimes suffer from internal and external parasites. Wild-caught individuals have been reported with cestodes (tape-worms) in the alimentary tract and digenetic parasites (trematodes). They can also contract saltwater ich (*Cryptocaryon irritans*). Bigeyes can be treated with copper, formalin, and other antiparasitics commonly available at aquarium stores.

If the tank is large enough, more than one member of the genus *Priacanthus* can be housed in the same aquarium. The chances of success will be greatly increased if all bigeyes are introduced to the tank simultaneously and if each individual has its own hiding place. The *Pristigenys* species usually occur singly in their natural habitat and are best kept that way in the aquarium.

The bigeyes will acclimate more readily if housed with tank-mates that rarely behave aggressively, such as frogfishes, scorpionfishes, flying gurnards, comets, cardinalfishes, drums, sweetlips, grunts, batfishes, goatfishes, butterflyfishes, and *Genicanthus* angelfishes. Do not house priacanthids with larger squirrelfishes, larger hawkfishes, large damselfishes, angelfishes, *Thalassoma* wrasses, or triggerfishes. Be aware that bigeyes, although mild-mannered, do have large mouths and will eat smaller fishes.

BIGEYE SPECIES

Genus *Heteropriacanthus*

Heteropriacanthus cruentatus (Lacépède, 1801)
Common Names: Bloody Bigeye, Glasseye Snapper.
Maximum Length: 32 cm (12.5 in.).
Distribution: Circumtropical.
Biology: The Bloody Bigeye is a resident of lagoon reefs, the reef crest, and fore-reef slopes at depths of 1 to over 20 m (3.3 to 66

Heteropriacanthus cruentatus, Bloody Bigeye: mottled phase.

Heteropriacanthus cruentatus, Bloody Bigeye: typical overall-red phase.

Priacanthus arenatus, Atlantic Bigeye: forms juvenile schools of up to 5,000.

ft.). It usually occurs singly or in small groups during the day, at which time it refuges in crevices and under rocks. Solitary individuals are often observed hovering near the entrance of small caves. Individuals may venture out from their hiding places on overcast days, or when strong surge temporarily forces them out of reef crest crevices. At dusk, this species emerges from shelter, and some form large aggregations that move offshore and up into the water column to capture larger zooplankton, such as errant polychaetes and the larvae of crustaceans, cephalopods, and fishes. Individuals often assume a pale silver coloration overall when feeding well above the substrate. Those Bloody Bigeyes that migrate away from the reef at night usually return to their daytime haunts about 40 minutes before sunrise. Not all join large migrating aggregations at dusk; some remain near the reef, where they capture polychaete worms, shrimps, mantis shrimps, crabs,

isopods, and fishes off or near the seafloor. In certain locations, this species also feeds heavily on octopuses. Not only does it hunt these cephalopods when they are active at night, it also captures them in reef crevices during the day. Some individuals have specific "home" caves where they refuge in the daytime.

Captive Care: This species will readily adjust to a captive lifestyle if placed in a larger tank with plenty of suitable hiding places. It will eat a variety of aquarium foods, including feeder fish, grass shrimp, chopped seafoods, and frozen preparations; live food may be needed to entice newly introduced individuals to feed. The Bloody Bigeye is not aggressive toward its tankmates, but it will consume fish small enough to swallow. This species will eat many of the motile invertebrates housed in reef aquariums, but it can be kept with soft and stony corals and other sessile invertebrates. It is more likely to adjust quickly and spend more time in the open in a dimly lit tank. Therefore, deep-water reef tanks make better living quarters than the typical brightly lit shallow-water habitat.

Aquarium Size: 100 gal. **Temperature:** 21 to 27°C (70 to 81°F).
Aquarium Suitability Index: 4.

Remarks: This species is usually red overall, although it will display bands or blotches if frightened or will assume a pale silver color overall when feeding in the water column. The median fins, especially the tail, have conspicuous small dark spots. The caudal fin margin is convex, rather than concave.

Genus *Priacanthus*

Priacanthus arenatus Cuvier & Valenciennes, 1829
Common Name: Atlantic Bigeye.
Maximum Length: 30 cm (11.7 in.).
Distribution: Massachusetts and Bermuda, south to Argentina.
Biology: This species occurs on fore-reef slopes and rocky reefs, at depths of 1.5 to 200 m (4.9 to 656 ft.), but is most commonly encountered at depths greater than 20 m (66 ft.). It usually hovers in the open during the day, but does not move far from a crevice or ledge into or under which it retreats if threatened. Adults of this species are frequently seen in small schools of four to eight fish, hanging in the water column near prominent reef features, like large sea fans. In some areas, they may form migratory schools at certain times of the year. Juveniles are observed in large schools that can number more than 5,000 individuals. The Atlantic Bigeye feeds more on zooplankton than on benthic organisms. Its diet is comprised mainly of fishes (including larval and small schooling species) and shrimps, but it also eats polychaete worms (including fireworms), crabs, crustacean larvae, and cephalopods. In the southern Gulf of Mexico, this

species spawns in March (the dry season) and young recruits show up on the reef between March and June. This species is fed upon by the Amberjack (*Seriola dumerili*); one specimen examined had eaten seven Atlantic Bigeyes.

Captive Care: The Atlantic Bigeye can be more difficult to acclimate than some of its close relatives. It will often refuse to eat anything but live food (e.g., grass shrimp or guppies) and should be housed with less aggressive tankmates. Suitable hiding places are essential to ensure acclimation.

Aquarium Size: 100 gal. **Temperature:** 22 to 27°C (72 to 81°F).

Aquarium Suitability Index: 3.

Priacanthus blochii Bleeker, 1853

Common Name: Bloch's Bigeye.

Maximum Length: 30 cm (11.7 in.).

Distribution: Gulf of Aden to Samoa, north to the Philippines, and south to the northern Great Barrier Reef.

Biology: Bloch's Bigeye occurs on lagoon reefs, reef faces, and fore-reef slopes at depths from 15 to 30 m (49 to 98 ft.). It lives under ledges and in caves during the day.

Captive Care: Care for this species is the same as for *Heteropriacanthus cruentatus*, page 180.

Aquarium Size: 100 gal. **Temperature:** 22 to 27°C (72 to 81°F).

Aquarium Suitability Index: 4.

Remarks: This species is red overall or silvery white on the head and body with red blotches. It is often confused with the Crescent-tail Bigeye (*Priacanthus hamrur*), but Bloch's Bigeye does not have the obvious crescent-shaped tail.

Priacanthus hamrur (Forsskål, 1775)

Common Names: Crescent-tail Bigeye, Goggle-eye.

Maximum Length: 40 cm (15.6 in.).

Distribution: Southern Africa and Red Sea to the Marquesas, north to southern Japan, and south to northern Australia.

Biology: This species occurs on deep lagoon pinnacles, back-reef areas, and fore-reef slopes, at depths from 8 to 250 m (26 to 820 ft.). It is most abundant at depths of 30 to 50 m (98 to 164 ft.). It is usually solitary, and feeds on larger zooplankters, small fishes, and benthic invertebrates. In some areas, the Crescent-tail Bigeye reproduces in the fall and may form spawning aggregations.

Captive Care: Care for this species is the same as for *Heteropriacanthus cruentatus*, page 180. Keep only one Crescent-tail Bigeye per tank.

Aquarium Size: 100 gal. **Temperature:** 22 to 27°C (72 to 81°F).

Aquarium Suitability Index: 4.

Remarks: This species has a strongly lunate, or crescent-shaped, tail and is red overall or has light bands on the body.

Priacanthus blochii, Bloch's Bigeye: may be red or silvery white with blotches.

Priacanthus hamrur, Crescent-tail Bigeye: typical solid-red phase.

Priacanthus hamrur, Crescent-tail Bigeye: barred phase may indicate fright.

Priacanthus hamrur, Crescent-tail Bigeye: note lunate (crescent-shaped) tail.

Priacanthus meeki, Hawaiian Bigeye: colors shift rapidly from red to silver.

Priacanthus meeki Jenkins, 1903

Common Name: Hawaiian Bigeye.
Maximum Length: 30 cm (11.7 in.).
Distribution: Hawaiian Islands, including Midway.
Biology: This species is found on fore-reef slopes, among coral or lava boulders, at depths of 3 to 50 m (9.8 to 164 ft.), although

it is more common at greater depths than the sympatric Bloody Bigeye. It usually occurs singly in reef caves and crevices, but it is occasionally observed in small schools in the open.
Captive Care: Care for this species is the same as for *Heteropriacanthus cruentatus*, page 180. Keep only one Hawaiian Bigeye per tank.
Aquarium Size: 100 gal. **Temperature:** 21 to 27°C (70 to 81°F).
Aquarium Suitability Index: 4.
Remarks: This species is very closely related to the Crescent-tail Bigeye (*Priacanthus hamrur*).

Priacanthus sagittarius (Starnes, 1988)

Common Names: Blackspot Bigeye, Arrow Bigeye.
Maximum Length: 35 cm (13.7 in.).
Distribution: Red Sea and Réunion Island east to Japan, northern Australia, and Samoa.
Biology: This bigeye is found on open sand and rocky bottoms at depths of 10 to at least 100 m (33 to 328 ft.)—but is most common at depths in excess of 60 m (197 ft.). Juveniles sometimes occur in aggregations near the seafloor or in midwater. This species probably feeds on crustaceans and fishes.
Captive Care: Challenging to collect in its usual deep-water habitats, this species is seldom seen in the aquarium trade. However, the occasional rare individual may show up in a dealer's tank.
Aquarium Size: 100 gal. **Temperature:** 22 to 27°C (72 to 81°F).
Aquarium Suitability Index: 3.
Remarks: *Priacanthus sagittarius* has posterior dorsal spines that are much longer than the anterior spines (the tenth dorsal spine is also about twice as long as the second). It has a black spot on the base of the pelvic fins and has black blotches (sometimes faint) on the membrane between the first two dorsal fin spines, toward the top of the fin. Like others in the family, it can quickly change color—shifting itself from reddish silver or pale yellowish to mostly silver overall. It can also assume a mottled appearance. Juveniles are often silver overall.

Genus *Pristigenys*

Pristigenys alta (Gill, 1862)

Common Name: Short Bigeye.
Maximum Length: 30 cm (11.7 in.).
Distribution: Massachusetts and Bermuda; northern Gulf of Mexico south to South America.
Biology: This species is found on deep rocky and coral reefs, usually at depths greater than 100 m (328 ft.), to a maximum depth of at least 300 m (984 ft.). Off the North Carolina coast, the

Short Bigeye is most abundant at depths of 34 to 98 m (112 to 321 ft.). Here it is found hanging near invertebrate-encrusted rocks, scattered on the sand near the reef slope. There is usually a burrow under one side of each rock that is occupied by one or two Short Bigeyes. Young individuals are often found at the surface among *Sargassum* algae; specimens between 2.5 and 7.5 cm (1 and 2.9 in.) can be encountered in shallow inshore waters in the spring and summer months.

Aquarium Size: 75 gal. **Temperature:** 18 to 26°C (64 to 79°F).

Aquarium Suitability Index: 4.

Captive Care: Juvenile Short Bigeyes are shy and prone to hiding when the aquarist is near the tank. In contrast, the adults are bold and will spend much of their time in the open. This is a voracious carnivore with a large mouth capable of ingesting large prey items. Smaller fishes are certainly not safe with this species, and ornamental crustaceans are also potential prey. This is a solitary species, so only one should be housed per tank.

Remarks: Juveniles of this species have orange spots on the dorsal, pelvic, and the base of the anal fin.

Pristigenys serrula (Gilbert, 1891)

Common Name: Popeye Catalufa.

Maximum Length: 33 cm (12.9 in.).

Distribution: Central California to Peru, including the central and lower Gulf of California, the Galapagos Islands, and other offshore islands.

Biology: The Popeye Catalufa occurs on rocky reefs at depths from 3 to 100 m (9.8 to 328 ft.). This species hides in reef crevices and caves during the day, but comes out to forage on the reef and adjacent sand substrates at night. It eats small fishes, polychaete worms, and crustaceans. It is sometimes found sharing its diurnal haunts with the Barspot Cardinalfish (*Apogon retrosella*) and Panamic Soldierfish (*Myripristis leiognathus*), but usually is found in deeper water than these species.

Captive Care: Care for this species is the same as for *Pristigenys alta*, above, and should be kept singly except in very large aquariums. This appealing fish is the most common member of the genus in the marine aquarium trade.

Aquarium Size: 75 gal. **Temperature:** 18 to 24°C (64 to 75°F).

Aquarium Suitability Index: 4.

Remarks: At one time, this species was placed in the genus *Pseudopriacanthus*.

References

Anderson et al. (1972), Caldwell (1962), Caldwell & Bullis (1971), Fitch & Crooke (1984), Myers (1999), Parker & Ross (1986), Quinn (1988), Salmon & Winn (1966), Starnes (1988).

Priacanthus sagittarius, Blackspot Bigeye: mottled color phase.

Pristigenys alta, Short Bigeye: cute juveniles become bold, voracious adults.

Pristigenys serrula, Popeye Catalufa: most common bigeye in aquarium trade.

FAMILY CIRRHITIDAE
HAWKFISHES

NOT THE MOST CONSPICUOUS FISHES ON THE REEF, these aquatic raptors are nonetheless of great interest to divers, snorkelers and aquarists who discover them. Careful inspection of several coral heads on any Indo-Pacific reef will usually turn up at least one of these vigilant little predators perched and ready to swoop out at passing prey. Because most species tend to be quite bold and colorful, they are popular subjects with neophyte fish photographers, who often find them some of the easiest fishes on the reef to photograph.

Not only are hawkfishes important members of reef communities, they are also ubiquitous in aquarium stores—and for good reason. Hawkfishes are fascinating to watch, extremely hardy, often quite colorful, and several species do reasonably well in mini-reef aquariums. But there are usually two sides to every coin, and this is certainly the case with hawkfishes. The less desirable side of hawkfish behavior includes a predisposition to be aggressive, a taste for smaller fishes and ornamental shrimps, and a tendency to lose their vivid coloration.

Classification and Biology

The hawkfish family consists of 35 to 36 species and nine or ten genera. At least 15 of these species show up in North American aquarium stores. All have cirri (hairlike filaments) on their single dorsal fin, cirri behind the anterior nostrils, and 14 pectoral rays that are stout and unbranched (these fishes rest on their pectoral rays when they sit on the bottom). To the delight of marine fish collectors, hawkfishes also lack a gas bladder. Because they do not possess this organ, they can be brought to the surface without long decompression stops.

While the hawkfishes are known from all tropical seas, most species are found in the Western Pacific and Eastern Indian Oceans. A number exhibit fairly narrow geographical ranges. For example, the Bicolor Hawkfish (*Paracirrhites bicolor*), Nisos Hawkfish (*P. nisus*), and the Golden Hawkfish (*P. xanthus*) are only found on reefs around certain Polynesian islands. The Spottedtail Hawkfish (*Cirrhitichthys calliurus*) is limited in distribution to the Northern Indian Ocean (the Gulf of Oman to the Gulf of Aden), while the Splendid Hawkfish (*Cirrhitus splendens*)

Paracirrhites forsteri, Freckled Hawkfish: likened to underwater raptors, members of this family perch with vigilance, ready to swoop upon passing prey.

has only been reported from Lord Howe Island and New South Wales, Australia (it is uncommon in the latter location). Two of the widest-ranging species are Falco's Hawkfish (*Cirrhitichthys falco*) and the Coral Hawkfish (*C. oxycephalus*), found from the Eastern Pacific to the Red Sea. Only three cirrhitids are known from the Atlantic Ocean (*Amblycirrhitus pinos, A. wilhelmi,* and *Cirrhitus atlanticus*). The majority of the cirrhitids associate with coral or rocky-reef substrate and are found in relatively shallow water.

Most hawkfishes spend their days sitting on or at the base of coral heads, using their enlarged pectoral rays to perch on the substrate. When prey comes close, the hawkfish will dart out from its ambush site to capture it. Hawkfish species can be divided up into two major groups based on the types of prey that predominate in their diets. The first group consists of those species with smaller mouths that feed heavily on more diminutive crustaceans. Members of this guild include the Coral (*Cirrhitichthys oxycephalus*), the Falco's (*C. falco*), and the Flame Hawkfishes (*Neocirrhites armatus*). Those in the second group have more capacious mouths and consume larger shrimp, crabs, and small fishes. The Freckled (*Paracirrhites forsteri*), Arc-eye (*P. arcatus*), and Stocky Hawkfishes (*Cirrhitus pinnulatus*) are members of this large-mouthed group.

Most hawkfishes are thought to be protogynous hermaphrodites (see the Yellow Hawkfish, *Cirrhitichthys aureus*, account below for a possible exception), and most species exhibit a haremic social structure, with the territory of a single male being occupied by one or more females. The Flame and Longnose Hawkfishes (*Oxycirrhites typus*) are exceptions—they are usually found in monogamous pairs. In at least some of the haremic species, a larger female will typically change sex when the territory-holding male disappears. However, in some cases, these females will engage in early sex change. Once they transform into males, they may try to steal one or more females from the harem they occupied or from neighboring social groups.

Hawkfish courtship occurs just prior to sunset. Some cirrhitids spawn every night, others may court on a daily basis but do not always spawn. Those hawkfishes in subtropical to warm temperature environments may have defined spawning seasons. Courtship behavior is similar (with minor variations) in most cirrhitids. It begins when the male swims circles around the female

Oxycirrhites typus, Longnose Hawkfish: an appealing, hardy aquarium fish, but one that is not at all safe with small fishes and ornamental shrimps.

Captive Care

What are the drawbacks to keeping hawkfishes in the home aquarium? One big problem is that they can be hostile, especially toward tankmates introduced after they are established or that exhibit similar behavior (i.e., sit on the substrate). The least aggressive species are the Longnose, the Lyretail (*Cyprinocirrhites polyactis*), and the Flame Hawkfishes, but even these species are not above reproach. Members of the genus *Paracirrhites* are extremely aggressive. They will attack, maim, and occasionally ingest fish tankmates. Small damselfishes, dottybacks, wrasses, gobies, and blennies are potential prey for Arc-eye and Freckled Hawkfishes. The *Paracirrhites* species will even attack fishes larger than themselves. I had an Arc-eye Hawkfish that charged and bit a Moon Wrasse (*Thalassoma lunare*) and another specimen that attacked and almost dispatched a Tobacco Bass (*Serranus tabacarius*) three times its own length. Members of the genus *Cirrhitus* and *Cirrhitops* can be equally as aggressive, while the *Cirrhitichthys* species have also been known to chase new arrivals and eat smaller fishes. Because of its aggressive tendencies, it is imperative that your hawkfish be the last fish placed in your community tank, unless of course it is being kept with fishes that are considerably larger or more aggressive.

It is possible to keep more than one hawkfish of the same species together. This is a more difficult thing to do with members of the genus *Paracirrhites* and *Cirrhitus*. In some cases, hawkfishes kept in the same aquarium for a long period of time may suddenly begin to squabble. It is not uncommon in these situations for the larger specimen to kill or severely damage a smaller conspecific tankmate. One reason that this may occur is because the smaller specimen may suddenly change sex, from female to male, and the larger specimen may then attempt to drive the rival member of the same sex out of its territory. Of course, in a relatively small glass box, there is no place for the subordinate male to go. If it is not removed by the aquarist, it is eliminated by the larger conspecific. Be warned: just because a pair of hawkfishes seems peaceful now, they may not be that way forever.

Another potential problem for the hawkfish owner is that all of these fishes have been implicated in attacks on ornamental shrimp. Even the apparently innocuous needle-nosed member of the clan, the Longnose Hawkfish, will occasionally grasp shrimp in its plierslike jaws and bash them against the substrate until they are broken into bite-size morsels. Lyretail Hawkfish are the least likely to eat your shrimp, while the Flame Hawkfish cannot be trusted in this regard. If you want to try to keep shrimp with a cirrhitid, add the shrimp first and keep larger varieties (e.g., boxer shrimps, *Stenopus* spp.). Hermit crabs and arrow crabs are also at risk from hawkfish predation.

and eventually comes to rest next to her. The female responds by leading the male around the courtship site. The male stimulates the female by nudging her with his snout, sitting on top of her, and quivering his body. Just prior to spawning, the male and female raise their heads up and lift their bodies off the substrate by flexing their pectoral fins. The pair then make a rapid spawning ascent, releasing their gametes at the top. Aquarium spawning has been reported for the Longnose Hawkfish, Hubbard's Hawkfish (*Cirrhitops hubbardi*), and the Yellow Hawkfish (*Cirrhitichthys aureus*). Unfortunately, the latter two species are rarely available in the North American aquarium trade. If you want to obtain a male-female pair, purchasing specimens that differ significantly in size will increase your chances, as all the hawkfishes studied have males larger than females. Differences in male-female coloration have been reported in aquarium studies conducted on the Longnose Hawkfish, but these observations have not been confirmed in field studies.

Cirrhitichthys aureus, Yellow Hawkfish: displaying the typical capacious hawkfish maw that is used to grasp prey items with lightning speed.

Of some concern to the reef aquarist is the irritation that hawkfishes can cause to corals when perching on them. For example, when a hawkfish lights on a piece of soft coral, it will cause the coral's polyps to contract. If an individual consistently rests on the same coral, this could interfere with the cnidarian's normal behavior.

Certain hawkfishes are also prone to losing their vivid color. This applies specifically to the bright red pigments found in the Longnose, Flame, Blood Red, and some of the "spotted hawkfishes" (*Cirrhitichthys* spp.). The key to maintaining their brilliance is to feed them as varied a diet as possible. Some of the newer frozen foods with added amino acids, pigments, and vitamins are particularly good staples. Salmon flesh is also helpful in chromatic maintenance, while live freshwater fish (e.g., mollies, guppies, goldfish) are greedily accepted, but should not be the mainstay of any marine fish's diet. Color may also fade if the hawkfish is suffering from a parasitic infection.

On the plus side, these are very rugged fishes, with a well-demonstrated resistance to disease. I have known hawkfish to thrive during parasitic outbreaks that killed every other fish in the aquarium. (Of course, one should always take all the precautions and administer the prescribed treatments even if a hawkfish is in an infected tank.) Another good cirrhitid feature is that they are not overly sensitive to poor water quality and some (e.g., *Cirrhitichthys* spp., *Cirrhitops* spp., *Paracirrhites* spp.) can even be used to "cycle" a new tank.

The only problem with using them to start an aquarium is that they are so territorial that any fish introduced afterward is likely to be abused.

HAWKFISH SPECIES

Genus *Amblycirrhitus*

Amblycirrhitus bimacula (Jenkins, 1903)
Common Name: Twospotted Hawkfish.
Maximum Length: 8.5 cm (3.3 in.).
Distribution: East Africa to the Hawaiian and Mangareva Islands, north to Taiwan.
Biology: The Twospotted Hawkfish occurs most frequently in the surge zone of spur and groove areas on the reef crest or reef face. It lives at depths from 2 to 15 m (6.6 to 49 ft.), and although it is common in many areas, it is rarely seen due to its secretive lifestyle. *Amblycirrhitus bimacula* remains hidden in brush corals, reef interstices, or among coral rubble. It is haremic or forms monogamous pairs depending on the availability of mates and the microhabitat occupied. For example, pairs have been observed in heads of *Pocillopora* coral. The pair behaves aggressively toward other species that inhabit the coral head during the day, like coral crouchers (*Caracanthus* spp.), small scorpionfishes, and damselfishes. They are especially aggressive as the sun sets when other fishes, like small groupers and surgeonfishes, attempt to use the same coral head as refuge for the night. This hawkfish probably feeds on small, cryptic crustaceans and polychaete worms.
Captive Care: The Twospotted Hawkfish will do well in a fish or reef aquarium, although it is rather cryptic and will be seen less frequently than some of the other cirrhitids. It is not as belligerent as most other members of the family, but it may defend a preferred hiding place or portion of the aquarium decor from

Amblycirrhitus bimacula, Twospotted Hawkfish: somewhat meek and retiring.

Amblycirrhitus pinos, Redspotted Hawkfish: the only Caribbean hawkfish.

Cirrhitichthys aprinus, Spotted Hawkfish: spawns daily in the wild.

intrusion or may attack other fishes that move about on the substrate (e.g., sand perches, gobies, and blennies). If you keep it with fishes that are aggressive feeders, you may have some trouble providing food to this hawkfish because of its reclusiveness. By placing it in a tank full of live rock, you will provide it with access to some natural food items. The Twospotted Hawkfish may eat small ornamental shrimps and tubeworms, but otherwise is no threat to invertebrates. This species is also less likely to agitate your sessile invertebrates by perching on them.

Aquarium Size: 20 gal. **Temperature:** 22 to 27°C (72 to 81°F).
Aquarium Suitability Index: 4.
Remarks: *Amblycirrhitus bimacula* is white overall with ten light orange to dark brown bars or rows of spots on the body.

Amblycirrhitus pinos (Mowbray, 1927)

Common Name: Redspotted Hawkfish.
Maximum Length: 9.5 cm (3.7 in.).
Distribution: South Florida to Venezuela, east to St. Helena.
Biology: The Redspotted Hawkfish occurs on lagoon coral heads, on the edge of the reef flat, the reef face, and fore-reef slopes in areas of heavy coral and sponge growth. This species is also very common on invertebrate-encrusted pier pilings, where it perches on or among orange cup corals (*Tubastraea* sp.) and sponges. It occurs at depths from 3 to 25 m (9.8 to 82 ft.). The Redspotted Hawkfish feeds mostly on zooplankton (including copepods and shrimp larvae), but it also includes small shrimps, isopods, crabs, and polychaete worms in its diet.
Captive Care: The Redspotted Hawkfish is quite shy when initially introduced to the aquarium. However, after it has settled in it may bully newly introduced tankmates, especially in a smaller tank. More then one specimen can be kept in a medium

to large aquarium if they are introduced simultaneously, are not of equal size, and if adequate hiding places are provided. This species will spend most of its time sitting in the open. It is an excellent reef aquarium fish, although it may eat smaller, more delicate shrimps.

Aquarium Size: 20 gal. **Temperature:** 22 to 27°C (72 to 81°F).
Aquarium Suitability Index: 5.
Remarks: The Redspotted Hawkfish is one of only three cirrhitids present in the Atlantic and the only species that occurs in the Caribbean. It is replaced at Ascension Island by **Earnshaw's Hawkfish** (*Amblycirrhitus earnshawi*) **Lubbock, 1978,** which is the only all-white hawkfish. The Redspotted Hawkfish is dark green overall with a brown line down its head, brown bands on the body, and a black spot under the soft portion of the dorsal fin. The face, back, and dorsal fin are peppered with orange or red spots. **Wilhelm's Hawkfish** (*Amblycirrhitus wilhelmi*) (**Lavenberg & Yañez, 1972**) is another member of the genus with a very restricted range. It is only known from Easter Island.

Genus *Cirrhitichthys*

Cirrhitichthys aprinus (Cuvier, 1829)

Common Names: Spotted Hawkfish, Threadfin Hawkfish, Blotched Hawkfish.
Maximum Length: 12.5 cm (4.9 in.).
Distribution: East Indies, north to southern Japan, and south to the Great Barrier reef.
Biology: This species occurs on coastal coral and rocky reefs, in turbid estuarine conditions, and on encrusted shipwrecks. It often lives in areas with rich sponge growth and is commonly found in repose on large barrel sponges. It occurs at depths from 5 to

40 m (16 to 131 ft.). The Spotted Hawkfish is haremic, with these social units typically consisting of one male and one to five females. Male territories typically cover an area of 25 m² (278 ft.²). Females and from one to nine juveniles reside in the male's territory. Fighting between males is uncommon because they rarely encounter one another, but female-female aggression occurs frequently within harems. Occasionally harems include a congener. For example, female Falco's Hawkfish (*Cirrhitichthys falco*) and female Coral (*C. oxycephalus*) Hawkfish were observed in *C. aprinus* harems. Male Spotted Hawkfish have also been observed courting and spawning with female Falco's Hawkfish, and laboratory investigations have shown that these spawnings will produce some viable eggs. This fish spawns daily. Reproductive behavior occurs just prior to and right after sunset, with males visiting the courtship sites of all the females in his harem. This species displays shorter but more frequent courtship bouts than its congeners. The spawning ascent takes the pair from 0.25 to 1 m (.8 to 3.3 ft.) above the substrate. Groupers and scorpionfishes have been observed trying to prey upon male Spotted Hawkfish as they move from one spawning site to another or as they court females.

Captive Care: The Spotted Hawkfish is hardy but is a potentially aggressive aquarium inhabitant. It cannot be trusted with small fishes or ornamental shrimps. It can be kept in male-female pairs, and although they are not sexually dichromatic, males are usually larger than females. Territorial males are larger in body size than the females within their social unit, but may be smaller than females in other harems. Therefore, the greater the disparity in body size between individuals, the more likely they are of the opposite sexes.

Aquarium Size: 20 gal. **Temperature:** 22 to 27°C (72 to 81°F).

Aquarium Suitability Index: 5.

Remarks: The Spotted Hawkfish has a dark spot with a pale outline on its gill cover and three or more diagonal lines below each eye. The body and fins are blotched. There are two color phases: red and brown. Donaldson (1990) reported that the adult female *C. aprinus* he observed ranged in total length from 4 to 8.5 cm (1.6 to 3.3 in.), while adult males were 6 to 10 cm (2.3 to 3.9 in.) in total length.

Cirrhitichthys aureus (Temminck & Schlegel, 1843)

Common Names: Yellow Hawkfish, Golden Hawkfish.

Maximum Length: 14 cm (5.5 in.).

Distribution: Southern Indonesia, the Philippines, south China, and southern Japan.

Biology: The Yellow Hawkfish is a resident of reef faces and fore-reef slopes, where it occurs at depths of 5 to 60 m (16 to 197

Cirrhitichthys aureus, Yellow Hawkfish: colors vary in this uncommon species.

ft.). In more tropical seas, it is usually found at greater depths (in excess of 25 m [82 ft.]). It is usually seen on sponges and is almost always solitary. This species defends a larger territory than many of its congeners and is less site-attached. The sexuality of this fish is also different from that of other hawkfish species studied: it is capable of changing sex in either direction (female to male or male to female). According to Sadovy and Donaldson (1995) it exhibits a sexual pattern intermediate between a simultaneous and sequential hermaphrodite. Reproduction in this species is seasonal.

Captive Care: *Cirrhitichthys aureus* is not common in the aquarium trade. Its care requirements are similar to those of *C. aprinus* (see species account above).

Aquarium Size: 20 gal. **Temperature:** 19 to 27°C (66 to 81°F).

Aquarium Suitability Index: 5.

Remarks: The color of this species varies from bright yellow to brown overall. Some individuals sport dark blotches similar to those of *C. aprinus*.

Cirrhitichthys calliurus Regan, 1905

Common Name: Spottedtail Hawkfish.

Maximum Length: 12 cm (4.7 in.).

Distribution: Gulf of Oman to the Gulf of Aden.

Biology: This species is found at depths of 15 to 30 m (49 to 98 ft.). It rests on coral heads and rocky substrate waiting for prey to pass by.

Captive Care: The Spottedtail Hawkfish is rare in the aquarium

Cirrhitichthys calliurus, Spottedtail Hawkfish: rarely seen by aquarists.

Cirrhitichthys falco, Falco's Hawkfish: color variant lacking usual red patches.

Cirrhitichthys falco, Falco's Hawkfish: small, attractive, and very hardy.

trade, but general husbandry rules for other members of this genus should apply.

Aquarium Size: 20 gal. **Temperature:** 19 to 27°C (66 to 81°F).

Aquarium Suitability Index: 5.

Remarks: This deeper-bodied hawkfish, similar to the Yellow Hawkfish (*C. aureus*), is pinkish red or orangish overall with darker blotches, a black caudal peduncle, and a white tail with black spots and a dark rear margin. It is very closely related to **Bleeker's Hawkfish** (*Cirrhitichthys bleekeri*) **Day, 1874.** Unlike *C. calliurus* and *C. aureus*, the pelvic fins of *C. bleekeri* do not reach the anus. Known only from the coast of India, *C. bleekeri* is a rosy color overall with pale longitudinal lines and an obscure blotch below the posterior portion of the dorsal fin.

Cirrhitichthys falco Randall, 1963

Common Names: Falco's Hawkfish, Dwarf Hawkfish.

Maximum Length: 7 cm (2.7 in.).

Distribution: Red Sea and southern Africa to Panama, north to the Marianas, and south to New Caledonia.

Biology: Falco's Hawkfish occurs on the reef crest, the reef face, and fore-reef slopes with moderate to rich coral growth. It is also found on rubble slopes. *Cirrhitichthys falco* is found at depths from 4 to 46 m (13 to 151 ft.), normally sitting at the base of coral heads. Juveniles are usually solitary, while the adults are haremic. An adult social unit consists of one male and one to seven females. Some social groups may also contain "sneaker" males that attempt to split the harems of the dominant male. Females of this species have been observed spawning with the Spotted Hawkfish (*C. aprinus*). Spawning occurs daily in *C. falco*.

Captive Care: This durable species is a great fish for beginning hobbyists. It is slightly smaller in size and poses less danger to its tankmates than most of its congeners, but it should not be trusted with small, nonaggressive fishes (e.g., dartfishes, small gobies, some anthias, flasher wrasses, and other small, inoffensive wrasses), especially in a smaller tank. In an aquarium with less aggressive species, it should be the last fish introduced.

Aquarium Size: 15 gal. **Temperature:** 22 to 27°C (72 to 81°F).

Aquarium Suitability Index: 5.

Remarks: *Cirrhitichthys falco* has a white body with red or reddish brown spots, most of which are grouped to form five bars; the darkest of the bars is in front of the dorsal fin. Color varies from one habitat to another. Those specimens that occur in sandy areas are often lighter than those who live where stony corals predominate. Falco's Hawkfish also has two bars under each eye.

Donaldson (1990) reported that the adult female *C. falco* he observed ranged in total length from 3.5 to 6 cm (1.4 to 2.3 in.), while adult males were 5.5 to 8 cm (2.1 to 3.1 in.) in total length.

Cirrhitichthys oxycephalus (Bleeker, 1855)

Common Names: Coral Hawkfish, Pixy Hawkfish, Coral Hawkfish.

Maximum Length: 8.5 cm (3.3 in.).

Distribution: Red Sea and South Africa to Panama and the middle Gulf of California, north to the Marianas, and south to New Caledonia.

Biology: The Coral Hawkfish occurs on lagoon coral heads, reef channels, reef faces, fore-reef slopes, shipwrecks, and rocky reefs at depths from 1 to 40 m (3.3 to 131 ft.)and most often at depths of less than 12 m (39 ft.). It is often found in habitats with lush stony coral growth. For example, in the southern Gulf of California, it is most common on *Pocillopora* and *Porites* reefs. In other parts of the Gulf, it is found among colonies of the orange cup coral (*Tubastraea* sp.). In some regions, it most often occurs at the base of coral colonies, rather than on or among the branches. It will also sit between the branches of *Sinularia* soft corals or among tunicates and sponges. It is found in both sheltered microhabitats and those exposed to considerable surge. This hawkfish feeds on small crustaceans, small fishes, fish eggs, and polychaete worms. It is haremic, with social units varying greatly from one geographical area to another. In the southern Gulf of California, where suitable habitat for these fish is in short supply, males may have a harem of one to seven females. Males defend a territory in which the females reside (the females spend most of their time in a certain part of the male's territory but are not territorial themselves). In areas of the Indo-Pacific, where this species occurs at lower densities, males usually have no more than two females in their harem. One female will occupy a coral head with the male, while a second female may live up to 3 m (9.8 ft.) away. Reproduction occurs daily just before dusk. The male will begin visiting the females in his territory, possibly to assess their reproductive readiness. The females will move to a prominent feature in their home range and wait for the male to return. When the male revisits a ripe female, he will begin to nudge her and the pair will begin "hopping" around the spawning area. They will then move to the top of the prominent topographical feature, rest side by side for 10 to 30 seconds, and then commence the spawning ascent.

Captive Care: This pugnacious fish should not be housed with smaller, less aggressive species. I have seen it relentlessly pick on small dottybacks, grammas, pygmy angelfishes, butterflyfishes, sand perches, gobies, and dartfishes. I have also had this species

Cirrhitichthys oxycephalus, Coral Hawkfish: pretty, but notoriously pugnacious.

Cirrhitichthys oxycephalus, Coral Hawkfish: color variant with light pigments.

attack small Arc-eyed Hawkfish (*Paracirrhites arcatus*) introduced after the Coral Hawkfish became a well-established resident of the tank. To keep this species with less aggressive fishes, make sure it is the last fish added to the tank. It is also a threat to ornamental shrimps.

Aquarium Size: 20 gal. **Temperature:** 22 to 27°C (72 to 81°F).

Aquarium Suitability Index: 5.

Remarks: The Coral Hawkfish has a white body with red or reddish brown spots; it also has spots, rather than lines, under the eye. **Guichenot's Hawkfish (*Cirrhitichthys guichenoti*) (Sauvage, 1880)** is very similar to *C. oxycephalus*, but it has a much longer snout, and higher fin and scale counts. It is also limited in distribution to Mauritius and Reunion Islands. Donaldson (1990)

Cirrhitops fasciatus, Blood Red Hawkfish: possible female color phase.

Cirrhitops fasciatus, Blood Red Hawkfish: probable male color phase.

reported that the adult female *C. oxycephalus* he observed ranged in total length from 3.5 to 5 cm (1.4 to 2 in.), while adult males were 4.5 to 5.5 cm (1.8 to 2.1 in.) in total length.

Genus *Cirrhitops*

Cirrhitops fasciatus (Bennett, 1828)
Common Names: Blood Red Hawkfish, Redbar Hawkfish, Banded Hawkfish.
Maximum Length: 12.7 cm (5 in.)
Distribution: Japan, Hawaii, Madagascar, and Mauritius.
Biology: This species occurs at depths of 2 to 52 m (6.6 to 171 ft.). In Hawaii, it occurs on both coral and basalt reefs. It often sits in exposed positions during both the day and night and does not usually associate with live stony corals, as do some of the other hawkfishes. It feeds mainly on small fishes, xanthid crabs, and shrimps, but also consumes zooplankters (including larval shrimps, copepods, amphipods, and larval gastropods), octopuses, sipunculid worms, and serpent stars on occasion. Unlike most hawkfishes, this species feeds both day and night.
Captive Care: *Cirrhitops fasciatus* is a very durable aquarium fish. It is a threat to small fishes and crustaceans and is best housed with larger or more aggressive species like angelfishes, larger pseudochromoids (e.g., Red Dottyback [*Labracinus cyclophthalmus*], Australian Dottyback [*Ogilbyina novaehollandiae*], Arabian Bluelined Dottyback [*Pseudochromis aldabraensis*]), larger wrasses, pufferfishes, and triggerfishes. It will eat almost anything, including flake and frozen prepared foods, but should be fed a varied diet, including some natural color-enhancing foods like krill and shrimp.

Aquarium Size: 20 gal. **Temperature:** 22 to 27°C (72 to 81°F).
Aquarium Suitability Index: 5.
Remarks: The Blood Red Hawkfish is white with red or brownish bars on the body, spots on the head, and a large black spot on the caudal peduncle. It has yet to be determined whether this species is sexually dichromatic, but in a pair that I kept, the male was bright red overall while the smaller female was reddish brown. The similar **Hubbard's Hawkfish** (*Cirrhitops hubbardi*) (Schultz, 1943) is known from the Ogasawara Islands of Japan west to the islands of Oceania (excluding the Hawaiian Islands). Rather than having vertical bars like *C. fasciatus*, Hubbard's Hawkfish has four rows of pale spots running down the body and a large black spot on the caudal peduncle. There are also small white spots on the head and back and white lines on the lips.

Genus *Cirrhitus*

Cirrhitus pinnulatus (Forster, 1801)
Common Names: Stocky Hawkfish, Chinese Hawkfish.
Maximum Length: 28 cm (10.9 in.).
Biology: This nocturnal hawkfish spends most of its days under ledges and in crevices in the surging shallow waters of the spur-and-groove zone. It occurs at depths of 0.3 to 3 m (1 to 9.8 ft.). Although nocturnally active, individuals are sometimes observed interacting with one another during the day and occasionally darting from one hiding place to another. It feeds primarily on crabs, but also eats shrimps, fishes, sea urchins, and brittle stars. It has even been reported to feed on cleaner wrasses. Like most other hawkfishes, this species forms harems. Males occupy a territory that is inhabited by one or more females and defend their

courtship sites from consexuals just before courtship begins (just prior to sunset). In the case of shared courtship sites, larger females dominate smaller, subordinate individuals. During the courtship period, males chase smaller females away and spawn with larger females. The male will not spawn with all the females in his harem in a single evening of courtship. This species makes a spawning ascent of 1.5 m (4.9 ft.).

Captive Care: In the aquarium, as in nature, the Stocky Hawkfish will remain hidden much of the time, peering out from reef crevices. It will greedily accept live and prepared foods and will make short work of most shrimps and small fishes.

Aquarium Size: 75 gal. **Temperature:** 22 to 27°C (72 to 81°F).

Aquarium Suitability Index: 5.

Remarks: *Cirrhitus pinnulatus* is an olive color overall with white blotches on the side and a white belly. The head and body are sprinkled with reddish brown or orange-brown spots. The Stocky Hawkfish is one of the largest cirrhitids. Donaldson (1990) reports that adult females are 6 to 17 cm (2.3 to 6.6 in.) in total length, while males are 15 to 21 cm (5.9 to 8.2 in.) long. The only member of the genus in the Atlantic Ocean is the **West African Hawkfish** (*Cirrhitus atlanticus*) **Osório, 1893**, which has been reported from the Ivory Coast of Africa to the island of São Tomé. This hawkfish attains a maximum length of 18 cm (7 in.).

Cirrhitus rivulatus (Valenciennes, 1846)

Common Names: Giant Hawkfish, Chino Mero, Hieroglyphic Hawkfish.

Maximum Length: 52 cm (20.3 in.).

Distribution: Central Gulf of California south to Colombia, as well as most of the offshore islands, including the Galapagos.

Biology: *Cirrhitus rivulatus* is a resident of shallow water and rocky reefs. It resides among large boulders, fragmented rocks, and on reef walls, at depths from 4 to 23 m (13 to 75 ft.). Smaller individuals are most common in areas of strong wave action and spend most of their time hiding. Adults often perch in exposed areas, although they are also found under overhangs, in crevices, and at the entrances of caves. This hawkfish is nocturnal and feeds on crustaceans and fishes. It appears to be a solitary species.

Captive Care: The Giant Hawkfish, not regularly seen in the aquarium trade, is a durable species that will eat chopped seafood, cubes of frozen preparations, feeder fish, and live grass shrimp. It will also make short work of smaller fishes and ornamental crustaceans. Only one Giant Hawkfish should be kept per aquarium. Small individuals can be housed with other hawkfish species, but larger *C. rivulatus* may eat smaller congeners. This fish is usually not overly aggressive toward other fish species. It

Cirrhitus pinnulatus, Stocky Hawkfish: large, but with a tendency to hide.

Cirrhitus rivulatus, Giant Hawkfish: fascinating and formidible fish.

will require a larger tank than any of the other hawkfishes and should be provided with crevices or ledges to hide in or under. Small individuals are very secretive, while larger fish will spend most of their daylight hours perched in the open.

Aquarium Size: 135 gal. **Temperature:** 20 to 27°C (68 to 81°F).

Aquarium Suitability Index: 5.

Remarks: The body of the adult Giant Hawkfish is olive in color, with darker spots edged in light blue to bluish green. The spots on the head form bands that radiate from the eyes. There are two light spots under the posterior dorsal fin. The juveniles lack the spots and are banded instead. The Spanish name, *Chino Mero*, means Chinese Bass. The **Splendid Hawkfish** (*Cirrhitus splendens*) (**Ogilby, 1889**) is an amazing fish that is a resident of Lord Howe Island (stragglers have been reported around islands

Cirrhitus splendens, Splendid Hawkfish: rarity from Lord Howe Island.

Cyprinocirrhites polyactis, Lyretail Hawkfish: possibly an anthias mimic.

off the coast of New South Wales). It attains a maximum length of 20 cm (7.8 in.). Unfortunately, this beauty is not regularly seen in the aquarium trade.

Genus *Cyprinocirrhites*

Cyprinocirrhites polyactis (Bleeker, 1874)
Common Names: Lyretail Hawkfish, Swallowtail Hawkfish.
Maximum Length: 14 cm (5.5 in.).
Distribution: East Africa to Australia, north to southern Japan, south to southern Queensland.
Biology: The Lyretail Hawkfish lives on reef faces and fore-reef slopes of coral reefs, on rocky reefs, and in macroalgae/sponge beds. It tends to occur in current-prone habitats at depths from 10 to 132 m (33 to 433 ft.) and is most common at depths in excess of 20 m (66 ft.). This species often rests on large sponges or perches on stony corals, gorgonians, or macroalgae. On a number of occasions, I have also seen this hawkfish resting near the base and even among the tentacles of the Magnificent Sea Anemone (*Heteractis magnifica*). *Cyprinocirrhites polyactis* is truly the "black sheep" of the hawkfish family. Not only does it spend time resting on the substrate (like its relatives), it also swims and feeds up in the water column. On occasion, it will even join groups of plankton-feeding anthias. This has led some naturalists to suggest that it may be a social mimic of certain *Pseudanthias* species, like the Luzon Anthias (*Pseudanthias luzonensis*). The Lyretail Hawkfish feeds on zooplankton, including crustacean larvae and copepods. It typically occurs in pairs or in small groups, although solitary individuals are occasionally encountered.
Captive Care: The Lyretail Hawkfish will spend most of its time in repose on the reef structure, unless the tank has a considerable amount of water movement, in which case it will often swim against the current up in the water column. On occasion, it will hide near the base and under the tentacles of large anemones (especially *Heteractis* spp.) or large-polyped corals (i.e., *Goniopora* spp.). Although not as aggressive as most other hawkfishes, it will often dominate smaller tankmates. It might also behave aggressively toward more passive fishes that are introduced after it has established itself. For example, I once had a specimen that beat up on a fairy wrasse and a Blue Assessor (*Assessor macneilli*). Keeping more than one *C. polyactis* in anything but an extra large tank is risky. Males will fight, although a single male may tolerate a female conspecific. If you want to try to keep more than one, add them to the tank at the same time.
Aquarium Size: 20 gal. **Temperature:** 22 to 27°C (72 to 81°F).
Aquarium Suitability Index: 5.
Remarks: Like many other fish species that enter the water column to feed on plankton, this hawkfish is built to make a hasty retreat if danger threatens. It has a lunate tail and is laterally compressed. It is typically pinkish red with or without mottling on the body and fins (the mottled pattern is often present at night or when the fish is stressed). The eyes are a deep blue or green, depending on the angle from which it is viewed.

Genus *Neocirrhites*

Neocirrhites armatus Castlenau, 1873
Common Name: Flame Hawkfish.
Maximum Length: 9 cm (3.5 in.).
Distribution: Ryukyus to the Line Islands and Mangareva, south to the Great Barrier and Austral Islands.

Neocirrhites armatus, Flame Hawkfish: offering instant appeal to human observers, this species can be a great addition to a branching stony coral reef tank.

Biology: The Flame Hawkfish occurs on upper reef slopes and channels, often in areas with significant surge, typically at depths of less than 11 m (36 ft.). This species is considered an obligatory coral dweller, always found in association with stony corals. Individuals may remain in the same coral colony for a period of years. The Flame Hawkfish is monogamous or haremic, with one male and from one to four females living together among the branches of live *Pocillopora* corals (especially *Pocillopora elegans, P. eydouxi,* and *P. verrucosa*). (There is a correlation between the abundance of Flame Hawkfish and the abundance of live *Pocillopora* colonies.) When threatened by a predator, this hawkfish will withdraw into the deepest recesses of its coral head where it becomes very difficult to extract. The size of a Flame Hawkfish social group is dependent upon the size of the coral head. The larger the coral head, the more females in a male's harem. (Males may defend and court with females in coral colonies as far as 1.5 m [4.9 ft.] away.) While these fish are usually found in pairs, on rare occasions a male may have up to four females in its harem. It is not uncommon for a coral head to contain a single fish as well. Males defend their territories (which may consist of all or a part of a coral head) from other males and from large females. The males usually ignore smaller females and juveniles. Apparently, males chase away larger females because they are more likely to undergo a rapid sex change and compete with the

Neocirrhites armatus, Flame Hawkfish: may attack snails, limpets, shrimps.

resident male for mates. Females will chase off intruding females of greater or equal size, but also tend to be indifferent toward smaller females and juveniles. Reproduction occurs year round. Courtship begins just before and after the sun goes down and ends after dusk. During spawning, their red coloration may serve to make them less conspicuous to potential predators when light levels are low. Sadovy and Donaldson (1995) demonstrated that this species is a protogynous hermaphrodite.

Captive Care: Although this striking creature is one of the most

Oxycirrhites typus, Longnose Hawkfish: prefers to associate with gorgonians.

larger fish and one (or more) smaller individuals. (This will increase the chances you will get a male and a female or juveniles.)

Aquarium Size: 20 gal. **Temperature:** 22 to 27°C (72 to 81°F).

Aquarium Suitability Index: 4.

Remarks: The overall color of the Flame Hawkfish is brilliant red, the eye is encircled in black, and there are black bands running down each side of the dorsal fin. An occasional specimen lacks the black dorsal markings. Within a social group in the wild, the male is always the largest individual. In a study conducted by Donaldson (1989), females ranged from 3.7 to 6.2 cm (1.4 to 2.4 in.) in total length, while males were 4.5 to 7 cm (1.8 to 2.8 in.) long.

Genus *Oxycirrhites*

Oxycirrhites typus Bleeker, 1857

Common Name: Longnose Hawkfish.

Maximum Length: 13 cm (5.1 in.).

Distribution: East Africa and Red Sea east to the Eastern Pacific.

Biology: The Longnose Hawkfish is found on coral and rocky reefs. It occurs on reef pinnacles and fore-reef slopes at depths of 15 to 150 m (49 to 492 ft.). (In at least some regions, it is most common at depths in excess of 20 m [66 ft.].) This fish associates with large gorgonians (e.g., *Subergorgia* spp., *Melithaea* spp.) and black coral trees (*Antipathes* spp.), and their distribution on the reef is influenced by the presence of these corals. Donaldson (1989) reported that this species prefers gorgonians with a diameter greater than 1.8 m (5.9 ft.) and black corals greater than 1.6 m (5.2 ft.) in height. This fish's elongated snout aids it in extracting shrimps from reef crevices, but it also feeds on planktonic crustaceans and even small fishes. (Don't let their unusual jaw anatomy fool you—I have seen photos of adult Longnose Hawkfish with juvenile Lyretail Anthias [*Pseudanthias squamipinnis*] and small baitfish in their mouths.) When this hawkfish captures prey items that are too large to swallow whole, it will bash the prey against the substrate until it is smashed into bite-size pieces. *Oxycirrhites typus* usually occurs singly or in pairs, but it occasionally displays a haremic social system. These harems consist of a male and two females that live on different gorgonians or soft corals adjacent to one another. The male visits and spawns with both females in a single evening. Spawning occurs just before the sun sets and ends at dusk. Although once thought to be a demersal spawner, field observations confirm that like most hawkfishes, this species produces pelagic eggs.

Captive Care: The Longnose Hawkfish will adapt to most reef-type settings, but will look most natural if provided with gorgonians or similar decor in which to perch. It can be kept in

suitable for the invertebrate aquarium, it too has a somewhat dubious reputation. It will occasionally behave aggressively toward other bottom-dwelling fishes and those introduced after it has established its territory. This can be a chronic problem if you have a smaller aquarium (under 55 gallons). Another unfavorable *N. armatus* behavior involves gastropods and hermit crabs. In captivity, these fish have been observed to jerk upended hermit crabs, limpets, and turbo snails out of their shells and eat them. They will even knock snails off the glass in order to make them vulnerable to attack. Christmas Tree Worms (*Spirobranchus giganteus*) are occasionally grasped and extracted from their calcareous tubes by hungry Flame Hawkfish. They will also eat ornamental shrimps, including cleaner shrimps (*Lysmata* spp.) and anemone shrimps (*Periclimenes* spp.). Unfortunately for the aquarist, these fish are difficult to sex, but if you are trying to keep a pair you should have a large tank with plenty of hiding places, and there should be a great size disparity between the individuals selected. In the aquarium they will sometimes refuge next to the base and under the tentacles of large Magnificent Sea Anemones (*Heteractis magnifica*). The movements of this species within a head of stony coral may facilitate water circulation within the colony, and their feces provide a source of nitrogen for coral tissue growth. Another characteristic of this fish that makes it less appealing than some of its congeners is that it is often quite secretive, spending less time in full view. To keep more than one in the same tank, provide plenty of hiding places (ideally, some live *Pocillopora* corals or their replicas) and add one male-female pairs, but both specimens should be introduced simultaneously. Longnose battles usually consist of the combatants circling in a head-to-tail orientation, and raising and lowering their dorsal fins. If the fighting escalates, they may lock jaws and try to inflict physical damage. If individuals start fighting, they should be separated immediately to prevent serious injury. This species tends to be beaten up by most other hawkfishes. Although it is one of the best hawkfishes for the mini-reef aquarium, it will occasionally eat ornamental shrimps (e.g., cleaner shrimps [*Lysmata* spp.] dancing shrimps [*Rhynchocinetes* spp.]). Some *O. typus* will also attack fishes with elongated bodies, such as firefishes and dart gobies. I even had an individual eat two Neon Gobies (*Gobiosoma oceanops*), which are thought to be noxious, and another Longnose attempted to eat a small Yellow Clown Goby (*Gobiodon okinawae*). Large adult *O. typus* are an even greater threat to a wider range of more diminutive fish tankmates. This species will often jump out of uncovered aquariums, so it is a good practice to cover the top of their tank with fiberglass screening.

Aquarium Size: 20 gal. **Temperature:** 22 to 27°C (72 to 81°F).

Aquarium Suitability Index: 5.

Remarks: Males can be distinguished from females on the basis of size and possibly color (although the disparity in size between males and females is not as great as seen in some other cirrhitids). One author reported that males have a darker red lower jaw and black edges on the pelvic and caudal fins (observations of wild social units have not led researchers to similar conclusions). Its exaggerated snout, red checkerboard color pattern, and gregarious personality in the aquarium make it one of the most popular species of hawkfish.

Genus *Paracirrhites*

Paracirrhites arcatus (Cuvier, 1829)

Common Name: Arc-eye Hawkfish.

Maximum Length: 14 cm (5.5 in.).

Distribution: East African to the Hawaiian, Line, and Mangareva Islands, north to southern Japan, and south to New Caledonia and Rapa Island.

Biology: The Arc-eye Hawkfish occurs on lagoon patch reefs, reef faces, and fore-reef slopes. While it has been reported from depths of less than 1 to 91 m (3.3 to 298 ft.), it is usually found in shallow water (less than 12 m [39 ft.]). It is most common in areas where preferred perching sites (e.g., branching stony corals like *Acropora* spp., *Pocillopora elegans, P. eydouxi, P. meandrina* [especially in the Hawaiian Islands], and *Stylophora mordax*) are present. *Paracirrhites arcatus* spends about 95% of its time during the

Paracirrhites arcatus, Arc-eye Hawkfish: best for an aggressive community.

Paracirrhites arcatus, Arc-eye Hawkfish: black, shallow-water color phase.

day perched on the outer portions of branching coral heads and on top of rocks. Juveniles are more common in small colonies of *Pocillopora verrucosa* and *Acropora* spp., while large adults are often found in repose on massive heads of *Porites* corals or lava rock (larger fish have fewer predators and therefore are more likely to be found in the open). At night, or when threatened, the Arc-eye Hawkfish shelters between the branches of the stony corals on which it perches. *Paracirrhites arcatus* is an ambush predator that feeds primarily on bottom-dwelling crustaceans, including shrimps and crabs, but also eats small fishes swimming near the substrate or in the water column. De Martini (1996) reported that 60% of 329 feeding bites observed were directed at benthic (bottom-dwelling) prey (usually on lava rock or dead coral), while 40% were directed at prey in the water column. This hawkfish also feeds on the *Trapezia* crabs that co-occur within

Paracirrhites arcatus, Arc-eye Hawkfish: colors vary by habitat and region.

its coral shelter. Although most feeding occurs during the day, individuals may occasionally feed on swarming copepods and shrimps after dark. This species forms male-dominated harems, with males defending one to several females. (As in most hawkfishes, the male in a social group is larger than the female members.) In areas where its preferred microhabitat is in short supply, as many as 11 *P. arcatus* have been observed in a single *Pocillopora* colony (this was after a hurricane had reduced the number of coral colonies available in the area). Females live in a home range within a male's territory. Juveniles live in small heads of coral, often within the boundaries of male territories as well. Males interact aggressively at territory boundaries, but ignore females. While females are not territorial per se, they may occasionally squabble over a coral head or shelter site within the male's territory. Members of a social unit often perch less than 1 to 5 m (3.3 to 16 ft.) apart. Spawning may take place year round in many locations, but in the Hawaiian Islands it occurs from March through May. Courtship and spawning coincide with the dusk period, just before and after sunset. Courtship in this species is less complex than that of the Freckled Hawkfish (*Paracirrhites forsteri*). Males may consecutively court as many as four females, but do not necessarily spawn with all the females in their harem in the same evening. The spawning ascent usually takes the pair 1 to 1.4 m (3.3 to 4.6 ft.) into the water column where they release eggs and sperm.

Captive Care: The Arc-eye Hawkfish is a larger species that does best in an aggressive community setting. It will display hostility toward fishes introduced after it, even if the new fishes are considerably larger. For example, I have had *P. arcuatus* attack larger seabasses, damselfishes, anemonefishes, and wrasses. I have also had it prey on other fishes. In one instance, I had a medium-sized individual that grasped a Yellowtail Blue Damselfish (*Chrysiptera parasema*) by the tail section. It was having difficulty swallowing it, so it struck the fish against the substrate several times, then spat it out, grasped it by the head and proceeded to swallow it. Although it will not harm corals (except for possible mechanical damage), it will eat small crabs, cleaner, boxer, anemone, and *Saron* shrimps, as well as small fishes. A known male-female pair can be kept in a larger aquarium together, but otherwise place only one individual per aquarium. You can increase the chances of acquiring a pair if you purchase individuals that differ significantly in size (males are typically larger than females).

Aquarium Size: 30 gal. **Temperature:** 22 to 27°C (72 to 81°F).
Aquarium Suitability Index: 5.

Remarks: The Arc-eye Hawkfish is one of several hawkfishes with a postocular marking (a chromatic feature behind the eye). In the case of this species, it consists of a ring of orange, red, and blue behind and around the eye. There are three main *P. arcatus* color morphs. The one most commonly observed by divers and in aquarium stores is the white-striped form, which is pink overall with a white streak on each flank. Another color morph has a reddish olive body without the white markings. (An intermediate color form has also been described with the reddish olive body and the white stripes as well.) The third major color morph (a melanistic form) is olive or dark brown overall with a postocular marking but no other chromatic features. All of the color morphs have dark-edged, orange bars on the gill cover. It has been shown that these color variations are not related to the size or sex of the individual. However, one study demonstrated that the melanistic form is more common in shallow water, while the white-striped form typically occurs at greater depths (this can vary from one location to the next). In the Hawaiian Islands, the melanistic morph is also most common on leeward reefs off the islands of Oahu and Hawaii. Donaldson (1990) reported that the adult females he observed ranged in total length from 4 to 7 cm (1.6 to 2.7 in.), while adult males were 5 to 9.5 cm (2 to 3.7 in.) in total length.

Paracirrhites forsteri (Schneider, 1801)

Common Names: Freckled Hawkfish, Forster's Hawkfish, Blackside Hawkfish.

Maximum Length: 22.5 cm (8.8 in.).

Distribution: Red Sea to Hawaiian, Line, Marquesas and Ducie Islands, north to southern Japan, and south to Norfolk and the Austral Islands.

Paracirrhites forsteri, Freckled Hawkfish: beautiful pair in their usual element—ramose or branching *Pocillopora* corals. This species is a voracious fish predator.

Biology: The Freckled Hawkfish perches on ramose stony corals (including *Acropora* spp. and *Pocillopora* spp.), fire corals (*Millepora* spp.), and on top of massive hard corals or boulders. It occurs at depths from 3 to 30 m (9.8 to 98 ft.). This diurnal predator feeds primarily on fishes (including wrasses), but also consumes shrimps (e.g., *Saron* spp.) and xanthid crabs. It moves infrequently, remaining still and waiting for its quarry to move past. When a potential prey item moves within range, the hawkfish makes a quick, explosive dash to try to capture it. This species is haremic, with social groupings consisting of one male and one to three females. Males are sexually dimorphic, attaining a larger size than females. The large territories held by males contain one or more large coral heads (e.g., *Pocillopora eydouxi* and/or *Acropora palifera*) that the male moves between and uses as ambush sites, places to hide, and spawning sites. Males interact aggressively along territory borders; females, although they rarely interact, commonly behave aggressively toward each other at spawning sites. Juveniles live within the male territories as well but rarely interact with adult individuals. Courtship takes place just before and after sunset, while spawning occurs from 1 to 47 minutes afterward. Courtship may last from 2.5 to 12.6 minutes. Spawning ascents ranged from 1.5 to 2.5 m (4.9 to 8.2 ft.). The male spawns with more than one female in an evening.

Captive Care: This is a voracious fish-eater and is aggressive toward fishes with similar behavior and those introduced after it. These hardy fish should be excluded from the invertebrate aquarium and are best kept with larger, more aggressive species (e.g., triggerfishes, large angelfishes, large surgeonfishes).

Aquarium Size: 75 gal. **Temperature:** 22 to 27°C (72 to 81°F).
Aquarium Suitability Index: 5.

Remarks: Like the Arc-eye Hawkfish (*P. arcuatus*), this species exhibits a number of different color forms. One adult color morph is quite common (it represents about 70% of *P. forsteri* populations in most areas), and there are eight other less common adult color forms. There are also three juvenile color morphs (one common, two uncommon). The body color of the adults may be light pink, brown, or olive, with or without light streaks down the sides and under the base of the dorsal fin. Another color phase

Paracirrhites forsteri, Freckled Hawkfish: juvenile in Papua New Guinea. One of many color forms.

Paracirrhites forsteri, Freckled Hawkfish: juvenile photographed in the Red Sea.

Paracirrhites forsteri, Freckled Hawkfish: adult specimen from the Red Sea.

Paracirrhites forsteri, Freckled Hawkfish: adult color variant in the Red Sea.

Paracirrhites forsteri, Freckled Hawkfish: the so-called *typee* phase—maroon body and a yellow tail.

Paracirrhites forsteri, Freckled Hawkfish: large mouth capable of engulfing large prey items.

(originally described as a different species, *Paracirrhites typee*), has a deep maroon body with a yellow tail. Juveniles, up to about 8 cm (3.1 in.), are also distinctly colored and maintain this chromatic pattern until they join a harem. They are usually white ventrally and orangish red or brown dorsally. In all color morphs, the face is peppered with red or black spots. Donaldson (1990) reported that the adult females he observed ranged in total length from 6 to 14.5 cm (2.3 to 5.7 in.), while adult males were 8 to 18 cm (3.1 to 7 in.) in total length.

Paracirrhites hemistictus (Günther, 1874)
Common Names: Whitespot Hawkfish, Halfspotted Hawkfish.
Maximum Length: 29 cm (11.3 in.).
Distribution: Cocos-Keeling and Christmas Island to the Marquesas and Ducie Island, north to the Bonins, south to New Caledonia and the Austral Islands.
Biology: The Whitespot Hawkfish is found on the reef crest, reef face, and fore-reef slope of exposed outer reefs. It occurs at a depth range of 1 to 18 m (3.3 to 59 ft.). There are two color morphs (described below) that appear to have different microhabitat preferences. (See Remarks section for more informa-

tion). Courtship begins at sunset, at which time females behave aggressively toward one another (there is a size-related dominance hierarchy among females in an area). Males, which are larger than the females in their harems, defend a large territory (up to 150 m^2 [1,667 ft.^{2}]), while females reside in smaller home ranges within the male's territory. The focal point of the male's territory is usually a prominent topographical feature, like a large colony of *Pocillopora* coral, a stand of fire coral (*Millepora* spp.), a boulder, or a ledge. A group of Whitespot Hawkfish may share a preferred coral head with congeners (Freckled Hawkfish [*Paracirrhites forsteri*]), the coral-feeding Leopard Blenny (*Exallias brevis*), and Johnston's Damsel (*Plectroglyphidodon johnstonianus*). A social unit (harem) can consist of one male and up to four females. The male and females rendezvous at dusk and courtship begins. The females will quarrel among themselves and with female *P. forsteri*. (There is usually a dominant female in each harem.)
Captive Care: The Whitespot Hawkfish is a voracious fish-eater and is aggressive toward fish with similar behavior and those introduced after it. These hardy fish are best excluded from the invertebrate aquarium and are best kept with larger, more ag-

Paracirrhites hemistictus, Whitespot Hawkfish: a big, predatory species that must be housed with other large fishes that are not easily attacked or intimidated.

gressive species (e.g., triggerfishes, large angelfishes, large surgeonfishes). Only one should be kept per tank, unless your aquarium is very large and you can acquire a male-female pair.

Aquarium Size: 75 gal. **Temperature:** 22 to 27°C (72 to 81°F).

Aquarium Suitability Index: 5.

Remarks: This species exhibits two adult color morphs. One is pale overall with black spots on the flanks and a broad white band down the middle of the side (this is known as the "hemistictus" phase). The second morph is maroon or black overall with black spots on the body and a single spot in the middle of the flank (this morph was once thought to represent a separate species, *Paracirrhites polyactis*). Individuals with color patterns intermediate to these two color phases have also been reported. These two color morphs segregate by depth and habitat. The "polyactis" morph occurs at shallower depths than its paler counterpart and is most often found under overhangs in the upper surge zone in spur-and-groove habitats. The pale color morph is found in the lower surge zone and on reef terraces. It often rests on fire corals, encrusting stony corals, and rocks and is occasionally observed

sharing branching coral colonies with the Arc-eye Hawkfish (*P. arcatus*). Donaldson (1990) reported that the adult females he observed ranged in total length from 12 to 22 cm (4.7 to 8.6 in.); adult males were 20 to 24 cm (7.8 to 9.4 in.) in total length.

Paracirrhites xanthus Randall, 1963

Common Name: Golden Hawkfish.

Maximum Length: 12 cm (4.7 in.).

Distribution: Phoenix, Society, Tuamotu and Gambier Islands (most common at Caroline Atoll in the Phoenix Islands).

Biology: This beautiful hawkfish is found in reef passes and on exposed outer-reef faces and slopes. It usually associates with colonies of the stony coral *Pocillopora* at depths of 3 to 25 m (9.8 to 82 ft.) and will take refuge in the coral if threatened. Unlike most other hawkfishes, which are inconspicuous against the variegated reef background, the bright coloration of *P. xanthus* causes it to stick out prominently. It feeds on crustaceans.

Captive Care: Unfortunately, this beauty is rarely seen in the aquarium trade. Most that are collected probably go to more lu-

Paracirrhites xanthus, Golden Hawkfish: a glorious fish but rarely collected.

Paracirrhites nisus, Nisus Hawkfish: rare, Polynesian species.

Paracirrhites xanthus, Golden Hawkfish: color variant nestled in coral.

Paracirrhites xanthus, Golden Hawkfish: color variant with dark markings.

crative markets in Japan. Its behavior and care requirements are similar to those of the Arc-eye Hawkfish (*P. arcuatus*).

Aquarium Size: 30 gal. **Temperature:** 22 to 27°C (72 to 81°F).

Aquarium Suitability Index: 5.

Remarks: The Golden Hawkfish is bright yellow overall, with a brownish yellow back and a black postocular mark that is edged in light yellow. The color will sometimes fade in captivity. Two other rarely seen members of this genus also have postocular markings and very limited distributions. The **Nisus Hawkfish** (*Paracirrhites nisus*) **Randall, 1963** is known only from the Tuamotus and Cook Islands. The body of this fish is light brown with a pale band edged with black. (Its common and species name comes from a fabled Greek king, Nisus, who was changed into an osprey, or fish hawk.) It has been reported from the outer-reef faces of atolls, at depths of 8 to 14 m (26 to 46 ft.). The second species is the **Bicolor Hawkfish** (*Paracirrhites bicolor*) **Randall, 1963,** which is limited in distribution to Caroline Atoll. This hawkfish is dark brown except for the caudal peduncle and the lower portion of the body behind the pelvic fins. Almost unknown, it was collected in 4.6 m (15 ft.) on an outer atoll reef. To the best of my knowledge, neither of these two hawkfishes has been reported in the North American aquarium trade.

References

Debelius (1986), De Martini (1996), De Martini & Donaldson (1996), Donaldson (1987, 1989b, 1990), Donaldson & Colin (1989), Hiatt & Stratsburg (1960), Hobson (1974), Kobayashi & Suzuki (1992), Lobel (1974, 1976), Randall (1963a, 1967, 1985, 2001), Sadovy & Donaldson (1995), Takeshita (1975), Tanaka et al. (1985), Tanaka & Suzuki (1991), Talbot (1984), Thresher (1984).

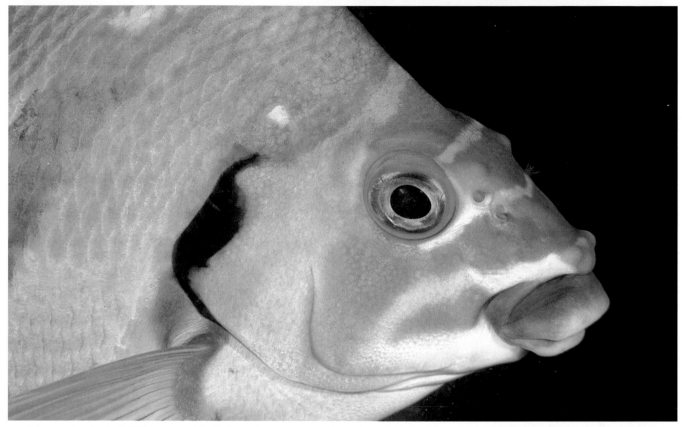

Goniistius zonatus, Spottedtail Morwong: rarities in the marine aquarium world, members of this family have large, fleshy lips that facilitate bottom feeding.

Known as Moki in New Zealand and fingerfins in South Africa, the morwongs are unusual fishes thought to be closely related to the hawkfishes. Although rarely seen in the aquarium trade, they are occasionally encountered by divers who spend time in the Western Pacific, especially in warm-temperate seas. In these regions, morwongs are an important food fish. The flesh of some species is reported to be firm and white, while others are reported to be somewhat rubbery. Australian marine aquarists are familiar with their husbandry, and some of the more attractive and interesting species are occasionally collected and are of interest to rare-fish enthusiasts.

The Family Cheilodactylidae consists of 5 different genera with approximately 18 species. The members of this family are found in subtropical to warm-temperate waters in the Indo-Pacific. The greatest concentration of species is found in Australia's cooler waters, where 14 different morwongs have been reported. They are also quite common around Lord Howe Island, Norfolk Island, the Kermadec Islands, New Zealand, New Caledonia, and Japan. Outside of the Western Pacific, one species is found around the Hawaiian Islands and another is known from Rapa and Easter Island. A single species occurs in Peruvian waters and yet another off Chile. There are also six species known from southern Africa (some of these range into the Atlantic) and at least two species off eastern South America.

The morwongs are characterized by large, fleshy lips, with a small mouth and small teeth. The mouth is often downturned

Goniistius quadricornis, Fourhorn Morwong: often found on rocky reefs, these carnivorous fishes feed on a wide array of substrate-dwelling invertebrate life.

and in a terminal position. The pectoral rays and those toward the center of the fin are equipped with elongated rays. These specialized fin rays are used to perch on the substrate like their relatives the hawkfishes and as stabilizers during feeding. The long pectoral rays are also employed to scratch the sides of their bodies (and possibly to dislodge parasites) when they are irritated. The morwongs have a forked caudal fin, and the dorsal fin is very long, with numerous spines and soft rays. The anterior portion of the dorsal fin is sometimes sail-like. While many are deep-bodied, some morwongs are more elongate. Many species are attractively marked with bands and stripes. Others are silver overall. The Queen Morwong (*Nemadactylus valenciennesi*) is especially attractive: bright blue overall with yellow markings on its head.

Biology

The morwongs are found both on inshore shallows and offshore at depths of less than 1 m (3.3 ft.) to as far down as 400 m (1,312 ft.). While the morwongs are most common on rocky reefs, they are also found near pier pilings, in estuaries, on sand flats, and on sand slopes. Only a few species have been reported from coral reefs. Those species that are found in rocky habitats shelter in the labyrinthine structure (e.g., holes and tunnels) of the reef. Some of the reef-dwelling morwongs can be found resting among large macroalgae, like kelp. While many of the morwongs prefer more structured reef habits, others spend much of their time over or resting on open bottoms. While many morwongs spend much of their time resting on the substrate, some species do hover over the bottom, at least for short periods of time. At night, some reef-dwelling forms seek shelter in caves and crevices.

Morwongs are distributed somewhat sporadically in the habitats they prefer. However, they can be locally abundant. For example, as many as 2,000 Banded Morwongs (*Goniistius spectabilis*) have been reported for each kilometer (0.6 mi.) of rocky reef in northern New Zealand. In this species, their numbers are directly correlated with the topographical complexity of the seafloor—the more complex, the more of these morwongs you are likely to find.

Feeding and Interspecific Interactions

The morwongs are carnivores that feed mainly on a wide variety of benthic invertebrates, including foraminiferans, polychaete worms, mollusks, chitons, amphipods, crabs, shrimps, serpent stars, and heart urchins. Some morwongs also feed on more mobile prey, including squids and small fishes, with certain species concentrating their feeding efforts on the sand between rocks and boulders—a place where certain prey organisms concentrate. Others spend more time grazing over algal material on hard substrates, sucking food items from foliose and turf algae and from around the holdfasts of kelp. Some morwongs scrape prey, along with microalgae and benthic debris, from rock surfaces.

When they feed, morwongs usually tilt their heads down as they beat their large pectoral fins. These large fins are often spread downward as the fish adopts a vertical orientation and feeds on the substrate. The large fins serve to stabilize the "headstanding" morwongs, preventing the fish from rolling to the side. With its head oriented toward the substrate, the morwong propels itself forward with a flick of the tail and presses its rubbery lips against the substrate. Those cheilodactylids that feed from algal turf use the fine teeth in their jaws to rake in prey items. Food is sucked into the mouth by a rapid increase in the size of the buccal cavity (it can expand up to seven times its "normal" volume). The materials ingested are sorted in the mouth. Inedible material is expelled out through the gills or spit from the mouth. The gill rakers act, at least to some degree, as a sieve to prevent some prey items from being expelled along with debris. Most of the sediment is expelled during this process, as this material is rarely found in the gut contents of morwongs.

In some species, the adult size and the distribution of the morwong determines the diet. Studies have shown that larger Spottedtail Morwong (*Goniistius zonatus*) consume less epifaunal ("surface-dwelling") crustaceans and more infaunal invertebrates than do smaller conspecifics. Other studies have documented that in certain locations, *G. zonatus* of varying sizes show no differences in their dietary preferences. The Banded Morwong (*G. spectabilis*) also exhibits dietary shifts as it grows. Juveniles feed primarily on gammarid amphipods, while large adults ingest more ophiuroids. A sudden shift in the diet was noted when the fish attained a standard length of 25 cm (9.8 in.), with the predominance of amphipods in the diet dropping abruptly. Adults do feed on some amphipods, but these are usually larger than those ingested by the juveniles. Because adults can create greater suction with their mouthparts, they are able to suck prey items from among kelp holdfasts and small crevices—something the juveniles are physically unable to do. As a result, the adults are able to exploit a wider range of prey items. Juveniles are reported to feed more frequently than adults, behavior typical in most fish species as the juveniles have greater metabolic demands.

Morwongs vary in their patterns of feeding activity, with some being nocturnal hunters. For example, groups of Red Morwongs (*Goniistius fuscus*) disperse at dusk to feed. Some morwongs also feed during the day. In the Banded Morwong (*Goniistius spectabilis*), larger individuals do most of their feeding during midday, while smaller size classes are crepuscular, showing peaks of foraging at dusk and dawn.

Some morwong species undergo feeding migrations. Others maintain feeding territories. The Spottedtail Morwong forages in staple feeding territories, which they defend from conspecifics. The feeding territories of these morwongs overlap between the various size classes. However, individuals will try to exclude competitive conspecifics of a similar size, while tending to ignore conspecifics in different size classes. At one location, *G. zonatus* exhibits dietary differences (food-habit partitioning) between size classes. This may explain why they tolerate conspecifics of different sizes in their territories—unless they are perceived as directly competitive for food, they are ignored.

Territory size for the Spottedtail Morwong is in part dependent on prey density. The feeding territory covered by a morwong in an area where prey densities are low may be ten times larger than in a location where food is more abundant. Those morwongs in areas with high densities of prey often are fatter, have heavier reproductive organs, and grow faster, due to the fact that they have to invest less energy in covering large distances when they forage. However, one study documented that Spottedtail Morwongs that occupy larger territories often have larger livers, even though they are less fatty, than those from small territories. It has been suggested that this is because glycogen rather than fat accumulates in the livers of these morwongs. Glycogen, an important source of "quick fuel," is important for the more active lifestyle of a morwong that has to do more swimming.

Morwong feeding behavior often attracts the attention of unrelated opportunists. For example, in Japan, wrasses of the genus *Pseudolabrus* often associate with the Spottedtail Morwong. In one study, wrasses associating with this morwong were reported to enjoy greater hunting success than members of their same species feeding on their own. It has also been reported that wrasses more often associate with morwongs that engage in a feeding method called "repeated-feeding." This is where the morwong repeatedly pecks at a particular portion of the substrate and spends less time swimming from one location to another. The other foraging mode is called "single-feeding." This is where a morwong sporadically nips at the substrate while moving about its feeding territory. Morwongs that feed in areas with patches of calcareous algae engage more in repeated-feeding and, as a result, more often are accompanied by wrasses.

In turn, morwongs are fed on by large piscivores, including sharks. In Australian waters, they share their habitat with wobbegongs (Orectolobidae), a group of benthic sharks that ambush larger prey items, including morwongs. Australian morwongs often visit the cleaning stations of the Eastern Cleaner Clingfish (*Cochleoceps orientalis*). These clingfish move over the body surface of the morwong and apparently feed on parasites (e.g., isopods), as well as the hosts slime and scales. In warmer seas, they are also cleaned by cleaner wrasses (*Labroides* spp.).

Social Structure

Much of the information available on the social behavior of cheilodactylids comes from studies conducted on the Banded Morwong. In this species, there is an ontogenetic change in the social behavior. At a length of about 10 cm (3.9 in.), this species forms feeding territories at water depths of from 3 to 10 m (9.8 to 33 ft.). These individuals exclude conspecifics that are smaller or of similar size, although they allow Banded Morwongs that are 25 cm (9.8 in.) in length or longer to feed in their territories; they will even feed along side one another. Smaller Banded Morwongs will also defend a preferred shelter site.

Larger members of this species give up their feeding territories and are home ranging, moving over distances as great as 1 km (0.6 mi.). Their home ranges overlap those of other adults as well as small *G. spectabilis*. However, most individuals concen-

Goniistius zonatus, Spottedtail Morwong: cleaner wrasse grooms a specimen resting lightly on the substrate—a typical pose for members of this family.

trate their activities around a specific patch reef. Larger morwongs tend to spend their time at greater depths (usually greater than 20 m [66 ft.]), with males more often moving into deeper water than adult females. Studies also show that males occupy a larger home range than females.

While some morwongs form feeding territories, others aggregate in preferred areas and remain in the same location for many years. For example, groups of over 100 Douglas Morwongs (*Nemadactylus douglasii*) have been observed off northern New Zealand. The Red Morwong (*Goniistius fuscus*), a species from temperate Australian seas, is an aggregating species that forms groups numbering from 3 to over 100 individuals. In *G. fuscus*, the size of the aggregation is variable, and individuals cover a larger home range during the nonreproductive period (i.e., midsummer). During the day, groups of Red Morwongs are found in boulder habitats. At night, they disperse into a variety of different habitats to feed. Lowry and Suthers (1998) found that the mean daytime home range for the Red Morwong was 1,850 m^2 (20,555 ft.^{2}). At night they moved over a larger area—the mean nocturnal home range was 3,639 m^2 (40,433 ft.^{2}). These researchers also found that displaced Red Morwongs would find their way back to the place where they were captured. Fish that were moved 200 to 900 m (656 to 2,952 ft.) away made their way back in 1 to 3 days.

Reproduction

Sexual dimorphism has been reported in morwongs. In some species, females tend to be larger than males and mature at a later age. In others, males are reported to get larger than females.

It is possible that the horns (projections) above the eye in some morwong species differ in size between the sexes (it has been suggested that those of the male are more pronounced). In one morwong species, females reach sexual maturity at an age of five years, while males are sexually mature at four.

Many of the species studied spawn in the summer and early autumn. It appears that many morwongs form groups during the spawning season. In some species, these groups can be quite large. In one of these, the Jackass Fish or Tarakihi (*Nemadactylus macropterus*) spawning occurs at the edge of the continental shelf around New Zealand. At night, these large groups of fish move high into the water column. From the large aggregation, smaller groups of *N. macropterus* rise up into the water and group spawn. After spawning, these fish will then sink back down and rejoin the larger group.

Studies conducted on *G. spectabilis* off the northeast coast of New Zealand found that spawning occurs during summer and autumn. At this time, large males form spawning territories at the edge of rocky reefs. Males were also reported to return to the same spawning territory over a number of years. It was determined that males that have a conspicuous cave in their territory have greater reproductive success. This species has been observed to spawn within caves. The Banded Morwong spawns at dusk.

Postlarval morwongs are large and often silver in overall color. They usually have deep, thin bodies (they have been described as paperlike), and they lack the elongated pectoral fins of their parents. The transformation of the body and fins apparently takes place soon after they settle to the bottom. The post-larvae remain in the plankton for some time—7 to 10 months in some species. At this time, they often associate with flotsam to avoid predators and to aid in dispersal. When they finally shift from a planktonic to benthic lifestyle, the juvenile fish are often quite large. For example, one species does not settle out until it reaches a length of about 10 cm (3.9 in.). In some morwongs, the newly settled juveniles form groups on sandy bottoms. Others occur singly, seeking protection in rocky crevices, under rocks, and among macroalgae. The juveniles of some morwong species are commonly found in tidepools.

The young morwongs feed often. For example, juvenile Banded Morwongs (*Goniistius spectabilis*) spend up to 83% of their time feeding. The rate of feeding decreases as the fish grows, with adult Banded Morwongs spending only 20% of the daylight hours feeding. Young morwongs grow quickly. The Douglas Morwong (*Nemadactylus douglasii*) reaches a length of 25 to 28 cm (9.8 to 11 in.) in 12 months and may attain 38 cm (14.8 in.) in two years. Studies have shown that some morwongs may live for as many as 60 years.

Captive Care

Little information is available on the husbandry of these fishes because they so rarely enter the North American aquarium trade. There are a few collectors in Australia and Japan that occasionally export them. In general, morwongs are considered to be fairly hardy aquarium residents. They readily eat prepared frozen and fresh seafoods. Norton Chan of the Waikiki Aquarium states that they housed one Hawaiian Morwong (*Goniistius vittatus*) at the aquarium that ate so much gel food that its anus ruptured. From that point on, they restricted the amount of food provided to the fish during each feeding bout. Chan reports that this species is relatively easy to keep.

The morwongs should be provided with a moderate-to-large-sized aquarium with suitable hiding places, such as rocky caves and overhangs. Be sure to provide plenty of swimming room for these fishes, although they spend much of their time resting on the substrate. They could be housed in a reef tank with a more open reef structure. However, they will eat a variety of motile invertebrates, including ornamental crustaceans and some desirable worm species. Larger individuals may pester small tridacnid clams.

According to professional aquarist Jay Hemdal, morwongs will do best in a tank without conspecifics. If kept together, it is not unusual for the more dominant fish to intimidate smaller or subordinate conspecifics. Field studies indicate that at least some species are more territorial as juveniles (the size class most likely to make it into the aquarium trade) than adults. Morwongs are known to suffer from digenean infections in the wild.

Goniistius vestitus, Crested Morwong: adults develop bony "horns" on head.

Goniistius quadricornis, Fourhorn Morwong: young specimen without "horns."

MORWONG SPECIES

Goniistius vestitus (Castelnau, 1879)

Common Name: Crested Morwong.
Maximum Length: 35 cm (13.7 in.).
Distribution: New South Wales and Queensland, Australia, New Caledonia, and Lord Howe Island.
Biology: This morwong has been reported from shallow estuaries and inshore rocky and coral reefs. However, according to Kuiter (1993), it is most common at depths of 20 m (66 ft.). It occurs singly or in small groups.
Captive Care: Little information is available on the husbandry of this species. See the general comments on morwong husbandry, above.
Aquarium Size: 100 gal. **Temperature:** 20 to 25°C (68 to 77°F).
Aquarium Suitability Index: 4.
Remarks: Adults have pairs of bony protuberances, or horns, in front of the eyes and on the tip of the snout. This species was formerly placed in the genus *Cheilodactylus* (some authors continue to place it in this taxon). The **Fourhorn Morwong** (*Goniistius quadricornis*) (Günther, 1860) is a similar species that is found off the coast of Japan. It has six dark diagonal bars on the head and body and a dark patch on the lower lobe of the caudal fin. (*Goniistius vestitus* has a dark line running along the base of the dorsal fin and down onto the lower caudal lobe and three bars on the head and front of the body.) The Fourhorn Morwong attains a length of 40 cm (15.6 in.). It is usually found at moderate depths of 25 m (82 ft.) or deeper.

Goniistius vittatus (Garrett, 1864)

Common Name: Hawaiian Morwong.
Maximum Length: 40 cm (15.6 in.).

Goniistius vittatus, Hawaiian Morwong: hardy but best kept singly.

Goniistius zonatus, Spottedtail Morwong: note characteristic spots on tail fin.

Goniistius zebra, Redlip Morwong: attractive species from Japanese waters.

Distribution: New Caledonia, Lord Howe, and Hawaiian Islands.
Biology: This fish is usually found on rocky reef faces and slopes, most often at depths in excess of 18 m (59 ft.). It feeds on a variety of small, benthic invertebrates, including foraminiferans, polychaete worms, mollusks, crabs, shrimps and other crustaceans, and heart urchins. The Hawaiian Morwong is typically a solitary species.
Captive Care: This is a durable aquarium fish. For more information on its husbandry, see the general remarks on the captive care of these fishes, page 207.
Aquarium Size: 135 gal. **Temperature:** 19 to 25°C (66 to 77°F).
Aquarium Suitability Index: 4.
Remarks: Adults have two pairs of bony projections, or horns—one pair in front of the eyes and one pair on the tip of the snout. This species was formerly placed in the genus *Cheilodactylus* (some authors continue to place it in this taxon).

Goniistius zonatus (Cuvier, 1830)
Common Name: Spottedtail Morwong.
Maximum Length: 45 cm (17.6 in.).
Distribution: Japan, south China sea to Taiwan.
Biology: This species is known from depths of 1 to 12 m (3.3 to 39 ft.) on rocky reef faces and slopes. It spends most of the daylight hours sucking benthic invertebrates from calcareous algae or the algal mat veneer of rocky substrates. The Spottedtail Morwong forages in stable feeding territories, which it defends from conspecifics—particularly those of a similar size. Feeding *G. zonatus* are often followed by *Pseudolabrus* wrasses, which feed on worms and crustaceans exposed by the morwongs' activities.
Captive Care: Little information is available on the husbandry of this species, but this fish is probably best kept singly except in very large aquariums. See the general remarks on the captive care of these fishes, page 207.
Aquarium Size: 135 gal. **Temperature:** 19 to 25°C (66 to 77°F).
Aquarium Suitability Index: 4.
Remarks: This attractive morwong is easily identified by the white spots on the caudal fin. The **Redlip Morwong** (*Goniistius zebra*) (**Döderlein, 1883**) is also found in Japanese waters. As the name implies, the lips are red. It is reported from depths of 3 to 30 m (9.8 to 98 ft.).

References
Ayling & Cox (1984), Bruno et al. (2000), Hirara et al. (1996), Leum & Choat (1980), Lowry & Suthers (1998), Matsumoto (2001), Matsumoto & Kohda (2000, 2001a, 2001b), McCormick (1989, 1998), Schroeder & Lowry (1994), Wohler & Sanchez (1994), Van Der Elst (1985).

Archamia zosterophora, Girdled Cardinalfish: eminently vulnerable to predators, aggregations of cardinalfishes commonly refuge within *Acropora* spp. corals.

DESPITE THEIR ABUNDANCE AND KEY ROLES IN THE interlacing food chains on a coral reef, some smaller fishes are often overlooked because of their diminutive dimensions and shy demeanors. The Family Apogonidae, commonly known as cardinalfishes, is one such group. This family makes up one of the largest families of reef fishes, with 22 genera and approximately 250 species. They are important predators of zooplankton and benthic invertebrates, as well as being principal prey for the many piscivores that lurk around the coral realms. Though many sport radiant hues or attractive color patterns and exhibit interesting behaviors (especially in the area of reproductive biology), they are often overlooked by divers and snorkelers.

Many are also nocturnal and are rarely seen out in the open during the day.

Not only are cardinalfishes underappreciated by many underwater naturalists, relatively few are encountered in saltwater aquariums. This is unfortunate, as many cardinalfishes are attractively colored, hardy, and well-behaved in both a fish tank or a reef aquarium. Recently, there has been increased interest in the family because of one unique apogonid, the Banggai or High-fin Cardinalfish (*Pterapogon kauderni*). Although this is a truly spectacular fish that readily spawns in captivity, there are many other species in the genus equally worthy of the marine hobbyist's consideration.

Apogon semilineatus, Semilined Cardinalfish: a vital part of the food web on many reefs, apogonids often form social groups to find safety in numbers.

Classification and Biology

The cardinalfishes have two dorsal fins, the first of which has six to eight spines. The anal fin has two spines, they have large eyes, a large, oblique mouth, and a single, flat opercular spine, which is often very small. There is also a ridge on the preopercle preceding the margin. Most of the cardinalfishes are also relatively small, attaining maximum lengths of less than 10 cm (3.9 in.). The common name is apparently derived from the fact that some of the better known members of the family (especially those from the Atlantic) are bright red, like their avian namesakes.

Habitat Preferences and Predators

Although some cardinalfishes live in temperate seas, most members of the family are found on tropical coral reefs or in adjacent seagrass meadows and/or mangrove habitats. On tropical reefs, cardinalfishes are most abundant in areas where coral cover is profuse and there is relatively little wave action. For example, on a barrier reef off Madagascar, only two species were found in seagrass areas in a lagoon that was lacking coral heads. In this same region, only two species were found on the boulder tract, and six species were found in the surge zone, but only one of these species was abundant there. All of these areas were subjected to swell, breaking waves, or surge, and/or relatively few hiding places. In contrast, 10 cardinalfish species were reported on the outer-reef slope, 12 on the outer-reef flat, 12 on the inner-reef flat, and 12 more from coral heads in seagrass beds. These reef zones are characterized by an abundance of hiding places and are protected from excessive water motion. While some cardinalfishes are restricted in their ranges to a specific biotope, others occur over a wide range of reef habitats. For example, in Madagascar, the Narrowlined Cardinalfish (*Archamia fucata*) is found only on the reef face, while the Broadstriped Cardinalfish (*Apogon angustatus*) occurs in a number of different habitats. Not all cardinalfishes occur in the marine environment: members of the genus *Glossamia* are found only in freshwater.

Cardinalfishes have few if any special anatomical defenses against predators. Some species form schools or shoals to reduce the possibility of predation. Many species are very cryptic, spending the daylight hours, when they would be more vulnerable to being attacked by piscivores, hiding in reef crevices or caves. There are a number of cardinalfish species that associate with invertebrates for protection. The Bluestreak (*Apogon leptacanthus*) and Coral Cardinalfish (*Siphamia corallicola*) live among the branches of live stony coral colonies. The Sawcheek (*Apogon quadrisquamatus*) and the Bridle Cardinalfish (*Apogon aurolineatus*) from the tropical Western Atlantic associate with the Giant Sea Anemone (*Condylactis gigantea*) or the Corkscrew Sea Anemone (*Bartholomea annulata*), while the Moluccan Cardinalfish (*Apogon moluccensis*) will hang out among the tentacles of the Magnificent Sea Anemone (*Heteractis magnifica*). A number of cardinalfishes, especially during the juvenile stages of their life cycles, hide among the spines of *Diadema* urchins. Some apogonids even utilize the venomous thorns of the Crown-of-Thorns Sea Star (*Acanthaster planci*) for protection. Three cardinalfishes, the Conch Cardinalfish (*Astrapogon stellatus*), the Blackfin (*A. puncticulatus*), and the Bronze Cardinalfish (*A. alutus*), live in the mantle cavities of live conchs (*Strombus* spp.). Several other cardinalfishes refuge in the lumens of large tube sponges (e.g., *Aplysina* spp.) during the day.

Cardinalfishes are preyed upon by a number of reef fishes. Lizardfishes, trumpetfishes, frogfishes, scorpionfishes, groupers, and flounders are all known to eat apogonids. Some of these species hunt them after dark, others feed on them during the day. The cardinalfishes are most vulnerable to attack when they are away from shelter (e.g., when they are feeding out over the sand or searching for potential mates). Some cardinalfishes are also known to eat other apogonids.

Activity Patterns and Food Habits

Most cardinalfishes conceal themselves in, or hover near, reef crevices, holes, or caves during the day, leaving these hiding places at night to feed. Some nocturnal cardinalfishes rise into the water column and capture zooplankton (e.g., errant polychaete worms). These species will ingest an enormous number of smaller prey items in a single night. For example, zooplankton-feeding cardinalfishes have been observed to eat as many as 160 planktonic organisms in a single night. These nocturnal zooplanktivores rise higher in the water column on moonless nights, because they are less vulnerable to predators when they are not backlit by moonlight. Other cardinalfishes swim just over the substrate and capture bottom-dwelling invertebrates (e.g., worms, crustaceans) and small fishes. I have seen one *Apogon* sp. thrusting its snout into the sand and filtering the substrate through its gills. The benthic carnivores feed on far fewer large prey items than their zooplankton feeding counterparts. Many of the nocturnal cardinalfishes are opportunistic, feeding on prey items that share their hiding places during the day.

Some cardinalfishes are inactive at night and hunt during the day. Members of this group either feed on small fishes and benthic crustaceans or on zooplankton. For example, some *Cheilodipterus* cardinalfishes feed primarily on small fishes during the day, while certain of the *Archamia* spp. consume zooplankton at this time. The young of some nocturnally active cardinalfish species, such as the Bluestreak Cardinalfish (*Apogon leptacanthus*), also feed on zooplankton during daylight hours.

While most cardinalfishes occur singly, in pairs, or in small aggregations, some species live in large, dense groups during the day. For example, many of the members of the genus *Archamia*, the Artus Cardinalfish (*Cheilodipterus artus*), and several of the *Siphamia* spp. occur in dense aggregations. Some of these cardinalfishes will also form large mixed groups. For example, the Goldbelly Cardinalfish (*Apogon apogonides*), Bridled Cardinalfish (*A. fraenatus*), Narrowlined Cardinalfish (*Archamia fucata*), and Blackbelted Cardinalfish (*A. zosterophora*) will aggregate together over large stands of staghorn coral (*Acropora* spp.).

Sphaeramia nematoptera, Pajama Cardinalfish: one of many ideal species that adapt readily to captive conditions, even thriving for novice aquarists.

Reproduction

A few cardinalfishes are known to be sexually dimorphic. For example, males of the genus *Siphamia* are smaller than females on average and have deeper bodies and a larger, deeper head. In a number of other cardinalfishes, it has been determined that females are larger than males on average. Permanent sexual dichromatism has been reported for one species, but temporary color change during courtship is relatively common in this family. In such species, the male's color typically becomes lighter and the female exhibits more vivid colors than the male.

Many cardinalfishes live in pairs when they reach sexual maturity. Even those species that live in shoals often form and maintain pairs within these groups. Some species adopt temporary spawning territories during the breeding period, which the female actively defends as the male broods the eggs. After spawning takes place, the pair breaks up in some species, while in others the bond is maintained year-round. Some cardinalfishes are promiscuous, with males and/or females spawning with a number of mates during the breeding period. Because the female is freed from parental care, she is able to desert her mate once they spawn and find another male. For this reason, polyandry (one female, two or more males) has been reported in some apogonids.

Before spawning occurs, the female becomes conspicuously swollen with eggs and stops eating. Courtship and spawning can take several forms and may last minutes or hours, depending on the species in question. Courtship includes behaviors such

Apogon monospilus, Yelloweyed Cardinalfish: cardinalfish courtship begins.

Apogon monospilus, Yelloweyed Cardinalfish: typical parallel swimming.

Apogon monospilus, Yelloweyed Cardinalfish: male trembles beside female.

Apogon monospilus, Yelloweyed Cardinalfish: note light face of male fish.

as flicking the dorsal and pelvic fins, parallel swimming, circling, chasing, and nipping. In some species, the male will wrap his anal fin around the urogenital opening of the female, the two fish will quiver, and an egg ball will be extruded. The male immediately turns and ingests the egg ball. In other cardinalfishes, the male approaches a group of females, undulates, and curves its body into an S-shape. A female follows the male, and they swim side-by-side intermittently until the male finds a clear spot on the bottom. He approaches this spot and begins to tremble. The female places her abdomen on the bottom and releases an egg ball, which the male sucks into his mouth. In most species, the male and female bring their abdomens close together, at which time the female extrudes a gelatinous egg mass. The male turns around and sucks it into his mouth. It has been suggested that one species of cardinalfish practices internal fertilization.

Chave (1971) reported that among *Apogon kallopterus,* males fertilize the eggs while still in the female. The egg mass is released a few hours after it has been fertilized, at which time the male takes the eggs into his mouth. In most other species, fertilization occurs within several minutes after the egg mass is extruded. In at least some species, the eggs are fertilized while in the mouth of the male: the males swim in circles in the area where the sperm are released, opening and closing their mouths rapidly, apparently to facilitate fertilization.

The egg ball is held together by threads that extend from each egg. In at least some species, there may also be a membrane that surrounds them. The egg ball ranges from 5 to 30 mm in diameter and contains approximately 600 to more than 3,500 eggs, ranging in diameter from 0.24 to 0.7 mm. The males of some species may carry egg balls from several spawns, so the total number of eggs being orally incubated at any one time may range from 75 to 22,000, depending on the species. (Some cardinalfishes only incubate the egg mass from one spawn at a time.) While brooding the eggs, the male fasts. In studies conducted on a cardinalfish from Japan, it was estimated that males are incubating eggs for 78% of the spawning period, which occurs from May to August. Because his food intake is limited during this time, the physical condition of the male cardinalfish will gradually deteriorate during the breeding season. Studies have shown that males are more likely to eat some or all of the entire brood of eggs later in the reproductive period when their physical condition has declined. In some cases, eating the eggs may partially compensate for not feeding during the spawning period. Brood cannibalism is more common in those species that are more abundant (i.e., there is a high level of mate availability so re-mating is more likely). In some cases, a male cardinalfish may eat part of a brood when the egg mass is too large to be held in his mouth. If the buccal cavity becomes too crowded, oxygen levels may drop, which will lead to greater egg mortality. For this reason, females will often select larger males—those that have larger mouths—as mates (this is especially true with those apogonids that form groups).

There are several accounts suggesting that in some species the females incubate the eggs, but this is apparently erroneous. It appears that some researchers have mistaken males with swollen abdomens (from eating an egg ball), for females. The brooding male will occasionally spit out and suck in the eggs to reposition and aerate them. Those species living in tropical seas typically hold the eggs in their mouths for about one week (in some species it may be as long as 14 days) until they hatch. When they hatch, the larvae are between 2 and 4 mm and enter the plankton for about 60 days. This long planktonic phase allows them to disperse over a greater area. When the juveniles settle out of the plankton they can range in size from 10 to 25 mm, and at least one species has been reported to grow 6.4 mm per month. The Banggai Cardinalfish (*Pterapogon kauderni*) not only incubates the eggs in its mouth, but orally broods the young (for more on this species, see pages 257-261).

Captive Care
Cardinalfishes are hardy aquarium inhabitants suitable for aquarists of all levels of experience. Because most do not get very large, they can be housed in smaller aquariums. For example, a standard 20-gallon tank is a suitable home for one or more cardinalfishes. It is important for such an aquarium to be replete with cover and not be home to any overly aggressive tankmates.

Live rock, replica corals, coral skeletons, limestone, and PVC

Apogon leptacanthus, Bluestreak Cardinalfish: many species do best with live rock caves, overhangs, and crevices to provide a natural sense of security.

pipe can be used to fashion ledges, overhangs, crevices, and caves that cardinalfishes can shelter in. Some cardinalfishes hide among the branches of live staghorn corals in nature, so a small-polyped stony coral aquarium would be an ideal habitat for them. Not only will the coral provide shelter, but the nitrogen released in the fish's feces will accelerate the coral's growth. The movement of the apogonids among the coral's branches may also serve to mix stale water with fresh, oxygenated water within these small interstices.

As in nature, many cardinalfish will hide under a ledge or in a hole, or hang near the entrance of a preferred shelter site when the aquarium lights are on. Secretive species will spend more time in the open in a dimly lit aquarium. If they are kept in a shallow-water reef tank, they will begin to emerge from their hiding places when the more intense bulbs (e.g., metal halides) are extinguished, or after all the lights are turned off. Some individuals, however, are reclusive when first placed in the aquarium and may begin spending more time in full view when the lights are on once they have acclimated to their new home. One technique that can be employed to observe nocturnally active apogonids is to light the tank with a red fluorescent or red incandescent bulb, or one of the newer moonlight lamps that cast a realistic faint bluish glow into the tank. Cardinalfishes are not overly sensitive to red light and will behave as if there is no light at all. A bulb that mimics moonlight can allow the aquarist to see how cardinalfishes behave on a typical moonlit night on the reef. It has been suggested in the older aquarium literature that some reclusive car-

Apogon aureus, Ringtailed Cardinalfish: beautiful social aggregations can be replicated in captivity if a sufficiently large aquarium can be provided.

dinalfishes will go blind if they are not given adequate places to shelter in a brightly lit tank. Though I have never observed it, there is a possibility that overexposure to intense lighting could damage their optic system.

Cardinalfish species that are diurnally active are more likely to remain in the open, even if they are placed in a tank with intense illumination. These species are obviously better display animals for the shallow-water reef aquarium than their more secretive cousins.

Feeding

Cardinalfishes will accept a wide variety of aquarium foods, including finely chopped seafoods, frozen preparations, frozen brine and mysid shrimps, and flake foods. The more diverse the diet, the more healthy your apogonids will remain. The colors of certain species are prone to fade in captivity, but this process can be arrested if a cardinalfish is fed a varied diet (including frozen or flake foods containing added pigments). Species that feed only on zooplankton should be fed several times a day, while those that feed on benthic invertebrates should be fed twice a

day in a tank without live rock, and several times a week in a tank with a good macro-invertebrate fauna (e.g., amphipods and polychaete worms). In either case, keep a close eye on the condition of the fish. If it is getting thin, feed it more. If it appears to be getting too fat, feed it less.

Compatibility

Cardinalfishes are more likely to be the victims of aggression than the aggressors. It is important to house your apogonids with passive tankmates. For example, dottybacks, damselfishes, hawkfishes, some pygmy angelfishes, and triggerfishes have been known to pester apogonids, especially in smaller tanks. If they are bullied by more aggressive fishes, they will hide and may refuse to feed. Their small size makes them vulnerable to predation if kept with piscivorous species. Certain invertebrates pose a threat to cardinalfishes as well. For example, they are vulnerable prey to Elephant-ear Anemones (*Amplexidiscus fenestrafer*), carpet sea anemones (*Stichodactyla* spp.), and larger, more destructive crustaceans (e.g., hermit and brachyuran crabs).

On the other side of the coin, some cardinalfishes will definitely eat small fishes and ornamental shrimps. Members of the genus *Cheilodipterus*, for example, are inclined to eat any fish tankmates that they can swallow whole. Likewise, adults of some of the larger *Apogon* spp., like the Fyeshadow (*A. exostigma*), Iridescent (*A. kallopterus*), and the Blackstripe Cardinalfish (*A. nigrofasciatus*), are a threat to smaller fishes and crustacean tankmates. Some of these species will even eat other apogonids. Smaller, more delicate crustaceans, like some of the anemone shrimps (*Periclimenes* spp.), are potential prey for a large number of cardinalfishes.

Although many cardinalfishes can be observed in groups in the wild, not all species will tolerate the presence of their own kind in the confines of a smallish aquarium. If you want to keep a group of cardinalfishes together, it is best to house them in a larger tank (55 gallons or more) that contains plenty of hiding places. Some species can be housed together in smaller tanks, but even in these species a hierarchy will be formed within the group, with larger fish dominating smaller individuals. In these species, keeping a larger number of individuals (five or more) in the same tank will help to prevent any one member of a group from being bullied. Also, juvenile individuals tend to be more tolerant of each other than adults. If adult individuals form a male-female pair, they may become intolerant of conspecifics. In this case, either the pair or the other members of that particular species will have to be separated or the latter are likely to become victims of intraspecific aggression. Be aware that some cardinalfishes will not only pick on conspecifics, they will also behave aggressively toward other apogonids. Cardinalfishes do not tend to harass unrelated fishes. They may defend a preferred hiding place from other secretive species, but most tend to be rather docile.

Captive Breeding

The cardinalfishes are ideal candidates for captive breeding because they attain sexual maturity at a small size, they orally incubate their eggs, and their larvae are relatively large at hatching. One species that has proven to be relatively easy to breed is the Banggai Cardinalfish (*Pterapogon kauderni*). This species is the only marine fish that is known to brood its young in its mouth, as well as its eggs. (See pages 260-261 for more details on breeding this species.)

Finding a male-female pair of apogonids can be difficult, because most species are not known to be sexually dimorphic. In some species, females are larger than males, so placing two individuals together that are different in size may increase the chances that they are of opposite sexes. Another way to pair them is to place a small aggregation (five or more) in a tank. Individuals within the group will often form obvious pairs. The other fish in the tank can then be removed to isolate the pair, or all individuals can be left in together if the tank is large enough. In some species, one of the pair, or both, will systematically attack, and may even kill, other conspecifics left in the tank.

To induce spawning, it is important to provide plenty of hiding places for the pair and ample supplies of food. Live foods, such as vitamin-fortified adult brine shrimp, will often help to encourage these fishes to breed. Once they spawn, the male can be isolated with a tank divider or placed in a breeder trap or net. Be cautious when moving an incubating male, as he may spit out the egg mass or even eat it if overly agitated. If the egg mass is rejected, place it in a container of saltwater and aerate it heavily. When the eggs hatch, separate the larvae from the male (and other fish species) immediately.

CARDINALFISH SPECIES

Before we plunge into the cardinalfish species accounts, the reader should know that there are some differing opinions available on apogonid taxonomy. Many of these differences among experts appear to be a function of whether the researcher is a "lumper" or a "splitter." That is, some lump similar, separated populations that exhibit color differences into one species, believing that these populations could easily interbreed and thus fail to conform to the classic definition of a species. Others split such groups into two or more valid species, based on geographical isolation and chromatic disparities. Kuiter and Kozawa's (1999) massive treatise of the Indo-Pacific apogonids approaches the group from a "splitters" point of view. Since I am not an apogonid expert, I present both perspectives in these accounts whenever possible.

Genus *Apogon* (Cardinalfishes)

Apogon angustatus (Smith & Radcliffe, 1911)
Common Name: Broadstriped Cardinalfish.
Maximum Length: 10 cm (3.9 in.).
Distribution: Red Sea to the Line and Gambier Islands, north to Taiwan, and south to New Caledonia.
Biology: The Broadstriped Cardinalfish is found on coastal reefs, the outer-reef flat, the reef face, and fore-reef slopes, at depths from 1 to 65 m (3.3 to 213 ft.). It is often seen in the open, over sand or rubble substrates. It is also found in caves and in crevices. *Apogon angustatus* occurs singly or in pairs. It feeds primarily at night on benthic crustaceans (including amphipods, copepods, and shrimps), polychaete worms, and small fishes.
Captive Care: The Broadstriped Cardinalfish is a hardy aquarium species. The amount of time it spends in the open is a function of the fishes it is kept with. If housed with less aggressive species, it will remain in the open much of the time. Do provide it with plenty of suitable caves and crevices in which to refuge. It is a solitary fish, so I would recommend keeping only one per tank, unless the aquarium is large. It has been known to pick on congeners in smaller aquariums. Larger *A. angustatus* may eat delicate ornamental shrimps and small fishes.

Apogon angustatus, Broadstriped Cardinalfish: note spot at base of tail fin.

Apogon apogonides, Goldbelly Cardinalfish: large, uncommon species.

Apogon aureus, Ringtailed Cardinalfish: handsome with black tail ring.

Aquarium Size: 30 gal. **Temperature:** 22 to 28°C (72 to 82°F).
Aquarium Suitability Index: 5.
Remarks: This species is very similar to the Blackstripe Cardinalfish (*Apogon nigrofasciatus*) and the Sevenstriped Cardinalfish (*A. novemfasciatus*). It can be differentiated from these congeners by its color pattern. In *Apogon angustatus* there is a distinct spot at the base of the caudal fin (this spot is more obvious in some specimens), and the spaces between the dark body stripes are about equal to the width of the stripes. In *Apogon nigrofasciatus* the stripes are broader (the interspaces between them are much narrower than the width of the stripes themselves), and there is no obvious spot at the base of the tail. Finally, in *Apogon novemfasciatus* the stripes extend onto the base of the caudal fin, and the upper and lower stripes curve toward the middle stripe near the tail.

Apogon apogonides (Bleeker, 1856)

Common Names: Goldbelly Cardinalfish, Plain Cardinalfish.
Maximum Length: 12 cm (4.7 in.).
Distribution: East Africa to eastern Indonesia, north to the Izu Islands, Japan, and south to the Great Barrier Reef.
Biology: The Goldbelly Cardinalfish is found on coastal reefs, lagoon patch reefs, reef faces, and fore-reef slopes. It occurs at depths of 12 to 30 m (39 to 98 ft.). In the Coral Sea, it is most common around coral heads at depths of about 30 m (98 ft.). *Apogon apogonides* lives in coral reef crevices and among branching stony corals. It occurs singly, in small groups and in large shoals. It sometimes forms heterospecific shoals with other cardinalfishes, like the Bridled Cardinalfish (*Apogon fraenatus*), the Narrowlined Cardinalfish (*Archamia bigutatta*), and the Blackbelted Cardinalfish (*Archamia zosterophora*).
Captive Care: The Goldbelly Cardinalfish is rarely seen in the aquarium trade. Because it attains a larger size than some of its congeners, it is a greater threat to small fishes and crustaceans. Otherwise, its care requirements are similar to that of other apogonids.
Aquarium Size: 30 gal. **Temperature:** 22 to 28°C (72 to 82°F).
Aquarium Suitability Index: 5.
Remarks: This species is very similar to the **Capricorn Cardinalfish** (*Apogon capricornis*) **Allen & Randall, 1993**, which is restricted in distribution to the Capricorn Group of the Great Barrier Reef, the Chesterfield Islands in the Coral Sea, and New South Wales, Australia. It differs from *A. apogonides* by having a spot on the caudal peduncle. *Apogon capricornis* has been reported from depths of 3 to 15 m (9.8 to 49 ft.).

Apogon aureus (Lacépède, 1802)

Common Name: Ringtailed Cardinalfish.
Maximum Length: 14 cm (5.5 in.).
Distribution: East Africa to Tonga, north to southern Japan, and south to New Caledonia and New South Wales.
Biology: The Ringtailed Cardinalfish inhabits coastal reefs, lagoon reefs, fore-reef slopes, and walls. It is found at depths of 1 to 50 m (3.3 to 164 ft.), although it is most common at depths of less than 30 m (98 ft.). *Apogon aureus* occurs singly, in pairs, or in small to large shoals. Adult individuals will often maintain male-female pair bonds within groups. The Ringtailed Cardinalfish often occurs beneath overhangs, as well as out in the open during the day. It never strays far from cover when on its own, but shoals will spend more time in the open.
Captive Care: *Apogon aureus* makes a beautiful display fish, but unfortunately it is rarely seen in the aquarium trade. It should be kept singly, unless you have a very large tank (100 gallons or

Apogon bandanensis, Threesaddle Cardinalfish: shy, secretive species.

Apogon binotatus, Barred Cardinalfish: night color of common Caribbean fish.

more), in which case a pair or trio can be kept if all individuals are introduced to the tank simultaneously. The Ringtailed Cardinalfish is a greater threat to smaller fish and crustaceans than many other cardinalfishes because it attains a larger size.
Aquarium Size: 30 gal. **Temperature:** 22 to 28°C (72 to 82°F).
Aquarium Suitability Index: 5.
Remarks: Juvenile *A. aureus* lack the characteristic ring around the caudal peduncle, but have a spot on each side instead. Kuiter and Kozawa (1999), have suggested that the valid name for this species is *Apogon fleurieu* (Lacépède, 1801).

Apogon bandanensis Bleeker, 1854
Common Names: Threesaddle Cardinalfish, Banda Cardinalfish, Bigeye Cardinalfish.
Maximum Length: 10 cm (3.9 in.).
Distribution: East Indies to Samoa, north to Ryukyu Island, and south to the Great Barrier Reef.
Biology: The Threesaddle Cardinalfish lives on coastal reefs, lagoon reefs, outer-reef flats, reef faces, and reef slopes at depths from 10 to 34 m (33 to 112 ft.). It is most common on silty reefs, where it hides in holes and interstices during the day and comes out to feed after dark. It is a solitary species.
Captive Care: Although *A. bandanensis* will readily acclimate to the home aquarium if provided with plenty of hiding places, it is a secretive species that will spend most of the daylight hours under cover. Therefore, it is not the best apogonid for captivity. It is likely to spend more time in the open in an aquarium that is in a low-traffic area and is dimly lit. It will eat crustaceans and small fishes.
Aquarium Size: 30 gal. **Temperature:** 22 to 28°C (72 to 82°F).
Aquarium Suitability Index: 3.

Remarks: The **Gray Cardinalfish** (*Apogon fuscus*) (**Quoy & Gaimard, 1825**) and the **Guam Cardinalfish** (*Apogon guamensis*) **Valenciennes, 1832** are similar to the Threesaddle Cardinalfish. They differ in having a smaller eye than *A. bandanensis,* and in the shape of the markings under the eye. *Apogon bandanensis* also has yellow on the tail margin and on the tips of the second dorsal and anal fins.

Apogon binotatus (Poey, 1867)
Common Name: Barred Cardinalfish.
Maximum Length: 10 cm (3.9 in.).
Distribution: Southeastern Florida and Bermuda, south to Venezuela.
Biology: This is a common Caribbean species that occurs on lagoon patch reefs, reef flats, fore-reef slopes, and dropoffs. It is found over a depth range of 1 to 58 m (3.3 to 190 ft.). The Barred Cardinalfish hides between stony coral branches, in reef crevices, caves, and under overhangs during the day and comes out at night to feed on zooplankton. It feeds close to the bottom, usually over sand substrates. *Apogon binotatus* will emerge from diurnal hiding places at dusk to begin feeding, and will return to its refuge at dawn. During the day, *A. binotatus* will sometimes aggregate in preferred hiding places—groups can number up to 70 individuals. It is occasionally found mixing with the similar Belted Cardinalfish (*Apogon townsendi*).
Captive Care: *Apogon binotatus* is a hardy aquarium species that will spend much of its time hiding in, or hovering near, entrances to caves and crevices. Feed it a varied diet that includes color-enhancing foods. It can be kept singly or in small groups. It is not a threat to smaller fish tankmates and is of little threat to ornamental shrimps, but it is a potential target for aquarium bullies.

Apogon cavitiensis, Caviti Cardinalfish: attractive yellow wash.

Apogon chrysotaenia, Highfin Cardinalfish: larger fish, best kept singly.

Apogon chrysotaenia, Highfin Cardinalfish: variant. Note high second dorsal.

Aquarium Size: 30 gal. **Temperature:** 22 to 28°C (72 to 82°F).
Aquarium Suitability Index: 5.
Remarks: This species is similar to the Belted Cardinalfish (*Apogon townsendi*). It differs by having two stripes on the body and caudal peduncle, rather than three as in *A. townsendi*. The Barred Cardinalfish can change its color from red to a pale pink, but the two bars are always present.

Apogon cavitiensis Jordan & Seale, 1907
Common Name: Caviti Cardinalfish.
Maximum Length: 6 cm (2.3 in.).
Distribution: Singapore to Bali, north to the Philippines, south to northern Australia.
Biology: *Apogon cavitiensis* is found in mangrove swamps and sand slopes at depths of 1 to 18 m (3.3 to 59 ft.). It is reported to be most common at depths of less than 7 m (23 ft.). It usually stays near sheltering structures, such as coral colonies or rocky outcrops.
Captive Care: Although it occasionally makes it into aquarium stores, *A. cavitiensis* is by no means commonly seen. Though it is a durable aquarium charge, it is best housed with passive tankmates. If you do keep it with more pugnacious species, it must be kept in a large tank with numerous hiding places and it should be one of the first fish introduced. It is a highly desirable reef aquarium fish.
Aquarium Size: 20 gal. **Temperature:** 22 to 28°C (72 to 82°F).
Aquarium Suitability Index: 4.

Apogon chrysotaenia Bleeker, 1851
Common Name: Highfin Cardinalfish.
Maximum Length: 12 cm (4.7 in.).
Distribution: Indonesia to northwest Australia.
Biology: The Highfin Cardinalfish occurs on fringing coastal reefs or patch reefs at depths from 1.5 to 10 m (5 to 33 ft.). It is found among stony and soft corals or boulders. *Apogon chrysotaenia* occurs singly or in pairs. It spends its days in the open, but never strays far from a hiding place. At night, it moves away from its diurnal haunts to feed over the surrounding sand or mud.
Captive Care: This species is not regularly encountered in the aquarium trade. It should be kept singly, unless of course you want to attempt to breed them.
Aquarium Size: 30 gal. **Temperature:** 22 to 28°C (72 to 82°F).
Aquarium Suitability Index: 5.
Remarks: Young *A. chrysotaenia* have bold stripes that fade as the fish grows. There is a spot at the base of the caudal fin that darkens or lightens, depending on the fish's mood. This cardinalfish has a high second dorsal fin.

Apogon compressus (Smith & Radcliffe, 1911)
Common Names: Ochrestriped Cardinalfish, Blue-eye Cardinal-fish.
Maximum Length: 12 cm (4.7 in.).
Distribution: Malaysia to the Solomon Islands, north to the Ryukyus, and south to the Great Barrier Reef.
Biology: The Ochrestriped Cardinalfish is most abundant on coastal and lagoon patch reefs, with adults typically occurring in small to large groups. Juveniles usually occur singly. It is found at a depth range of less than 1 to 20 m (3.3 to 66 ft.). It often hides among branching small-polyped stony corals or over large-polyped stony corals (e.g., *Euphyllia ancora*) during the day. It leaves its diurnal shelter at night to feed on zooplankton.
Captive Care: The Ochrestriped Cardinalfish is a durable aquarium inhabitant that will spend much of its time in the open during the day. It can be kept in groups of five or more in tanks of 75 gallons or larger. It is a good choice for the shallow- or deep-water reef tank; however, it will eat ornamental shrimps.
Aquarium Size: 30 gal. **Temperature:** 22 to 28°C (72 to 82°F).
Aquarium Suitability Index: 5.
Remarks: The young of *A. compressus* have a spot on the caudal peduncle (which is yellow) and resemble some of the juvenile largetoothed cardinalfishes (*Cheilodipterus* spp.). The adults have stripes that can be rusty brown to black. Their eyes are blue.

Apogon cookii Macleay, 1881
Common Name: Blackbanded Cardinalfish.
Maximum Length: 10 cm (3.9 in.).
Distribution: East Africa to the Great Barrier Reef, north to the Ryukyus.
Biology: This cardinalfish is found on coastal fringing reefs and lagoon patch reefs at depths of 1 to 10 m (3.3 to 33 ft.). It is also found around debris in seagrass beds. Often solitary, it also regularly forms shoals in areas where it is common.
Captive Care: *Apogon cookii* is not frequently encountered in the aquarium trade. It should be provided with plenty of hiding places. This cardinalfish will eat ornamental crustaceans and smaller fish tankmates.
Aquarium Size: 30 gal. **Temperature:** 22 to 28°C (72 to 82°F).
Aquarium Suitability Index: 5.
Remarks: The Blackbanded Cardinalfish has silver-white stripes on the body with light to dark brown interspaces. There is a stripe that starts at the snout, runs above the eye and converges with the middle body stripe.

Apogon cyanosoma Bleeker, 1853
Common Name: Yellowstriped Cardinalfish.

Apogon compressus, Ochrestriped Cardinalfish: juvenile with spot near tail.

Apogon compressus, Ochrestriped Cardinalfish: note blue eye in adult fish.

Apogon cookii, Blackbanded Cardinalfish: one of a host of similar species.

Apogon cyanosoma, Orangestriped Cardinalfish: bold, colorful and hardy.

Apogon properupta, Coral Cardinalfish: part of the *A. cyanosoma* complex.

Apogon rubrimacula, Orangespot Cardinalfish: new species or synonym?

Maximum Length: 8 cm (3.1 in.).

Distribution: This species is apparently restricted in distribution to the Western Pacific (from southern Japan to Queensland, Australia). According to Kuiter and Kozawa (1999), seven similar species have been confused with this fish, hence the wider range often ascribed to this species.

Biology: The Yellowstriped Cardinalfish is most prevalent on coastal reefs, lagoon patch reefs, reef faces, and fore-reef slopes at depths of 1 to 49 m (3.3 to 161 ft.). It occurs singly, in pairs, in small, loose groups, or in large shoals. It spends the day swimming or hovering near the entrances of crevices or holes in the reef. It will occasionally take up residence among the long spines of *Diadema* sea urchins, near the tentacles of sea anemones, or the polyps of the Longtentacled Plate Coral (*Heliofungia actiniformis*). *Apogon cyanosoma* feeds both day and night on planktonic crustaceans that live near the substrate. These include amphipods, shrimps, errant polychaetes, and copepods. This species has been observed to spawn around midday. mouthbrooding males are sometimes chased by groups of wrasses (e.g., Moon Wrasses, *Thalassoma lunare*). The wrasses try to get the male cardinalfish to spit out their eggs, which the labrids then eat.

Captive Care: The Yellowstriped Cardinalfish is one of the most ubiquitous apogonids in the marine aquarium trade, in part because it is very colorful and hardy. It is also a bolder species that spends much of its time in the open. However, it usually does not move far from cover. *Apogon cyanosoma* is best kept singly, in pairs, or in small groups of five to seven individuals (all the members of a group should be introduced to the tank simultaneously, and the aquarium should be 75 gallons or more). This species can be housed in a shallow- or deep-water reef tank. Although it is much less of a threat to small fishes and ornamental crustaceans than some of its relatives, it might prey on more delicate ornamental shrimps (e.g., anemone shrimps, *Periclimenes* spp.).

Aquarium Size: 20 gal. **Temperature:** 22 to 28°C (72 to 82°F).

Aquarium Suitability Index: 5.

Remarks: This species can be recognized by the width of the orange stripes on its body. On the upper part of the body, they are narrower than the gray spaces between them. They get wider toward the ventrum until they are about equal in width to the interspaces on the ventrum.

Apogon dispar Fraser & Randall, 1976

Common Name: Whitespot Cardinalfish.

Maximum Length: 5 cm (2 in.).

Distribution: Cocos-Keeling to Fiji, north to the Yaeyamas.

Biology: The Whitespot Cardinalfish is a resident of reef slopes (often on walls) from depths of 15 to 58 m (49 to 190 ft.). It is

Apogon cyanosoma Complex:
A Taxonomic Enigma

The mild-mannered cardinalfishes, perhaps surprisingly, are the subject of some real taxonomic feuding among ichthyologists. Some fish experts have been separating species with apparent abandon, taking one recognized species and separating it into two or more "valid" species based only on color form and geographical range. Others are more prudent, using characteristics like gill-raker numbers along with color variations to distinguish very similar forms. Making matters more confusing is the fact that there seem to be no objective standards. The same ichthyologist may distinguish two species based on color alone, but then lump two others that differ only in color characteristics. To the taxonomically challenged, it sometimes seems like an arbitrary guessing game. One cardinalfish group that has been the subject of much controversy is the *Apogon cyanosoma* complex. The basis of this complex is the **Yellowstriped Cardinalfish (*Apogon cyanosoma*)**, originally described by **Bleeker, 1853** from a specimen collected off Solor Indonesia.

Apogon sp., Izu Cardinalfish: one of many fishes similar to *Apogon cyanosoma* and the subject of lively controversy among taxonomists.

The Randall & Kulbicki Description

A paper published in 1998 by Randall and Kulbicki recognizes **four distinct species** in this complex aside from *Apogon cyanosoma*. They indicate that *Apogon cyanosoma* is known from the Red Sea and the east coast of Africa to the Western Pacific, where it occurs from southern Japan to the Great Barrier Reef. They consider **Wassink's Cardinalfish (*Apogon wassinki*) Bleeker, 1860** to be a valid species that ranges from Western Australia, Sabah, and Bintan Island, Indonesia. They report that it has three yellow stripes that run along the body to the base of the caudal fin (with a very narrow stripe along the upper edge of the body that ends at the rear of the second dorsal fin base). Comparatively, *Apogon cyanosoma* has six narrow yellow stripes on the body (including one that runs along the back and ends at the upper base of the caudal fin). The **Coral Cardinalfish (*Apogon properupta*) (Whitley, 1964)** is also considered valid by these authors. They suggest that this species is limited in distribution to Eastern Australia and the Coral Sea. In this paper, the authors describe the **Yellow Cardinalfish (*Apogon luteus*)** and the **Orangespot Cardinalfish (*Apogon rubrimacula*)** as new species. The Yellow Cardinalfish (*A. luteus*) is known from the Marshall, Mariana, and Caroline Islands. It is easy to distinguish from the others in the complex because of its highly divergent coloration. *Apogon luteus* is entirely yellow overall or has two bluish gray stripes.

The Kuiter & Kozawa Description

Kuiter and Kozawa (1999) recognize **eight species** in this complex aside from *Apogon cyanosoma*. Here is the *cyanosoma* story according to these two authors. The **Pacific Yellowstriped Cardinalfish (*Apogon* sp.)** is an undescribed form from Malaysia, Indonesia, Taiwan and southern Japan. It differs from *A. cyanosoma* in having orange stripes that are wider than the gray interspaces. This species is apparently most common on inner and coastal reefs, while *A. cyanosoma* is more abundant in the clear waters of outer-reef faces and slopes. The **Coral Cardinalfish (*Apogon properupta*)** has orange stripes on the upper half and middle of the body, while the lower half is orange overall, except for a silver gray or blue stripe along the cheek. This species is known from Papua New Guinea to northern New South Wales, Australia. In Micronesia, one finds the **Yellow Cardinalfish (*Apogon luteus*)**. It is entirely yellow overall with a dark snout and white lines on the head and through the eyes. The **Izu Cardinalfish (*Apogon* sp.)** is endemic to southern Japan. It has a central orange stripe that extends onto the caudal fin, and there are a series of silver gray spots on the belly. **Wassink's Cardinalfish (*Apogon wassinki*)** is known only from the Timor Sea and Western Australia. It is mainly pale with fewer orange stripes. The **Indian Yellowstriped Cardinalfish (*Apogon* sp.)** occurs in the western Indian Ocean and Red Sea. It has very narrow orange stripes. The **Maldivian Cardinalfish (*Apogon* sp.)** is found from the Maldives to Java. Most individuals have narrow silver or white interspaces between the wide orange stripes, although some individuals are pale yellow overall with silver stripes restricted to the head. The **Hibernia Cardinalfish (*Apogon* sp.)** is found in the Timor Sea and has five orange stripes, four of which extend to the base of the caudal fin. Kuiter and Kozawa consider *A. rubrimacula* to be a color variant of *A. cyanosoma*.

Confused yet? Taxonomists who fall into the "lumper" category consider some of Kuiter and Kozawa's proposed species to be simply geographical color variants of *Apogon cyanosoma*.

Apogon dispar, Whitespot Cardinalfish: small schooling fish.

Apogon parvulus, Redspot Cardinalfish: semi-transparent with telltale red dot.

Apogon neotus, Mini Cardinalfish: measures just 3 cm (1.2 in.) as an adult.

Apogon doederleini, Fourline Cardinalfish: handsome fish occurs in Japan.

commonly seen hovering in caves and associating with black coral. It usually occurs in schools and feeds on zooplankton.

Captive Care: A school of these delicate-looking little cardinalfish would make an interesting display in the reef aquarium. Its small size makes it vulnerable to being picked on, sometimes even eaten, by fish tankmates, so select them carefully. *Apogon dispar* is not a threat to ornamental crustaceans.

Aquarium Size: 20 gal. **Temperature:** 22 to 28°C (72 to 82°F).

Aquarium Suitability Index: 4.

Remarks: The Whitespot Cardinalfish is recognized by the black spot, with the white spot above it, on the caudal peduncle. There is also a red to black stripe along the middle of the body. The **Blackvent Cardinalfish** (*Apogon melanoproctus*) **Fraser & Randall, 1976** is a similar species, but it has a black area around its anus. It is known from Palau and the Solomon Islands. The

Redspot Cardinalfish (*Apogon parvulus*) **Smith & Radcliffe, 1912** is another small, semi-transparent cardinalfish, but it has a larger red spot on the caudal peduncle and lacks the black spot. Like its other two close relatives, *A. parvulus* is often found in large schools. It ranges from Indonesia to southern Japan. Finally, the **Mini Cardinalfish** (*Apogon neotus*) **Allen, Kuiter & Randall, 1994** is a tiny fish (3 cm [1.2 in.] total length) that has a black spot on the caudal peduncle and lacks a red spot. There is also a dark stripe in the middle of the body and black around the mouth.

Apogon doederleini Jordan & Snyder, 1901

Common Names: Fourline Cardinalfish, Doederlein's Cardinalfish.

Maximum Length: 12 cm (4.7 in.).

Distribution: Southern Japan. This species has been reported from other areas in the Indo-west Pacific, but these range records may be based on similar but different species.

Biology: The Fourline Cardinalfish is found on coral and rocky reefs. It sometimes occurs on reefs with extensive macroalgae growth. This cardinalfish lives in caves and crevices at depths of 3 to at least 30 m (3.9 to 98 ft.). While it shelters in the reef during the day, at night *A. doederleini* leaves its hiding places to feed. It will return to the same refuges (or at least the same general area) by sunrise. The Fourline Cardinalfish usually occurs singly, but is sometimes found in loose aggregations numbering up to ten individuals. Individuals in aggregations often exhibit aggression toward one another, including mouth-gaping and chasing. During the spawning season (May to August), individuals will migrate to the home range of a potential mate. The male and female *A. doederleini* will swim close to one another, engage in parallel circling (swimming in circles with the female on the outside, her snout adjacent to the middle of the male's body), and trembling (the female trembles as the pair swims in a circle). The body stripes and spot on the caudal peduncle fade during courtship and spawning. When the female is ready to spawn, she will release the egg mass (about 2 to 3 cm in diameter) as the pair maintains a parallel orientation after circling. The male turns and takes the egg mass into his mouth. After mating, the pair will continue parallel circling for more than an hour. The courting and spawning pair are often approached by other cardinalfishes, damselfishes, and wrasses. The Fourline Cardinalfish will chase these potential egg-predators away from the area, with the female exhibiting more aggression than the male. The male will mate again, two to four days after the eggs hatch (they spawn every 9 to 12 days). In some cases, males will eat part or all of the egg mass. The incidence of brood cannibalism in this species is reported by Okuda et al. (1997) to be about 16%. Much of what we know about the biology of this fish comes from Kuwamuru (1985).

Captive Care: This handsome cardinalfish is not often encountered by aquarists. It should be provided with ample caves and crevices in which to shelter. Keep singly, unless you can acquire a pair. The Fourline Cardinalfish is a threat to small fishes and crustaceans.

Aquarium Size: 30 gal. **Temperature:** 19 to 25°C (66 to 77°F).

Aquarium Suitability Index: 5.

Remarks: Kuiter and Kozawa (1999) separate the Japanese population from the more southern form of *Apogon "doederleini."* They state that there are differences in body depth (the Japanese population has a deeper body) and subtle color variations. More study is needed to confirm the relationship between the various populations. The **Copperstriped Cardinalfish** (*Apogon holotae-*

nia) **Regan, 1905** has light brown or copper stripes running down the body, but differs from similar species in that the middle stripe runs into the caudal fin. This species is found from the Arabian Gulf to the Gulf of Tomini, Sulawesi, Indonesia.

Apogon endekataenia Bleeker, 1832

Common Name: Candystripe Cardinalfish.

Maximum Length: 13 cm (5.1 in.).

Distribution: Singapore to Japan, south to northwest Australia. (See Remarks below for more on distribution.)

Biology: This cardinalfish is found on coral and rocky reefs. It often occurs in caves and in crevices and has been reported at a depth range of about 2 to 60 m (6.6 to 197 ft.).

Captive Care: The Candystripe Cardinalfish is not readily seen in the aquarium trade. It should be provided with suitable hid-

Apogon holotaenia, Copperstriped Cardinalfish: note stripe running into tail.

Apogon endekataenia, Candystripe Cardinalfish: a threat to smaller fishes.

Apogon evermanni, Oddscale Cardinalfish: most adundant in deep water and hard to collect.

Apogon exostigma, Eyeshadow Cardinalfish: hardy but best kept in a dimly lit or deep-water aquarium.

Apogon exostigma, Eyeshadow Cardinalfish: variant without usual dark spot on caudal peduncle.

ing places. Keep only one per tank unless you can acquire a male-female pair. This large cardinalfish is a threat to ornamental crustaceans and small fishes.

Aquarium Size: 30 gal. **Temperature:** 22 to 28°C (72 to 82°F).
Aquarium Suitability Index: 5.
Remarks: The taxonomy of this cardinalfish also appears to be somewhat enigmatic. Kuiter and Kozawa (1999) use the name *Apogon endekataenia* to refer to a dark-striped cardinalfish known in Singapore and Papua New Guinea, and *Apogon schlegeli* for the Japanese form of this fish. They separate the two species based on the size of the spot on the caudal peduncle. This species has probably been confused with similarly colored Australian forms; thus, its actual distribution is uncertain.

Apogon evermanni Jordan & Snyder, 1904
Common Names: Oddscale Cardinalfish, Evermann's Cardinalfish, Cave Cardinalfish.
Maximum Length: 15 cm (5.9 in.).
Distribution: East Africa to the Marquesan and Hawaiian Islands and tropical Western Atlantic.
Biology: This wide-ranging cardinalfish lives on reef faces, fore-reef slopes, and dropoffs. It occurs at depths of 8 to 70 m (26 to 230 ft.) but is more abundant in water deeper than 23 m (75 ft.). It tends to inhabit deep caves and crevices during the day, often swimming upside down with its ventrum near the cave ceiling. *Apogon evermanni* comes out at night to feed. It is usually a solitary species.
Captive Care: The Oddscale Cardinalfish is rarely collected because of its reclusive nature and predilection for deeper water. Because it is sensitive to light, it should be kept in a dimly lit tank with relatively passive fish tankmates. In this venue, you are more likely to see it in the open. Provide it with a cave in which to find security. Its greater maximum length means that it is more of a threat to smaller fishes and ornamental crustaceans.

Aquarium Size: 30 gal. **Temperature:** 22 to 28°C (72 to 82°F).
Aquarium Suitability Index: 3.
Remarks: What is currently referred to as *A. evermanni* may actually represent more than one species. Kuiter and Kozawa (1999) suggest that the Japanese population tends to differ in body depth and coloration from those in other parts of the Western Pacific. The common name Oddscale is derived from the fact that all the body scales are small, except those that form the lateral line.

Apogon exostigma (Jordan & Starks, 1906)
Common Names: Eyeshadow Cardinalfish, Oneline Cardinalfish.
Maximum Length: 11 cm (4.3 in.).
Distribution: Red Sea to the Line and Gambier Islands, north to Ryukyu Island, and south to the Great Barrier Reef and Austral Island.
Biology: The Eyeshadow Cardinalfish lives on coastal and lagoon reefs, outer-reef flats, reef faces, and fore-reef slopes at depths of 12 to 40 m (39 to 131 ft.). It feeds on small fishes, including gobies of the genus *Eviota*, shrimps, xanthid crabs, and polychaete worms.
Captive Care: The Eyeshadow Cardinalfish is a hardy aquarium inhabitant that will spend much of its time hiding or hovering near a place to refuge when the aquarium lights are on. It is more likely to spend time in the open in a dimly lit tank, so it is best kept in a fish-only tank or a deep-water reef tank. Only one *A. exostigma* should be housed per tank unless the aquarium is larger than 55 gallons. This species will eat small fishes and ornamental crustaceans.

Aquarium Size: 30 gal. **Temperature:** 22 to 28°C (72 to 82°F).
Aquarium Suitability Index: 5.
Remarks: This species is similar to the Bridled Cardinalfish (*Apogon fraenatus*). They differ in the position (or presence) of the spot on the caudal peduncle. In the Eyeshadow Cardinalfish the

spot is smaller and above the lateral line, while the Bridled Cardinalfish has a larger spot that is level with the lateral line. However, there is some debate about the taxonomic status of this and related cardinalfishes.

Apogon fraenatus Valenciennes, 1832

Common Name: Bridled Cardinalfish.
Maximum Length: 12 cm (4.7 in.).
Distribution: Red Sea to the Line and Tuamotu Islands, north to the Ryukyus, and south to New South Wales.
Biology: The Bridled Cardinalfish lives in estuaries, on lagoon reefs, outer-reef flats, reef faces, and fore-reef slopes at depths from 3 to 35 m (9.8 to 115 ft.). It is usually found in caves or under ledges. *Apogon fraenatus* feeds mainly at night on invertebrates that live on or near the bottom, but it will also take some prey items during the day. It occurs singly or in small groups.
Captive Care: The Bridled Cardinalfish is a hardy aquarium inhabitant that will spend much of its time hiding or hovering near a place to refuge when the aquarium lights are on. It is more likely to spend time in the open in a dimly lit tank, so it is best kept in a fish-only tank or a deep-water reef tank. Only one individual should be housed per tank, unless the aquarium is 55 gallons or more. *Apogon fraenatus* will eat small fishes and ornamental crustaceans.
Aquarium Size: 30 gal. **Temperature:** 22 to 28°C (72 to 82°F).
Aquarium Suitability Index: 5.
Remarks: This species is similar to the Eyeshadow Cardinalfish (*Apogon exostigma*). They differ by the position of the spot on the caudal peduncle. In *A. exostigma*, the spot is smaller and above the lateral line, while in *A. fraenatus* there is a larger spot that is level with the lateral line. Kuiter and Kozawa (1999) consider *A. exostigma* to be a synonym of *A. fraenatus*. They claim the presence, size, and position of the spot relative to the central body stripe can vary from one population to the next. The spot may also disappear in the late afternoon or at night or be absent in individuals from deeper water. These authors state that this has caused much confusion. In their coverage of the family, Kuiter and Kozawa (1999) also recognize the **Spinyeye Cardinalfish** (*Apogon melanorhynchus*) **Bleeker, 1852.** They indicate that this species usually has a larger spot (the size of the pupil) on the caudal peduncle that is centered at the end of the stripe on the side of the body. However, individuals from Bali sometimes lack the spot all together. This species is said to be greenish gray dorsally and pink below the midbody stripe. More intensive study is needed to determine the taxonomic status of the cardinalfishes in the *Apogon fraenatus* complex.

Apogon fragilis Smith, 1961

Common Name: Fragile Cardinalfish.
Maximum Length: 5 cm (1.9 in.).
Distribution: East Africa to the Marshall Islands and Samoa, north to the Ryukyus, and south to the Great Barrier Reef.
Biology: The Fragile Cardinalfish is a resident of lagoon reefs, where it is found at depths from 1 to 15 m (3.3 to 49 ft.). It forms large groups in reef crevices and among branching stony corals.
Captive Care: This diminutive apogonid is rarely collected for the aquarium trade. If acquired, it should be kept in groups of five or more and housed with very peaceful tankmates, like chromises, flasher wrasses, dartfishes, razor gobies, smaller shrimp gobies, and dragonets. Its small size makes it more vulnerable to predators, even some of the larger cardinalfish species. *Apogon fragilis* should be provided with plenty of hiding places and is a perfect addition to the deep- or shallow-water reef aquarium.
Aquarium Size: 20 gal. **Temperature:** 22 to 28°C (72 to 82°F).
Aquarium Suitability Index: 4.
Remarks: Kuiter and Kozawa (1999) state that *A. fragilis* is limited in distribution to the Indian Ocean. They refer to the Pacific form as the **Bluespotted Cardinalfish** (*Apogon* sp.), stating it

Apogon fraenatus, Bridled Cardinalfish: hardy but shy and fond of hiding in caves and under ledges.

Apogon fraenatus, Bridled Cardinalfish: easily confused with the Eyeshadow Cardinalfish (page 224).

Apogon fragilis, Fragile Cardinalfish: best kept in groups of five or more, with peaceful tankmates.

Apogon gilberti, Gilbert's Cardinalfish: eyecatching species for reef tanks.

Apogon griffini, Sicklefin Cardinalfish: note long extension of second dorsal.

differs from the true *A. fragilis* in coloration (e.g., it lacks the blue spots and dashes seen on adult individuals of the Pacific form).

Apogon gilberti (Jordan & Seale, 1905)
Common Name: Gilbert's Cardinalfish.
Maximum Length: 5 cm (2 in.).

Distribution: Philippines and Indonesia.
Biology: Gilbert's Cardinalfish is found in lagoons at depths of 2 to 4 m (6.6 to 13 ft.). Groups of these fish shelter among the branches of staghorn corals (*Acropora* spp.). It feeds on zooplankton.
Captive Care: A school of these delicate-looking cardinalfish makes an eyecatching display in the reef aquarium. Because of their small size and passive disposition, they are likely to be picked on by bullies and eaten by piscivorous tankmates. Choose their tankmates very carefully.
Aquarium Size: 20 gal. **Temperature:** 22 to 28°C (72 to 82°F).
Aquarium Suitability Index: 4.
Remarks: *Apogon gilberti* has a black spot on the gill cover, and the lobes of the caudal fin are black-tipped. There is a filament extending from the first dorsal fin.

Apogon griffini (Seale, 1910)
Common Name: Sicklefin Cardinalfish.
Maximum Length: 15 cm (5.9 in.).
Distribution: Philippines and northern Borneo.
Biology: This large cardinalfish is found on shallow coastal reefs. It has been reported at depths of 2 to 8 m (7 to 26 ft.). Adults typically occur in pairs.
Captive Care: The Sicklefin Cardinalfish is a handsome display fish. Keep singly, unless you can acquire a male and female. It will be right at home in a shallow-water reef aquarium. *Apogon griffini* is a larger species that is a threat to smaller fish and crustacean tankmates.
Aquarium Size: 30 gal. **Temperature:** 22 to 28°C (72 to 82°F).
Aquarium Suitability Index: 4.
Remarks: *Apogon griffini* gets its common name from the long extension on the second dorsal fin. *Apogon sabahensis* is a synonym. The **Norfolk Island Cardinalfish** (*Apogon norfolcensis*) **Ogilby, 1888** also has a high, falcate second dorsal fin, but differs radically in coloration. It is gray overall, with a white stripe just under the eye and one on the cheek. It is only known from Norfolk Island, Lord Howe Island, and New Caledonia. It is reported to be common in some areas.

Apogon hartzfeldii Bleeker, 1852
Common Names: Hartzfeld's Cardinalfish, Silverlined Cardinalfish.
Maximum Length: 10 cm (3.9 in.).
Distribution: Philippines to western New Guinea, south to Northwestern Australia.
Biology: Hartzfeld's Cardinalfish occurs on coastal reefs, sheltered reef flats, and lagoon patch reefs, at depths from 1 to at least

8 m (3.3 to 26 ft.). It can be found over mud, rubble, or live coral. *Apogon hartzfeldii* occurs singly or in small to large shoals. It will occasionally join shoals of Seale's Cardinalfish (*Apogon sealei*) and may form mixed aggregations with other apogonids as well.

Captive Care: This is a durable aquarium species that it is best kept on its own, unless you have a larger tank replete with cover. Hartzfeld's Cardinalfish is a moderately shy species that will stay close to cover in a brightly lit tank. This cardinalfish will eat smaller fishes and ornamental crustaceans.

Aquarium Size: 30 gal. **Temperature:** 22 to 28°C (72 to 82°F).

Aquarium Suitability Index: 5.

Remarks: Juvenile *A. hartzfeldii* have two white stripes running down the middle of each side of the body. The posterior portion of these stripes usually fades as the fish grows. The overall coloration ranges from gray to a coppery brown overall. There is also a black spot on the caudal peduncle. This species has been mistaken for closely related forms, and thus the distribution of *A. hartzfeldii* is somewhat nebulous.

Apogon hoevenii Bleeker, 1854

Common Name: Frostfin Cardinalfish.

Maximum Length: 5 cm (2 in.).

Distribution: Borneo to Great Barrier Reef, north to southern Japan.

Biology: The Frostfin Cardinalfish is most abundant on coastal sand or mud flats, slopes, or lagoon reefs, at depths between 20 to 30 m (66 to 98 ft.). It has also been reported from estuaries. This cardinalfish lives in shoals and often associates with crinoids, sponges, and even sea anemones. In seagrass areas, *A. hoevenii* regularly refuges among the spines of longspined sea urchins (*Diadema* spp.). It feeds on zooplankton.

Captive Care: This small cardinalfish species is rarely encountered in the aquarium trade. It should be kept with smaller, more docile tankmates, such as dartfishes, smaller shrimp gobies, razor gobies, worm gobies, and dragonets. *Apogon hoevenii* does best when kept in shoals comprised of five or more individuals. Provide them with plenty of shelter sites (you may want to add one or more longspined sea urchins to the tank for them to refuge in). This species can be kept in either a shallow- or deep-water reef tank.

Aquarium Size: 20 gal. **Temperature:** 22 to 28°C (72 to 82°F).

Aquarium Suitability Index: 4.

Remarks: The overall coloration of *A. hoevenii* is gray to greenish yellow. The first dorsal fin has a distinct white margin, and there are usually white spots on the posterior portion of the body and caudal peduncle.

Apogon hartzfeldii, Hartzfeld's Cardinalfish: typical daylight coloration.

Apogon hartzfeldii, Hartzfeld's Cardinalfish: pale nighttime appearance.

Apogon hoevenii, Frostfin Cardinalfish: refuges among spines of sea urchins.

Apogon kallopterus, Iridescent Cardinalfish: solitary cave dweller in the wild.

Apogon kallopterus, Iridescent Cardinalfish: color variant.

Apogon kiensis, Rifle Cardinalfish: interesting when displayed in schools.

Apogon kallopterus Bleeker, 1856

Common Name: Iridescent Cardinalfish.

Maximum Length: 15 cm (5.9 in.).

Distribution: Red Sea to the Hawaiian, Marquesas, and Pitcairn Islands, north to southern Japan, and south to Lord Howe and Rapa Islands.

Biology: The Iridescent Cardinalfish occurs on coastal fringing reefs, lagoon patch reefs, in seagrass beds, on outer reef flats, reef faces, and fore-reef slopes at depths of less than 1 to 158 m (3.3 to 518 ft.). This is a solitary species that hovers in caves and crevices during the day. At night, *A. kallopterus* moves out over sand patches and flats and remains near the seafloor. Its diet consists mainly of benthic and planktonic crustaceans, including shrimps (e.g., snapping shrimps, genus *Alpheus*), xanthid crabs, brachyuran crabs, amphipods, and isopods. It also feeds on polychaete worms, serpent stars, and small fishes (including smaller cardinalfishes). The Iridescent Cardinalfish feeds during both the day and night, although hunting activity does increase after dark. It is reported to consume an average of five prey organisms per night.

Captive Care: *Apogon kallopterus* is a durable aquarium species that will spend much of the time in the open, even when the lights are on. However, it is not highly sought after because of its drab appearance under daylight. Only one individual should be kept per aquarium, and it should be provided with crevices and caves to shelter in. It will eat small fishes, including other cardinalfishes, and ornamental crustaceans.

Aquarium Size: 30 gal. **Temperature:** 22 to 28°C (72 to 82°F).

Aquarium Suitability Index: 5.

Remarks: This species common name is derived from its blue-green iridescent coloration, which is only displayed at night. In the old scientific literature this species was often referred to as *Apogon snyderi* or *Pristiapogon snyderi*. Kuiter and Kozawa (1999) call this fish *Apogon urostigma* (Bleeker, 1874) and argue that *A. kallopterus* was originally applied to *A. fraenatus*.

Apogon kiensis Jordan & Snyder, 1901

Common Name: Rifle Cardinalfish.

Maximum Length: 8 cm (3.1 in.).

Distribution: East Africa and the Red Sea, north to Japan, south to New South Wales, Australia.

Biology: *Apogon kiensis* lives in estuaries, bays, and lagoons and is usually found in seagrass beds, on sand flats, and on sand slopes. It occurs to a depth of at least 25 m (82 ft.). This apogonid usually associates with remote coral heads, soft corals, large sea anemones, and tube anemones.

Captive Care: Because of its muted coloration, it is not highly

Apogon lachneri, Whitestar Cardinalfish: reclusive and averse to bright light.

Apogon leptacanthus, Bluestreak Cardinalfish: note filament on first dorsal.

sought after by aquarists. However, a school of these cardinals makes for an interesting display in a seagrass or sand slope biotope aquarium. It will swim around large sea anemones and tube anemones in the aquarium. Although it may ingest small, ornamental shrimps, it is less of a threat to tankmates than some of its larger kin.

Aquarium Size: 20 gal. **Temperature:** 22 to 28°C (72 to 82°F). **Aquarium Suitability Index:** 4.

Remarks: The Rifle Cardinalfish has a dark lateral stripe that extends onto the caudal fin, bordered by a white stripe above and below it. There is also a dark stripe on the dorsum with a white stripe above it. Kuiter and Kozawa (1999) recognize several species as valid that are usually considered color variants of *A. kiensis*. This includes a separate species from the Indian Ocean, Lembeh Strait (Sulawesi), and Japan. They suggest that the true *Apogon kiensis* is limited in distribution to Japan.

Apogon lachneri Böhlke, 1959

Common Name: Whitestar Cardinalfish.

Maximum Length: 6.5 cm (2.5 in.)

Distribution: Southern Florida and the Bahamas, south to Belize.

Biology: The Whitestar Cardinalfish is a denizen of fore-reef slopes and dropoffs, where it lives in caves and crevices. Although it occurs at depths from 5 to 70 m (17 to 230 ft.), it is more frequently found in water deeper than 24 m (79 ft.). In some areas (e.g., Belize, Honduras) it is the most common apogonid captured at depths between 24 and 30 m (79 to 98 ft.).

Captive Care: This reclusive species should be provided with plenty of shelter sites in which to refuge when the lights are on and should be housed with docile tankmates. It will spend most of its time in hiding during the day, but will leave the sanctuary

of the aquarium decor at night to hunt. It will spend more time in the open in a dimly lit tank, and is thus better suited to the deep-water, rather than shallow-water, reef aquarium. It is not a threat to other fishes or ornamental crustaceans.

Aquarium Size: 20 gal. **Temperature:** 22 to 28°C (72 to 82°F). **Aquarium Suitability Index:** 4.

Remarks: *Apogon lachneri* is reddish pink overall, with a square black blotch near the rear base of the second dorsal fin. There is also a white spot near the rear of the black blotch.

Apogon leptacanthus Bleeker, 1856

Common Names: Bluestreak Cardinalfish, Threadfin Cardinalfish.

Maximum Length: 6 cm (2.3 in.).

Distribution: Red Sea to Samoa, north to the Ryukyus, south New Caledonia, and Tonga.

Biology: This delicate-looking little cardinalfish is a resident of lagoon patch reefs at depths from 1 to 12 m (3.3 to 39 ft.). It is usually found in large shoals, hanging above the branches of certain stony corals (e.g., *Acropora* spp.). It will move into the safety of the coral branches when a threat approaches. Shoals comprised of 2,000 or more *A. leptacanthus* are commonly encountered, and one researcher reports seeing a shoal that consisted of over 24,000 individuals. At night, *A. lachneri* disperses over adjacent sand substrates to feed on crab larvae. It will also feed on zooplankton during the day. They return to their diurnal haunts before dawn.

Captive Care: Although the Bluestreak Cardinalfish is not often encountered in the aquarium trade, it would be a welcome addition to a more docile fish-only tank or a small-polyped stony coral aquarium. This species should be kept in groups consisting of five or more individuals and should never be kept with aggressive tankmates. They make great display animals for ei-

Apogon sp., Bluebarred Cardinalfish: possible new Indonesian species.

Apogon luteus, Yellow Cardinalfish: Micronesian beauty.

ther shallow- or deep-water reef aquariums. *Apogon leptacanthus* is not a threat to other fishes or to ornamental crustaceans.
Aquarium Size: 10 gal. **Temperature:** 22 to 28°C (72 to 82°F).
Aquarium Suitability Index: 4.
Remarks: The Bluestreak Cardinalfish has a long filament on the first dorsal fin, blue eyes, and often has blue streaks on the side of the body surrounded by patches of orange coloration. Kuiter and Kozawa (1999) report a similar species from Flores, Indonesia, that lacks the long filament on the first dorsal fin and has more thinner blue lines on the body (some individuals lack the lines altogether) and a black spot on the caudal peduncle. This species, which they refer to as the **Bluebarred Cardinalfish** (*Apogon* sp.), is reported to school within mangrove prop roots and staghorn corals in lagoons.

Apogon luteus Randall & Kulbicki, 1998
Common Name: Yellow Cardinalfish.
Maximum Length: 5 cm (2 in.).
Distribution: Palau to the Marshalls, possibly north to the Bonins.
Biology: The Yellow Cardinalfish is found in sheltered clear-water lagoons and on outer-reef faces and slopes. It is found at a depth range of 1 to 49 m (3.3 to 161 ft.). It aggregates under ledges, in holes, caves, and among the spines of urchins. At night, it moves from its diurnal refuges to feed on plankton and small benthic crustaceans. It will also do some feeding during the day.
Captive Care: *Apogon luteus* is another hardy cardinalfish that is well-suited to aquariums of various sizes. A small group makes an attractive display in the reef aquarium. It poses a minimal threat to small fishes and crustaceans, although large adults may ingest small, delicate shrimps. Its small size makes it a target to piscivores—do not keep it with overly aggressive tankmates.

Aquarium Size: 20 gal. **Temperature:** 22 to 28°C (72 to 82°F).
Aquarium Suitability Index: 5.
Remarks: The Yellow Cardinalfish is yellow overall, with white lines on the head that pass through the eyes.

Apogon maculatus (Poey, 1861)
Common Name: Flamefish.
Maximum Length: 10.5 cm (4.1 in.)
Distribution: Massachusetts, Bermuda and northeast Gulf of Mexico, south to Venezuela. Not common north of Florida.
Biology: The Flamefish is found in a variety of reef habitats, including cobble and rubble tracts, seagrass beds, mangrove areas, tidepools on reef flats, lagoon patch reefs, reef faces, fore-reef slopes and dropoffs. It occurs at a depth range of less than 1 to 127 m (3.3 to 417 ft.). It is one of the few cardinalfishes in the tropical Western Atlantic that is frequently found on the reef crest—a habitat exposed to high wave energy. *Apogon maculatus* spends the daytime hovering in or near holes, crevices, or under overhangs, and moves out over surrounding sand substrate to feed at night (it usually emerges from its diurnal refuge at about 6:15 P.M. and returns to the same hiding place at approximately 6:00 A.M.). Individuals have been observed to use the same hiding place for as long as two months. It feeds mostly on planktonic crustaceans, including shrimp larvae and copepods. It will also eat benthic prey, like shrimps, crabs, isopods, amphipods, and polychaete worms. It may occasionally feed during the day on cryptic prey that shares its hiding places. The Flamefish is a solitary species that rarely associates with other apogonids. In some areas, it will live among the spines of *Diadema* sea urchins. Courtship in *A. maculatus* includes circling behavior, in which the pair swim in a tight circle for several hours with the male keeping his anal

fin under the anus of the female. Spawning apparently occurs after dark, yielding an egg mass containing 75 to 100 eggs.

Captive Care: Because of its abundance on reefs of the tropical Atlantic and its bright red coloration, the Flamefish is one of the most common cardinalfish species in the aquarium trade. Unfortunately, its color often fades after it has been in captivity for some time, especially if it is not fed a varied diet, including enriched, pigment-enhancing foods. It is a great fish for hobbyists at any level, although it will often spend a considerable amount of time peering from holes and crevices, especially in well-illuminated tanks. *Apogon maculatus* will stake out a small territory in its captive home and will chase away any other cardinalfish that intrudes into its defended area. For this reason, it is advisable to keep only one Flamefish per tank, unless the aquarium is of sufficient size. If you want to keep more than one in the same tank, add two individuals simultaneously to a tank of 55 gallons or larger. Other cardinalfishes are also apt to get pestered if placed into a small tank with an *A. maculatus*.

Aquarium Size: 30 gal. **Temperature:** 22 to 28°C (72 to 82°F).

Aquarium Suitability Index: 5.

Remarks: *Apogon maculatus* is similar to the Twospot Cardinalfish (*Apogon pseudomaculatus*), but *A. maculatus* usually has a dark marking behind the eye and no spot on the peduncle (often has a band).

Apogon maculiferus Garrett, 1863

Common Name: Spotted Cardinalfish.

Maximum Length: 14 cm (5.5 in.).

Distribution: Hawaiian Islands (most common in the northeastern portion of the chain).

Biology: The Spotted Cardinalfish is found on rocky and coral reefs, at depths of 1 to 153 m (3.3 to 502 ft.). In most areas, this fish is most common at depths in excess of 20 m (66 ft.). Adults live under ledges and in caves during the day. Juveniles occur in shallower water than adults and are found in aggregations at cave entrances or under ledges. At night, this fish feeds above the seafloor. When moonlight is present, *A. maculiferus* may stray as high as 2 to 3 m (6.6 to 9.8 ft.) above the substrate. On darker nights when no moon is present, this fish may even rise higher into the water column. They occur singly or form loose aggregations. *Apogon maculiferus* feeds mainly on crustaceans, but also consumes fishes, polychaetes, and gastropods. Most of their feeding takes place at dawn.

Captive Care: This cardinalfish is rare in the trade. Adult *A. maculiferus* may pester each other, especially in smaller aquariums, so it is prudent to keep only one individual unless you can acquire a male-female pair or if you have a large aquarium. This is

Apogon maculatus, Flamefish: needs varied diet to retain bright colors.

Apogon maculatus?, Flamefish: possible hybrid or odd color form.

Apogon maculiferus, Spotted Cardinalfish: large species from Hawaii.

Apogon margaritophorus, Redstriped Cardinalfish: lovely smaller species.

Apogon moluccensis, Moluccan Cardinalfish: associates with sea anemones.

Apogon moluccensis: ventrifasciatus phase.

a larger cardinalfish that is a greater threat to ornamental crustaceans and small fishes. *Apogon maculiferus* tends to prefer slightly cooler water.

Aquarium Size: 30 gal. **Temperature:** 22 to 24°C (72 to 75°F).
Aquarium Suitability Index: 4.
Remarks: The Spotted Cardinalfish is easily recognized. It is pinkish orange overall, with rows of dark spots along the side of the body and an obscure spot at the base of the caudal fin.

Apogon margaritophorus Bleeker, 1854

Common Names: Redstriped Cardinalfish, Pearly Cardinalfish.
Maximum Length: 7 cm (2.7 in.).
Distribution: Malaysia to the Solomon Islands.
Biology: The Redstriped Cardinalfish is a resident of seagrass beds adjacent to coastal reefs. It occurs at a depth of less than 1 to 10 m (3.3 to 33 ft.). It sometimes shelters near sea urchins or sea anemones, as well as in seagrass. This apogonid usually occurs in groups, with individuals forming pairs within these aggregations.
Captive Care: This lovely cardinalfish occasionally shows up as an "Assorted Cardinalfish." A small group makes an especially nice display in a medium-size reef tank or a seagrass aquarium. Do not keep it with aggressive tankmates or piscivores, as its small size makes it particularly vulnerable. It is a minimal threat to small crustaceans and mild-mannered with other fish species. However, it is prone to be picked on by more pugnacious tankmates, including squirrelfishes and larger cardinalfishes.
Aquarium Size: 20 gal. **Temperature:** 22 to 28°C (72 to 82°F).
Aquarium Suitability Index: 4.
Remarks: The Redstriped Cardinalfish has two central stripes running along the side of the body with bars that connect the stripes. There are also stripes along the back, ranging from coppery brown to bright reddish orange.

Apogon moluccensis Valenciennes, 1828

Common Name: Moluccan Cardinalfish.
Maximum Length: 8.5 cm (3.3 in.).
Distribution: Philippines to Queensland, Australia.
Biology: The Moluccan Cardinalfish is found on coastal fringing reefs, lagoon patch reefs, and on the reef face at depths of 3 to 25 m (9.8 to 82 ft.). It occurs in pairs or in shoals, and in some areas it lives among the tentacles of large anemones (e.g., *Heteractis crispa* and *H. magnifica*). Even when forming groups, adults usually form pairs. The juveniles will aggregate around the tentacles of the Elegance Coral (*Catalaphyllia jardinei*) and the Corkscrew Tentacle Sea Anemone (*Macrodactyla doreensis*).
Captive Care: This is a great species for the aquarium, especially

Apogon monospilus, Yelloweyed Cardinalfish: distinguished by its eye color.

Apogon monospilus, Yelloweyed Cardinalfish: note blue coloration under eye

the reef tank, because it is not reclusive during the day. It can be kept in pairs or small groups and is less of a threat to crustaceans that its larger kin. Even so, it may attempt to eat small, delicate shrimps, like some anemone shrimps (*Periclimenes* spp.).

Aquarium Size: 20 gal. **Temperature:** 22 to 28°C (72 to 82°F).

Aquarium Suitability Index: 5.

Remarks: The Moluccan Cardinalfish is somewhat variable in color. It has two white lines on the head that run through the eyes, a conspicuous white spot at the base of the second dorsal fin, and distinct bars on the abdomen. Some individuals have light stripes along the dorsum. That said, it is reported that they often change their coloration when feeding or during courtship. The **Yelloweyed Cardinalfish (*Apogon monospilus*) Fraser, Randall & Allen, 2002** differs from *A. moluccensis* in having yellow eyes with a blue stripe under the eye. There may or may not be a white spot present at the base of the second dorsal fin—when it is present, it is not as large and conspicuous. This species also ranges from the Philippines to Queensland, Australia. Kuiter and Kozawa (1999) also suggest that *Apogon ventrifasciatus* Allen, Randall & Kuiter, 1995, is simply a color variant of *A. moluccensis*. They report having seen the common color form of *A. moluccensis* rapidly changing into the *A. ventrifasciatus* phase.

Apogon multilineatus Bleeker, 1853

Common Name: Multistriped Cardinalfish.

Maximum Length: 10 cm (3.9 in.).

Distribution: Sumatra to the Solomon Islands, north to the Philippines

Biology: The Multistriped Cardinalfish occurs on coastal and lagoon reefs, at depths from 3 to 25 m (9.8 to 82 ft.). It usually

Apogon multilineatus, Multistriped Cardinalfish: daytime coloration.

occurs singly or in small groups, hiding out under ledges or in reef crevices during the day and moving out over the sand at night to feed. It presumably feeds on worms and crustaceans, including planktonic and benthic forms.

Captive Care: This species does well in fish-only or reef aquariums. Be sure to provide it with plenty of good crevices and caves. It will also do better if you keep it with passive species. This medium-sized apogonid is a threat to smaller crustaceans, and large adults may ingest small fish tankmates.

Aquarium Size: 30 gal. **Temperature:** 22 to 28°C (72 to 82°F).

Aquarium Suitability Index: 4.

Remarks: The Multistriped Cardinalfish has numerous fine stripes running down the side of the body and a thicker dark stripe through the eye. The head is often darker than the rest of the body, while the fins often have a pink hue.

Apogon nigrofasciatus, Blackstripe Cardinalfish: fins often have pink hues.

Apogon notatus, Spotnape Cardinalfish: shoaling species.

Apogon nigrofasciatus Lachner, 1953

Common Name: Blackstripe Cardinalfish.

Maximum Length: 9 cm (3.5 in.).

Distribution: Red Sea to the Tuamotus, north to southern Japan, and south to New Caledonia and Rapa Island.

Biology: The Blackstripe Cardinalfish is found on coastal reefs, rocky estuaries, reef faces, fore-reef slopes, and on lagoon patch

reefs at depths from 3 to 50 m (9.8 to 164 ft.). During the day, it often lives under ledges and in reef interstices, but it will also hover in the open near the entrance to a hiding place. At night, it leaves its hiding place to feed. *Apogon nigrofasciatus* is usually a solitary species and is reported to feed on shrimp and polychaete worms.

Captive Care: Although not spectacular in appearance, the Blackstripe Cardinalfish does well in the home aquarium. It will accept most aquarium foods and should be provided with a varied diet that includes meaty foods (e.g., chopped seafoods, frozen preparations). It will spend much of the daylight hours peering from reef cracks and crevices. It may have a difficult time competing for food with more pugnacious species. It usually occurs singly in the wild and should be kept on its own in the aquarium. *Apogon nigrofasciatus* is a threat to smaller, delicate shrimps.

Aquarium Size: 30 gal. **Temperature:** 22 to 28°C (72 to 82°F).

Aquarium Suitability Index: 5.

Remarks: *Apogon nigrofasciatus* is one of several dark-striped species. There are apparently two basic color forms. One has white between the dark stripes, while the other has yellow interspaces. The fins of *A. nigrofasciatus* are often pink in hue. This species is similar in overall appearance to *Apogon angustatus* and *A. novemfasciatus*. For more on separating these species, see the Remarks section in the *A. angustatus* species account (page 216).

Apogon notatus (Houttuyn, 1782)

Common Name: Spotnape Cardinalfish.

Maximum Length: 10 cm (3.9 in.).

Distribution: Philippines to New Caledonia, north to southern Japan, south to the Great Barrier Reef.

Biology: *Apogon notatus* is found around rocky and coral reefs in harbors and bays, occurring at depths of 1 to 45 m (3.3 to 148 ft.). During certain parts of the year (autumn to spring in some areas), it regularly forms large, dense aggregations during the day, hovering near reef crevices, caves, or coral heads. It sometimes forms mixed schools with the Halfstriped Cardinalfish (*Apogon semilineatus*).

The Spotnape Cardinalfish exhibits a polyandrous mating system. About two months before spawning, when the water temperature exceeds 16°C (61°F), females set up territories on rocky substrate. Males join the females in these territories and they form a mating pair. Females sometimes initiate pairing by chasing a male away from the group. The territory-holding pair will chase off conspecifics that move too close, with the female attacking intruders more than the male. During most of the day, the pair remains in a side-by-side orientation. The fish will engage in a number of courtship behaviors. Kuwamaru (1983) reports that females engage in a motor pattern known as "warping." This is where the female fish, as she swims toward her mate, twists her body toward the male, with the abdomen pointing in the direction of her partner. During the reproductive season, spawning occurs daily, usually in the early afternoon. Spawning begins when the water temperature rises above 20°C (68°F). The morning of spawning, the female's abdomen swells as a result of egg hydration. About five hours before spawning, the female begins to nuzzle the male's genital area with her snout, which causes the male to open his mouth wide. About two hours before spawning, the male and female adopt a parallel orientation with their abdomens in contact. While in this position, they swim in circles. The male continues to perform mouth-opening and begins to nuzzle the genital area of the female. This behavior occurs intermittently until they spawn. The female extrudes an egg mass about 2 cm in diameter (it contains several thousand eggs), which catalyzes the male (usually swimming parallel to the female) to turn around and suck up the eggs. The pair then engage in rapid circling for a few minutes while the male rapidly opens and closes his mouth. Sperm release (fertilization) occurs from the time when the male turns to ingest the eggs until the rapid circling behavior ends (most of the eggs are fertilized while in the mouth of the male, within a few minutes of the spawning). Some egg-incubating males remain with their female partners, while others enter aggregations and exhibit no aggression. Females often engage in "pushing up," after spawning: she pushes her snout up against the ventral surface of the male's lower jaw. Kuwamaru (1983) suggests that this serves to drive the male into an aggregation, which enables the female to find another mate. The female will usually find a new mate within a day of spawning. Females have been reported to maintain their spawning territories for several weeks after the last spawning event. The eggs hatch in 8 to 14 days, depending on the water temperature. Wrasses sometimes interrupt the spawning process. In some cases, they dash in and eat the eggs as they are extruded from the female's genital pore.

At night, Spotnape Cardinalfish, whether in pairs or aggregations, disperse into midwater to feed. They will return to the aggregation or territory before the sun comes up. The diet of *A. notatus* consists of crustaceans (including decapods, amphipods, and copepods) and small fishes (including other cardinalfishes). This fish has a maximum lifespan of about 7 years.

Captive Care: This handsome species does not regularly enter the aquarium trade. If you do obtain one, offer it a varied diet of meaty foods (including frozen preparations for carnivores). It is a threat to crustaceans and small fishes.

Aquarium Size: 30 gal. **Temperature:** 19 to 24°C (66 to 75°F).

Apogon novemfasciatus, Sevenstriped Cardinalfish: stripes converge on tail.

Aquarium Suitability Index: 5.

Remarks: Kuiter and Kozawa (1999) recognize a second similar species that has long been considered a form of *A. notatus*. They call it the **False Earspot Cardinalfish (*Apogon jenkinsi*) Evermann & Seale, 1907.** It differs in that it lacks the dark V-shaped markings above the eyes, and the dark spot on the nape is often smaller or faded. This form is found from southern Japan to northern Australia, while Kuiter and Kozawa (1999) state that the true *A. notatus* is limited to Japan. The **Blackrim Cardinalfish (*Apogon nigrocincta*) Smith & Radcliffe, 1912** is another similar species that has been reported from Northern Australia to the Philippines. It occurs on sand or mud slopes and flats, where it associates with patch reefs and coral heads. It is light purple or pinkish overall, with a black edge on the distal margin of the first dorsal fin, and black lines along the base of the second dorsal, anal, and caudal fins.

Apogon novemfasciatus Cuvier, 1828

Common Name: Sevenstriped Cardinalfish
Maximum Length: 9 cm (3.5 in.).
Distribution: Cocos-Keeling Island to the Line Islands, north to the Izu Islands, and south to the Great Barrier Reef and Samoa.
Biology: The Sevenstriped Cardinalfish is abundant on reef flats and around coral heads in shallow lagoons at depths from less than 1 to 4 m (3.3 to 13 ft.). This fish often occurs in pairs or in small, loose groups (usually no more than three individuals). It hides under ledges and in reef crevices during the day, rarely seen more than 60 cm (23 in.) away from cover. After dark, *A. novemfasciatus* disperses and hunts for food. It feeds mainly on

Apogon ocellicaudus, Taileye Cardinalfish: small, easily bullied species.

small fishes (including anemonefishes, other damselfishes, wrasses, gobies, and blennies) and crustaceans (including shrimps and crabs). It will feed during the day as well, if the opportunity presents itself.

Captive Care: *Apogon novemfasciatus* readily acclimates to life in captivity and will spend a considerable amount of time in the open, especially in a dimly lit aquarium. It is prone to squabbling with members of its own species and may also pick on other cardinalfishes in smaller tanks. The Sevenstriped Cardinalfish will eat delicate ornamental shrimps (e.g., anemone shrimps) and will prey on small fishes. Other than its taste for potential tankmates, it is ideally suited for the reef aquarium.

Aquarium Size: 30 gal. **Temperature:** 22 to 28°C (72 to 82°F).
Aquarium Suitability Index: 5.
Remarks: This is one of several dark-striped cardinalfishes. For more on how to separate it from similar species, see the Remarks section of the *Apogon angustatus* species account (page 216).

Apogon ocellicaudus Allen, Kuiter & Randall, 1994

Common Name: Taileye Cardinalfish.
Maximum Length: 5 cm (2 in.).
Distribution: Sulawesi and Flores, Indonesia and the Timor Sea.
Biology: This cardinalfish is found on coastal reefs, often on isolated patch reefs, on sand slopes, or under ledges at the base of the reef face. It tends to prefer current-swept habitats. This cardinalfish usually lives at depths of 15 to 30 m (49 to 98 ft.). It occurs in pairs, small groups, or large shoals.

Captive Care: This lovely little cardinalfish is not readily found in the aquarium trade. It can and probably should be kept in pairs or small groups. It is a minimal threat to smaller shrimps and is not a threat to fish tankmates. On the other hand, it is prone to being picked on or eaten by bullies and piscivores. It tends to prefer dimly lit aquariums.

Aquarium Size: 20 gal. **Temperature:** 22 to 28°C (72 to 82°F).
Aquarium Suitability Index: 5.
Remarks: This beautiful little cardinalfish has a distinct black spot that is surrounded by lighter pigment at the base of the tail. A stripe (which varies in its degree of conspicuousness and is either yellow or orange) runs down the middle of the body. The **Faintbanded Cardinalfish** (*Apogon franssedai*) **Allen, Kuiter & Randall, 1994** is a similar species that is known from southern Indonesia to northern Australia. It has the spot at the base of the caudal fin, but differs from *A. ocellicaudus* in having two stripes on the body (one along the middle of the body and one along the back).

Apogon perlitus Fraser & Lachner, 1985

Common Names: Pearly Cardinalfish, Lagoon Cardinalfish.
Maximum Length: 5.5 cm (2.2 in.).
Distribution: Philippines to northwestern Australia, east to the Caroline Islands.
Biology: The Pearly Cardinalfish is found in lagoons, often on silt-covered reefs. It occurs in shoals that usually inhabit branching stony corals. It may also be found among the spines of longspined sea urchins (*Diadema* spp.). It feeds on zooplankton.

Captive Care: This little silver cardinalfish may occasionally come into the aquarium trade. A shoal of these fish makes an interesting display in the reef aquarium. Its small size makes it vulnerable to being picked on or eaten by fish tankmates. It is not a threat to crustaceans.

Aquarium Size: 20 gal. **Temperature:** 22 to 28°C (72 to 82°F).
Aquarium Suitability Index: 5.
Remarks: This species is similar to the Fragile Cardinalfish (*Apogon fragilis*). It differs in having a black patch along the edge of the anal fin base. The jaws are often yellow, the body is blue and silver, there is a white spot near the rear edge of the second dorsal fin base, and a black spot on the caudal peduncle. The **Mangrove Cardinalfish** (*Apogon lateralis*) **Valenciennes, 1829** is a similar species that is silver overall with a black line in the middle of the body and a small black spot on the caudal peduncle. The anterior edge of the first dorsal fin is also black. *Apogon lateralis* is found from East Africa to Samoa, north to Taiwan. It lives in river mouths and shallow lagoons, where it occurs in large shoals among mangrove prop roots, algae clumps, and rubble.

Apogon perlitus, Pearly Cardinalfish: silvery shoals are a lovely sight.

Apogon lateralis, Mangrove Cardinalfish: often found in shallow lagoons.

Apogon phenax, Mimic Cardinalfish: note iridescent turquoise-blue sheen.

Apogon pillionatus, Broadsaddle Cardinalfish: excellent for deep-water reefs.

Apogon phenax Böhlke & Randall, 1968
Common Name: Mimic Cardinalfish.
Maximum Length: 7.5 cm (3 in.).
Distribution: Florida Keys and the Bahamas to Curacao.
Biology: This solitary apogonid is found on rock and coral patch reefs, reef faces, and dropoffs, at depths of 3 to 50 m (9.8 to 164 ft.). It is most often encountered at about 12 m (39 ft.). A cave and crevice dweller, it hides during the day and comes out to feed at night.
Captive Care: The Mimic Cardinalfish is not common in the aquarium trade. It is a durable aquarium fish that will spend much of its time in the open when the lights are on. House only one per tank, unless your aquarium is large. It may quarrel with apogonids having similar color patterns (e.g., *Apogon maculatus*). It is possible to keep a small group in a medium-sized aquar-

ium. Do not house it with aggressive tankmates. This fish is a threat to small ornamental shrimps.
Aquarium Size: 20 gal. **Temperature:** 22 to 28°C (72 to 82°F).
Aquarium Suitability Index: 5.
Remarks: *Apogon phenax* is red overall with a dark triangle-shaped patch at the base of the second dorsal fin. There is also a wide bar at the base of the caudal fin. This fish exhibits an iridescent turquoise sheen at night.

Apogon pillionatus Böhlke & Randall, 1968
Common Name: Broadsaddle Cardinalfish.
Maximum Length: 6 cm (2.3 in.).
Distribution: Florida Keys and Bahamas, south to northern South America.
Biology: The Broadsaddle Cardinalfish is found on deep reef faces,

Apogon planifrons, Pale Cardinalfish: pearly nighttime coloration.

Apogon pseudomaculatus, Twospot Cardinalfish: may be kept in groups.

Apogon quadrisquamatus, Sawcheek Cardinalfish: sheltering near anemone.

reef slopes, and walls at depths of 6 to 93 m (20 to 305 ft.). In the Bahamas, it is most often seen at 26 to 46 m (85 to 151 ft.). This secretive species hides in reef crevices during the day and comes out to feed at night. It occurs singly and in pairs.

Captive Care: This little cardinalfish is a great addition to the deep-water reef aquarium. It will spend more time hiding in a brightly lit aquarium or if housed with aggressive tankmates. It is possible to keep more than one in the same tank, but larger congeners may pick on this species. It is not a significant threat to ornamental crustaceans.

Aquarium Size: 20 gal. **Temperature:** 22 to 28°C (72 to 82°F).

Aquarium Suitability Index: 5.

Remarks: The Broadsaddle Cardinalfish is easily recognized by the black saddle on the caudal peduncle, the white line in front of the saddle (there is sometimes a second white line behind the saddle), and a black bar under the second dorsal fin.

Apogon planifrons Longley & Hildebrand, 1940

Common Name: Pale Cardinalfish.

Maximum Length: 10 cm (3.9 in.).

Distribution: South Florida and the Bahamas, south to Venezuela.

Biology: The Pale Cardinalfish lives on lagoon patch reefs, reef faces, fore-reef slopes, and dropoffs at a depth range of 3 to 30 m (9.8 to 98 ft.), but is most common at depths greater than 12 m (39 ft.). This reclusive species lives deep in crevices and caves during the day. At night, it leaves the protection of the reef to forage on zooplankton in the open water. It is a solitary species.

Captive Care: This secretive species will spend more time in full view if the aquarium is not brightly lit. However in time, most individuals will learn to come out to take food when the lights are on. Only one individual should be housed per tank, unless the aquarium is larger in size (70 gallons or larger). Even then, it is best to add all individuals simultaneously. This fish is a threat to small ornamental crustaceans.

Aquarium Size: 30 gal. **Temperature:** 22 to 28°C (72 to 82°F).

Aquarium Suitability Index: 5.

Remarks: This species is a pale pink overall, with a dark bar extending from the rear of the dorsal fin to the ventrum (this is not triangular as for *A. phenax*), and a bar or area near the caudal fin base (less conspicuous in larger individuals). The bar at the base of the caudal fin is wider than that of the Barred Cardinalfish (*Apogon binotatus*). At night, this fish exhibits bluish and yellow highlights and often has a pearly appearance.

Apogon pseudomaculatus Longley, 1932

Common Name: Twospot Cardinalfish.

Maximum Length: 10.5 cm (4.1 in.).

Apogon quadrisquamatus, Sawcheek Cardinalfish: great choice for grouping in a Caribbean biotope aquarium with a Giant Sea Anemone (*Condylactis gigantea*).

Distribution: Massachusetts and Bermuda, south to Brazil.
Biology: The Twospot Cardinalfish is found among pier pilings, on lagoon patch reefs, the reef face, deep-reef slopes, and dropoffs at depths from 2 to 400 m (6.6 to 1,312 ft.). In most areas, it appears to be common at greater depths. This species is sometimes found in the same hiding places as the closely related Flamefish (*A. maculatus*). It usually hides in reef crevices and caves during the day and comes out at night to feed on zooplankton.
Captive Care: The Twospot Cardinalfish will do well in the home aquarium as long as it is kept with docile tankmates and provided with plenty of hiding places. It will eat most aquarium fare (as long as the food is suspended in the water column) and will not behave aggressively toward other fishes. It can be kept singly or in small groups. It will spend more time in the open in a dimly lit tank. Larger individuals may bother smaller, delicate, ornamental shrimps, such as anemone shrimps (*Periclimenes* spp.). The color of this fish may fade in captivity unless offered a pigment-enhancing diet.
Aquarium Size: 30 gal. **Temperature:** 22 to 28°C (72 to 82°F).
Aquarium Suitability Index: 5.
Remarks: This apogonid is similar to the Flamefish (*Apogon maculatus*). For information on how to differentiate these two similar species see the *A. maculatus* Remarks section (page 231).

Apogon quadrisquamatus Longley, 1934

Common Name: Sawcheek Cardinalfish.
Maximum Length: 7 cm (2.7 in.).
Distribution: Southern Florida and the Bahamas to northern South America.
Biology: The Sawcheek Cardinalfish is found in lagoons, the reef face, and fore-reef slopes at depths of 1 to 75 m (3.3 to 246 ft.), often over sand, rubble, and gravel substrates. This apogonid associates with the Longspine Sea Urchin (*Diadema antillarum*), tube sponges, and sea anemones. It will swim at the periphery of, and among, the expanded tentacles of the Curleycue Anemone (*Bartholomea annulata*) and the Giant Sea Anemone (*Condylactis gigantea*). It will occasionally contact and be stung by these cnidarians, which results in lesions and scars on the body. Even so, *A. quadrisquamatus* will sometimes seek shelter among the stinging tentacles in sandy areas where hiding places are in short supply. Anemone-associated individuals have been observed being attacked and eaten by Slippery Dick Wrasses (*Halichoeres bivittatus*). This species leaves its daytime hiding places at night and feeds close to the substrate. It eats zooplankton.
Captive Care: This pretty little cardinalfish can be an interesting addition to the home aquarium—especially if kept in a group with a large *Condylactis gigantea*. It should not be housed with ag-

Apogon rhodopterus, False Threespot Cardinalfish: muted fish, tends to hide.

Apogon trimaculatus, Threespot Cardinalfish: note spot on gill cover.

gressive tankmates or with fish-eating species, as its small size makes it an easy target. A simple biotope aquarium would include a small group of these fish with a few pieces of live rock and one or more Curleycue or Giant Sea Anemones.
Aquarium Size: 20 gal. **Temperature:** 22 to 28°C (72 to 82°F).
Aquarium Suitability Index: 4.
Remarks: This is a plain pink cardinalfish (sometimes with a bronze hue) with a dark area in front of the caudal fin base. It can rapidly darken or lighten its hue. The **Bridle Cardinalfish** (*Apogon aurolineatus*) (**Mowbray, 1927**) is a similar species that also associates with sea anemones. *Apogon aurolineatus* lacks the dark marking on the caudal peduncle. The Bridle Cardinalfish is occasionally found living among the tentacles of *B. annulata* and *C. gigantea*, but also occurs in seagrass beds and open sand bottoms. It has been reported to share sea anemone hosts with *A. quadrisquamatus*. Colin and Heiser (1973) report having collected 26 *A. quadrisquamatus* and nine *A. aurolineatus* from a single Curleycue Sea Anemone. It has been reported from depths of 1 to 75 m (3.3 to 246 ft.).

Apogon rhodopterus (Bleeker, 1854)

Common Name: False Threespot Cardinalfish.
Maximum Length: 15 cm (5.9 in.).
Distribution: Malaysia to the Solomons, north to the Ryukyus.
Biology: The False Threespot Cardinalfish occurs inshore, in sheltered reefs, and on more exposed outer reefs. It is found at depths of 1 to 35 m (3.3 to 115 ft.) on rocky reefs, coral patch reefs, reef faces, and reef slopes. *Apogon rhodopterus* typically resides deep in crevices and caves during the day. At night, it moves out to feed on benthic invertebrates.
Captive Care: Because of its rather muted coloration, *A.*

rhodopterus is not highly sought after by aquarists. It is also quite secretive and thus will spend much of its time hiding in the aquarium. Provide it with plenty of suitable shelter sites. It may have a difficult time getting enough to eat if kept in a pugnacious community tank. The False Threespot Cardinalfish is a definite threat to crustaceans and small fishes.
Aquarium Size: 40 gal. **Temperature:** 22 to 28°C (72 to 82°F).
Aquarium Suitability Index: 2.
Remarks: The False Threespot Cardinalfish is gray to light brown overall, with a pale digestive tract. The **Threespot Cardinalfish** (*Apogon trimaculatus*) (**Cuvier, 1828**) is a similar species. It differs in having a spot (often pale) on the gill cover. Juveniles of this species have more distinct markings, including a black and white first dorsal fin. It ranges from Malaysia to Samoa, north to the Ryukyus, south to northwestern Australia and the Great Barrier Reef. Its husbandry requirements are similar to those of the *A. rhodopterus*. *Apogon rhodopterus* and *A. trimaculatus* are known to hybridize. The **Red Cardinalfish** (*Apogon rufus*) **Randall & Fraser (1999)** is brownish red overall, with a black digestive tract. It also has a spot on the gill cover, two dark saddles on the back, and a spot on the caudal peduncle. It occurs from Indonesia to Fiji, north to the Ryukyus, and south to Papua New Guinea.

Apogon robinsi Böhlke & Randall, 1968

Common Name: Roughlip Cardinalfish.
Maximum Length: 11 cm (4.3 in.).
Distribution: Bahamas to Belize.
Biology: This cardinalfish is found on patch reefs, outer reef faces and fore-reef slopes at depths of 3 to 30 m (9.8 to 98 ft.). In the Bahamas, it is reported to be most common at depths of 2 to 15 m (6.6 to 49 ft.). During the day, *A. robinsi* lurks in deep crevices.

Apogon robinsi, Roughlip Cardinalfish: hides in deep crevices during daylight.

Apogon savayensis, Samoan Cardinalfish: cryptic and a challenge to keep.

At night, it comes out to feed.

Captive Care: The Roughlip Cardinalfish is much rarer in the aquarium trade than many of its Western Atlantic congeners. It is a secretive species that will spend most of its time hiding, unless kept in a dimly lit aquarium. This fish may be pestered by overly pugnacious tankmates, but is not as susceptible to being picked on as smaller apogonids. It is a threat to ornamental crustaceans and small fish tankmates.

Aquarium Size: 30 gal. **Temperature:** 22 to 28°C (72 to 82°F).
Aquarium Suitability Index: 4.

Remarks: *Apogon robinsi* is pink overall and is characterized by reddish patches on the dorsal and anal fins, darker red caudal fin margins, a dark red bar that extends from the base of the second dorsal fin to the ventrum, and a wide dark bar on the caudal peduncle. In large adults, the tooth patches extend outside the mouth. It also has more pointed second dorsal and anal fins and a longer caudal peduncle than similar apogonids. At night, this species exhibits a turquoise iridescence on the head and body.

Apogon savayensis Günther, 1871
Common Name: Samoan Cardinalfish
Maximum Length: 11 cm (4.3 in.).
Distribution: Red Sea to the Line and Tuamotu Islands, north to the Ryukyus, south to the Great Barrier Reef and Rapa Island.
Biology: This secretive apogonid is found on sheltered reefs in lagoons, on outer reef faces, and on fore-reef slopes at depths of 3 to 25 m (9.8 to 82 ft.). *Apogon savayensis* spends its days hidden deep in reef crevices and caves. At night, it comes out to feed on polychaete worms and crustaceans (including ostracods, amphipods, and shrimps).
Captive Care: This fish is not a great display animal because of

its muted coloration and cryptic habits. It will spend most of its time deep in crevices or behind aquarium decor. If it is not provided with suitable hideouts, it will stop feeding and hang in the upper corners of the aquarium. It may be difficult to feed in a tank full of vigorous feeders. You may have to add small feeder fish when the lights are turned out. The Samoan Cardinalfish is prone to being picked on by fish tankmates that defend reef caves and crevices. This includes squirrelfishes, groupers, and dottybacks. It is a threat to crustaceans and small fishes.

Aquarium Size: 30 gal. **Temperature:** 22 to 28°C (72 to 82°F).
Aquarium Suitability Index: 3.

Remarks: This species is silvery gray overall, with a black saddle on the caudal peduncle. There is a thin black line running diagonally (toward the tail) from the lower edge of the eye. The similar Banda Cardinalfish (*Apogon bandanensis*) has a black band around the caudal peduncle (rather than a saddle), and the marking under the eye is darker and tapers more toward the distal end. The **Guam Cardinalfish** (*Apogon guamensis*) **Valenciennes, 1852** is a similar large-eyed species. This fish has no band or saddle on the caudal peduncle (if a band is present, it is very obscure), it is usually gray or brownish gray overall, and the line under the eye is very thin. The **Blackring Cardinalfish** (*Apogon annularis*) **Rüppell, 1829** is gray overall, with a white caudal peduncle and a black band around the peduncle. The line under the eye is thick and distinct. There are apparently several undescribed species that are similar to these three species. One of these, which Kuiter and Kozawa (1999) refer to as the **Yellowedged Cardinalfish** (*Apogon* sp.) has yellow margins on all the fins except the first dorsal (they are very conspicuous on the caudal fin). They report that this species is found in the tropical eastern Indian Ocean and Western Pacific. They also describe the

Apogon sealei, Seale's Cardinalfish: handsome, ideal aquarium species.

Apogon chrysopomus, Cheekspot Cardinalfish: note orange cheek markings.

Zebra Cardinalfish (*Apogon* sp.), which has white lines along the body, a black patch on the anterior part of the first dorsal fin, and a black band on the caudal peduncle. The Zebra Cardinalfish is found in the Red Sea and eastern Indian Ocean. More study is required to determine if these different color forms are simply color variants or true species. All of these species tend to prefer sheltered inshore habitats and spend their days deep in reef crevices. They come out at night to feed.

Apogon sealei Fowler, 1918
Common Name: Seale's Cardinalfish.
Maximum Length: 8 cm (3.1 in.).
Distribution: Malaysia to the Solomon Islands, north to the Ryukyus, and south to the Great Barrier Reef.
Biology: Seale's Cardinalfish is usually found on coastal fringing reefs or patch reefs at depths of 3 to 10 m (9.8 to 33 ft.). It is often found in pairs or in small groups among branching corals. I have also encountered this species hanging over reefs composed mainly of large-polyped stony corals (including *Euphyllia ancora* and *Plerogyra sinuosa*). They hover above these corals until threatened, at which time they seek hiding places provided by the corals' calcareous skeletons. Groups of *A. sealei* are sometimes joined by other apogonids, like juvenile Ochrestriped Cardinalfish (*Apogon compressus*) and the Coral Cardinalfish (*A. properupta*).
Captive Care: This is an ideal aquarium inhabitant because it will swim about the tank, even if it is brightly illuminated. It should be kept in pairs or small groups, and, as with most cardinalfishes, it needs to be housed with peaceful tankmates. *Apogon sealei* is a threat to smaller shrimps.
Aquarium Size: 20 gal. **Temperature:** 22 to 28°C (72 to 82°F).
Aquarium Suitability Index: 4.
Remarks: Seale's Cardinalfish is very similar to the **Cheekspot Cardinalfish (*Apogon chrysopomus*) Bleeker, 1854.** Both species have orange markings on the gill covers, lines on the body, and a black spot on the caudal peduncle. In *A. chrysopomus* there are orange spots on the gill cover and "cheeks," while in *A. sealei* the gill cover is adorned with orange bars and has no markings on the "cheeks." In some parts of its range, the Cheekspot Cardinalfish has rows of spots, rather than lines, on its body. The Cheekspot Cardinalfish is known from Indonesia and the Philippines. It attains a maximum length of 11 cm (4.3 in.). This species occurs on protected coastal and lagoon reefs, at depths from 3 to 10 m (9.8 to 33 ft.). It is usually found in groups over or among branching stony corals. The Cheekspot Cardinalfish is not readily available in the aquarium trade, but it can be kept singly, in pairs, or if you have a larger aquarium you can keep it in small groups. It will eat crustaceans and fishes small enough to fit into its mouth.

Apogon selas Randall & Hayashi, 1989
Common Names: Meteor Cardinalfish, Bandspot Cardinalfish, Shooting Star Cardinalfish.
Maximum Length: 5.5 cm (2.2 in.).
Distribution: Philippines to Solomon Islands, north to the Ryukyus, south to the Great Barrier Reef.
Biology: The Meteor Cardinalfish is found in sheltered lagoons or coastal reefs at depths of 4 to 42 m (13 to 138 ft.). It is most common at depths in excess of 15 m (49 ft.). It is usually found in small shoals.
Captive Care: This attractive apogonid is not common in the aquarium trade. Provide it with suitable hiding places and do

not keep it with aggressive tankmates. Its small maximum size means it is less of a threat to crustacean tankmates.

Aquarium Size: 20 gal. **Temperature:** 22 to 28°C (72 to 82°F).

Aquarium Suitability Index: 5.

Remarks: *Apogon selas* has a central coppery brown stripe from the tip of the snout to near the base of the tail. A pair of white stripes start on the snout and run through the eye and along some of the central body stripe. There is a large black spot on the caudal peduncle. This species is similar to the **Anklet Cardinalfish** (*Apogon pselion*) **Randall, Fraser & Lachner, 1990.** This apogonid occurs in the northern Red Sea. It has an orange central body stripe with a large black spot near the caudal fin base.

Apogon semilineatus Schlegel, 1843

Common Names: Semilined Cardinalfish, Barface Cardinalfish.

Maximum Length: 12 cm (4.7 in.).

Distribution: Philippines north to southern Japan.

Biology: The Semilined Cardinalfish is most commonly encountered on rocky reefs with varying amounts of coral cover. It occurs over a depth range of 12 to 100 m (39 to 328 ft.). During the day it remains near hard substrate, but at night it moves out onto surrounding sandy areas to feed. The diet of *A. semilineatus* consists mainly of gammarid amphipods that live in tubes in the substrate (moving out of their holes into the water column at night). It will also eat ostracods, copepods, mysid shrimp, polychaete worms, and small fishes on occasion. It is usually found in large groups and forms long-term pair bonds. It sometimes joins shoals of Spotnape Cardinalfish (*Apogon notatus*).

Captive Care: The Semilined Cardinalfish is a durable aquarium species that will spend much of its time in the open when the lights are on. It can be kept singly, in pairs, or in small aggregations, but will tend to be bolder if more than one is kept per tank. If individuals pair up, they may exclude conspecifics, as well as other cardinalfishes, from a certain part of the tank. Because of its larger size, this species is a greater threat to smaller fish and crustaceans than the closely related *Apogon sealei.*

Aquarium Size: 30 gal. **Temperature:** 20 to 26°C (68 to 79°F).

Aquarium Suitability Index: 4.

Remarks: *Apogon semilineatus* has a pair of dark stripes that run from the snout, through the eye, and onto the back and side. There is also a yellow patch on the abdomen, and the rear portion of the body and caudal peduncle is salmon orange or pinkish.

Apogon semiornatus Peters, 1876

Common Name: Halfbanded Cardinalfish.

Maximum Length: 7 cm (2.7 in.).

Distribution: Red Sea and Gulf of Oman, east to Australia, north

Apogon selas, Meteor Cardinalfish: interesting but rarely seen by aquarists.

Apogon semilineatus, Semilined Cardinalfish: forms long-term pairs.

Apogon semiornatus, Halfbanded Cardinalfish: shy, solitary species.

Apogon townsendi, Belted Cardinalfish: likes sheltering ledges and crevices.

Apogon townsendi, Belted Cardinalfish: nocturnal coloration with fused belts.

to Japan and south to Natal, South Africa.

Biology: This secretive species is found on coastal reefs. It occurs at depths of 2 to 30 m (6.6 to 98 ft.) and is usually is found under rocks or in caves.

Captive Care: Provide *A. semiornatus* with plenty of hiding places. It may spend more time in the open in an aquarium that is dimly lit. It is also prone to being picked on by aggressive tankmates, especially those that may compete with it for holes and crevices (e.g., dottybacks).

Aquarium Size: 20 gal. **Temperature:** 20 to 26°C (68 to 79°F).

Aquarium Suitability Index: 3.

Remarks: The Halfbanded Cardinalfish has a thick stripe that starts behind the head and extends onto the caudal fin, and a short stripe that begins at the back of the eye and ends at the base of the anal fin. There is a red stripe in front of the eye.

Apogon townsendi (Breder, 1927)

Common Name: Belted Cardinalfish.

Maximum Length: 6.5 cm (2.6 in.).

Distribution: South Florida and Bahamas, south to northern South America.

Biology: This species is found on the reef face and slopes at depths of 3 to 55 m (9.8 to 180 ft.). It hovers between the branches of stony corals, in crevices, caves, and beneath overhangs during the day. Aggregations of *A. townsendi* often form in preferred hiding places (groups can number up to 40 individuals) and may include the closely related Barred Cardinalfish (*Apogon binotatus*). It moves onto sand patches or adjacent flats at night to feed on zooplankton. It is reported to feed higher in the water column (up to 2.5 m [8 ft.] above the substrate) than *A. binotatus*. In one study where numerous individuals were collected for internal examination, females outnumbered males 5 to 1.

Captive Care: This Western Atlantic native is regularly encountered in the aquarium trade. Provide it with plenty of crevices and ledges to shelter in or under. More than one Belted Cardinalfish can be kept in the same tank. It is not a threat to most ornamental crustaceans, but may be picked on or eaten by larger fish tankmates.

Aquarium Size: 30 gal. **Temperature:** 22 to 28°C (72 to 82°F).

Aquarium Suitability Index: 5.

Remarks: The Belted Cardinalfish has a dark bar that extends from the rear of the second dorsal fin to the anal fin, a bar on the caudal peduncle, and a more obscure bar at the base of the caudal fin (these two bars are often so close together that they form a single dark-edged bar). The similar Barred Cardinalfish (*Apogon binotatus*) lacks the third bar at the base of the caudal fin. At night, a wide bar or saddle appears on the caudal peduncle of *A. townsendi* (i.e., the area between the bars on the caudal peduncle darkens).

Genus *Archamia* (Deepbodied Cardinalfishes)

The 16 members of the genus *Archamia* are deepbodied, have more soft anal fin rays, and more fill rakers than the *Apogon* spp. These fishes often occur in large groups during the day. They will consume zooplankton from the midwater during both day and night. At night, they move up to 6 m (20 ft.) from their daytime hideouts. The genus *Archamia* contains several delightful cardinalfish species that are ideally suited for the reef aquarium. Unfortunately, none of them are regularly collected for the aquarium trade.

Archamia bigutatta Lachner, 1951

Common Name: Twinspot Cardinalfish.

Maximum Length: 11 cm (4.3 in.).

Distribution: Sumatra to Samoa, north to the Ryukyus and the Marianas.

Biology: The Twinspot Cardinalfish is found in sheltered bays and lagoons, where it associates with coastal fringing reefs and lagoon patch reefs. It occurs at depths of 5 to 10 m (16 to 33 ft.). It usually lives in dense shoals at the entrances of caves or among branching corals. It has occasionally been observed singly.

Captive Care: If you happen to run across *A. bigutatta* at your local fish store, buy it—or better yet, buy several. It will do best if kept in groups in either a shallow- or deep-water reef aquarium. Although they are normally nocturnal feeders, they will learn to readily accept most aquarium fare when the lights are on. They shouldn't be placed in a tank with aggressive fishes, as they tend to be picked on.

Aquarium Size: 30 gal. **Temperature:** 22 to 28°C (72 to 82°F).

Aquarium Suitability Index: 4.

Remarks: *Archamia bigutatta* has a black spot just over its gill cover and one just in front of the caudal fin. It also has a black band under the eye. This species can also have fine orange lines on the sides of the body and caudal peduncle.

Archamia fucata (Cantor, 1850)

Common Names: Narrowlined Cardinalfish, Orangelined Cardinalfish.

Maximum Length: 8 cm (3.1 in.).

Distribution: Red Sea to Samoa, north to the Ryukyus, south New Caledonia.

Biology: The Narrowlined Cardinalfish is found on coastal fringing reefs and lagoon patch reefs at depths of 3 to 28 m (9.8 to 92 ft.). It forms shoals over stands of branching stony corals. This species is sometimes found in heterospecific aggregations that include the Girdled (*Archamia zosterophora*), Goldbelly (*Apogon apogonides*), and Bridled Cardinalfish (*A. fraenatus*). It feeds on zooplankton.

Captive Care: This beautiful little cardinalfish is a great addition to the passive community tank (especially the reef aquarium). It will do best if kept in small groups. Provide *A. fucata* some branching corals (or a similar shelter site) to refuge in, especially if you have potential bullies in the tank. If picked on, this species is likely to hide constantly or hang in the upper corners of the aquarium. Feed it a varied diet that includes color-enhancing foods.

Aquarium Size: 30 gal. **Temperature:** 22 to 28°C (72 to 82°F).

Aquarium Suitability Index: 4.

Archamia bigutatta, Twinspot Cardinalfish: a nice find for reef aquarists.

Archamia fucata, Narrowlined Cardinalfish: shoaling species.

Archamia fucata, Narrowlined Cardinalfish: color variant.

Archamia lineolata, Lined Cardinalfish: distinctive nighttime coloration.

Archamia macroptera, Faintlined Cardinalfish: note dark caudal peduncle.

Remarks: This silver fish has a yellow snout with two blue stripes, and has fine orange lines on the body and caudal peduncle. There is also a large black spot at the base of the caudal fin (it may be absent during the spawning period) and a white tip on the anal fin. The **Faint Earspot Cardinalfish** (*Archamia dispilus*) **Lachner, 1951** is a similar species, but it has a faint spot above the pectoral fin base as well as a large spot on the caudal peduncle. This apogonid may be limited in distribution to the Philippines and southern Japan.

Archamia lineolata (Cuvier, 1828)

Common Names: Lined Cardinalfish, Shimmering Cardinalfish.
Maximum Length: 10 cm (3.9 in.).
Distribution: East Africa and Red Sea, east to Papua New Guinea.
Biology: This is a lagoon dweller that is found in shallow water

(usually in 3 to 7 m [9.8 to 23 ft.]). It forms shoals, often creating mixed groups with other *Archamia* spp. It is highly secretive, spending the daylight hours among stony coral branches, in caves, or in crevices. It comes out at night to feed.
Captive Care: *Archamia lineolata* should be housed in a reef aquarium or a fish tank that has plenty of shelter sites. It should not be kept with pugnacious species (e.g., squirrelfishes, groupers, dottybacks, surgeonfishes). The Lined Cardinalfish will do best if kept in small groups. Feed them frequently, at least twice a day.
Aquarium Size: 30 gal. **Temperature:** 22 to 28°C (72 to 82°F).
Aquarium Suitability Index: 4.
Remarks: This species has dark lines on the body and a dark spot on the caudal peduncle. According to Kuiter and Kozawa (1999) this species is limited in its range to the Red Sea and western Indian Ocean. They suggest that it has been confused with other species from the Pacific Ocean. The **Mozambique Cardinalfish** (*Archamia mozambiquensis*) **Smith, 1961** is only found in the tropical western Indian Ocean. It is silver overall with an orange stripe running down the side of the body (the line breaks up into a series of spots as the fish ages). It also has a black spot at the base of the caudal fin.

Archamia macroptera (Cuvier & Valenciennes, 1828)

Common Name: Faintlined Cardinalfish.
Maximum Length: 10 cm (3.9 in.).
Distribution: West Pacific.
Biology: This species is found in estuaries, sheltered bays, or lagoons at depths of 2 to 15 m (6.6 to 49 ft.). It forms large shoals, often hanging over or sheltering within branching stony corals during the day. In Lembeh Strait, Sulawesi, it is found on coastal reefs comprised of large-polyped stony corals (e.g. *Euphyllia ancora*) and can be found grouped with other apogonids. At night, it disperses and feeds in adjacent habitats on zooplankton.
Captive Care: The Faintlined Cardinalfish will do well in the peaceful community aquarium. It can be housed with other apogonids, including members of its own kind. Like others in the genus, it feeds out of the water column and is inclined to ignore food once it hits the substrate. Feed it a varied diet of meaty foods, including finely chopped table shrimp, frozen preparations for carnivores, and flake foods. It is not a threat to most ornamental crustaceans or to small fishes.
Aquarium Size: 30 gal. **Temperature:** 22 to 28°C (72 to 82°F).
Aquarium Suitability Index: 4.
Remarks: The Faintlined Cardinalfish has a yellow snout (without blue stripes), dull orange lines on the body, and a dark caudal peduncle (sometimes with a dark spot at the caudal fin base). There is a conspicuous white tip on the anal fin.

Archamia zosterophora, Girdled Cardinalfish: bandless color form.

Archamia ataenia, Andaman Cardinalfish: very similar to Girdled Cardinalfish.

Archamia zosterophora (Bleeker, 1856)

Common Names: Girdled Cardinalfish, Blackbelted Cardinalfish.

Maximum Length: 8 cm (3.1 in.).

Distribution: Moluccas and Philippines to the Solomon Islands, north to Ryukyus, and south to New Caledonia.

Biology: The Girdled Cardinalfish is found in sheltered bays and lagoons, where it can be found associating with fringing and patch reefs. It occurs at depths of 2 to 45 m (6.6 to 148 ft.)—it is most often seen in less than 15 m (49 ft.) of water. This species forms dense shoals over heads of *Acropora* spp. and *Porites cylindrica*. It will also form groups near the entrances of caves or among black coral trees. The Girdled Cardinalfish moves out onto adjacent substrates to feed after dark.

Captive Care: A group of these tetra-like apogonids makes an attractive addition to the reef aquarium. They are very susceptible to being bullied or picked on by more pugnacious fishes, so select their tankmates carefully. Feed them finely chopped seafoods (e.g., shrimps) and frozen prepared foods. They can be housed in the shallow- or deep-water reef aquarium.

Aquarium Size: 30 gal. **Temperature:** 22 to 28°C (72 to 82°F).

Aquarium Suitability Index: 4.

Remarks: *Archamia zosterophora* is easily identified by two red lines behind the eyes. They may or may not have a wide black band on the body. The colors of the Girdled Cardinalfish may be enhanced during spawning.

The **Andaman Cardinalfish** (*Archamia ataenia*) **Randall & Satapoomin, 1999** has been reported from the Andaman Sea coast of Thailand and from the Mentawai Islands, West Sumatra. This species is very similar to the Girdled Cardinalfish. It differs in having no black band on the body, otherwise the color is very similar. Kuiter and Kozawa (1999) state that the width and even the presence of the band of *A. zosterophora* may vary from one population to the next. The Girdled Cardinalfish is also known to lose the black band and the two red lines at night. *Archamia ataenia* differs from *A. zosterophora* in having 14 pectoral rays (usually 13 in *A. zosterophora*) and usually 20 gill rakers (22 for *A. zosterophora*). The Andaman Cardinalfish reaches at least 5 cm (2 in.) in total length.

Genus *Astrapogon*

This group of tropical Atlantic cardinalfishes is dark in overall color, with short bodies and enlarged pelvic fins. While they all have been reported to associate with live shells (in particular conchs, *Strombus* spp.), the Conch Cardinalfish (*Astrapogon stellatus*) is regularly found in the mantle of these large gastropods. They are nocturnal.

Astrapogon puncticulatus (Poey, 1867)

Common Name: Blackfin Cardinalfish.

Maximum Length: 6.5 cm (2.6 in.).

Distribution: South Florida and the Bahamas to Brazil.

Biology: The Blackfin Cardinalfish is found in tidepools, lagoon seagrass beds, mangrove habitats, lagoons, reef flats, and reef faces. It occurs over sand or rubble/cobble substrates. This cardinalfish often hides in empty gastropod shells. It has also been reported from the mantle cavity of live Hawkwing Conchs (*Strombus raninus*). *Astrapogon puncticulatus* hangs just above the bottom, remaining close to a refuge during the day. At night, it roams farther from its hiding place.

Captive Care: This fish makes an interesting addition to the Western Atlantic seagrass biotope tank. Provide some empty conch shells, or other large types of sea shells, for it to hide in. It should

Astrapogon puncticulatus, Blackfin Cardinalfish: frequents shallow waters.

Astrapogon alutus, Bronze Cardinalfish: may live in mantle cavity of conchs.

Astrapogon stellatus, Conch Cardinalfish: associates with live Queen Conchs.

not be housed with aggressive tankmates, especially species that will compete with it for places to hide. If it cannot find a suitable refuge, it will pine away in the aquarium.

Aquarium Size: 20 gal. **Temperature:** 22 to 28°C (72 to 82°F).

Aquarium Suitability Index: 4.

Remarks: This fish has black pelvic fins that reach the middle of the anal fin base when laid against the body. It is similar to the **Bronze Cardinalfish (*Astrapogon alutus*) (Jordan & Gilbert, 1882)**, which has dark brown pelvic fins (with a bronze hue) that do not reach the middle of the anal fin base (they only extend about one-third of the way along the fin base). The Bronze Cardinalfish has been reported from the mantle cavity of *Strombus pugilis*. It also occurs in seagrass beds.

Astrapogon stellatus (Cope, 1867)

Common Names: Conch Cardinalfish, Conchfish.

Maximum Length: 6.5 cm (2.6 in.).

Distribution: Bermuda, Florida, and the Bahamas to the Lesser Antilles.

Biology: *Astrapogon stellatus* is found in sheltered bays, lagoons, and sand slopes at depths of 1 to 40 m (3.3 to 131 ft.). This unusual cardinalfish lives in the mantle cavity of the living Queen Conch (*Strombus gigas*). However, this relationship is not obligatory, as they will also inhabit tube sponge lumens, pen shells (*Pinna* spp.), and the bivalve *Atrina rigida*. The Queen Conch is not adversely affected by the cardinalfish, nor does the association benefit the gastropod (this type of symbiosis is often referred to as endoecism). *Astrapogon stellatus* remains in its refuge during the day, but comes out at night to feed on small crustaceans. It hangs over open sand bottoms or hard reef substrate as it feeds. Just before sunrise, it reenters its host through the anterior siphonal canal. As many as five *A. stellatus* have been found in the same conch.

Captive Care: This fish makes an interesting addition to the Western Atlantic seagrass biotope tank. Provide a live conch or some empty conch shells, or other large types of sea shells, for it to hide in. Keep it with peaceful tankmates that will not evict it from its hiding places. You may have to feed it at night, at least initially. With time, it may be trained to come out and ingest food floating past when the lights are on. Do not keep it with aggressive tankmates, as it is likely to be picked on.

Aquarium Size: 20 gal. **Temperature:** 22 to 28°C (72 to 82°F).

Aquarium Suitability Index: 4.

Remarks: *Astrapogon stellatus* has black pelvic fins that are longer than than those of the aforementioned congeners (the pelvics reach the rear third of the anal fin base when laid against the body).

Genus *Cheilodipterus* (Bigtoothed Cardinalfishes)

The genus is comprised of 14 to 15 species that have canine teeth in both jaws. The juveniles of most forms, and the adults of several, are gray or cream-colored overall with a number of black stripes from the snout to the tail and a black spot on the caudal peduncle. The bigtoothed cardinalfishes are found in a variety of reef habitats. These are sleek predators with canine teeth in both jaws. They feed on small fishes, worms, and crustaceans. They often float near coral crevices, in caves, or above stony corals during the day, and move farther afield to feed after dark. The *Cheilodipterus* spp. are regularly encountered by divers and are occasionally seen by aquarists. Three species are known to be Batesian mimics of fangblennies (*Meiacanthus* spp.).

Cheilodipterus artus Smith, 1961

Common Name: Artus Cardinalfish.
Maximum Length: 12 cm (4.7 in.).
Distribution: Red Sea to French Polynesia, north to southern Japan, south to the Seychelles and the Great Barrier Reef.
Biology: This species is most abundant in estuaries, coastal reefs, and lagoons at a depth range of 3 to 10 m (9.8 to 33 ft.). It is occasionally observed on reef faces and fore-reef slopes to depths of 20 m (66 ft.). In the Maldives, it is usually found at depths greater than 20 m. *Cheilodipterus artus* often hides near or among staghorn corals (*Acropora* spp.), among stands of large-polyped stony corals, around boulders, under ledges, or in caves. Juveniles sometimes aggregate among sea urchin species. Adults occurs singly, in small groups, or even in large shoals (more than 100 individuals). They feed on small fishes and benthic crustaceans.
Captive Care: This cardinalfish is not often seen in the aquarium trade. It will spend most of its time in the open when the lights are on. More than one can be housed per tank, but be sure the aquarium is large, with plenty of hiding places. Like others in this genus, it is a threat to smaller fishes and crustaceans.
Aquarium Size: 30 gal. **Temperature:** 22 to 28°C (72 to 82°F).
Aquarium Suitability Index: 5.
Remarks: Kuiter and Kozawa (1999) conclude that the true *C. artus* is limited in distribution to the Indian Ocean and that the species referred to as *C. artus* from the Western Pacific is an undescribed species. Individuals from the Indian Ocean have a yellow area around the spot on the caudal peduncle. There is also a creamy blotch in front of this dark spot. Those from the Pacific lack the creamy spot and the caudal peduncle often becomes dark as the fish grows, hiding the black spot on the peduncle. More study is required to determine if these two populations represent two distinct species. The **Intermediate Cardinalfish** (*Cheilodipterus intermedius*) **Gon, 1993** has darker stripes than

Cheilodipterus artus, Artus Cardinalfish: juveniles refuge with sea urchins.

Cheilodipterus artus, Artus Cardinalfish: variant; spot on caudal peduncle.

Cheilodipterus intermedius, Intermediate Cardinalfish: lives in aggregations.

Cheilodipterus macrodon, Largetoothed Cardinalfish: adolescent coloration.

Cheilodipterus octolineatus, Allen's Cardinalfish: note black tip on dorsal fin.

Cheilodipterus nigrotaeniatus, Blackline Cardinalfish: fangblenny mimic.

C. artus and narrower stripes than the Largetoothed Cardinalfish (*C. macrodon*). The Intermediate Cardinalfish is found from Vietnam to the Solomon Islands, north to the Ryukyus, and south to the Great Barrier Reef. It is typically found over mud and sand substrates, near patch reefs, at depths of 1 to 21 m (3.3 to 69 ft.). This species typically occurs in small aggregations.

Cheilodipterus macrodon (Lacépède, 1802)
Common Name: Largetoothed Cardinalfish.
Maximum Length: 25 cm (9.8 in.).
Distribution: Indonesia to Papua, north to the Philippines, and south to Great Barrier Reef.
Biology: The Largetoothed Cardinalfish occurs on reef faces and outer-reef slopes at depths of 4 to 30 m (13 to 98 ft.), or on lagoon patch reefs at depths of 15 to 35 m (49 to 115 ft.). It is a solitary species that often hangs under ledges or in caves and is a voracious predator that feeds mainly on small fishes, including blennies.
Captive Care: *Cheilodipterus macrodon* is rarely encountered by aquarists. It is a larger species that is a threat to smaller fishes and ornamental crustaceans. This solitary fish is best not housed with conspecifics, as they are likely to squabble. Except for its being a threat to crustaceans, this apogonid is well-suited for the reef aquarium. It may jump out of an open aquarium if startled.
Aquarium Size: 75 gal. **Temperature:** 22 to 28°C (72 to 82°F).
Aquarium Suitability Index: 5.
Remarks: The color of *C. macrodon* changes significantly as the fish grows. The juveniles are light overall, with a black spot at the base of the caudal fin. Kuiter and Kozawa (1999) consider *C. macrodon* to be a synonym of *C. lineatus.* They also differentiate between the Indian Ocean and Pacific Ocean forms of *C. lineatus* (= *C. macrodon*). They refer to the Pacific form as *Cheilodipterus heptazona* Bleeker, 1849. They also state that the Pacific "species" attains a maximum length of 16 cm (6.2 in.), while the Indian Ocean "species" is much larger (getting to about 25 cm [9.8 in.] in length). There are also some slight differences in coloration. The **Allen's Cardinalfish** (*Cheilodipterus alleni*) **Gon, 1993** is another species with coppery brown lines, but it is easily distinguished by the distinct black tip on the first dorsal fin. It is a solitary species that is found on coral and rocky reefs. It attains a maximum length of 22 cm (8.6 in.).

Cheilodipterus nigrotaeniatus Smith & Radcliffe, 1912
Common Name: Blackline Cardinalfish.
Maximum Length: 7 cm (2.7 in.).
Distribution: Philippines and the Moluccas.
Biology: The Blackline Cardinalfish is a resident of coastal fring-

Cheilodipterus parazonatus, Mimic Cardinalfish: mimics venomous blenny.

Cheilodipterus zonatus, Golden Mimic Cardinalfish: great display animal.

ing reefs. I have observed adults in 7 to 10 m (23 to 33 ft.) of water at the edge of stands of leather and stony corals. This species mimics the Striped Fangblenny (*Meiacanthus grammistes*) and the Striped Fangblenny Mimic (*Petroscirtes breviceps*). It not only looks like these fishes, it also acts like them. Rather than being secretive during the day, like many of the cardinalfishes, this species hangs up in the water column, away from shelter, and does not make a hasty retreat when approached.

Captive Care: This interesting cardinalfish is not often encountered in the aquarium trade. It will remain in the open, even in a brightly lit aquarium. Keeping this fish with its model, either *M. grammistes* (which is more common in aquarium stores) or *P. breviceps*, makes an interesting display. Like its congeners, it is a threat to fishes or crustaceans that will fit into its long jaws. However, its relatively small size means it is a threat to a narrower range of tankmates.

Aquarium Size: 20 gal. **Temperature:** 22 to 28°C (72 to 82°F).

Aquarium Suitability Index: 5.

Remarks: The color of *C. nigrotaeniatus* is white or grayish overall, with four dark brown stripes that end as dots and dashes at the base of the caudal fin. The head is yellow. Juveniles have more distinct black stripes and a brighter yellow head. The Blackline Cardinalfish becomes sexually mature at a length of about 7 cm (2.8 in.).

Cheilodipterus parazonatus Gon, 1993

Common Name: Mimic Cardinalfish.

Maximum Length: 8 cm (3.1 in.).

Distribution: Papua New Guinea, Solomon Islands, and the Great Barrier Reef.

Biology: The Mimic Cardinalfish is found in lagoons, on reef faces, and on fore-reef slopes. It is usually found at depths of 1 to 15 m (3.3 to 49 ft.), but has been found as deep as 35 m (115 ft.). It is a Batesian mimic of the fangblenny (*Meiacanthus vittatus*). Its resemblance to this venomous fanged blennioid affords it some degree of protection from predators. As a result, it is often found swimming above the reef (like *M. vittatus*) and is not as shy as most other apogonids. It is also diurnal, hunting small fishes and benthic invertebrates during the day.

Captive Care: The Mimic Cardinalfish is rarely seen in the aquarium trade. It makes a great display animal, because it is diurnal and spends more time away from shelter. Feed it meaty foods, like frozen mysid and adult brine shrimp, frozen prepared foods for carnivores, and baby guppies (if necessary to initiate a feeding response). Keeping this fish with *M. vittatus* will make an interesting display of Batesian mimicry.

Aquarium Size: 20 gal. **Temperature:** 22 to 28°C (72 to 82°F).

Aquarium Suitability Index: 5.

Remarks: This is the only species in the genus that is pale green to gray overall with a single gradually tapering stripe running down the middle of its body (there is a white border on either side of the stripe).

It has often been confused with the similar **Golden Mimic Cardinalfish** (*Cheilodipterus zonatus*) **Smith & Radcliffe, 1912,** which is known to occur in the Philippines, Malaysia, and the Solomon Islands. The Golden Mimic Cardinalfish is golden-yellow below the midbody stripe and white above it. The dorsum is gray. This cardinalfish mimics the Golden Fangblenny (*Meiacanthus geminatus*) and is found at depths of 2 to 12 m (6.6 to 39 ft.) in protected habitats. Kuiter and Kozawa (1999) consider *C. parazonatus* and *C. zonatus* as color forms (synonyms) of *C. nigrotaeniatus*.

Cheilodipterus singapurensis, Truncate Cardinalfish: male with eggs.

Cheilodipterus quinquelineatus, Fivelined Cardinalfish: common, durable fish.

Cheilodipterus singapurensis Bleeker, 1859

Common Names: Truncate Cardinalfish, Singapore Cardinalfish.
Maximum Length: 19 cm (7.4 in.).
Distribution: Sumatra to New Guinea, north to the Philippines.
Biology: *Cheilodipterus singapurensis* is found on coastal reef faces and on lagoon patch reefs at depths of 2 to 10 m (6.6 to 33 ft.). It often lives in silty habitats. Adult *C. singapurensis* are solitary and can be found among boulders, under plate corals, among soft corals, or in seagrass meadows. Juveniles often swim among the spines of sea urchins.
Captive Care: This fish is not regularly encountered in aquarium stores, although the juvenile may show up as an "Assorted Cardinalfish." Although you should provide it with suitable hiding places, it will spend most of the time in the open or hovering near the entrance of a cave or crevice. The adults get quite large and are

a threat to crustacean and fish tankmates.
Aquarium Size: 75 gal. **Temperature:** 22 to 28°C (72 to 82°F).
Aquarium Suitability Index: 5.
Remarks: Juvenile *C. singapurensis* are light overall, with obvious body stripes and a dark spot at the base of the caudal fin. There is a characteristic white spot at the posterior second dorsal fin base. The adults are darker in color (brown over much of the body, darker on the snout, top of the head, and the body above the lateral line) with fainter body stripes. Mature males over 7 cm (2.7 in.) in standard length have a black spot around the anus. The area covered by the black spot increases as the fish grows.

Cheilodipterus quinquelineatus Cuvier, 1828

Common Name: Fivelined Cardinalfish.
Maximum Length: 12 cm (4.7 in.).
Distribution: Red Sea to Ducie Island, north to southern Japan, and south to Lord Howe Island.
Biology: The Fivelined Cardinalfish occurs on coastal reefs, lagoon patch reefs, reef flats, reef faces, and fore-reef slopes, at depths from 2 to 40 m (6.6 to 131 ft.). Adults of this species are usually observed near crevices and branching corals during the day. In some cases, adults will form loose aggregations in larger holes in the reef. Solitary juveniles often hang over the tentacles of large sea anemones (*Heteractis crispa, H. magnifica*) or aggregate among the spines of *Diadema* sea urchins. The Fivelined Cardinalfish feeds mainly on fishes, crustaceans (including shrimps and crabs), and small gastropods. It will feed both day and night but actively moves over sand and rubble areas after dark. The Fivelined Cardinalfish tends to be site-specific, returning to the same general area to refuge during the day. Females will visit males about one hour before sunset. Courtship starts with tail quivering. The male and female will alternate tail quivering in front of each other. The female will also approach the male from behind, with her head tipped down. Her body will quiver as she approaches her mate. The male may respond by opening his mouth slightly. If a conspecific should approach the courting pair, both the female and male often attack it. The pair engage in these courtship behaviors for about two hours prior to spawning. About one hour before they spawn, the male and female begin adopting a parallel orientation. While in this position, the female extrudes an egg ball about 3 cm (1.2 in.) in diameter. The male then drops behind the female to ingest the egg mass.
Captive Care: This common species is a durable aquarium inhabitant, but it will eat smaller fishes and ornamental crustaceans. It will spend most of its time in exposed portions of the tank, but will rarely move far from a place to take shelter, except when presented with food. Although *C. quinquelineatus* prefers

Cheilodipterus isostigmus, Tailspot Cardinalfish: note spot location.

Foa fo, Weedy Cardinalfish: with a mouthful of eggs.

live baby guppies and live ghost shrimp, it will also eat frozen brine shrimp and chopped seafoods.

Aquarium Size: 30 gal. **Temperature:** 22 to 28°C (72 to 82°F).

Aquarium Suitability Index: 5.

Remarks: *Cheilodipterus quinquelineatus* is very closely related to the **Tailspot Cardinalfish** (*Cheilodipterus isostigmus*) (**Schultz, 1940**). It lacks canine teeth at the front of the lower jaw, and the black spot on the caudal peduncle lines up with the mid-body stripe (in *C. quinquelineatus* the spot is above the midbody stripe and may actually extend onto the dorsal surface of the caudal peduncle). It has been reported from scattered localities in the Western Pacific (Philippines south to Vanuatu). The Tailspot Cardinalfish is found among stony corals or in caves, at depths of 4 to 40 m (13 to 131 ft.). The **Twospot Cardinalfish** (*Cheilodipterus novemfasciatus*) **Rüppell, 1838** is a similar species that has a white spot over the black caudal peduncle spot, while the black stripe on the abdomen is thickened. It is only found in the Red Sea and usually among the spines of sea urchins (*Diadema* spp.) on sheltered reefs. The **Dwarf Toothy Cardinalfish** (*Cheilodipterus pygmaios*) **Gon, 1994** is another Red Sea endemic. It differs from the Twospot Cardinalfish in usually having a black spot on the dorsal and ventral surface of the caudal peduncle. The lateral stripe over the abdomen is not thickened as in *C. novemfasciatus.*

Genus *Foa* (Secretive Cardinalfishes)

This small, seldom-seen genus is comprised of 4 species. The *Foa* spp. have teeth on the palatine bone on the roof of the mouth and an incomplete lateral line. They are usually found in shallow, sheltered habitats, often among vegetation or rubble. The *Foa* spp. are sometimes encountered by naturalists who engage in muck diving. Although not targeted by fish collectors, they occasionally show up in the aquarium trade and are sold as "Assorted Cardinalfish."

Foa fo Jordan & Seale, 1906

Common Names: Weedy Cardinalfish, Bay Cardinalfish.

Maximum Length: 4 cm (1.6 in.).

Distribution: Maldives to the Society Islands, north to southern Japan, south to Australia.

Biology: This solitary fish is typically found in estuaries, bays, and coastal seagrass meadows. It often lives under rocks, among sponges, algae, or seagrass. A shallow-water apogonid, it is most common at depths of less than 15 m (49 ft.), where it most likely feeds on small, nocturnal invertebrates.

Captive Care: This fish can be kept in a quiet community tank, although it is quite shy and will spend most of its time under cover. Getting your Weedy Cardinalfish to eat enough may mean feeding it when light levels are low or when the lights have been turned off. Live enriched adult brine shrimp is a good first food. Because it is a very small fish, it is likely to fall prey to a wide range of tankmates (both invertebrate and vertebrate). You can keep more than one individual in a moderate-sized tank (it is likely to disappear in a large reef aquarium).

Aquarium Size: 10 gal. **Temperature:** 23 to 28°C (73 to 82°F).

Aquarium Suitability Index: 4.

Remarks: The Weedy Cardinalfish is highly variable in color but typically displays one of various shades of brown or dark green with some degree of lighter mottling. There are often three small spots at the base of the caudal fin, and the front margins of the first dorsal and pelvic fins are white. This species is apparently synonymous with *Foa brachygramma* (Jenkins, 1903).

Foa hyalinus, Sharpsnout Cardinalfish: prefers to hide in soft coral colonies.

Fowleria variegata, Variegated Cardinalfish: may mimic small scorpionfish.

Fowleria vaiulae?, Mottled Cardinalfish: possible color variant.

Foa hyalinus Smith & Radcliffe, 1912

Common Name: Sharpsnout Cardinalfish.
Maximum Length: 4 cm (1.6 in.).
Distribution: New Guinea and Palau.
Biology: This unusual and extremely secretive cardinalfish is reported to live among the branches of *Sinularia* soft corals. Because of its small size and cryptic behavior, little is known about its biology or its distribution. It has been reported from depths of 14 m (46 ft.).
Captive Care: Although a true oddity, *F. hyalinus* is very reclusive and a poor prospect as a display fish. It will spend most of its time hiding in the recesses of the aquascaping. The best situation for this fish is a small aquarium with a few other secretive or peaceful fishes. You can use red or pale blue moonlight lamps to view it at night. Be sure to provide it with plenty of suitable shelter sites. Do not keep it with aggressive tankmates or with piscivores. Reef aquarists with large *Sinularia* colonies might consider this fish as a realistic addition, but a cryptic one to be sure.
Aquarium Size: 10 gal. **Temperature:** 22 to 28°C (72 to 82°F).
Aquarium Suitability Index: 4.
Remarks: *F. hyalinus* has a light orange body with darker reddish orange lines on the head and body. It has a narrow head with a long snout.

Genus *Fowleria* (Spotcheek Cardinalfishes)

There are six species in this genus, all of which have a reduced lateral line. Many members of the genus *Fowleria* have a conspicuous eyespot on each gill cover. These nocturnal fishes tend to inhabit shallow, sheltered habitats, hiding among rocks, stony corals, or vegetation. At least one species is thought to mimic a small scorpionfish.

Fowleria variegata (Valenciennes, 1832)

Common Name: Variegated Cardinalfish.
Maximum Length: 8 cm (3.1 in.).
Distribution: Red Sea and the Arabian Gulf to Samoa, north to the Ryukyus and Bonins, south to the southern Great Barrier Reef.
Biology: The Variegated Cardinalfish is found in lagoons and estuaries among rubble and seagrass. It has been suggested that *F. variegata* may mimic some of the smaller scorpaenids, especially the Guam Scorpionfish (*Scorpaenodes guamensis*). This would be a case of Batesian mimicry, where *F. variegata* derives an antipredation advantage by resembling the venomous scorpaenid.
Captive Care: Provide this cardinalfish with rocks and rubble to hide among and under. This fish is secretive and may not be seen often, but it will spend more time in the open in a dimly lit aquarium. The Variegated Cardinalfish may eat any small

fishes or ornamental crustaceans that will fit into its mouth. To create an educational display, keep it with a similarly sized *Scorpaenodes*.

Aquarium Size: 20 gal. **Temperature:** 22 to 28°C (72 to 82°F).
Aquarium Suitability Index: 3.
Remarks: *Fowleria variegata* has a black ocellus on the gill cover and brown mottling on the head, body, and fins. The **Spotcheek** or **Peppered Cardinalfish** (*Fowleria punctulata*) (Rüppell, 1838) is a similar species that has a spot on the gill cover and a white line, with a dark border, running from the back of the eye to the edge of the gill cover. There are also rows of black spots on the body. Unlike *F. variegata*, this apogonid does not have spots on the fins. *Fowleria punctulata* ranges from the Red Sea east to the Tuamotus, north to southern Japan and south to Rapa Island. The **Mottled Cardinalfish** (*Fowleria vaiulae*) (Jordan & Seale, 1906) sports brown mottling like *F. variegata*, but lacks the eye-spots on the opercula and has six to eight light bars on the body. The Mottled Cardinalfish occurs from the Red Sea and the Arabian Gulf, east to the Society Islands, north to the Ryukyus, and south to the Great Barrier Reef.

Genus *Pseudamia*

This genus includes seven species of elongated, round-tailed cardinalfishes that have cycloid scales covering their bodies. They tend to be very secretive, hiding during the day in reef caves or crevices, beneath ledges, or among seagrass and mangrove roots. They are active nocturnally. The *Pseudamia* spp. are only encountered by divers who inspect the back of caves and crevices with a flashlight, or those who often dive at night. It has been confirmed that these species orally incubate their eggs like other apogonids. They are occasionally seen in the aquarium trade, but most of these individuals are probably collected with drugs.

Pseudamia amblyuroptera (Bleeker, 1856)

Common Names: Whitejaw Cardinalfish, Crocodile Cardinalfish.
Maximum Length: 10 cm (3.9 in.).
Distribution: Malaysia and the Philippines to the Solomon Islands, south to the Great Barrier Reef.
Biology: The Whitejaw Cardinalfish is a shallow-water form that is usually found in less than 2 m (6.6 ft.) of water. However, it can be found as deep as 30 m (98 ft.). *Pseudamia amblyuroptera* occurs in estuaries, among mangrove roots, or in saltwater creeks. It has also been reported from tidepools, seagrass beds, and among macroalgae. This fish is often found in turbid water. It is very cryptic, spending its days hiding.
Captive Care: In the aquarium, *P. amblyuroptera* hides among the tank decor or behind filtering equipment. The aquarist is only

Pseudamia amblyuroptera, Whitejaw Cardinalfish: crocodile-like species.

likely to see it when live food is introduced to the tank or when a red light is used to view the tank at night. It is a voracious predator that will make short work of smaller fishes housed in the same tank. The feeding behavior of this fish explains why one of its common names is Crocodile—it will hang motionless in the water column, then with incredible speed it will swoop down to capture its prey. Because this species is so secretive, most individuals are probably taken with cyanide. Nevertheless, it seems to hold up well in captivity if given plenty of hiding places and live food (e.g., feeder fish).

Aquarium Size: 30 gal. **Temperature:** 22 to 28°C (72 to 82°F).
Aquarium Suitability Index: 3.
Remarks: The Whitejaw Cardinalfish can be distinguished from the Gelatin Cardinalfish (*Pseudamia gelatinosa*) by the presence of a white area on the posterior half of the upper jaw (in *P. gelatinosa* the upper jaw is light brown with dark brown spots). *Pseudamia amblyuroptera* also tends to be darker in color overall than *P. gelatinosa*. **Hayashi's Cardinalfish** (*Pseudamia hayashii*) **Randall, Lachner, & Fraser, 1985** is also similar in appearance to these two species, but has larger scales and is translucent, sporting red and golden hues. It also has tiny golden spots on the body. *Pseudamia hayashii* occurs from the Gulf of Aden to Samoa, north to southern Japan, and south to Rowley Shoals and Queensland. **Tarr's Cardinalfish** (*Pseudamia tarri*) **Randall, Lachner & Fraser, 1985** is a resident of the Persian Gulf. It is translucent with small black spots.

Pseudamia gelatinosa, Gelatin Cardinalfish: has translucent body.

Rhabdamia gracilis, Graceful Cardinalfish: great schooling fish (see pg. 262).

Pseudamia zonata, Paddlefin Cardinalfish: rare find, likes to hide in caves.

Pseudamia gelatinosa Smith, 1954

Common Name: Gelatin Cardinalfish.

Maximum Length: 10 cm (3.9 in.).

Distribution: East Africa and the Red Sea, east to French Polynesia, north to the Ryukyus, and south to New South Wales, Australia.

Biology: Unlike its close relative the Whitejaw Cardinalfish(*P. amblyuroptera*) *P. gelatinosa* is most common on coral reefs at depths from less than 1 to 40 m (3.3 to 131 ft.). It typically occurs in protected habitats, like lagoons, bays, and harbors, and seems to prefer clear water. It lives in caves or beneath coral ledges. It is a secretive species rarely seen by divers during the day. It is assumed that *P. gelatinosa* does come out from cover at night to hunt.

Captive Care: The care of this species is similar to that of the Whitejaw Cardinalfish. Its smaller size makes it less of a threat to potential tankmates, although it will ingest any crustaceans or small fishes that fit into its mouth. It is very secretive and does not make a good display animal. If kept with more pugnacious feeders, it is likely to starve unless target fed.

Aquarium Size: 30 gal. **Temperature:** 22 to 28°C (72 to 82°F).

Aquarium Suitability Index: 3.

Remarks: The body of the Gelatin Cardinalfish is translucent in color, with light gold or silver on the sides of the body and head and large brown spots that surround a golden dot. There is a large black spot at the base of the caudal fin.

Pseudamia zonata Randall, Lachner, & Fraser, 1985

Common Name: Paddlefin Cardinalfish.

Maximum Length: 15 cm (5.9 in.).

Distribution: Philippines to Fiji, north to the Ryukyus, south to Vanuatu.

Biology: This cryptic cardinalfish is found on reef faces and slopes. It occurs in caves and deep reef crevices at depths of 10 to 31 m (33 to 102 ft.).

Captive Care: If you are lucky enough to acquire this fish at your local aquarium store, you will want to construct a large cave where it will be able to take shelter. This will allow it to acclimate more readily and make it easier to view (occasionally use a flashlight to see it in the back of its cave). If you reduce the amount of lighting over the aquarium and place the system in a room with limited activity, you are also more likely to see more of this fish. Live food (baby guppies or mollies) may be required to initiate a feeding response.

Aquarium Size: 40 gal. **Temperature:** 22 to 28°C (72 to 82°F).

Aquarium Suitability Index: 2.

Remarks: The Paddlefin Cardinalfish has alternating dark and light bands on the body and tail.

The Banggai Cardinalfish: From Remote Indonesia, a Newfound Beauty

Pterapogon kauderni, Banggai Cardinalfish: an instant favorite with graphic beauty, "new" species cachet, and mouthbrooding habits.

One of the most popular members of the cardinalfish family, and a relative newcomer to the marine hobby, is the Banggai Cardinalfish (*Pterapogon kauderni*). Although this fish was originally described by Koumans in 1933, it was rediscovered by Dr. Gerald Allen and Roger Steene in 1994. They went to observe what they suspected might be a new species, at remote Banggai Island, Sulawesi, Indonesia. Allen and Steene did find the fish and were able to glean important information on its natural history. Soon after, Dr. Allen made the handsome, unusual fish known to the aquarium world at a U.S. marine aquarium conference. Since then, the Banggai Cardinalfish has been the subject of intense study (Vagelli 1999, 2002). Vagelli reports having found this fish around 16 islands in the Banggai Archipelago and at Luwuk Harbor in central Sulawesi.

In 1998, the Banggai Cardinalfish was also found in Lembeh Strait, northern Sulawesi. The growing population there was apparently from individuals accidentally released by a marine fish collector/exporter. They have established a strong "fin-hold" there and are now one of the more common apogonids at a number of the dive sites.

The Banggai Cardinalfish is special for a number of reasons. First, it is a very striking fish. The color pattern consists of bold black stripes and small white spots on a silver body. The pelvic fins are relatively large and are black with white spots. This cardinalfish is also noteworthy for its recent discovery and relatively limited distribution. But the most fascinating characteristic of the Banggai Cardinalfish is its reproductive mode—which also is responsible for its restricted range. Not only does it incubate its eggs orally, like other cardinalfishes, but the young shelter in the male's mouth for the first few weeks after hatching. This reproductive strategy has

continued on next page

Pterapogon kauderni, Banggai Cardinalfish: as they appear in nature, over sandy bottoms and in close proximity to the protective spines of urchins.

not been observed in any other species of marine fish. Because of this unique mouthbrooding behavior, this species does not have a planktonic dispersal phase—a fact that explains its apparent confinement to a few isolated areas in Indonesia.

Habitat

The Banggai Cardinalfish is most often found in shallow water (less than 4.5 m [15 ft.]) in coastal habitats on rubble flats and slopes, sand flats, seagrass and macroalgae beds, mangroves, and around pier pilings. The most important determinant is the presence of proper microhabitat, especially proper shelter sites. These cardinalfish hide among the branches of stony corals, in the spines of the urchin *Diadema setosum*, in and near sea anemones, fire corals, and among mangrove prop roots. They live in turbid and clear water and in habitats that are well protected as well as those exposed to moderate current flow. This species is reported from a water temperature range of 25 to 31°C (77 to 88°F).

Banggai Cardinalfish are usually found in aggregations, although adults are sometimes observed in pairs and juveniles may occur singly. Groups can consist of over 80 fish, with the bulk being composed of juveniles or subadults. In some cases, entire groups are comprised of young fish. In Lembeh Strait, before this fish become more common, you could regularly see a single adult pair living in a sea anemone, along with one to several juveniles. Larger groups of juveniles and adolescents were often found among longspined urchins and cnidarians. But as the population of *P. kauderni* grew in the Strait, sea anemones began to abound with adults and juveniles. At night, groups of these fish are often found lying torpid on the substrate, near a sea anemone or sea urchins.

Banggai Cardinalfish and Sea Anemones

A number of cardinalfishes associate with sea anemones. Several common Western Pacific species are well-known for this behavior. For example, the Yellowstriped Cardinalfish (*Apogon cyanosoma*) and the Moluccan Cardinalfish (*Apogon moluccensis*) occasionally associate with the Leathery Sea Anemone (*Heteractis crispa*) and/or the Magnificent Sea Anemone

(*H. magnifica*). In some cases cardinalfishes simply swim near the stinging tentacles. In other cases they readily contact and shelter within them. The Banggai Cardinalfish was originally reported to shelter among the spines of *Diadema* sea urchins. Recent observations on the population in Lembeh Strait demonstrate that this species—both adults and juveniles—also regularly associates with cnidarians. I have often seen them swimming near the Leathery Sea Anemone, the Corkscrew Tentacle Sea Anemone (*Macrodactyla doreensis*), the Giant Carpet Anemone (*Stichodactyla gigantea*), and Haddon's Carpet Anemone (*S. haddoni*). It will actually contact and swim among the tentacles of the Leathery Sea Anemone. In the case of the other three sea anemones, the cardinals usually swim very close to them, but rarely come in contact with their stinging cells. Vagelli (2002) reports that in the Banggai Archipelago, these cardinalfish will also inhabit the Bubble Tentacle Sea Anemone (*Entacmaea quadricolor*). On one occasion, I also witnessed a juvenile Banggai swimming around and between (but not contacting) the tentacles of the deadly Hells-fire Sea Anemone (*Actinodendron* sp.). Juveniles will also swim among the tentacles of the anemone-like stony coral *Heliofungia actiniformis*. Vagelli (1999) found that small juveniles that had recently left the care of the parent were more often found in sea anemones than were larger juveniles or adults.

As mentioned earlier, in areas where population numbers are low, a single sea anemone will usually harbor an adult pair of Banggai Cardinalfish, and occasionally one or two juveniles. These anemone hosts often provide a home for anemonefishes as well. I have seen the Banggais living alongside pairs of Clark's Anemonefish (*Amphiprion clarkii*) and Pink Skunk Anemonefish (*A. perideraion*). One patch of three medium-sized *H. crispa* was home to a pair of Banggai Cardinals, a breeding pair of Clark's, and a pair of Pink Skunks. In this and other cases observed, the anemonefish paid little attention to the cardinalfish, even when the anemonefish were guarding eggs. In locations where the density of *P. kauderni* are higher, a single anemone may be home to dozens of these cardinalfish.

Feeding and Parasites

Banggai Cardinalfish feed during the day on zooplankton. Vagelli (2002) reports that they feed most heavily on copepods, but also consume some isopods, cirripedians, ostracods, urochordates, eucarids, and amphipods. Their prey was in the size range of 0.1 to 14 mm. Vagelli also found that 27% of the individuals he examined were parasitized by endoparasites, including trematodes, nematodes, and encysted isopods.

Reproduction

The reproductive behavior of this interesting cardinalfish is relatively well studied. Most of this has occurred in captivity, as *P. kauderni* readily spawns in the aquarium. Vagelli reports that spawning occurs year-round in the laboratory, generally in the early afternoon. I have also found this to be the case in Lembeh Strait. There I observed that pairs inhabiting cnidarians usually were incubating eggs at the same time. Vagelli (2002) reports a lunar periodicity in spawning in wild Banggai Cardinalfish. He found that they spawn during a few days preceding, during, and a few days after the full moon, with some reproductive activity also occurring at the time of the new moon.

***Pterapogon kauderni*, Banggai Cardinalfish: an ideal choice as a beginning marine breeder's fish, with easy-to-raise fry and strong consumer demand.**

During one courtship and spawning episode that I observed, the female appeared to initiate spawning. She swam next to the male so they were parallel to another, then trembled and pushed against the male for 4 to 8 seconds. The male then swam forward. The female once again assumed the parallel orientation and trembled. Parallel orientation and trembling occurred every 15 to 30 seconds. After one last trembling event, the male dropped behind the female with his snout near her anal fin. A light orange ball suddenly appeared from the female's vent and the male immediately sucked it up. (I am not sure when fertilization of the egg mass occurred.) The female remained in close proximity to the male, who occasionally spat the eggs partially out of his mouth. The male looked rather "distressed" about having a mouthful of

continued on next page

eggs. This spawning event occurred at about 1:00 P.M. Although the pair spent much of their time in close proximity prior to spawning, the female spent much less time near the male when he was incubating the eggs.

Vagelli (1999) describes female trembling behavior in captive *P. kauderni*. He also reports that the receptive male responds by sporadically opening his mouth, and his lower jaw darkens. He reports that these behaviors can begin several hours to a few days before actual spawning. Trembling behavior increases in frequency before spawning occurs.

The male takes an average of 45 large eggs (between 2.7 to 3 mm in diameter) into his mouth. A number of these eggs will be infertile eggs and will be spit out early in the incubation period. Vagelli (1999) found that in many cases (60% of the clutches), males kept in community tanks either swallow or spit out the egg clutch because of conspecific harassment. The male holds the eggs for about 20 days. At hatching, the embryos (called eleuthroembryos or free embryos) remain in the mouth for another 6 to 10 days (a few may be released earlier). The male then spits out several to as many as 62 young,

Pterapogon kauderni, **Banggai Cardinalfish: adult male with swelling eggs in mouth. Young will emerge as tiny, perfect miniatures of their parents.**

sometimes over a couple of days. According to Vagelli's research on captive *P. kauderni*, the average number of young per brood is about 40, with females able to spawn about every 25 to 30 days.

At hatching, the embryos are 5 to 6 mm in Standard Length (from the tip of the snout to the start of the caudal fin). When the young fish are finally released from the male's mouth, they are about 8 mm in SL and pigmented much like the adult. For the entire approximately 30-day incubation and brooding period, the male does not feed. According to Vagelli, this species is sexually mature in nine months at a SL of around 3.5 cm and reaches a total length of around 8 cm (3.1 in.).

Captive Care

Banggai Cardinalfish are very hardy aquarium residents that will quickly acclimate to life in a well-maintained tank. They will eat most aquarium foods, although they prefer brine shrimp, live black worms, and finely chopped seafoods. Although they aggregate in the wild, it is risky to keep these fish in groups in captivity, unless you have a large aquarium (100 gallons or more). Although they may behave peacefully toward one another when first introduced to the aquarium, a pair of fish will often start chasing and nipping their conspecific tankmates. If they are being kept in a larger tank, individuals will disperse throughout the aquarium, which will decrease the number of aggressive encounters. But in small and even medium-sized tanks (e.g., 75 gallons or smaller) subordinate individuals will often end up dead or cowering in the upper regions of the tank. Of course, it is possible to crowd a tank with so many of these fish that no one individual is picked on to the point of being killed.

The Banggai Cardinalfish is usually indifferent toward other fish species, except when they are tending eggs. At this time the pair, especially the female, will chase any fish that approaches too near. Banggais should not be housed with pugnacious tankmates. Their relatively peaceful disposition makes them a prime target for more aggressive fishes (e.g., dottybacks, damselfishes, hawkfishes, certain pygmy angelfishes), while their long anal and dorsal fin filaments are attractive targets to fin nippers (e.g., tobies, some wrasses). Instead, house them with other nonaggressive fishes, like assessors, dart gobies, shrimp gobies, flasher wrasses, and firefishes. *Pterapogon kauderni* is a great reef fish. It will not harm desirable invertebrates, except for smaller ornamental shrimp, and it spends most of its time hanging in the water column, almost always in view.

Breeding in Captivity

The Banggai Cardinalfish is relatively easy to breed. One of the biggest challenges is acquiring a pair. Unfortunately, this species is not sexually dimorphic. According to Marini (1996), a male he kept had a longer second dorsal fin filament, a more "V-like" profile, and a "thicker lower jaw and squatty body," compared to that of its female partner. However, extensive studies conducted by Vagelli (2002), indicate there are no permanent differences between the sexes. The female will become more rotund before spawning (no doubt due to hydrated eggs) and the color of the male's lower jaw may darken during courtship. The potential Banggai breeder may just have to acquire a small group and wait for two individuals to pair up. If you keep a group of *P. kauderni*, the female will select a male and a guard him away from other members of the group. The pair becomes more aggressive at this time and will defend an area of the tank. As mentioned above, this may cause problems in a small tank. Vagelli (2002) reports that the female will often allow another male (the secondary male) to enter the pair's territory, and this male may even participate in territory defense. When it is time to spawn, the female may actually spawn with the secondary male if the original male is not receptive to her advances.

Once Banggai Cardinalfish pair up, it is usually just a matter of time before they spawn. To increase the chances of success, it is a good idea to feed the pair heavily (especially the male). The male will have to fast for about one month after the eggs are fertilized, so it is important that he be in good physical condition before spawning. Males carrying eggs are easily recognized: they refuse to feed and have a noticeably distended mouth region. The egg mass will also be visible as the male respires and when he occasionally readjusts the eggs.

In order to save the greatest number of fry, it is best to separate the male from other fishes that are likely to eat the young when they are fully developed (this is not always necessary, but can increase survivorship of the newly released young). As mentioned above, the male is more likely to eat the eggs or young if kept in a tank with other fishes (including conspecifics). This can occur anytime during the incubation period. In some cases, it may result from unviable eggs, while on other occasions it may simply be a case of hunger.

After the young are released from the male's mouth, they are large enough to eat brine shrimp nauplii or rotifers. Some aquarists have even reported having luck getting them to eat frozen baby brine shrimp. However, it is very important that the feed be enriched with highly unsaturated fatty acids for the first four months. Vagelli (2002) reports that if the young are not given an enriched diet, they are likely to die of stress-related shock: simply bumping against the tank or turning on the aquarium lights can cause the juvenile fish to engage in erratic swimming, increased respiration and/or sinking to the aquarium bottom with their gill covers spread open. In some cases the young fish snap out of this condition, but many also perish.

It is critical to separate the fry from the parents immediately, before they are eaten. Placing plastic plants, *Caulerpa*, or urchins in the tank or container with the mouthbrooding male will provide the young ones with a place to hide when they are spit out. (The young usually drop to the bottom of the aquarium when they are released.) The young are not only susceptible to being eaten by other piscivorous fishes, they may also get sucked up by mechanical filters.

It is possible for a pair of Banggai Cardinalfish to produce a brood every other month for years. However, allowing a colony of these fish to spawn *ad libitum*, keeping the progeny in the tank with the original broodstock, may lead to inbreeding and unusual mutations, including malformed jaws and fins.

Pterapogon kauderni, **Banggai Cardinalfish: juvenile, over *Stichodactyla* carpet anemone. Juveniles can be started on newly hatched brine shrimp.**

Conservation

There is one major potential problem associated with the sudden popularity of this fish. Because the larvae of most cardinalfishes have a planktonic stage, which can last as long as 60 days, they can be dispersed over a larger geographical area. In contrast, *P. kauderni* apparently has a very limited distribution because it lacks a planktonic larval stage and because adults are associated with shallow coastal areas and unlikely to move over deep water. It is not difficult to imagine that an isolated population of Banggai Cardinalfish could be rapidly decimated. Vagelli (2002) estimates that as many as 700,000 *P. kauderni* are collected per year (based on numbers from 2000 and 2001). To date, predictions that the Banggai might be fished out in certain areas have not come true, but concerned aquarists and environmentalists continue to advise caution. Organized efforts to breed this fish in captivity need to be encouraged to take some of the pressure off wild stocks. Aquarists and store owners can help by purchasing captive-bred specimens.

Genus *Rhabdamia* (Luminous Cardinalfishes)

This genus contains four species of small, slender cardinalfishes. They have rather elongated, transparent bodies and bioluminescent organs near the rear margin of the gill cover. The *Rhabdamia* species live in large schools that hover near patch reefs and rocks. At least some species feed during the day on zooplankton.

Rhabdamia gracilis (Bleeker, 1856)

Common Names: Graceful Cardinalfish, Slender Cardinalfish.
Maximum Length: 6 cm (2.3 in.).
Distribution: East Africa to the Marshall Islands.
Biology: *Rhabdamia gracilis* is found on lagoon patch reefs and outer reef faces, at depths of 1 to 13 m (3.3 to 43 ft.). It lives in large schools that rise into the water column to feed on zooplankton. It feeds during both the day and night.
Captive Care: A school of these tetra-like fishes makes an interesting display in the larger reef aquarium. In fact, they do best in captivity if housed in groups. While they are not a threat to ornamental invertebrates or fish tankmates, their small adult size means they are vulnerable to being eaten by a wide range of piscivores. Feed them mysid and adult brine shrimp and finely chopped fresh shrimp. They may jump out of an open aquarium if suddenly startled.
Aquarium Size: 20 gal. **Temperature:** 22 to 28°C (72 to 82°F).
Aquarium Suitability Index: 3.
Remarks: The Graceful Cardinalfish is translucent, with white

Siphamia corallicola, Coral Siphonfish: hiding in soft coral tree.

on the abdomen. There are black tips on the end of each of the caudal fin lobes. The **Nosespot Cardinalfish** (*Rhabdamia cypselura*) **Weber, 1909** sometimes forms mixed schools with *R. gracilis*. The Nosespot Cardinalfish has two black spots in front of the eyes. It ranges from the Red Sea and Arabian Gulf to the Marshall Islands, north to the Ryukyus, and south to New Guinea. This cardinalfish occurs in dense schools during the day that disperse and feed in midwater at night. It tends to favor current-prone areas.

Genus *Siphamia* (Siphonfishes)

There are about 20 species in this genus of cardinalfishes, which are often referred to as siphonfishes. These apogonids are unique in that they possess a luminous organ inside the translucent thorax muscles and on the caudal peduncle. These light-emitting organs contain bioluminescent bacteria (*Photobacterium leiognathi*) that are apparently picked up during the planktonic stage of the fish's life cycle—the specialized organs are present even in the larvae. The *Siphamia* spp. have deep bodies and are quite small (most less than 5 cm [2 in.]). Some of the members of this genus associate with branching stony corals or spiny echinoderms, like sea urchins or Crown-of-Thorns Sea Stars (*Acanthaster planci*). Others do not form these symbiotic associations.

Siphamia corallicola Allen, 1993

Common Names: Coral Siphonfish, Forktail Siphonfish.
Maximum Length: 3 cm (1.2 in.).
Distribution: Malaysia, Papua New Guinea.
Biology: The Coral Siphonfish is found in the sheltered habitats of inlets, bays, and lagoons. It occurs at a depth range of 6 to 22 m (20 to 72 ft.). This species lives in shoals, numbering up to 30 individuals. They hide among the branches of pocilloporid corals, especially *Seriatopora hystrix*, and among soft corals. This species often shares its coral home with Jebb's Siphonfish (*Siphamia jebbi*). Males may incubate as many as 162 eggs in a clutch. The larvae are 2.8 mm at hatching.
Captive Care: This small apogonid should be housed in groups. It should also be provided with branching stony corals in which to refuge. Do not keep it with more aggressive fishes or with piscivorous tankmates (the small size of *S. corallicola* makes it a target for even smaller predators). It is not a threat to ornamental crustaceans.
Aquarium Size: 20 gal. **Temperature:** 22 to 28°C (72 to 82°F).
Aquarium Suitability Index: 3.
Remarks: *Siphamia corallicola* is an elongate member of the genus with a lateral line that is only present on the anterior portion of the body. It has a mottled color pattern with a dark brown spot

on the caudal peduncle and a deeply incised tail. This fish is very similar to the **Elongate Siphonfish** (*Siphamia elongata*) **Lachner, 1953,** which is more elongate than the *S. corallicola* and tends to a have a dusky area at the base of the caudal fin.

Siphamia fistulosa (Weber, 1909)
Common Names: Fistulose Siphonfish, Short Siphonfish.
Maximum Length: 4 cm (1.6 in.).
Distribution: Philippines, Indonesia, and Guam.
Biology: The Fistulose Siphonfish is found in harbors and coastal reefs at depths of 4 to 18 m (13 to 59 ft.). It has been reported living among the branches of stony corals (e.g., *Pocillopora damicornis*). In northern Sulawesi, I observed a solitary individual living over the tentacles of the Longtentacled Plate Coral (*Heliofungia actiniformis*).
Captive Care: This fish is not common in the aquarium trade. Provide it with branching stony corals or *Heliofungia* corals to shelter within. It is prone to being bullied by more aggressive tankmates, so it must be placed in a passive community tank. Feed it frozen mysid and brine shrimp and finely chopped fresh shrimp. The small size of *S. fistulosa* makes it potential prey to many piscivores and larger crustaceans.
Aquarium Size: 20 gal. **Temperature:** 22 to 28°C (72 to 82°F).
Aquarium Suitability Index: 3.
Remarks: The Fistulose Siphonfish has seven spines in the first dorsal fin. It is bronze overall, with silver speckles.

Siphamia versicolor (Smith & Radcliffe, 1911)
Common Name: Onespot Urchin Siphonfish.
Maximum Length: 4.5 cm (1.8 in.).
Distribution: Philippines to southern Japan.
Biology: This cardinalfish is only found among the spines of the venomous sea urchins (*Asthenosoma* spp.). It usually occurs in groups and probably feeds on plankton. It rarely moves far from its sea urchin refuge.
Captive Care: This species may be exported from the Philippines. Provide it with a live sea urchin or a replica of this echinoderm. It will also do best if kept in a group.
Aquarium Size: 20 gal. **Temperature:** 22 to 28°C (72 to 82°F).
Aquarium Suitability Index: 3.
Remarks: This dark-colored cardinalfish has a single white spot at the rear base of the second dorsal fin and a white spot at the axil of the pectoral fin. Like many in the genus, it can turn off and on the longitudinal stripes on the head and body. According to Kuiter and Kozawa (1998) this species is often misidentified. The **Twospot Urchin Siphonfish** (*Siphamia tubifer*) **Weber, 1909** is a very similar species, but it has a white spot following each of the

Siphamia elongata, Elongate Siphonfish: note dusky area at base of tail.

Siphamia fistulosa, Fistulose Siphonfish: lives with protective stony corals.

Siphamia versicolor, Onespot Urchin Siphonfish: stays close to its sea urchin.

Sphaeramia nematoptera, Pajama Cardinalfish: juvenile specimen.

Sphaeramia orbicularis, Polka Dot Cardinalfish: hardy but drably colored.

two dorsal fins. The lower dark stripe on the body is narrow (much narrower than that of the Onespot Urchin Siphonfish). It is widespread in the Western Pacific Ocean, and is found on coastal reefs and outer lagoons.

The **Philippine Urchin Siphonfish** (*Siphamia fuscolineata*) **Lachner, 1953** is usually plain brown to black overall, with no white spots on the back or caudal peduncle. It can exhibit a striped color pattern, in which case the dark stripes are as wide as the light spaces between them (they are narrower in the other species). It is reported to associate with sea urchins and the Crown-of-Thorns Sea Star (*Acanthaster planci*). The Philippine Urchin Siphonfish is found in lagoons, where it inhabits the spaces between the spines of the Crown-of-Thorns Sea Star. It occurs at depths down to 7 m (23 ft.). It clusters in aggregations numbering up to 30 individuals.

Genus *Sphaeramia*

Sphaeramia nematoptera (Bleeker, 1856)
Common Name: Pajama Cardinalfish.
Maximum Length: 8 cm (3.1 in.).
Distribution: Java to Papua New Guinea, north to the Ryukyus, and south to New Caledonia.
Biology: *Sphaeramia nematoptera* lives in sheltered bays, lagoons, and along coastal fringing reefs, at depths of 1 to 10 m (3.3 to 33 ft.). Adults tend to form loose shoals among branching stony corals (e.g., *Acropora* spp.), while juveniles often occur singly. At night, adult groups disband and feed on small invertebrates near the seafloor.
Captive Care: The Pajama Cardinalfish has been a mainstay in the marine aquarium hobby for many years and is certainly one of the best beginner fishes available. It is inexpensive, has an eyecatching, even bizarre, color pattern, will eat most aquarium foods, and is virtually bullet-proof. On a number of occasions I have seen or heard of aquarists losing all the fishes in a tank to a disease or parasite except for *S. nematoptera*. This fish may do better if housed in small groups. Members of the group will set up a pecking order, with the largest individual being the most dominant. But aggressive exchanges in this species usually consist of the occasional chase or nudge, not warfare like many other reef fishes (including some of the other apogonids). Individuals may communicate with each other by flicking their pelvic fins. This fish should not be introduced into a tank with overly aggressive fishes, although once it acclimates it will usually compete well for food and is usually ignored by all but the most pugnacious tankmates. It is a great cardinalfish for the shallow-water reef aquarium, because it will spend most of its time in full view. This species is reported to spawn and mouthbrood eggs regularly in some home aquariums, although the fry are apparently unable to survive in a typical community tank setting.
Aquarium Size: 20 gal. **Temperature:** 22 to 28°C (72 to 82°F).
Aquarium Suitability Index: 5.
Remarks: The color of the juvenile differs from that of the adult (see accompanying photographs). Although it has yet to be confirmed by internal examination, males are reported to have a longer filament on the second dorsal fin than females.

Sphaeramia orbicularis (Cuvier, 1828)
Common Names: Polka Dot Cardinalfish, Orbiculate Cardinalfish.
Maximum Length: 10 cm (3.9 in.).
Distribution: East Africa to Kiribati, north to the Ryukyus, south to New Caledonia.
Biology: The Polka Dot Cardinalfish is most often found among

Sphaeramia nematoptera, Pajama Cardinalfish: a classic marine aquarium species, durable and fantastically patterned. Good candidate for captive breeding.

mangrove prop root systems and around pier pilings in shallow water. It occurs at the water's surface to a depth of 2 m (6.6 ft.). This species is crepuscular, hunting mostly at dusk and dawn. It feeds mainly on planktonic crustaceans, but will also consume insects, polychaete worms, small fishes, and fish eggs. It does some of its hunting near the water's surface or within the mangrove prop root system. This fish spawns every 19 to 33 days, and males incubate from 6,100 to 11,700 eggs at a time. Spawning in *S. orbicularis* is based on a semi-lunar cycle.

Captive Care: This common species is as hardy as the closely related *S. nematoptera,* but its appearance is drab by comparison. For this reason it is not a popular choice with marine enthusiasts—and some even regard it as a "feeder fish" for larger, hard-to-keep marine specimens. It can be housed in a variety of aquarium venues. It seems to prefer more sheltered conditions, so provide a quiet area in the tank for it to get out of strong water flow. It will also do better in a tank that lacks aggressive fish tankmates. The Polka Dot Cardinalfish is a threat to ornamental crustaceans and small fishes that it can swallow whole.

Aquarium Size: 30 gal. **Temperature:** 22 to 28°C (72 to 82°F).

Aquarium Suitability Index: 5.

Remarks: The color of this species is fairly consistent. Females are reported to mature at a total length of 6 cm (2.3 in.), while males are mature at 7 cm (2.7 in.).

References

Allen (1975, 1993, 1997), Allen & Steene (1995), Charney (1976), Chave (1978), Colin & Heiser (1973), Fishelson (1970), Gon (1993), Gon & Randall (1995), Greenfield et al. (1990), Hiatt & Stratsburg (1960), Hobson (1974), Hoover (1993), Humann & DeLoach (2002), Klocek & Kolman (1976), Kuiter (1992, 1993, 2001), Kuiter & Debelius (1994), Kuiter & Kozawa (1999), Kuwamura (1983, 1985, 1987), Lachner (1955), Morin (1981), Myers (1999), Okuda (1999, 2001), Randall (1967, 1996, 1998) Randall & Fautin (2002), Randall & Fraser (1999), Randall & Kulbicki (1998), Randall et al. (1985), Randall & Satapoomin (1999), Reed (1992), Robins et al. (1986), Sano et al. (1984), Siegel & Adamson (1983), Smith & Tyler (1972), Sudo & Azeta (1992), Thresher (1980, 1984), Tominaga (1964), Vagelli (1999), Vagelli & Erdmann (2002), Vivien (1975).

Hoplolatilus starcki, Bluehead Tilefish: sleek and capable of blinding bursts of speed, members of this family are found over sand or rubble bottoms.

ELONGATE, HOVERING FISHES THAT SELDOM STRAY far from the bottom, the tilefishes are noted both for their elegant beauty and flashing speed. They are capable of rapid bursts of motion—usually into their protective burrows at the first sign of a threat. Several species make brilliantly colorful and unusual display specimens, and one, *Hoplolatilus chlupatyi,* the Flashing Tilefish, is known for its astonishing ability to shift through a dynamic range of colors in a matter of seconds. Tilefishes are most often found on open sand bottoms, with at least two genera (*Hoplolatilus* and *Malacanthus*) well represented on sand and rubble slopes adjacent to, but not on, coral reefs.

Classification and Biology

There are two subfamilies in the tilefish family, Malacanthinae and Latilinae. Those from the Subfamily Malacanthinae are well known to hobbyists—especially the torpedo tilefishes (*Hoplolatilus* spp.). While neither aggressive nor difficult to feed, the torpedo tilefishes have special social and environmental needs that must be met in order to keep them successfully in captivity. These unusual fishes can be difficult to acclimate and maintain if not provided with a setting and conditions that reflect their natural habitat and behavioral patterns.

There are ten described species in the genus *Hoplolatilus,* and at least one undescribed (from deep reefs off Papua New Guinea) that is awaiting formal description. One of the described forms, *Hoplolatilus oreni*, is known only from a single specimen collected in the southern Red Sea, while the description of another, *H. geo*, was based on observations made from a submersible in 100 m (328 ft.) of water. Most of the members of this genus were described relatively recently, in the 1970s and 1980s. This is in part due to their affinity for deeper water. It wasn't until ichthyologists equipped with scuba equipment began exploring deeper fore-reef slopes that many "new" torpedo tilefishes were discovered.

In the wild, most torpedo tilefishes swim 1 m (3.3 ft.) or more above the bottom and feed on zooplankton as it floats past. However, the dentition of some species, along with aquarium observations, suggest that certain tilefishes may feed on larger benthic (bottom-dwelling) prey as well. For example, the Green Tilefish (*H. cuniculus*) has larger recurved teeth in the lower jaw, which suggest it may eat items such as annelid worms, crustaceans, or even small fishes. Likewise, aquarium observations suggest that Fourmanoir's Tilefish (*H. fourmanoiri*) feeds off the bottom and will even engage in hydraulic jetting (i.e., blowing water out of its mouth at the substrate) to expose buried prey.

When threatened, a torpedo tilefish will typically hang with its tail up and head down over the entrance to a burrow. If pressed

The Sand Tilefish Mound: A Micro-Ecosystem

The mounds created by the Sand Tilefish (*Malacanthus plumieri*) occur in areas near coral reefs where places to hide are often few and far between. By collecting and piling bits of debris in this habitat, the tilefish, in effect, creates an artificial reef that can be used as a sanctuary and a source of food by invertebrates and other fish species. The mound provides a hard substrate for algae and sessile invertebrates to grow on, which then attracts herbivores and carnivores (e.g., damselfishes, Rock Beauty [*Holacanthus tricolor*]) that browse on encrusting invertebrates. This micro-ecosystem also serves as a refuge for smaller motile invertebrates, like amphipods, crabs, shrimps, mantis shrimps, brittle stars, and pencil urchins, which in turn draws carnivorous fishes (e.g., Lantern Bass [*Serranus baldwini*]) that prey on them. Zooplankton feeders (e.g., Sunshine Chromis [*Chromis insolata*]) feed on the zooplankton that is swept over the tilefish's domicile by ocean currents and use the mound as a place to hide when threatened and as a sleeping site. Finally, piscivorous fishes (e.g., Red Lizardfish [*Synodus synodus*]) are attracted to the mound by all the smaller fishes that live among the debris. The tilefish itself also feeds on some of the fishes and invertebrates that take up resident in the pile of debris that it creates.

Certain fish species utilize different parts of the tilefish's mound as well. For example, scorpionfishes, Reef Bass (*Pseudogramma gregoryi*), and cardinalfishes live inside of the mound, lurking in the interstices and cavities. The Lantern Bass lives at the edge of the tilefish's domicile, while the Yellowhead Jawfish (*Opistognathus aurifrons*) builds burrows at the mound's periphery. The Cherub Angelfish (*Centropyge argi*) moves from interstice to interstice, and damselfishes live above the mound and disappear among the rubble if threatened.

The species most abundant in these mounds include the Bicolor Dam-

Sand Tilefish over a typical mound they have constructed of debris and coral rubble that gives them—and many other animals—refuge.

selfish (*Stegastes partitus*), Goldspot Goby (*Gnatholepis thompsoni*), Lantern Bass, Reef Bass, Sunshine Chromis, Flamefish (*Apogon maculatus*), Twospot Cardinalfish (*A. pseudomaculatus*), Sawcheek Cardinalfish (*A. quadrisquamatus*), and the Cherub Angelfish. The species that occasionally associate with tilefish mounds include the Red Lizardfish, juvenile Rock Beauty Angelfish, and the Sharpnose Puffer (*Canthigaster rostrata*).

Numerous other species have been observed in this microhabitat, but some may be transient or uncommon residents. This list includes the Goldentail Moray (*Gymnothorax miliaris*), Spotted Moray (*G. moringa*), Smoothcheek Scorpionfish (*Scorpaena isthmensis*), Deepreef Scorpionfish (*Scorpaenodes tredecimspinosus*), juvenile Creolefish (*Paranthias furcifer*), Chalk Bass (*Serranus tortugarum*), Blue Chromis (*Chromis cyanea*), Threespot Damselfish (*Stegastes planifrons*), Jackknife Fish (*Equetus lanceolatus*), Highhat (*Pareques acuminatus*), juvenile grunts (*Haemulon* spp.), young Banded Butterflyfish (*Chaetodon striatus*), Reef Butterflyfish (*C. sedentarius*), Rusty Goby (*Priolepis hipoliti*), Ocean Surgeonfish (*Acanthurus bahianus*), and the Atlantic Blue Tang (*A. coeruleus*).

Malacanthus latovittatus, Striped Blanquillo: small adult specimen.

further, it will dive, headfirst, into its refuge. Although no information exists on the reproductive behavior of the genus *Hoplolatilus,* other tilefishes are known to be pelagic spawners, releasing their eggs into the water column. Field observations suggest that the torpedo tilefishes maintain long-term pair bonds, but this has yet to be confirmed. These fishes are not known to be sexually dimorphic or dichromatic, with males and females showing no readily apparent external differences.

The second of the two genera in the Subfamily Malacanthinae is *Malacanthus,* the blanquillos. The blanquillos are streamlined fishes with long, continuous dorsal and anal fins. They move above the bottom, in a sinuous fashion, and typically live in and over sand and rubble. Some blanquillos make their own homes out of debris and coral rubble. Many of them attain a large size for an aquarium fish and need plenty of swimming room if they are going to thrive in captivity. They are much more durable and quick to acclimate to aquarium life than the *Hoplolatilus* species, but are more likely to eat small fishes and ornamental crustaceans. They are usually peaceful toward tankmates that they cannot ingest.

It is not known whether all tilefishes dig their own burrows or utilize those excavated by crustaceans or other fishes. However, at least three species live in large rubble mounds, which they construct by carrying coral rubble and shells in their mouths.

Tilefishes in the Subfamily Latilinae are typically found in deeper-water habitats and rarely encountered by aquarists.

Captive Care

Tilefishes should be housed in an aquarium of at least 55 gallons and preferably 100 gallons or more. In nature, they typically occupy an open habitat devoid of high-profile structures. For this reason, they require plenty of swimming space—a tank packed with live rock is not the proper setting. However, it is important to provide plenty of low-profile hiding places that they can dart into if threatened. Suitable refuges can be constructed by stacking live rock, piling mounds of coral rubble to create caves, or by laying a flat piece of live rock on a sand substrate with a depression formed underneath it. Torpedo tilefishes will also dig their own holes under rockwork. A larger tank with one or two low-profile coral heads and flattish rocks lying on a sand bed would be an ideal environment.

Most tilefishes do not harm sessile invertebrates and therefore can be kept in the reef aquarium. However, a specimen of *Hoplolatilus fourmanoiri* was observed biting tissue from, and killing, two specimens of Elegance Coral (*Catalaphyllia jardinei*). (It reportedly ate the coral's flesh, but this same tilefish did not bother other large-polyped stony corals, small-polyped stony corals, or corallimorpharians.) Some *Hoplolatilus* species may also attack delicate ornamental shrimps (e.g., *Periclimenes* spp.). Most tilefish species are found in water deeper than 30 m (98 ft.), which means they live under relatively low-light conditions (less than 7000 lux). Therefore, they are best kept in deep-water reef aquariums. Like most active zooplanktivores, tilefishes should also be fed at least once and preferably several times a day.

It is important to keep these tilefishes in pairs or trios with members of their own species, or in a group of mixed tilefishes. Most species are less likely to acclimate to captivity if they are kept on their own. For example, I had a Bluehead Tilefish (*H. starcki*) in a tank by itself, and it hid and did not eat. When I moved it into a tank containing a Fourmanoir's Tilefish, the Bluehead immediately paired up with the resident tilefish and spent most of its time swimming around in the water column. (Animals, including fishes, often learn from individuals around them; this is known as social facilitation.) Another technique you can use to acclimate a tilefish is to keep it with peaceful fishes that spend most of their time in the open. For example, Bar Gobies (*Ptereleotris zebra*) and Green Gudgeon Gobies (*Ptereleotris microlepis*) are hardy zooplanktivores that will act as "dither fish," that is, they will encourage your tilefish to spend more time in the water column and may even stimulate feeding in a finicky individual. Another thing to keep in mind is that smaller specimens often acclimate more readily to captivity than their larger counterparts.

Most tilefishes are rarely aggressive, although if you keep

TABLE 2

Torpedo Tilefish Tankmates

Pipefishes (Syngnathidae)
Anthias (*Pseudanthias* spp.)
Slender anthias (*Luzonichthys* spp.)
Comets and assessors (Plesiopidae)
Cardinalfishes (Apogonidae)
Spinecheeks (*Scolopsis* spp.)
Jawfishes (Opistognathidae)
Fairy wrasses (*Cirrhilabrus* spp.)
Flasher wrasses (*Paracheilinus* spp.)
Convict Blenny (*Pholidichthys leucotaenia*)
Dragonets (Callionymidae)
Shrimp gobies (*Amblyeleotris* spp.)
Dartfishes and wormfishes (Microdesmidae)
Trunkfishes (Ostraciidae)

two individuals of the same species it is prudent to add them simultaneously. I have had the occasional specimen chase or nip at small zooplankton feeders, like flasher wrasses (*Paracheilinus* spp.), but these interactions never ended in serious injury. The Golden Tilefish (*H. luteus*) and Fourmanoir's Tilefish are the most likely to behave aggressively toward conspecifics or peaceful heterospecifics (see species accounts, below).

Because of their propensity to dash about recklessly when first introduced to the aquarium, especially when the lights are turned off or when bullied by their tankmates, these fishes should not be housed with invertebrates that have a potent sting or the ability to snare errant fishes. This would include spider anemones (*Actinodendron* spp.), carpet anemones (*Stichodactyla* spp.), and the Elegance Coral (*Catalaphyllia jardinei*).

Although some captive tilefishes will accept a wide range of aquarium fare, it is often necessary to present live food to initiate feeding. The best choices are live adult brine shrimp or baby guppies. Frozen brine shrimp, *Mysis* shrimp, frozen black worms, blood worms, and some of the frozen preparations should be accepted in time. An occasional specimen may even eat flake food. Most tilefishes will only ingest food particles as they are floating about in the water column and will not pick food off the aquarium substrate. If kept with overly aggressive feeders, a flighty tilefish may have trouble competing for food, at least before it fully acclimates.

One common cause of tilefish mortality is this group's ability to jump, with a known ability to fly even through incredibly small gaps in an aquarium cover. They are especially prone to such behavior when first introduced to the tank, when the lights are extinguished, or if they are being picked on by their tankmates. A tight-fitting top is a must. If it is a glass top, be sure to keep the water surface in motion, with a powerhead, water return, or even an airstone, to prevent the buildup of carbon dioxide in the space between the water's surface and the glass. It is best to construct a top using fiberglass screen or plastic eggcrate material, which will allow better gas exchange at the water's surface. It is also advisable to place a small night light or moonlight over the tank to prevent the tilefishes from hurling themselves against the aquarium top, which can result in injuries.

Because these fishes often come from deeper water on forereef slopes, an environment of relatively homogenous conditions, the aquarist must attempt to maintain similar conditions in the aquarium. Avoid sudden changes in water parameters (e.g., salinity, water temperature) and maintain optimal water quality. A good protein skimmer, monthly water changes, and live rock and live sand will help to keep nitrogenous waste and dissolved organic levels down.

One common problem with tilefishes is improper decompression by collectors. If fishes in a dealer's tank are swimming with their heads down and their tails up, laboring to stay stationary in the water column, this is indicative of swim bladder problems resulting from being improperly brought up from deep water. Specimens suffering from this malady rarely survive.

TILEFISH SPECIES

Genus *Hoplolatilus* (Torpedo Tilefishes)

Selecting proper tankmates for torpedo tilefish is critical. They should never be housed with boisterous fish species like groupers, jacks, snappers, large angelfishes, big wrasses (e.g., *Thalassoma* spp.), large damselfishes, aggressive hawkfishes, surgeonfishes, or triggerfishes. If bullied, tilefishes will hide and never come out to feed, or will jump out of the aquarium. Being long and slender, they are also easier for piscivorous predators, like frogfishes, scorpionfishes, and groupers to ingest. For a list of appropriate torpedo tilefish tankmates see Table 2.

Hoplolatilus chlupatyi Klausewitz, McCosker, Randall & Zetzsche, 1978

Common Names: Flashing Tilefish, Chlupaty's Tilefish, Chameleon Tilefish.
Maximum Length: 13 cm (5.1 in.).
Distribution: Indonesia and the Philippines.

Hoplolatilus chlupatyi, Flashing Tilefish: extraordinary color-change artist.

Hoplolatilus chlupatyi, Flashing Tilefish: can change colors in an instant.

Biology: This species occurs over sand and rubble bottoms on fore-reef slopes, usually at depths exceeding 30 m (98 ft.) to at least 70 m (230 ft.). According to Keisuke Imai, a noted Japanese underwater photographer and naturalist, this species usually appears in small aggregations and does not appear to reside in a specific "home" burrow. Instead, they flee when threatened or make use of the burrows of other tilefish species that occupy the same habitat (e.g., *H. marcosi*).

Captive Care: This wonderful but delicate fish is not commonly seen in the aquarium trade, and many of the specimens that do show up suffer from swim bladder problems resulting from improper decompression. They should not be kept with aggressive tankmates and are best housed with a member of their own species or another tilefish species. (This seems to reassure the tilefish and results in more natural behaviors. I have seen larger in-

dividuals of this species do a 360-degree roll around their longitudinal axis in front of a smaller conspecific.) They should be provided with plenty of swimming space and numerous hiding places. It may take several days before they will accept live or frozen food. Frozen *Mysis* shrimp and brine shrimp are good first foods. This species can be kept in a reef aquarium, but because of its relatively deep water origins, it will more readily acclimate if kept under low light conditions. A deep-water reef tank with gentle lighting is a more appropriate home for one of these fish than a brightly lit shallow-water reef aquarium.

Aquarium Size: 55 gal. **Temperature:** 22 to 26°C (72 to 79°F).
Aquarium Suitability Index: 2.

Remarks: The common name of this species is derived from its unique ability to change its color with great rapidity. The overall dorsal coloration can be salmon, orange, green, violet, or blue. One specimen was reported to have displayed 24 different colors in a single 15-second period. It is possible that this species could be confused with the juveniles of the Bluehead Tilefish (*H. starcki*). Young Bluehead Tilefish have yellow lines on the edges of the caudal lobes and are stockier in build.

Hoplolatilus cuniculus Randall & Dooley, 1974
Common Names: Green Tilefish, Pale Tilefish.
Maximum Length: 15 cm (5.9 in.).
Distribution: South Africa to Mauritius to the Society Islands, north to the Ryukyus and Marshall Islands.
Biology: The species occurs over muddy and rubble substrates on fore-reef slopes at depths from 2 to 115 m (6.6 to 377 ft.). In most areas this species is found at depths greater than 30 m (98 ft.).
Captive Care: The Green Tilefish should be provided with plenty of swimming room and hiding places. It ought to be kept in pairs and will do best in a tank with lower light levels, but can be successfully transferred to a shallow-water reef aquarium once it has fully adjusted to captive life.
Aquarium Size: 55 gal. **Temperature:** 22 to 26°C (72 to 79°F).
Aquarium Suitability Index: 2.
Remarks: There appear to be three distinct populations of Green Tilefish: from French Polynesia, the Western Pacific, and Mauritius. Individuals from the three populations vary in coloration and maximum size.

Hoplolatilus fourmanoiri Smith, 1963
Common Names: Fourmanoir's Tilefish, Yellow-blotched Tilefish, Yellow-spotted Tilefish.
Maximum Length: 14 cm (5.5 in.).
Distribution: Vietnam, Philippines, and the Solomon Islands.

Hoplolatilus cuniculus, Green Tilefish: as with others in this family, needs ample swimming room.

Hoplolatilus cuniculus, Green Tilefish: color variant. Regional color differences have been recorded.

Hoplolatilus cuniculus, Green Tilefish: color variant. All tilefishes are adept at jumping.

Hoplolatilus fourmanoiri, Fourmanoir's Tilefish: variant with widespread yellow pigmentation.

Hoplolatilus fourmanoiri, Fourmanoir's Tilefish: one of the hardiest species in its genus.

Hoplolatilus fronticinctus, Stocky Tilefish: large species that needs hiding places for security.

Biology: This species has been collected at depths of 18 to 36 m (59 to 118 ft.) off South Vietnam and at 55 m (180 ft.) off Guadalcanal in the Solomon Islands. At the latter location, it was taken on a silty sand bottom with scattered coral rocks. Captive observations suggest this fish may feed on benthic invertebrates, such as infaunal worms, as well as zooplankton.

Captive Care: Fourmanoir's Tilefish is one of the hardiest species in the genus, although it may take a week or more before some individuals start feeding. It can be kept singly or in pairs, but when housing with other tilefish, they should all be introduced to the tank simultaneously. Fourmanoir's Tilefish can be aggressive toward unrelated fishes when the new fishes are introduced after the tilefish has grown accustomed to its aquarium home. For example, a specimen kept in a 120-gallon tank chased two fairy wrasses (*Cirrhilabrus* spp.) that were introduced after the tilefish was fully acclimated and had established its own territory. This species not only feeds on zooplankton, but also eats benthic invertebrates. A specimen I kept continually scanned the substrate, adopting a head-down swimming posture. It would blow streams of water out of its mouth at the bottom debris in an attempt to locate food. It ravenously consumed live grass shrimp, but also

fed on frozen prepared foods, live brine shrimp, and black worms. I have seen this species feed on cleaner shrimps (*Lysmata* spp.). One particular individual I had swam about the tank with the tail of a peppermint shrimp (*Lysmata wurdemanni*) sticking out of its mouth until it finally succeeded in swallowing it. A Fourmanoir's Tilefish was also implicated in an attack on a fleshy polyped stony coral (see the Captive Care section in the family account, page 268, for more details).

Aquarium Size: 55 gal. **Temperature:** 22 to 27°C (72 to 81°F).
Aquarium Suitability Index: 3.

Remarks: The color pattern of this species can vary between specimens, but all adults have a violet-black area on top of the head and a black spot on the operculum and on the tail. The spot on the head and tail are often lacking or indistinct in juveniles. Some individuals also have more yellow on the body than others.

Hoplolatilus fronticinctus Günther, 1887
Common Name: Stocky Tilefish.
Maximum Length: 20 cm (7.8 in.).
Distribution: Mauritius to the Solomon Islands, north to the Philippines, Belau, and the Marshall Islands.

Hoplolatilus luteus, Golden Tilefish: sometimes mistaken for a Midas Blenny.

Hoplolatilus marcosi, Skunk Tilefish: delicate, deeper-water beauty.

Hoplolatilus purpureus, Purple Tilefish: sensitive fish needing expert care.

Biology: This species is found in sandy areas at the base of reefs at depths from 40 to 70 m (131 to 230 ft.). It occurs in small groups that refuge in large mounds of coral rubble and shell. The Stocky Tilefish makes these piles, which can be as large as 5 x 3 x 1 m (16 x 9.8 x 3.3 ft.), by carrying pieces of debris in its mouth. The mounds are often built so close together that the edge of one mound is in contact with another.

Captive Care: This larger species often seems to have difficulty acclimating to the home aquarium. It should be housed in a tank of 135 gallons or more with a coral rubble and shell substrate. To encourage acclimation, build a large mound in the middle of the tank with rubble and live rock. Create several larger passageways into the mound that the tilefish can use to enter and leave the structure. This species is not common in the aquarium trade, so acquiring a pair will be difficult. Keeping it with a more durable tilefish species may increase the chances of success.

Aquarium Size: 135 gal. **Temperature:** 22 to 26°C (72 to 79°F).
Aquarium Suitability Index: 2.

Hoplolatilus luteus Allen & Kuiter, 1989
Common Names: Golden Tilefish, Yellow Tilefish.
Maximum Length: 14 cm (5.5 in.).
Distribution: Flores, Indonesia and possibly Bali.
Biology: The Golden Tilefish occurs near coastal reefs, over flat, silty bottoms, at a depth of 15 to 35 m (49 to 115 ft.). It occurs singly and in pairs, which swim very near the bottom. In some areas, they are found in turbid water.
Captive Care: *Hoplolatilus luteus* is the most durable and, along with *H. fourmanoiri,* one of the most aggressive members of the genus. For example, I have had these fish chase and nip each other when time had elapsed between the introduction of the first and second fish. I have also had them chase small zooplankton-feeding fishes introduced after them. This species will acclimate more rapidly than most other tilefishes if kept on its own. The Golden Tilefish can be kept in a deep-water or shallow-water reef aquarium.
Aquarium Size: 55 gal. **Temperature:** 22 to 27°C (72 to 81°F).
Aquarium Suitability Index: 3.
Remarks: Some ichthyologists have suggested that this species is simply a color form of *Hoplolatilus fourmanoiri.* The latter differs from *Hoplolatilus luteus* in having a black triangular spot in the middle of the tail and its body is mainly gray, rather than yellow, overall. There are no known differences in the appearances of males and females. The Golden Tilefish is sometimes erroneously sold in the aquarium trade as the Midas Blenny (*Ecsenius midas*).

Hoplolatilus marcosi Burgess, 1978

Common Names: Skunk Tilefish, Marcos' Tilefish, Redstripe Tilefish, Redback Tilefish, Coca-Cola Tilefish.

Maximum Length: 12 cm (4.7 in.).

Distribution: Indonesia and the Philippines.

Biology: The Skunk Tilefish occurs over sand and rubble in 30 to 80 m (98 to 262 ft.) of water. It is usually seen in pairs. In some areas, it is found in the same habitat as the Flashing and Stocky Tilefishes (*H. chlupatyi* and *H. fronticinctus*).

Captive Care: This is a sensitive species that must be kept with less aggressive fishes. It should be kept in pairs and must be provided with numerous hiding places. *Hoplolatilus marcosi* may hide for a week or more before regularly swimming in the open. Like most members of the genus, it is a great jumper and can find and leap through incredibly small openings in an aquarium cover. This species can be kept in a deep-water reef aquarium.

Aquarium Size: 55 gal. **Temperature:** 22 to 27°C (72 to 81°F).

Aquarium Suitability Index: 2.

Hoplolatilus purpureus Burgess, 1978

Common Name: Purple Tilefish.

Maximum Length: 13 cm (5.1 in.).

Distribution: Indonesia, the Philippines, and the Solomon Islands.

Biology: This species occurs on fore-reef slopes at depths from 18 to 80 m (59 to 262 ft.) over mud or mixed sand and rubble substrates. Adults are seen both singly and in pairs.

Captive Care: The Purple Tilefish is a relatively difficult species to keep. It often suffers from swim bladder problems, resulting from improper decompression when collected. It is very prone to jumping out of the aquarium or hurling itself into the cover glass. In either case, the behavior often proves fatal to the fish. Pairs of these tilefish should be kept with other peaceful fish species. Live food will probably be needed to elicit a feeding response. They can be housed in a deep-water reef aquarium with plenty of open sandy bottom.

Aquarium Size: 55 gal. **Temperature:** 22 to 27°C (72 to 81°F).

Aquarium Suitability Index: 2.

Hoplolatilus starcki Randall & Dooley, 1974

Common Names: Bluehead Tilefish, Blueface Tilefish, Starck's Tilefish.

Maximum Length: 15 cm (5.9 in.).

Distribution: Celebes, Indonesia to the Philippines, east to the Pitcairn Group, north to the Marianas, and south to New Caledonia.

Biology: The Bluehead Tilefish lives on steep fore-reef slopes and at the base of the fore reef at depths of 21 to 105 m (69 to 344

Hoplolatilus starcki, Bluehead Tilefish: juvenile shows overall blue coloration.

Hoplolatilus starcki, Bluehead Tilefish: typical adult color scheme.

ft.). It is most abundant at depths greater than 30 m (98 ft.) and usually occurs over coral rubble substrates. When feeding, it will swim up to 2 m (6.6 ft.) above the bottom, but if disturbed will rapidly dive into holes amid the rubble. Adults typically occur in pairs, while juveniles form loose aggregations and often mix with other zooplanktivores. For example, in the Fijian Islands, juvenile Bluehead Tilefish are often found amid aggregations of Purple Queen Anthias (*Pseudanthias pascalus*). At the depths at which these mixed groups occur, the Purple Queens, which are magenta, look blue, and thus resemble the juvenile *H. starcki*. This is known as social mimicry, in which one species resembles another and associates with it because there is less likelihood that it will be eaten if it is in a group. I have observed pairs of Bluehead Tilefish on a fore-reef slope off Madang, New Guinea, in 33 m (108 ft.) of water, that were mixing with other zoo-

Malacanthus brevirostris, Flagtail Blanquillo: needs room to swim and burrow.

Malacanthus latovittatus, Striped Blanquillo: adults often seen in pairs.

Malacanthus latovittatus, Striped Blanquillo: may mimic a cleaner wrasse.

plankton feeders, including the Squarespot Anthias (*Pseudanthias pleurotaenia*) and the Blackspot Angelfish (*Genicanthus melanospilos*).

Captive Care: Like the rest of the torpedo tilefish clan, this species acclimates more readily if kept with another tilefish. Although keeping it with a member of the same species is best, you can house it with other torpedo tilefishes. Debelius and Baensch (1992) report that this species is less social than other tilefish species, maintaining a greater distance between itself and conspecifics and rarely sharing the same hiding place with other tilefishes. On one occasion, I observed a juvenile Bluehead Tilefish picking at a conspecific that posed in the water column with its head up and tail down, as if one was "cleaning" the other. One of these juveniles would also occasionally chase a flasher wrasse (*Paracheilinus* sp.) and nip at its pectoral fin. Juveniles acclimate more readily to captivity than adult specimens. The Bluehead Tilefish can be housed in a reef tank if plenty of swimming room is provided. However, it will acclimate more readily in the low-light conditions of a deep-water reef aquarium.

Aquarium Size: 55 gal. **Temperature:** 22 to 26°C (72 to 79°F).

Aquarium Suitability Index: 2.

Remarks: There is no known sexual dichromatism in this species, but juveniles do differ in color from adults. Young specimens are entirely blue, with a yellow bar on the upper and lower caudal fin lobes.

Genus *Malacanthus* (Blanquillos)

Malacanthus brevirostris Guichenot, 1848

Common Names: Flagtail Blanquillo, Quakerfish.

Maximum Length: 30 cm (11.7 in.).

Distribution: Red Sea to Panama, north to southern Japan and the Hawaiian Islands, and south to Lord Howe Island.

Biology: The Flagtail Blanquillo lives in sandy areas on the back reef and on fore-reef slopes at depths of 10 to 45 m (33 to 148 ft.). It digs a burrow in the sand, usually adjacent to or under a rock, where it will retreat if threatened.

Captive Care: The Flagtail Blanquillo should be housed in a large tank with limited aquascaping, a sandy substrate, and several flat rocks under which it can burrow. This is a peaceful fish that should not be housed with more aggressive species. It can be kept in a reef aquarium provided the tank has a low-profile reef with plenty of exposed sandy bottom.

Aquarium Size: 100 gal. **Temperature:** 22 to 26°C (72 to 79°F).

Aquarium Suitability Index: 4.

Remarks: The tail of the juvenile is rounded, while that of the adult is truncate.

Malacanthus latovittatus (Lacépède, 1801)

Common Names: Striped Blanquillo, Blue Blanquillo, Blue Whiting, Dolphin Shark.

Maximum Length: 35 cm (13.7 in.).

Distribution: Red Sea to the Line Islands, north to southern Japan, south to New Caledonia and Cook Island.

Biology: The Striped Blanquillo occurs over rubble and coral pavement on reef flats and fore-reef slopes at depths from 5 to 40 m (16 to 131 ft.). Adults are often seen in pairs, while juveniles are solitary. It probably preys upon small fishes and motile invertebrates, such as crabs and shrimps.

Captive Care: This hardy aquarium fish needs plenty of swimming space. It should be kept in a larger tank with only a limited amount of decor or live rock. Large specimens will eat small fishes and crustaceans. Although the Striped Blanquillo will not harm sessile invertebrates, it is not well suited for most reef tanks, because it needs more swimming room than they usually provide.

Aquarium Size: 180 gal. **Temperature:** 22 to 27°C (72 to 81°F).

Aquarium Suitability Index: 4.

Remarks: The juvenile Striped Blanquillo resembles the juvenile Ring Wrasse (*Hologymnosus annulatus*) and the Bluestreak Cleaner Wrasse (*Labroides dimidiatus*). This species is not known to clean other fishes, but may mimic this wrasse to inhibit predators from eating it.

Malacanthus plumieri (Bloch, 1787)

Common Names: Sand Tilefish, Sand Blanquillo.

Maximum Length: 60 cm (23.4 in.).

Distribution: South Carolina and Bermuda to southern Brazil, east to Ascension Island.

Biology: The Sand Tilefish lives at a depth range of 2 to 50 m (6.6 to 164 ft.), being most abundant at depths greater than 9 m (30 ft.), and within 40 m (131 ft.) of the reef face. Sand Tilefish dig a burrow, which is used as a refuge from predators. The burrow consists of a horizontal tunnel within a mound of coral rubble, barnacle and bivalve shells, and stones. Staghorn coral fragments (*Acropora cervicornis*), measuring between 2 and 10 cm (0.8 to 3.9 in.) in length, are the most common components of the tilefish's home, but the debris used is dependent on the materials available in the fish's environment. For example, in areas where stony corals are sparse, stones are more commonly used. The size of the material used in the mound is also a function of the individual tilefish's size, with smaller specimens using smaller bits of debris. In fact, Sand Tilefish less than 18 cm (7 in.) in length usually just burrow under a rock or piece of coral and do not create mounds. The mounds of adult tilefish can range in diameter from 0.75 to over 2 m (2.5 to 6.6 ft.) and can extend up

Malacanthus plumieri, Sand Tilefish: young fish—good choice for large tanks.

to 1 m (3.3 ft.) below the sand surface.

The Sand Tilefish excavates a burrow by undulating its sinuous body in the sand. Sometimes, the tilefish will dig under or next to a rock that will later serve as a foundation for a growing mound. After the fish creates a tunnel 10 to 15 cm wide (3.9 to 5.9 in.), it begins picking up small bits of shell and coral fragments and dropping them over the depression. The tilefish then searches for larger debris up to 30 m (98 ft.) away from its mound and may even steal building materials from the refuges of neighboring conspecifics and jawfishes. When it locates an appropriately sized fragment, it picks it up in its mouth and carries it back to the burrow. In some areas, mounds are constructed around the sponge *Xestospongia muta*, which may initially serve to signal the tilefish that there is suitable material for building in the area. The sponge also helps reinforce the roof of the burrow. Just before sunset, the tilefish will lie near the burrow entrance and undulate its body to push sand into the opening; occasionally, it will even place bits of algae at the entrance. After completing its nocturnal preparations, the tilefish wriggles through the sand and into the burrow for the night. Tilefishes have to maintain their burrows constantly by piling new debris on the mound, or they will be buried by the shifting sand.

The Sand Tilefish lives in colonies and, with the exception of its mate, defends its burrow and the surrounding area from all conspecifics. This fish also chases other benthic carnivores, like goatfishes and wrasses, out of its territory. The borders of female territories are contiguous, while the area defended by a male

Malacanthus plumieri, Sand Tilefish: adult male with elongating tail fin tips.

may overlap the territories of up to six females. Female territories range in size from 43 to 301 m^2 (478 to 3,344 ft.^{2}) in area, while those of males can cover an area from 73 to 950 m^2 (811 to 10,556 ft.^{2}). Males are dominant over females and even break up skirmishes between females at territory boundaries. Females fight more among themselves than males do, but they are rarely aggressive toward males. Aggressive encounters include several behaviors: a display where the median and pelvic fins are erected, sudden upward swimming where the pelvic and median fins are spread, chasing, tail and fin biting, and head-to-tail circling.

This species is a protogynous hermaphrodite (functional females can develop into males), but sex change is not socially controlled; that is, if the territorial male is removed, a female in its harem does not automatically change sex and take his position. The Sand Tilefish reproduces year-round. Courtship commences just before sunset, when males begin displaying to females. This display consists of abrupt upward swimming, followed by a downward glide. When a female is ready to spawn, she ascends 1 to 3 m (3.3 to 9.8 ft.) above the substrate with her snout and tail pointed upward. The male then swims next to the female and the two fish rub against each other for 5 to 60 seconds. The male may leave the female and go through the same ritual as many as ten times before spawning occurs. When they are finally ready to mate, the pair begins the spawning ascent, with the male swimming above and slightly behind the female. When the fish are 2 to 4 m (6.6 to 13 ft.) above the substrate, they quiver and

release their gametes. Yellowtail Snapper (*Ocyurus chrysurus*) often follow behind tilefish during the spawning ascent, feeding on the freshly expelled eggs. After spawning, the fish dart back to the bottom. Males may spawn as many as ten times, with one to six partners, in a single evening, while females spawn up to three times, but almost always mate with the male whose territory encompasses their burrow.

The Sand Tilefish feeds primarily on serpent stars, crabs, mantis shrimps, and small fishes (including eels and wrasses), but will also eat polychaete worms, peanut worms, chitons, amphipods, shrimps, and heart urchins. It does all its feeding within its own territory.

Captive Care: This large, active fish adjusts well to aquarium life if it is kept in an extra-large tank (180 gallons or more). The aquarium should not contain a lot of decor, but should have a thick sand bottom with scattered shells, small bits of live rock, and coral rubble (see Biology section, above, for information on preferred size of debris). A large slab of live rock lying flat on the sand will provide your tilefish with a roof for its burrow. Only one of these tilefish should be kept per aquarium, as they are highly territorial and the areas they defend are very large. The Sand Tilefish will eat motile invertebrates (including crabs, shrimps, mantis shrimps, and brittlestars) and any fish that is small enough to fit into its mouth. It may also chase small carnivores, like wrasses and goatfishes. To introduce other fishes to an aquarium that contains a tilefish, choose species that make their homes in tilefish mounds. (For a listing of these species see "The Sand Tilefish Mound: A Micro-Ecosystem," page 267.) This fish is not well suited to most home reef aquariums because it needs more open space than they usually offer and will eat ornamental crustaceans. The Sand Tilefish will jump out of open aquariums if startled.

Aquarium Size: 180 gal. **Temperature:** 22 to 27°C (72 to 81°F).
Aquarium Suitability Index: 4.

Remarks: Male Sand Tilefish are typically larger than females, with filaments extending from the tips of the caudal fin and a steeper head profile. Males measure from 19 to 41 cm (7.4 in. to 16 in.) in standard length, while females measure from 15 to 31 cm (5.9 to 12.1 in.). The posterior portion of the juvenile's body is yellow, and there is a black blotch on the upper lobe of the caudal fin.

References

Allen & Kuiter (1989), Baird (1988), Baird & Baird (1992), Büttner (1996), Clark & Ben-Tuvia (1973), Clark et al. (1988), Clifton & Hunter (1972), Debelius & Baensch (1994), Earle & Pyle (1997), Kuiter & Debelius (1994), Randall (1981).

Photography Credits

All photographs by Scott W. Michael unless otherwise indicated.

ROGER STEENE: 27, 34(R), 40(TL), 41, 42(L), 43(BL), 50(T), 51(BR), 54(T), 55(T), 68(TL, TR), 74(B, C), 78(BL, BR), 79(BR), 82(TR), 83, 88(C), 90(C), 111(TL, TR), 112(T), 114, 117(R), 119(T), 134(BR), 136(T), 162, 165, 170(C), 173, 192(L, R), 193(B), 194(L), 208(C), 222(TL), 226(B, T), 229(R), 251(R), 258, 263(T), 272(CL), 276

RUDIE KUITER: 58(L), 96(T), 99(R), 100(C), 110(B), 121(TR), 129(L), 140(BC, TR), 152(B), 156(L, R), 158, 159(T, C), 207(T), 217(L), 220 (C, B), 222(TR, BL), 225(R), 228(B), 230(L, R), 241(R), 243(T), 254(C), 256(TR)

TAKAMOSA TONOZUKA: 51(BL), 64(T), 90(B), 134(TR), 136(C), 139(B), 140(TL), 174(C), 186, 218(T), 224(L, R), 237(TL), 242(B), 247(L), 256(TL, B), 271(TL, BR)

JOHN RANDALL: 32, 48(L), 59(T), 68(CL), 77(TR), 79(TL) 87, 125(T), 132(C), 133(BR), 134(TL BL), 140(BL), 190(TL), 223(T), 231(B), 246(T), 247(R), 263(B), 274(TL)

PAUL HUMANN: 30, 34(L), 47(T), 48(R), 49, 57, 62(T), 70(L, R), 71(R), 72(T), 73, 75, 92(R), 95, 174(B), 177(L), 180(B), 229(L), 237(BR), 238(B), 241(L), 248(B),

FRED BAVENDAM: 10, 25, 36(R), 38(T), 39, 44(B), 46(B), 52(R), 54(B), 60(T, B), 66, 67(B), 68(BL), 78(TL, TR), 209

JOHN P. HOOVER: 79(TR), 122(L), 131(L), 155(L), 182(B), 208(T)

GERALD ALLEN: 109(B), 112(C), 120(R), 133(TL), 139(T), 254(T)

JANINE CAIRNS-MICHAEL: 58(R), 181(T), 183(T), 233(TL)

MARY JANE ADAMS: 201, 202(TL, CL, TR, BL)

DENISE NIELSEN TACKETT: 29(R), 51(TR), 76, 140(TC)

TOSHIO TSUBOTA: 204, 207(B), 208(B), 210

HELMUT DEBELIUS / IKAN: 33(T), 133(TR)

KEISUKE IMAI: 96(B), 271(TC)

LADDIE ATKINS: 237(BL)

GLEN BARNELL: 119(B)

CLAY BRYCE: 164

DIETER EICHLER: 40(BR)

KLAUS FIEDLER: 65

FRED GOOD: 170(B)

BOO NILSSON: 175(L)

AARON NORMAN: 153

ILLUSTRATIONS:
All illustrations by Joshua Highter

Bibliography

Addison, B. 1994. Spawning and rearing the Blackcap Basslet (*Gramma melacara*). *SeaScope* 11(Fall):1, 3.

Aguilar-Perera, A. and W. Aguilar-Davila. 1996. A spawning aggregation of Nassau Grouper *Epinephelus striatus* (Pisces: Serranidae) in the Mexican Caribbean. *Environ. Biol. Fish.* 45:351-361.

Allen, G.R. 1975. The biology and taxonomy of the cardinalfish *Sphaeramia orbicularis* (Pisces: Apogonidae). *J. Royal Soc. West Aust.* 58:86-92

———1993. Cardinalfishes (Apogonidae) of Madang Province, Papua New Guinea, with descriptions of three new species. *Revue fr. Aquariol.* 20:9-20.

———1994. *Pseudochromis howsoni*, a new species of dottyback fish (Pseudochromidae) from Ashmore Reef, Timor Sea. *Revue fr. Aquariol.* 21:83-85.

———1997. *Marine Fishes of Tropical Australia and South-east Asia.* Western Australian Museum, Perth, 292 pp.

Allen G.R and R.H. Kuiter. 1989. *Hoplolatilus luteus*, a new species of malacanthid fish from Indonesia. *Revue. fr. Aquariol.* 2:39-41.

Allen, G.R. and D.R. Robertson. 1991. Four new species of jawfishes (Opistognathidae) from the tropical Eastern Pacific. *Revue fr. Aquariol.* 18:47-52.

Allen, G.R. and R.C. Steene. 1995. Notes on the ecology and behavior of the Indonesian cardinalfish (Apogonidae) *Pterapogon kauderni* Koumans. *Revue fr. Aquariol.* 22:7-9.

Anderson, W.W., D.K. Caldwell, J.F. McKinney and C.H. Farmer. 1972. Morphological and ecological data on the priacanthid fish *Cookeolus boops* in the western North Atlantic. *Copeia,* 1972: 884-885.

Asoh, K. and D.Y. Shapiro. 1997. Bisexual juvenile gonad and gonochorism in the Fairy Basslet, *Gramma loreto*. *Copiea,* 1997: 22-31.

Asoh, K. and T. Yoshikawa. 1996. Nesting behavior, male parental care, and embryonic development in the Fairy Basslet, *Gramma loreto. Copeia,* 1996:1-8.

Ayling, T. and G. J. Cox. 1984. *Collin's Guide to the Sea Fishes of New Zealand.* William Collins Publ. Auckland, 343 Pp.

Baez, J. 1998. Breeding the Marine Comet: a challenge for the best. *SeaScope* 15 (Summer):1,3.

Baird, T.A. 1988. Female and male territoriality and mating system of the sand tilefish, *Malacanthus plumieri. Environ. Biol. Fish.* 22:101-116.

Baird, T.A. and T.D. Baird. 1992. Colony formation and some possible benefits and costs of gregarious living in the territorial tilefish, *Malacanthus plumieri. Bull. Mar. Sci.* 50:56-65.

Barrall, G and A.C. Gill. 1997. Rare and Unusual Marines: The Gold-browed Dottyback (*Pseudochromis aurifrons)* Lubbock 1980. *Freshwat. Mar. Aquar.* 20(6):48-51.

Beukers, J.S. and G.P. Jones. 1998. Habitat complexity modifies the impact of piscivores on a coral reef fish population. *Oecologia,* 114:50-59.

Böhlke, J.E. and C.G. Chaplin. 1968. *Fishes of the Bahamas and Adjacent Tropical Waters.* University of Texas Press, Austin. 771 pp.

Böhlke, J.E. and J.E. Randall. 1963. The fishes of the Western Atlantic serranoid genus *Gramma. Proc. Acad. Nat. Sci. Phila.* 115:33-52.

Böhlke, J.E. and L.P Thomas. 1961. Notes on the West Atlantic jawfishes, *Opisthognathus aurifrons, O. lonchurus* and *Gnathypops bermudensis. Bull. Mar. Sci. of the Gulf and Caribb.* 11: 503-515.

Brons, R. 1995. Reproduction and captive breeding of two red sea dottybacks. *Freshwat. Mar. Aquar.* 19(6): 48-62.

Brulé, T., D.O. Avila, M.S. Crespo and C. Déniel, 1994 Seasonal and diel changes in diet composition of juvenile Red Grouper (*Epinephelus morio*) from Campeche Bank. *Bull. Mar. Sci.* 55:255-262.

Brulé, T. and L.G. Rodriguez Canche, 1993. Food habits of juvenile Red Groupers, *Epinephelus morio* (Valenciennes, 1828), from Campeche Bank, Yucatan, Mexico. *Bull. Mar. Sci.* 52:772-779.

Bruno, C., M. B. Cousseau and C. S. Bremec. 2000. Contribution of polychaetous annelids to the diet of *Cheilodactylus bergi* (Pisces, Cheilodactylidae) in Argentina. *Bull. Mar. Sci.* 67: 277-286.

Bullock, L.H., M.D. Murphy, M.F. Godcharles and M.E. Mitchell. 1992. Age, growth and reproduction of Jewfish *Epinephelus itajara* in the eastern Gulf of Mexico. *U.S. Fishery Bull.* 90: 243-249.

Bussing, W.A. 1980. *Liopropoma fasciatum*, a new serranid fish and only known member of the genus from the tropical eastern Pacific Ocean. *Rev. Biol. Trop.* 28:147-151.

Büttner, H. 1996. Rubble mounds of sand tilefish, *Malacanthus plumieri* (Bloch, 1787) and associated fishes in Colombia. *Bull. Mar. Sci.* 58:248-260.

Caldwell, D.K. 1962. Western Atlantic fishes of the family Pria-canthidae. *Copiea*, 1962:417-424.

Caldwell, D.K. and H.R. Bullis. 1971. An unusually large aggre-gation of prejuvenile bigeyes, *Priacanthus arenatus*, in the West Indies. *Copiea*, 1971:176.

Campbell, D.G. 1979. Marines: their care and keeping. Groupers and their allies: part 3. *Freshwat. Mar. Aquar.* 2(**11**):39-45, 71,72.

Charney, P. 1976. Oral brooding in the cardinalfishes *Phaeoptyx* and *Apogon maculatus* from the Bahamas. *Copeia*, 1976:198-200.

Chave, E.H. 1978. General ecology of six species of Hawaiian cardinalfish. *Pac. Sci.* 32:245-270.

Chave, E.H. and B.C. Mundy. 1994. Deep-sea benthic fishes of the Hawaiian archipelago, Cross seamount and Johnston atoll. *Pac. Sci.* 48:367-409.

Chlupaty, P. 1985. The Two-banded Grouper. *Trop. Fish Hobby.* 33 (5):70-74.

Choat, J.H. 1968. Feeding habits of and distribution of *Plectropo-mus maculatus* (Serranidae) at Heron Island. *Proc. R. Soc. Qd.* 80:13-18.

Clark, E. and A. Ben-Tuvia. 1973. Red Sea fishes of the family Branchiostegidae with a description of a new genus and species *Asymmetrurus oreni*. *Bull. Sea Fish. Res. Sta., Haifa,* no. 60:63-74.

Clark, E., J.S. Rabin and S. Holderman. 1988. Reproductive be-havior and social organization in the sand tilefish, *Malacan-thus plumieri*. *Environ. Biol. Fish.* 22:273-286.

Clifton, H.E. 1972. The Sand Tilefish, *Malacanthus plumieri*, and the distribution of coarse debris near west Indian coral reefs. *Nat. Hist. Mus. Los Angeles County Sci. Bull.*14:87-92.

Clifton, H.E. and R.E. Hunter. 1972. The sand tilefish, *Malacan-thus plumieri*, and the distribution of coarse debris near West Indian coral reefs. *Bull. Nat. Hist. L.A. Count.* 14:87-92.

Coleman, N. 1981. *Australian Sea Fishes North of 30 Degrees South.* Doubleday, Sydney, Aus. 297 pp.

Colin, P.L. 1971. Interspecific relationships of the Yellowhead Jawfish, *Opistognathus aurifrons* (Pisces: Opistognathidae). *Copeia*, 1971:469-473.

————1972. Daily activity patterns and effects of environmental conditions on the behavior of the Yellowhead Jawfish, *Opis-tognathus aurifrons*, with notes on the ecology. *Zoologica*, 57:137-169.

————1973. Burrowing behavior of the Yellowhead Jawfish, *Opistognathus aurifrons*. *Copeia*, 1973:84-89.

————1974. Observation and collection of deep-reef fishes of the coasts of Jamaica and British Honduras (Belize). *Mar. Biol.* 24:29-38.

————1976. Observations of deep-reef fishes in the Tongue of the Ocean, Bahamas. *Bull. Mar. Sci.* 26:603-605.

Colin, P.L. and D.W. Arneson. 1978. Aspects of the natural his-tory of the Swordtail Jawfish, *Lonchopisthus micrognathus* (Poey) (Pisces: Opistognathidae), in south-western Puerto Rico. *J. Nat. Hist.* 12:689-697.

Colin, P.L. and J.B. Heiser. 1973. Associations of two species of cardinalfishes (Apogonidae: Pisces) with sea anemones in the West Indies. *Bull. Mar. Sci.* 23:521-524.

Colin, P.L., D.Y. Shapiro and D. Weiler. 1987. Aspects of the re-production of two groupers, *Epinephelus guttatus* and *E. striatus* in the West Indies. *Bull. Mar. Sci.* 40:220-230.

Conde, B. 1986. Longevity of marine tropicals at the Nancy Aquarium. *SeaScope* 3 (Summer):1-3.

Courtenay, W.R. Jr. 1967. Atlantic fishes of the genus *Rypticus* (Grammistidae). *Proc. Acad. Nat. Sci. Phila.* 119:241-293.

Debelius, H. 1986. *Fishes for the Invertebrate Aquarium.* Reimer Hobbing GmbH, Essen. 160 pp.

————1987. *Underwater Guide. Red Sea Fishes.* Verlag Stephanie Naglschmid, Stuttgart, 167 pp.

————1993. *Indian Ocean Tropical Fish Guide.* Aquaprint Ver-lags, Neu Isenburg, 319 pp.

Debelius, H. and H.A. Baensch. 1994. *Marine Atlas.* Mergus-Ver-lag Gmbh, Melle, Germany, 1215 pp.

Dekker, L.N. 1987. Bewust kiezen...een serie praktische aquari-umtips/7. *Het Zee-Aquarium* 37:152-157.

Delbeek, J.C. 1991. Fishes for the invertebrate aquarium. *Aquar. Fish Mag.* 3: 18-31.

DeLoach, N. 1999. *Reef Fish Behavior.* New World Publ. Inc. Jacksonville, Fl. 359 pp.

DeMartini, E.E. 1996. Sheltering and foraging substrate uses of the Arc-eye Hawkfish *Paracirrhites arcatus* (Pisces: Cirrhiti-dae). *Bull. Mar. Sci.* 58:826-837.

DeMartini, E.E., and T.J. Donaldson. 1996. Color morph-habitat relations in the Arc-eye Hawkfish *Paracirrhites arcatus* (Pisces: Cirrhitidae). *Copeia*, 1996: 362-371.

Diamant, A. and D. Golani. 1984. Coloration and possible toxic-ity of juvenile soapfish *Grammistes sexlineatus* (Pisces: Gram-mistidae). *Copeia*, 1984:1015-1017.

Diamant, A. and M. Shpigel. 1985. Interspecific feeding associa-tions of groupers (Teleostei: Serranidae) with octopuses and moray eels in the Gulf of Eilat (Aqaba). *Environ. Biol. Fish.* 13:153-159.

Donaldson, T.J. 1987. Social organization and the reproductive behavior of the hawkfish *Cirrhitichthys falco* (Cirrhitidae). *Bull. Mar. Sci.* 41:531-540.

————1989a. Pair spawning of *Cephalopholis boenack* (Ser-ranidae). *Japan. J. Ichthyol.* 35:497-500.

————1989b. Facultative monogamy in obligate coral-dwelling hawkfishes (Cirrhitidae). *Environ. Biol. Fish.* 26:295-302.

————1990. Reproductive behavior and social organization of some Pacific hawkfishes (Cirrhitidae). *Japan. J. Ichthyol.* 36:439-458.

————1995a. Courtship and spawning behavior of the pygmy grouper *Cephalopholis spiloparaea* (Serranidae: Epinephelinae), with notes on *C. argus* and *C. urodeta. Environ. Biol. Fish.* 43:363-370.

————1995b. Partitioning behavior and intra- and interspecific interactions: a comparison between male and female groupers, *Cephalopholis spiloparaea* (Pisces: Serranidae: Epinephelinae). *Mar. Biol.* 121:581-584.

Donaldson, T.J. and P.L. Colin. 1989. Pelagic spawning of the hawkfish *Oxycirrhites typus. Environ. Biol. Fish.* 24:295-300.

Dubin, R. 1982. Behavioral interactions between Caribbean reef fish and eels (Muraenidae and Ophichthidae). *Copeia,* 1982:229-231.

Earle, J.L. and R.L. Pyle. 1997. *Hoplolatilus pohle,* a new species of sand tilefish (Perciformes: Malacanthidae) from the deep reefs of D'Entrecasteaux Islands, Papua New Guinea. *Copeia,* 1997:382-387.

Eggleston, D.B., J.J. Grover and R.N. Lipcius, 1998. Ontogenetic diet shifts in Nassau Grouper: trophic linkages and predatory impact. *Bull. Mar. Sci.* 63:111-126.

Esterbauer, H. 1990. *Pseudochromis fridmani*—a jewel of a reef fish. *Trop. Fish. Hobby.* 39(9): 66-71.

Ferreira, B. 1993. Reproduction of the inshore coral trout, *Plectropomus maculatus* (Perciformes: Serranidae) from the central Great Barrier Reef, Australia. *J. Fish Biol.* 42:831-844.

Ferreira, B.P. and G.R. Russ, 1993. Age validation and estimation of growth rate of the coral trout, *Plectropomus leopardus* (Lacépède, 1802) from Lizard Island, northern Great Barrier Reef. *Fish. Bull.* 92:46-57.

Fishelson, L. 1970. Spawning behavior of the cardinalfish, *Cheilodipterus lineatus,* in Eilat (Gulf of Aqaba, Red Sea). *Copeia,* 1970: 370-371.

Fitch, J.E. and S.J. Crooke. 1984. Revision of eastern Pacific Catalufas (Pisces: Priacanthidae) with description of a new genus and discussion of the fossil record. *Proc. Calif. Acad. Sci.* 43:301-315.

Freeman, S. and W. Alevizon. 1983. Aspects of the territorial behavior and habitat distribution of the Fairy Basslet *Gramma loreto. Copeia,* 1983:829-832.

García-Moliner Basora, G. 1986. Aspects of the social spacing, reproduction and sex reversal in the Red Hind *Epinephelus guttatus* (Linnaeus). p. 328-329. In Contribuciones. Department of Marine Sciences, University of Puerto Rico, Mayagüez. 336 p. (abstract of M.S. thesis).

Gardner, T. 1997. Commercial breeding of the dottybacks. Seascope 14 (Summer):1-2.

Gill, A.C. 2003. Revision of the Indo-Pacific Dottyback Fish Subfamily Pseudochrominae (Perciformes: Pseudochromidae). *Smithiana Monograph* 1, 213 pp.

————1993. Dottybacks for the marine aquarium. *Trop. Fish Hobby.,* 41:30-53.

Gill, A.C. and G.R. Allen. In press. *Pseudochromis lugubris* and *P. tonozukai,* two new dottybacks from the Indo-Australian Archipelago (Perciformes: Pseudochromidae: Pseudochrominae). *Zeylanica.*

————1996. *Pseudochromis viridis,* a new species of dottyback from Christmas Island, Indian Ocean (Teleostei: Perciformes: Pseudochromidae). *Revue fr. Aquariol.* 23:33-38.

Gill, A.C. and Edwards, A.J. 2002. Two new species of the Indo-Pacific fish genus Pseudoplesiops (Perciformes, Pseudochromidae, Pseudoplesiopinae). *Bull. Nat. Hist. Mus. London, Zool. Ser.* 68:19–26.

Gill, A.C. and J.K.L. Mee. 1993. Notes on dottyback fishes of the genus *Pseudochromis* off Oman, with a description of a new species (Perciformes: Pseudochromidae). *Revue fr. Aquariol.* 20:53-60.

Gill, A.C., R.L. Pyle and J.L. Earle. 1996. *Pseudochromis ephippiatus,* a new species of dottyback from the southeastern Papua New Guinea (Teleostei: Perciformes: Pseudochromidae). *Revue fr. Aquariol.* 23:97-100.

Gill, A.C. and J.E. Randall. 1998. Five new species of the dottyback genus *Pseudochromis* from Indonesia (Teleostei: Pseudochromidae). *Revue fr. Aquariol.* 25: 17-26.

————1992. *Pseudochromis steenei,* a new sexually dimorphic species of dottyback fish from Indonesia (Perciformes: Pseudochromidae). *Revue fr. Aquariol.* 19:41-45.

Gill, A.C., J.E. Randall and A.J. Edwards. 1991. *Pseudoplesiops collare,* a new species of fish from Indonesia, with lecotype designation for *Nematochromis annae* Weber (Perciformes: Pseudochromidae: Pseudochromidae). *Revue fr. Aquariol.* 18: 75-78.

Gill, A.C. and H. Senou. 2002. *Lubbockichthys tanakai,* a new species of pseudoplesiopine dottyback from the West Pacific (Perciformes: Pseudochromidae). *Aqua. Jour. Ichthyol. Aqua. Biol.* 6: 1-4.

Gill, A.C. and H. Tanaka. In press. *Pholidochromis cerasina,* a new species of pseudochromine dottyback from the West Pacific (Perciformes: Pseudochromidae). *Proc. Biol. Soc. Wash.*

Gill, A.C. and D.J. Woodland. 1992. Description of a new dottyback of the genus *Pseudochromis* (Pisces: Pseudochromidae) from Western Australia. *Rec. Aust. Mus.* 44: 247-251.

Goeden, G.B. 1978. A monograph of the coral trout, *Plectropomus leopardus* (Lacépède). *Queensland Fish. Serv. Res. Bull.* 1:1-42.

Gon, O. 1993. Revision of the cardinalfish genus *Cheilodipterus* (Perciformes: Apogonidae), with description of five new species. *Indo-Pac. Fishes,* 22:59 pp.

Gon, O. and J.E. Randall. 1995. Description of three new species of the cardinalfish genus *Archamia* (Perciformes: Apogonidae). *Israel J. Zool.* 41:539-550.

Greenfield, D.W. and R.K. Johnson. 1990. Heterogeneity in habitat choice in cardinalfish community structure. *Copeia,* 1990:1107-1114.

Grover, J.J. , D.B. Eggleston and J.M. Shenker. 1998. Transition from pelagic to demersal phase in early—juvenile Nassau Grouper *Epinephelus striatus*: pigmentation, squamation and ontogeny of diet. *Bull. Mar. Sci.* 62:97-113.

Gudger, E.W. 1927. Inquilism between the cheilopterid fish, *Apogonichthys punticulatus,* and the univalve mollusk, *Strombus bituberculatus. Zoologica, N.Y.* 9:193-200.

Harmelin-Vivien, M.L. and C. Bouchon. 1976. Feeding behavior of some carnivorous fishes (Serranidae and Scorpaenidae) from Tulear (Madagascar). *Mar. Biol.* 37: 329-340.

Heemstra, P.C. and J.E. Randall. 1986. Serranidae. p. 509-537. In M.M. Smith and P.C. Heemstra (eds.) *Smiths' Sea Fishes.* Springer-Verlag, Berlin.

———1993. FAO Species Catalogue. Vol. 16. *Groupers of the World. (Family Serranidae, Subfamily Epinephelinae). An Annotated and Illustrated Catalogue of the Grouper, Rockcod, Hind, Coral Grouper and Lyretail Species Known to Date.* FAO Fish. Synops. No. 125, Vol. 16.

Hess, H.C. 1993. Male mouthbrooding in jawfishes (Opistognathidae): constraints on polygyny. *Bull. Mar. Sci.* 52:806-818.

Hiatt, R.W. and D.W. Stratsburg. 1960. Ecological relationships of the fish fauna on coral reefs of the Marshall Islands. *Ecol. Monogr.* 30:65-127.

Hirara, T, T. Yamakawa, A. Iwata, S. Manabe, W. Hiramtsu and N. Ohnishi. 1996. Fish fauna of Kashiwa-jima Island, Kochi Prefecture, Japan. *Bull Mar. Sci. Fish. Kochi Univ.* 16, 177 Pp.

Hobson, E.S. 1965. Diurnal-nocturnal activity of some inshore fishes in the Gulf of California. *Copeia,* 1965:291-302.

———1968. Predatory behavior of some shore fishes in the Gulf of California. *Fish. & Wildlife Res. Rpt.* 73, 92 pp.

———1974. Feeding relationships of teleostean fishes on coral reefs in Kona, Hawaii. *Fishery Bull.,* 72:915-1031.

Hoese, D.F. and Kuiter, R.H. 1984. A revision of the Australian plesiopid fish genus *Paraplesiops,* with notes on other Australian genera. *Rec. Aust. Mus.*: 7-18.

Hoover, J.P. 1993. *Hawaii's Fishes; a Guide for Snorkelers, Divers, and Aquarists.* Mutual Publishing, Honolulu, 178 pp.

Humann, P. 1993. *Reef Fish Identification. Galapagos.* New World Publ. Jacksonville, FL 192 pp.

Humann, P. and N. DeLoach. 2002. *Reef Fish Identification (third edition).* New World Publ. Inc. Jacksonville, FL 481 pp.

Itzkowitz, M., M. Haley, C. Otis and D. Evers. 1991. A reconnaissance of the deeper Jamaican coral reef fish communities. *Northeast Gulf Sci.* 12:25-34.

Johannes, R.E. 1988. Spawning aggregation of the grouper, *Plectropomus areolatus* (Rüppell) in the Solomon Islands. *Proc. 6th Intern. Coral Reef Symp. Vol 2.* 751-755.

Kaplan, E.H. 1982. *A Field Guide to Coral Reefs of the Caribbean and Florida.* Houghton Mifflin Co., Boston, MA 289 pp.

Kerstitch, A. 1979. The first record of the courtship behavior of the Blue-spotted Jawfish. *Freshwat. Mar. Aquar.* 2(**9**):9-10.

———1988. Master builders. *SeaScope* 5 (Winter), 1, 4.

Kingsford, M. 1992. Spatial and temporal variation in predation on reef fishes by coral trout (*Plectropomus leopardus,* Serranidae). *Coral Reefs,* 11:193-198.

Klocek, R. and J. Kolman. 1976. *Marines (the Fishes).* Marine Hobbyist News, Normal, IL. 144 pp.

Kobayashi, K. and K. Suzuki. 1992. Hermaphroditism and sexual function in *Cirrhitichthys aureus* and the other Japanese hawkfishes (Cirrhitidae: Teleostei). *Japan. J. Ichthyol.* 38:397-404.

Kosaki, R.K., R.L. Pyle, J.E. Randall and D.K. Irons. 1991. New records of fishes from Johnston Atoll, with notes on biogeography. *Pac. Sci.* 45:186-203.

Kuiter, R.H. 1992. *Tropical reef-fishes of the Western Pacific: Indonesia and adjacent waters.* PT Gramedia Utama, Jakarta. 314 pp.

———1993. *Coastal Fishes of South-Eastern Australia.* University of Hawaii Press, Honolulu, 437 pp.

———1995. The juvenile Vermicular Cod *Plectropomus oligacanthus,* a mimic of the Slender Maori Wrasse, *Cheilinus celebicus. Revue fr. Aquariol.* 21:7778.

———2001. *Indonesian Reef Fishes.* Zoonetics CD ROM.

Kuiter, R.H. and H. Debelius. 1994. *Southeast Asia tropical fish guide.* IKAN-Underwasserarchiv, Frankfurt, 321 pp.

Kuiter, R.E. and T. Kozawa. 1999. *Pictorial guide to fishes of the Indo-west Pacific: Apogonidae.* CD-ROM, Zoonetics erbook.

Kuwamura, T. 1983. Spawning behavior and timing of fertilization in the mouthbrooding cardinalfish, *Apogon notatus. Japan. J. Ichthyol.* 30:61-71.

———1985. Social and reproductive behavior of three mouthbrooding cardinalfishes, *Apogon doederleini, A. niger* and *A. notatus. Environ. Biol. Fish.* 13:17-24.

———1987. Night spawning and paternal mouthbrooding of the cardinalfish *Cheilodipterus quinquelineatus. Japan J. Ichthyol.* 33:431-433.

Lachner, E.A. 1955. Inquilinsim and a new record for *Paramia bipunctata*, a cardinal fish from the Red Sea. *Copeia*, 1955:53-54.

Leong, T. and S. Wong. 1988. A comparative study of the parasite fauna of wild and cultured grouper (*Epinephelus malabaricus* Bloch and Schneider) in Malaysia. *Aquaculture* 68:203-207.

Leum, L.L. and J.H. Choat. 1980. Density and distribution patterns of the temperate marine fish *Cheilodactylus spectabilis* Cheilodactylidae in a reef environment. *Mar. Biol. (Berlin)* 57: 327-337.

Lieske, E. and R. Myers. 1994. *Collins Pocket Guide. Coral reef fishes: Indo-Pacific and Caribbean*. HarperCollins Publ., London, 400 pp.

Lobel, P.S. 1974. Sea spawnings—hawkfish. *Octopus,* 1:23.

———1976. Predation on a cleaner wrasse by a hawkfish (Cirrhitidae). *Copeia*, 1976:384-385.

Lowry, M.B. and I.M. Suthers. 1998. Home range, activity and distribution patterns of a temperate rocky-reef fish, *Cheilodactylus fuscus. Mar. Biol. (Berlin)* 132: 569-578.

Lubbock, R. 1975. Fishes of the family Pseudochromidae (Perciformes) in the northwest Indian Ocean and Red Sea. *J. Zool., Lond.* 176, 115-157.

———1976. Fishes of the family Pseudochromidae (Perciformes) in the central Indian Ocean. *J. Nat. Hist.* 10, 167-177.

———1980. Five new basslets of the genus *Pseudochromis* (Teleostei: Pseudochromidae) from the Indo-Australian archipelago. *Revue Suisse Zool.* 87: 821-834.

Lubbock, R. and Goldman, B. 1974. A new magenta *Pseudochromis* from the Pacific. *J. Fish Biol.* 6:107-110.

Manooch, C.S. 1987. Age and growth of snappers and groupers. p. 329-373. In J.J. Polovina and S. Ralston (eds.) *Tropical Snappers and Groupers: Biology and Fisheries Management*. Ocean Resour. Mar. Policy Ser. Westview Press, Inc., Boulder and London.

Matsumoto, K. 2001. Overlapping territory of a benthophagous fish, *Goniistius zonatus* (Teleostei: Cheilodactylidae). *Ecol. Res.* 16: 715-726.

Matsumoto, K. and M. Kohda. 2000. Energy allocation and foraging activities in the morwong, *Goniistius zonatus* (Cheilodactylidae). *Ichthyol. Res.* 47: 416-419.

Matzumoto, K. and M. Kohda. 2001a. Differences in gill raker morphology between two local populations of a benthophagous filter-feeding fish, *Goniistius zonatus* (Cheilodactylidae). *Ichthyol. Res.* 48: 269-273.

———2001b. Differences in feeding associations of benthophagous fishes in two locations. *Environ. Biol. Fish.* 61: 111-115.

McCarthy, L.V. 1979. Eastern Pacific *Rypticus* (Pisces: Grammistidae). *Copeia*, 1979:393-400.

McCormick, M.I. 1989. Reproductive ecology of the temperate reef fish *Cheilodactylus spectabilis* Pisces: Cheilodactylidae. *Mar. Ecol. Prog. Ser.* 55: 113-120.

———1998. Ontogeny of diet shifts by a microcarnivorous fish, *Cheilodactylus spectabilis*: Relationship between feeding mechanics, microhabitat selection and growth. *Mar. Biol. (Berlin)* 132:9-20.

Moe, M.A. 1989. *The Marine Aquarium Reference: Systems and Invertebrates*. Green Turtle Publ., Plantation, FL 512 pp.

———1992. *The Marine Aquarium Handbook: Beginner to Breeder*. Green Turtle Publications, Plantation, FL. 318 pp.

———1997. *Breeding the Orchid Dottyback: An Aquarists Journal*. Green Turtle Publications, Plantation, FL. 285 pp.

Montgomery, W.L. 1975. Interspecific associations of sea-basses (Serranidae) in the Gulf of California. *Copeia*, 1975:785-787.

Mooi, R.D. 1995. Revision, phylogeny, and discussion of biology and biogeography of the fish genus *Plesiops* (Perciformes: Plesiopsidae). *Life Sci. Contrib*. No. 159. 108 pp.

Mooi, R.D. and Randall, J.E. 1991. Three new species of the genus *Plesiops* (Teleostei: Plesiopidae) from tropical Australian and adjacent seas. *Copeia*, 1991:373-387.

Morin, J.G. 1981. Bioluminescent patterns in shallow tropical marine fishes. Proc. 4th Intern. *Coral Reef Symp. 2:* 570-574.

Myers, R.F. 1999. *Micronesian Reef Fishes: A Comprehensive Guide to the Coral Reef Fishes of Micronesia, 3rd revised and expanded edition*. Coral Graphics, Barrigada, Guam, 330 pp.

Nagelkerken, W. 1981. Distribution of the groupers and snappers of the Netherlands Antilles. Proc. 4th Intern. *Coral Reef Symp. Vol. 2:* 479-484.

Nemtzov, S.C., S.M. Kajiura and C.A. Lompart. 1993. Diel color phase changes in the Coney *Epinephelus fulvus* (Teleostei, Serranidae). *Copeia*, 1993: 883-885.

Okuda, N. 1999. Female mating strategy and male brood cannibalism in a sand-dwelling cardinalfish. *Animal Behav.* 58:273-279.

———2001. The costs of reproduction to males and females of a paternal mouthbrooding cardinalfish *Apogon notatus. J. Fish Biol.* 58:776-787.

Okuda, N. and Y. Yanagisawa. 1996. Filial cannibalism by mouthbrooding males of the cardinal fish , *Apogon doederleini*, in relation to their physical condition. *Environ. Biol. Fish.* 45:397-404.

Ormond, R.F.G. 1980. Aggressive mimicry and other interspecific feeding associations among Red Sea coral reef predators. *J. Zool., Lond.* 191: 247-262.

Parker, R.O. and S.W. Ross. 1986. Observing reef fishes from submersibles off North Carolina. *Northeast Gulf Sci.* 8:31-49.

Parrish, J.D. 1987. The trophic biology of snappers and groupers In: Polovina, J.J. and Ralston, S. (eds.) *Tropical Snappers and Groupers: Biology and Fisheries Management.* Westview Press Inc., Boulder, Co. p 405-463.

Potts, J.C. and C.S. Manooch, III. 1995. Age and growth of Red Hind and rock hind collected from North Carolina through the Dry Tortugas, Florida. *Bull. Mar. Sci.* 56:784-794.

Privitera, L.A. 1991. The Sunset Basslet, *Liopropoma aurora* (Jordan and Evermann). *Freshwater. Mar. Aquar.* 14(3):24-26.

Quinn, J.R. 1988. The eyes have it. *Trop. Fish. Hobby.* 37(1):85-87.

Randall, J.E. 1963a. Review of the hawkfishes (family Cirrhitidae). *Proc. U.S. Nat. Mus.* 114:389-451.

———1963b. Three new species and six new records of small serranoid fishes from Curacao and Puerto Rico. *Stud. Fauna Curacao and other Caribbean Islands* 80:77-110.

———1967. Food habits of reef fishes of the West Indies. *Stud. Trop. Oceanogr., Miami,* 5:665-847.

———1968. *Caribbean Reef Fishes.* T.F.H. Publications, Inc., Neptune City, NJ 318 pp.

———1981. A review of the Indo-Pacific sand tilefish Genus *Hoplolatilus* (Perciformes: Malacanthidae). *Freshwat. Mar. Aquar.* 4(12):39-46.

———1983. *Red Sea Reef Fishes.* Immel Publishing, London, 192 pp.

———1985. *Guide to Hawaiian Reef Fishes.* Harrowood, Newton Square, PA, 79 pp.

———1992. *Diver's Guide to Fishes of the Maldives.* Immel Publishing, London, 193 pp.

———1995. Coastal Fishes of Oman. University of Hawaii Press, Honolulu, 439 pp.

———1996. *Shore Fishes of Hawaii.* Natural World Press, Vida, OR, 216 pp.

———1998. Review of the cardinalfishes (Apogonidae) of the Hawaiian Islands, with descriptions of two new species. *Aqua* 3(1):25-38.

———2001. Revision of the generic classification of the hawkfishes (Cirrhitidae), with descriptions of three new genera, *Zootaxa,* 12:1-12.

Randall, J.E., G.R. Allen and R.C. Steene. 1997. *Fishes of the Great Barrier Reef and Coral Sea.* University of Hawaii Press, 557 pp.

Randall, J.E. and V.E. Brock. 1960. Observations on the ecology of Epinephelinae and lutjanid fishes of the Society Islands, with emphasis on food habits. *Trans. Am. Fish. Soc.* 891:9-16.

Randall, J.E. and D.G. Fautin. 2002. Fishes other than anemonefishes that associate with sea anemones. *Coral Reefs* 21:188-190.

Randall, J.E. and T.H. Fraser. 1999. Clarification of the western Pacific cardinalfish species *Apogon trimaculatus* and *A. rhodopterus,* with descriptions of a similar new species. *Raffles Bull. Zool.* 47:617-633.

Randall, J.E. and P.C. Heemstra. 1991. Revision of Indo-Pacific groupers (Perciformes: Serranidae: Epinephelinae), with descriptions of five new species. *Indo-Pac. Fishes,* 20:332 pp.

Randall, J.E. and D.F. Hoese. 1986. Revision of the groupers of the Indo-Pacific genus *Plectropomus* (Perciformes; Serranidae) *Indo-Pac. Fishes,* 13:31 pp.

Randall, J.E. and R.H. Kuiter. 1989. The juvenile Indo-Pacific grouper *Anyperodon leucogrammicus,* a mimic of the wrasse *Halichoeres purpurescens* and allied species, with a review of the recent literature on mimicry in fishes. *Revue fr. Aquariol.,* 16:51-56.

Randall, J. E. and M. Kulbicki. 1998. Two new cardinalfishes (Perciformes: Apogonidae) of the *Apogon cyanosoma* complex from the western Pacific, with notes on the status of *A. wassinki* Bleeker. *Revue fr. Aquariol.,* 25:31-40.

Randall, J.E., E.A. Lachner and T.H. Fraser. 1985. A revision of the Indo-Pacific apogonid fish genus *Pseudamia,* with descriptions of three new species. *Indo-Pac. Fishes,* 6:23 pp.

Randall, J.E. and U. Satapoomin. 1999. *Archamia ataenia,* a new species of cardinalfish (Perciformes: Apogonidae) from the Andaman Sea and Mentawai Islands. *Phuket mar. biol. Cent. Res. Bull,* 62:1-8.

———2000. *Cephalopholis polyspila,* a new species of grouper (Perciformes: Serranidae: Epinephelinae) from southwestern Thailand and Sumatra. *Phuket mar. biol. Cent. Res. Bull.,* 63:1-8.

Reed, S.E. 1992. *Astrapogon alutus* (Perciformes: Apogonidae) found in the mantle cavity of *Strombus pugilis* (Mesogastropoda: Strombidae). *Bull. Mar. Sci.,* 50:227.

Relyea, K., T. Vaughan and J. Ferguson. 1979. Notes on the *Pseudochromis* RUPPELL, 1835 in the northern Arabian Gulf (Pisces: Pseudochromidae). *Sendenbergiana biol.* 60, 141-146.

Rigby, M.C. and V. Dufour. 1996. Parasites of coral reef fish recruits, *Epinephelus merra* (Serranidae), in French Polynesia. *J. Parasitology* 82:405-408.

Robins, C.R. and P.L. Colin. 1979. Three new grammid fishes from the Caribbean Sea. *Bull. Mar. Sci.* 29:41-52.

Robins, C.R., G.C. Ray and J. Douglass. 1986. *A Field Guide to Atlantic Coast Fishes of North America.* Houghton Mifflin Co., Boston, 354 pp.

Sadovy, Y. and T.J. Donaldson. 1995. Sexual pattern of *Neocirrhites armatus* (Cirrhitidae) with notes on other hawkfish species. *Environ. Biol. Fish.* 42:143-150.

Sadovy, Y. J. and A.M. Eklund. 1999. Synopsis of Biological Information on *Epinephelus striatus*, the Nassau Grouper and *E.
itajara*, the Jewfish. *NOAA Technical Report,* **65 pp.**

Sadovy, Y.J., A. Rosario and A. Romain. 1994. Reproduction in
an aggregation grouper, the red hind, *Epinephelus guttatus*.
Environ. Biol. Fish. 41:269-286.

Salmon, M. and H.E. Winn. 1966. Sound production by priacanthid fishes. *Copeia*, 1957:155-156.

Samoilys, M.A. 1997. Movement in a large predatory fish: coral
trout *Plectropomus leopardus* (Pisces: Serranidae) on Heron
Reef, Australia. *Coral Reefs,* 16:151-158.

Samoilys, M.A. and L.C. Squire. 1994. Preliminary observations
on the spawning behavior of coral trout, *Plectropomus leopardus* (Pisces: Serranidae), on the Great Barrier Reef. *Bull. Mar.
Sci.* 54:332-342.

Sano, M., M. Shimizu and Y. Nose. 1984. Food habits of
teleostean reef fishes on Okinawa Island, southern Japan.
Univ. Mus. Univ. Tokyo Bull. 15:70 pp.

Sazima, I., J.L. Gasparini and R.L. Mourra. 1998. *Gramma
brasiliensis*, a new basslet from the western South Atlantic
(Perciformes: Grammatidae). *Aqua*, 3:39-44.

Schroeder, A. and M. Lowry. 1994. Sexual dimorphism in the
Red Morwong, *Cheilodactylus fuscus. Aust. J. Mar. Freshwat.
Res.* 45: 1173-1180.

Shapiro, D.Y., G. Garcia-Moliner and Y. Sadovy. 1994. Social system of an inshore stock of the Red Hind Grouper, *Epinephelus guttatus* (Pisces: Serranidae). *Environ. Bio. Fish.*
41:415-422.

Shapiro, D.Y., Y. Sadovy and M.A. McGehee. 1993. Periodicity of
sex change and reproduction in the Red Hind, *Epinephelus
guttatus. Bull. Mar. Sci.* 53:1151-1162.

Shinohara, G. 1999. A new jawfish, *Stalix toyoshio*, from Kyushu,
Japan (Perciformes: Opistognathidae). *Ichthyol. Res.*, 46:267-
270.

Siegel, J.A. and T.A. Adamson. 1983. Batesian mimicry between a
cardinalfish (Apogonidae) and a venomous scorpionfish
(Scorpaenidae) from the Philippine Islands. *Pac. Sci.* 37:75-
79.

Sluka, R., M. Chiappone, K.M. Sullivan, T.A. Potts, J.M. Levy,
E.F. Schmitt and G. Meester. 1998. Density, species, and size
distribution of groupers (Serranidae) in three habitats at El-
bow Reef, Florida Keys. *Bull. Mar. Sci.* 62:219-228.

Sluka, R.D and N. Reichenbach. 1996. Grouper density and diversity at two sites in the republic of Maldives. *Atoll Res. Bull.*
438: 16 pp.

Smith, C.L. 1971. Secondary gonochorism in the serranid genus
Liopropoma. Copeia, 1971:316-319.

Smith, C.L. and J.C. Tyler. 1972. Space resource sharing in a
coral reef fish community. *Los Angeles Co. Nat. Hist. Mus.
Sci. Bull.* 14:125-170.

Smith-Vaniz, W.F. 1989. Revision of the jawfish genus *Stalix*
(Pisces: Opistognathidae), with descriptions of four new
species. *Proc. Acad. Nat. Sci. Phila.* 375-407.

————1997. Five new species of jawfishes (*Opistognathus*: Opistognathidae) from the western Atlantic Ocean. *Bull. Mar.
Sci.* 60:1074-1128.

Snyder, D. 1999. Mimicry of the initial phase Bluehead Wrasse,
Thalassoma bifasciatum (Labridae) by juvenile Tiger Grouper,
Mycteroperca tigris (Serranidae). *Revue fr. Aquariol.*, 26:17-20.

Snyder, D.B., J.E. Randall and S.W. Michael. 2001. Aggressive
mimicry by the juvenile of the Redmouth Grouper, *Aethaloperca rogaa* (Serranidae). *Cybium,* 25:227-232.

Shpigel, M. and L. Fishelson. 1989a. Food habits and prey selection of three species of groupers from the genus *Cephalopholis* (Serranidae: Teleostei). *Environ. Biol. Fish.* 24:67-73.

————1989b. Habitat partitioning between species of the genus
Cephalopholis (Pisces: Serranidae) across the fringing reef of
the Gulf of Aqaba (Red Sea). *Mar. Ecol. Prog. Ser.* 58:17-22.

————1991. Territoriality and associated behavior in three
species of the genus *Cephalopholis* (Pisces: Serranidae) in the
Gulf of Aqaba, Red Sea. *J. Fish Biol.* 38:887-896.

Spotte, S. 1992. *Captive Seawater Fishes.* John-Wiley and Sons,
Inc., New York, 942 pp.

St. John, J. 1999. Ontogenetic changes in the diet of the coral reef
groups *Plectropomus leopardus* (Serranidae): patterns in taxa,
size and habitat of prey. *Mar. Ecol. Prog. Ser.* 180:233-246.

Starck, W.A. and P.L. Colin. 1978. *Gramma linki*—a new species
of grammid fish from the tropical Western Atlantic. *Bull.
Mar. Sci.* 28:146-152.

Starck, W.A. and W.R. Courtenay, Jr. 1962. *Choristium eukrines*, a
new serranid fish from Florida, with notes on related species.
Proc. Biol. Soc. Wash. 75:159-167.

Starnes, W.C. 1988. Revision, Phylogeny and biogeographic comments on the circumtropical marine percoid fish family Pria-
canthidae. *Bull Mar. Sci.* 43:117-203.

Sudo, H and M. Azeta. 1992. Selective predation on mature male
Byblis japonicus (Amphipoda: Grammaridea) by the barace
Cardinalfish, *Apogon semilineatus. Mar. Biol.* 114: 211-217.

Takeshita, G.Y. 1975. Long-snouted Hawkfish. *Mar. Aquar.* 6:27-
31.

Talbot, F.H. 1965. A description of the coral structure of the Tu-
tia reefs (East Africa) and its fish fauna. *Proc. Zool. Soc. London.* 145:431-470.

————1984. *The Reader's Digest book of the Great Barrier Reef.*
Reader's Digest, Sydney. 384 pp.

Tanaka, Y. and K. Suzuki. 1991. Spawning, eggs and larvae of the hawkfish, *Cirrhitichthys aureus*, in an aquarium. *Japan. J. Ichthyol.* 38:283-288.

Tanaka, Y., Y. Shiobara, M. Hayashi, T. Furukawa and M. Hattori. 1985. Spawning behavior, eggs and larvae of the hawkfish, *Cirrhitops hubbardi*, in an aquarium. *Advance Abstracts of the 18th Annual Meeting of the Ichthyological Society of Japan*, No. 58.

Tapia-Garcia, M., A. Yanez-Arancibia, P. Sanchez-Gil and M.C. Garcia-Abad. 1995. Distribution, abundance and reproduction of *Priacanthus arenatus* Cuvier (Pisces: Priacanthidae) on the continental shelf in the southern Gulf of Mexico. *Biotropica* 27:232-237.

Thompson, R. and J.L. Munro. 1978. Aspects of the biology and ecology of Caribbean reef fishes: Serranidae (hinds and groupers). *J. Fish Biol.* 12:115-146.

Thomson, D.A., L.T. Findley and A.N. Kerstitch. 1979. *Reef Fishes of the Sea of Cortez.* John Wiley and Sons, New York, 302 pp.

Thresher, R.E. 1980. *Reef fish: Behavior and Ecology on the Reef and in the Aquarium.* The Palmetto Publ. Co., St. Petersburg, 171 pp.

———1984. *Reproduction in Reef Fishes.* TFH Publications, Inc., Neptune City, NJ, 399 pp.

Thresher, R.E. and P.L. Colin. 1986. Trophic structure, diversity and abundance of fishes of the deep reef (30-300 m) at Enewetak, Marshall Islands. *Bull. Mar. Sci.* 38:253-272.

Thurmon, G. 1982. PH signaling by *Chromileptes altivelis. J. Aquaricul. and Aquat. Sci.,* 3(2) 28-30.

Tominaga, Y. 1964. Notes on the fishes of the genus *Siphamia* (Apogonidae), with a record of *S. versicolor* from the Ryukyu Islands, Japan. *Japan. J. Ichthyol.* 12:10-17.

Tucker, J.W., Jr. 1994. Spawning by captive serranids: A review. *J. World Aquacult. Soc.* 25:345-359.

Vagelli, A. 1999. The reproductive biology and early ontogeny of the mouthbrooding Banggai Cardinalfish, *Pterapogon kauderni* (Perciformes, Apogonidae). *Environ. Biol. Fish,* 56:9-92.

Vagelli, A. and M. Erdman. 2002. First comprehensive ecological survey of the Banggai Cardinalfish, *Pterapogon kauderni* (Perciformes, Apogonidae). *Environ. Biol. Fish,* 63:1-8.

Van Der Elst, R. 1985. *A Guide to the Common Sea Fishes of Southern Africa. 2nd Edition.* C. Struik Publ., Cape Town, 398 pp.

Vivien, M.L. 1975. Place of apogonid fish in the food webs of a Malagasy coral reef. *Micronesica* 11:185-196.

Walsh, J. 1994. Reproduction of Yellowhead Jawfish in captivity. *SeaScope* 11 (Winter) 1-2.

Wassink, H. and R. Brons, 1990. A Successful Cultivation of the Comet *Calloplesiops altivelis. SeaScope* 7 (Spring) 1-3.

Wilkie, D. 1986. *Aquarium fish.* Pelham Books Ltd., London, 214 pp.

Wohler. O.C and F. Sanchez. 1994. Feeding ecology of Castaneta (*Cheilodactylus bergi:* Pisces: Cheilodactylidae) in the southwestern Atlantic. *Aust. Jour. Mar. Freshwat. Res.* 45:507-520.

Young, F.A. 1982. The Yellowhead Jawfish—Breeding the Marine Mouthbrooder in Captivity. *Freshwat. Mar. Aquar.* 5(4):50-51.

Zeller, D.C. 1997. Home range and activity patterns of the coral trout *Plectropomus leopardus* (Serranidae). *Mar. Ecol. Prog. Ser.* 154: 65-77.

———1998. Spawning aggregations: patterns of movement of the coral trout *Plectropomus leopardus* (Serranidae) as determined by ultrasonic telemetry. *Mar. Ecol. Prog. Ser.* 162:253-263.

Index

About the Author

SCOTT W. MICHAEL is an internationally recognized writer, underwater photographer, and marine biology researcher specializing in reef fishes. He is a regular contributor to *Aquarium Fish Magazine* and is the author of the *PocketExpertGuide to Marine Fishes* (Microcosm/TFH), the *Reef Fishes Series* (Microcosm/TFH), *Reef Sharks & Rays of the World* (Sea Challengers), and *Aquarium Sharks & Rays* (Microcosm/TFH).

Having studied biology at the University of Nebraska, he has been involved in research projects on sharks, rays, frogfishes, and the behavior of reef fishes. He has also served as scientific consultant for National Geographic Explorer and the Discovery Channel. His research and photographic

Author Scott W. Michael in Bonaire.

endeavors have led him from Cocos Island in the Eastern Pacific to various points in the Indo-Pacific, including the Maldive Islands, Sulawesi, the Fiji Islands, Papua New Guinea, Australia's Great Barrier Reef, and Japan, as well as the Red Sea, the Gulf of Mexico, and many Caribbean reefs.

A marine aquarist since boyhood, he has kept tropical fishes for more than 30 years, with many years of extensive involvement in the aquarium world, including a period of retail store ownership. He is a partner in an extensive educational website on the coral reef environment, **www.coralrealm.com**.

Scott lives with his wife, underwater photographer Janine Cairns-Michael, and their Golden Retriever, Ruby, in Lincoln, Nebraska.

Author's Camera Equipment
Nexus F4 camera housing; Nikon F4 camera; Nikkor 60 and 105 mm macro lenses; TLC and Oceanic strobe arms; Nikon V with 20 mm lense; SB 105 Speedlights.

Future Editions
The author and editor are committed to making all future editions of this series as complete, accurate, and up-to-date as possible. Readers with suggestions, information, or photographs for possible publication are encouraged to contact one of the following in writing:

Reef Impressions
Attn: Scott W. Michael
4310 Garfield Street
Lincoln, NE 68506

Microcosm Ltd.
P.O. Box 550
Charlotte, VT 05445
e-mail: jml@microcosm-books.com